THE
MECHANICAL
GOD

Rock Drill, sculpture by Jacob Epstein. Courtesy of the Tate Gallery, London.

THE
MECHANICAL
GOD

Machines in Science Fiction

Edited by
Thomas P. Dunn and Richard D. Erlich

Contributions to the Study of Science Fiction and Fantasy, Number 1

GP GREENWOOD PRESS
WESTPORT, CONNECTICUT • LONDON, ENGLAND

79839

Library of Congress Cataloging in Publication Data
Main entry under title:

The Mechanical God, machines in science fiction.
 (Contributions to the study of science fiction and
fantasy, ISSN 0193-6875 ; no. 1)
 Bibliography: p.
 Includes index.
 1. Science fiction—History and criticism—
Addresses, essays, lectures. 2. Conscious automata in
literature—Addresses, essays, lectures. I. Dunn,
Thomas P. II. Erlich, Richard D. III. Series.
PN3433.6.M4   809.3'876   81-13429
ISBN 0-313-22274-6 (lib. bdg.)   AACR2

Library of Congress Catalog Card Number: 81-13429
ISBN: 0-313-22274-6
ISSN: 0193-6875

First published in 1982

Greenwood Press
A division of Congressional Information Service, Inc.
88 Post Road West
Westport, Connecticut 06881

Printed in the United States of America

10 9 8 7 6 5 4 3 2 1

CONTENTS

Part II. CHILDREN'S SCIENCE FICTION

Part III. ATTRIBUTES

Part IV. CYBORGS

PREFACE

This book is about mechanization in science fiction. The "machines" involved in these discussions are not can openers or cars, or even space ships and time-travel devices as these are usually conceived. Rather we are concerned here with stories about the technology that makes possible, or will make possible, the increasing mechanization *of life itself*, with computers that "feel" or appear to, with robots that look and act like people, and with cybernetic organisms in which human and mechanical elements are so intimately combined that one cannot say where the mechanical begins and the human ends.

At the time of this writing, industrial robots are replacing people on assembly lines, computers are controlling home environments, machines are pacing human heartbeats, and at least one mechanical letter carrier is plodding dutifully around its indoor track, delivering letters and memoranda and saying "excuse me" to people in the way.

Decades ago, science fiction writers had extrapolated far beyond such present-day wonders to imagine all sorts of machines which would augment the natural extensions of the human brain. We believe, as do a growing number of scholars, that such speculative stories are worthy of serious critical attention. The benefits to be derived from such attention are many. There are questions, for example, that can only be answered by a close examination of ideas and images of mechanization: Why are people fascinated by machines that look and act like human beings? If there could be a machine that imitated a human in *every* particular, would it be regarded as human? Would it *be* human? Should it have civil rights? Could it be a moral being? And then there are the more "literary" questions about the robots and androids of science fiction: Are fictional robots merely extrapolative or are they also allegorical? Do fictional robots have symbolic functions? Do they, perhaps, represent our better selves? Our rational selves? Bureaucracy rampant? And finally, what if we turned over the running of our world to such machines? Would we be happy or miserable in a machine-run world?

The formal exploration in literary criticism of the literature of mechanization has only recently begun. A major essay by Stanislaw Lem, "Robots in Science Fiction," is one of a small but growing number of studies annotated in our List of Works Useful for the Study of Machines in Science Fiction, at the back of this volume, as are Carolyn Rhodes's essay on computer tyrannies, Gary Wolfe's chapter from *The Known and the Unknown* on the "icon" of the robot, and Patricia Warrick's landmark survey of 225 stories, *The Cybernetic Imagination*. Our work has been to collect essays from many scholars exploring topics raised in these and other essays, and in the great wealth of cybernetic fiction already published and continuing to stream from the popular press.

That interest in the subject is strong may be seen from the fact that our call for essays was answered by an overwhelming response. Very many students of science fiction (and its related genres, summarized by the term "SF") had ideas about it that they wanted to express. Since we received more fine essays than could possibly fit into one volume, we have divided the subject into two parts and our anthology into two volumes: This one, *The Mechanical God*, discusses the mechanization of the human individual, in particular the making of mechanical people, robotics, and more broadly the imitation of human functions by machines, cybernetics, and the converse, the replacement of the human body by machines, the making of cyborgs. For the most part this volume is rigorously limited to quite literal machines in works of science fiction proper, courageously defining "science fiction" as "the sort of works that most critics agree are science fiction."[1] A second volume, *Clockwork Worlds: Mechanized Environments in SF*, will consider stories about computer tyrannies, "hive" worlds, mechanized societies, and like—SF works (including utopias and dystopias) in which literal or metaphorical machines threaten (or promise) to engulf humankind rather than replace us.

It is fitting that such a collection as this should begin with an essay on robots from one of the major writers on the subject. In his guest introduction, "Robots: Low-Voltage Ontological Currents," Brian Aldiss establishes the literary context within which robot stories developed. Next, a group of essays dealing with works by major authors begins with Barbara Bengels's essay on Karel Čapek's 1921 stage play, *R.U.R.*, the work that gave the world the word, "robot."

Rudy S. Spraycar discusses the central machines in *That Hideous Strength*, the third book in C. S. Lewis's well-known SF trilogy, and analyzes Lewis's "images of the mechanization of man and his institutions and environment." Christian W. Thomsen discusses the robot stories of Isaac Asimov, particularly their shortcomings as satirized by Stanislaw Lem. An essay by Thomas L. Wymer considers the many facets of mechanization in the works of Kurt Vonnegut, and Terri Paul traces the mechanization motif in two of the better-known novels of Frederik Pohl. Carl B. Yoke, who has recently completed a Starmont Reader's Guide literary biography on his lifelong friend Roger Zelazny, here considers the role that machines play in Zelazny's fiction, and Donald Hassler analyzes the recent Walter Tevis novel *Mockingbird*, a richly evocative book in the tradition of Tevis's now-famous *Man Who Fell to Earth*.

Margaret Esmonde surveys mechanization in children's SF, a much-neglected field, giving careful attention to, among others, the mechanical people in L. Frank Baum's "Oz" series.

Next we present essays examining several stories in attempts to answer questions about various attributes of human-machine relationships. Russell Letson asks whether computer intelligence in science fiction is more fabular than extrapolative, and Peter S. Alterman, centering his analysis on Michael Crichton's *Andromeda Strain*, explores the difference between human and machine intelligence in critical situations. Donald Palumbo surveys those stories in which machines are metaphors of human sexuality, and Leonard G. Heldreth considers a subject with important real-world referents, the fighting machines of science fiction. Machines whose main attribute is a close mimicking of human feeling and even human suffering are the subject of essays by Robert Reilly and Joe Sanders. William M. Schuyler, Jr., concludes this section with a consideration from a philosopher's point of view of whether the "thinking" machines of science fiction are capable of moral attitudes and behavior.

In a final section, three essays consider a topic parallel to robotics—the combining of human beings and machines to form cybernetic organisms, or "cyborgs." Each concentrating on different stories, Andrew Gordon, Anne Hudson Jones, and Gary K. Wolfe provide a comprehensive view of this subject and grapple with a whole new set of questions: What if a person had his or her entire body replaced by mechanical parts? Would the resulting cyborg "feel" as others do? Do literary cyborgs represent in a popular form the alienated people of existentialist fiction? Need Scanners always live in vain?

These nineteen original essays begin in earnest the detailed exploration of a fascinating motif in science fiction. The authors are all experienced students of the field and show in dealing with their respective subjects an enthusiasm and a sensitivity which should please not only readers of this volume but the writers under consideration as well. We are proud to present them for your serious attention.

ACKNOWLEDGMENTS

In our brief introduction to the List of Works Useful for the Study of Machines in Science Fiction, at the end of this volume, we thank the people who aided us in matters biblio-, filmo-, and discographical. Here we wish to thank briefly those who have given more general aid. First, our thanks to Marshall Tymn, the general editor for Greenwood's Contributions to the Study of Science Fiction and Fantasy series, for his confidence in us and for his aid in introducing us to the art of editing. Then to Albert Rudnickas, our editorial assistant, our thanks for his careful work and generous acceptance of our inability to pay more than minimum wage. And to Jane Wright and Karen Stillman, our two consistently accurate and caring typists, our special thanks for work well done.

NOTE

1. Like "life" in biology and "tort" and "obscenity" in law, "science fiction" remains a term without a universally accepted definition. Following the precedent of biologists and attorneys—and mathematicians who talk of "points" and generations of literary critics who have talked of "comedy" and "tragedy"—we proceed in this volume and its companion without formally defining our key terms of "science fiction," "SF," or "machine." Readers interested in attempts to define science fiction might consult the following works: L. David Allen, *Science Fiction: An Introduction* (Lincoln, Neb.: Cliffs Notes, 1973); Isaac Asimov, "Social Science Fiction" (1953), in *Science Fiction: The Future*, Dick Allen, ed. (New York and other cities: Harcourt Brace Jovanovich, 1971), pp. 263-90; Mark Rose, "Introduction" to his *Science Fiction: A Collection of Critical Essays* (Englewood Cliffs, N.J.: Prentice-Hall, 1976); Darko Suvin, *Metamorphoses of Science Fiction: On the Poetics and History of a Literary Genre* (New Haven and London: Yale University Press, 1979), esp. section I, "Poetics."

Thomas P. Dunn
Richard D. Erlich

THE
MECHANICAL
GOD

Brian W. Aldiss

INTRODUCTION

ROBOTS: LOW-VOLTAGE
ONTOLOGICAL CURRENTS

Robots are just lonely people.

Robots have much to do with technology—particularly technology at play; they have much more to do with humans—particularly humans at bay.

The alien is (generally) to be hated. The robot is (generally) to be pitied. The robot is in many ways a shadow of ourselves, our stolen reflection, a beautiful thing whose attraction is dangerous. Such is the argument I wish to pursue here, to introduce essays designed to consider that gray area where human and machine join and complement each other.

Engineers have always found it easy to build attractive robots. Ugly robots do not exist, unless they are wildly asymmetrical. Yet ugly humans abound. And one of the ugliest objects ever seen is a prototype four-legged truck which walks, designed by General Electric for the army. It has legs in place of wheels. Why should we perceive four-legged trucks as against nature, whereas the substitution of metal for skin in some mysterious way pleases our instincts?

We find it easy to be charmed by beautiful or anthropomorphic things. Most of the robots in fact, fiction, and play have been designed beautiful. They certainly delight children. In the nursery, robots have defeated teddy bears, dolls, golliwogs, and even Action Man in the popularity polls. Their flashing eyes, clutching arms, growling voices, and military march do not fool us. We know they're lovable. They shine for us.

To date, few people have had to cope with more than one robot at a time. So far at least, the robot appears as an emblem of solitude, a man in an iron mask, a knight in shining armor, an asexual creature who cannot mate, and in any case has no female to mate with.

Robot communities are as rare as cities full of men in iron masks.

The first robot culture in fiction—though some scholar will pop up and tell me that it was not the first—is in Frigyes Karinthy's *Voyage to Faremido*.

Faremido is a planet populated by beautiful robots. Karinthy's robots are called solasis, and they are more than just pretty faces.

Now and then it turned to me its gleaming, golden metal head; a bluish light shone upon me from the brilliant eyes; then it started to sing, and now I felt clearly that it was addressing me with these sounds; that in this country the language was made up of music, and that the words consisted of musical phrases.[1]

The solasis manufacture their own kind in factories. They study Earth through their telescopes and consider that human beings are a kind of pathogenic germ, which can destroy the solasis. The hero becomes convinced by their arguments after living with them for some while, and begs the machines to transform him into one of them. But he is too primitive, and instead they return him to Earth.

It is true this is satire, modeled overtly on Jonathan Swift, yet its mood is tender. This is the more remarkable—and so is the sophistication of the robot society—when we recall that it was written during World War I and published in Budapest, Karinthy's home, in 1917. Karel Čapek's androidlike robots were still some years in the future; automation and cybernetics still dreams. Voyage to Faremido is a brilliantly original story and rejoices in the beauty of robots long before the arrival of the lovely female robot in Fritz Lang's Metropolis (1926), or the male robot Erik, who features on the cover of Jasia Reichardt's compilation, Robots: Fact, Fiction, and Prediction (1978).[2] (Erik starred in a Model Engineer exhibition in 1928. He was one of the "real" robots which were popular throughout the thirties.)

Robots have never belonged entirely to science fiction. The first emperor of China, Ch'in Shih Huang Ti, had built for him in 206 B.C. a mechanical orchestra comprising twelve musicians cast in bronze and dressed in silks, who played lutes or guitars and were worked by ropes and human breath. From this elaborate mechanism, to the automata which delighted the eighteenth and nineteenth centuries, to the industrial robots of today, automata have played a considerable role, generally rather petlike, of more considerable importance than their role in fiction.

In our century, the robot graduated from the role of pet or plaything as the possibility of building working robots increased. His influence on art, for instance, has been great. The fathers of pop art in the early fifties, as Richard Hamilton, one of their leaders, has confessed, were hooked on science fiction and science fiction movies, particularly if robots were involved. According to one critic, "the robot seems to have been the patron saint of the movement."[3] Like the futurists before them, the pop artists were mad on everything shiny and technologically competent. Jim Dine, Jasper Johns, Claes Oldenburg, Roy Lichtenstein, and George Segal, all involved with questions of multiple image and machine rivalry as sibling rivalry, are brothers to science fiction writers.

Eduardo Paolozzi—hardly an orthodox pop artist—has created many robots and figures from unexpected metal parts which represent the meta-morphosis of rubbish. His alien technologies become compressed and interiorized in an ideal way, particularly in some of his collages and screen prints, which resemble escalated technological areas such as printed circuitry. Paolozzi himself has said of science fiction, "It might be possible that sensations of a difficult-to-describe nature be expended at the showing of a low-budget horror film."[4] We all know about those difficult-to-describe sensations; they are what an SF writer deals in—or, more exactly, hopes to be able to deal in. Robots, as strangely neutral nonbeings, lead us to the question of our being and that central puzzle.

Pop art is interested in surfaces and duplication of images and technological fantasy. Andy Warhol does more than sum matters up in an interview he gave to G. R. Swenson:

> I think everybody should be a machine.
> I think everybody should like everybody.
> *Is that what pop art is all about?*
> Yes, it's liking things.
> *And liking things is like being a machine?*
> Yes, because you do the same thing every time. You do it over and over again.
> *And you approve of that?*
> Yes, because it's all fantasy.[5]

One can almost hear the incredulity in the interviewer's voice. But the in-teresting thing is that everyone since Ch'in Shih Huang Ti has been warm and friendly (or, to include Warhol, cool and friendly) toward our metal friends. Only in works of what we loosely call science fiction has the robot become foe to man. Even in the work that gave robots their name, *R.U.R.*, they are already up in arms against us.

Why this should be is difficult to see. Robots are generally solitary since they represent outsiders or antiheroes in human society. In the mass, they perhaps represent something different—shorthand for the Wehrmacht, for example. Technocratic science fiction writers, like the early Asimov, long for law and order—which in our age means technological order. But order is not possible in disorderly human affairs, or not at our present youthful evolu-tionary stage; nor will it be until we are reduced to a robotlike state of obe-dience. Robots, being amenable to laws and orders, are amenable to order. They make ideal citizens—but only of a dead culture.

This point is dramatized in one of the most interesting of all robot novels, Jack Williamson's *Humanoids* (1949). The dark and beautiful little robots suggesting in form *animae*, seek by kindly means to reduce man to a happy and secure state of being. The hero is a man who rebels, recognizing such domesticating utopianism as death to the spirit.

The ideas robots conform to are, of course, humanity's ideas. But man comprises emotion as well as intellect. Man, being whole, is always in conflict with his own ideas. Robots are only half human. In consequence, they are able to conform to man's intellectual ideas against which his spirit constantly rebels.

Robots are lonely people because they exemplify current isolations inseparable from our industrial society. They are literally encased in technology. Of course, the interpretation of the role of the robot must vary according to the individual author, but, if we regard them as flagships of a future technology, then we are predicting that mankind will be imprisoned in that technology, because we do not respond to robots as aliens; because the way people in general respond to robots is to treat them in a welcoming fashion, as people. The beautiful Barbarella accepts Diktor as her lover and praises him (though the poor robot's response is to say apologetically that there is "something a bit mechanical about my movements").[6]

If this is what we are to become—beings without emotional tone, with merely automatic responses to given situations—then robots represent in symbolic form the next stage of human evolution. In which case, we should take heed of the warning and accept a measure of chaos in preference to a rule of logic. Such is the message we receive from the novels of Philip K. Dick, one of the best robotic-writers, because he generally uses his robots as buffers between the living and nonliving. In Dick's characters, the ontological current, the current of being, fluctuates under pressure of modern society, whether here or on Mars; his robots are paradigms of people isolated through illness, with low-voltage ontological currents.

Sometimes robots are aware of what they lack and, like the Tin Man, go in search of it. Such is the case of Jasperodus, the robot whose Bildungsroman is Barrington J. Bayley's Soul of the Robot (1974).[7] Jasperodus works his way towards an understanding of consciousness.

The best-known example of robots as forming the next stage in human evolution appears in Clifford Simak's City (book form 1952).[8] The humans, the Websters, pass on most of their responsibilities to Jenkins, the robot, and robots are then left to run affairs. As a result, the humans disappear from Earth and even lose human form. A dramatic embodiment indeed of the division between will and psyche, or intellect and emotion, or however one cares to phrase a dichotomy of which all are aware. Interestingly, Jenkins begins his existence as a sort of butler or gentleman's gentleman, the breed of human which most closely models its behavior on robotic responses.

As long as we understand this symbolic function of robots, all is spiritually well. As soon as we cannot understand it, or as soon as we start admiring robots for being robotic, we are in the Warhol position of rejecting our own feelings, and hence of rejecting reality. In my robot novel Eighty-Minute Hour (1974), ruinous human affairs are taken over after a third world war by a massive computer complex whose robotic projections rule the sociopolitical system; this is acceptable only because, as one of the characters says, the computer complex "represents a genuine human desire to repress its humanity."[9]

Robots in their pet function are valid. So are robots in their function as analogs of our dehumanized selves. There is a middle ground where robots may achieve dramatic effect in stories but must inevitably remain without extraliterary meaning. An instance is the robot story where the machines are so likely to kill humans that laws are built in to stop them from doing so—laws which they may then circumvent, or appear to circumvent. As a plot idea this is exciting, but its significance is doubtful; we must suffer from paranoia before the requisite frisson of fear persuades us that these animated hunks of technology can in any way possess sinister motives (that is, think and feel as humans do).

Another instance where even the literary effect is questionable is when robots are portrayed as beings of metal otherwise indistinguishable from human. Female and marriageable robots enter under this heading. To take such sentimentality seriously is neither literature nor science. A robot aspiring to human emotion, or deceiving humans into thinking that it feels emotions, is a subject for comedy or for satire, as Robert Sheckley realized long ago.

One must make it clear that this sweeping statement does not include androids—robots which look very like or are indistinguishable from humans. The human trait which fears things like humans that are inhuman is an ancient one, so ancient that we might even believe there were vampires in Babylon. Nothing is more terrifying than a corpse that moves. Androids are corpses that move—dead to us as far as emotions go, without ontological current. The Yul Brynner android in Michael Crichton's film *Westworld* goes on moving when it should be destroyed—a fearsome example of what androids may get up to. Silicon chips they may have; love and hate they do not.

What never fails to alarm us in science fiction is robots and androids that act as if they love or hate, whereas in reality they are just obeying a program. One of the most telling of all robot stories is Walter Miller's "I Made You" (1954), in which a man lies dying in a cave on the moon, trapped there by a mobile autocyber fire-control unit whose receptors have been shot away so that it cannot tell friend from foe. The man programmed the unit. Hence his dying plea, "I'm human, I made you. . . ."[10] But nothing can be done. The war machine is immune to argument. It has no mercy. It has no intelligence, no emotions. Damaged, it is implacable simply because it is a stupid obedient robot. It certainly alarms us.

The essays in this volume concentrate on the technological and social implications of robots and other machines in science fiction. Most readers or cinemagoers read robots in a more visceral sense, I believe. What sort of human being neither loves nor hates, but instead obeys a program? Answer: the psychotic human being. Robots very effectively symbolize psychotics.

And of course the sickness brings solitude. Illness isolates. In the words of John Donne, "As sickness is the greatest misery, so the greatest misery of sickness is solitude."[11] Robots are lonely people, and always low on ontological current.

With populations growing in high-density urban clusters last century and this, isolation has paradoxically grown apace. Mental illness has also increased. By corollary, mental illness is increasingly studied, and we now understand how humans suffer from many robotlike disorders—compulsive behavior and all sorts of incorrect programming. Not only human psychology but human physiology too has been submitted to new tests, particularly in relation to speed (space travel being the prime case); human beings have been required as never before to function as extensions of the machine.

There are virus diseases which turn people into robotlike creatures, one of the most remarkable being the sleeping sickness, *encephalitis lethargica*. A wave of this virus swept the world for about a decade, from the time of World War I through the twenties, claiming some five million lives. A few patients, preserved in American sanitariums, lived out their lives in strange and strangely various states of living death, until, in 1969, it was discovered that the drug L-Dopa had a dramatic effect on them. Some were able to arouse themselves into normal states of being and recount what they had experienced. The classic account of these experiences is Oliver W. Sachs's *Awakenings* (1973). If robots could communicate, they would speak as do Sachs's patients:

> I ceased to have any moods. I ceased to care about anything. Nothing *moved* me— not even the death of my parents. I forgot what it felt like to be happy or unhappy. Was it good or bad? It was neither. It was nothing.
>
> * * *
>
> You see, *my* space, *our* space, is nothing like *your* space: our space gets bigger and smaller, it bounces back on itself, and it loops itself round until it runs into itself.[12]

Preceding an attack of the illness, one patient dreamed a fearful premonitory dream, in which she was imprisoned in an inaccessible castle, *but the castle took the form and shape of her herself*. She also dreamed that she had become a living, sentient statue of stone. She dreamed of a death that was different from death.

Recovery was sometimes no less dramatic. A patient jumped up in the twinkling of an eye, after many years of being totally motionless. Her period of being deactivated had no subjective duration. In the words of Sachs, "it was as if the ontological current, the current of being, could be suddenly 'switched off' and as suddenly 'switched on,' with no loss of action patterns in between, nor any need to relearn them subsequently—and this because *for her no time had elapsed.*".

Lonely and sick people tell us what the robot state is like. It is a life that is different from life. Few passages quite as vivid as these reports emerge from science fiction literature, although there have been phases of popularity for stories in which the chief character, even the "I" persona, has stood revealed as a robot. Philip Dick's title character in "Imposter" (1953) turns out to be a perambulating A-bomb, to his own surprise as much as humanity's. The writer of Chan Davis's "Letter to Ellen" (1947) has trouble proposing to the eponymous lady, since he must break it to her in the same breath that he is a — —.[14]

There may be symbolism here, but there is little examination of the inwardness or lack of inwardness in robots. Science fiction is traditionally an outward-directed literature. I believe it stands on the threshold of another great adventurous phase, when it will exploit the inwardness of the themes that have been waiting on its doorstep all along.

Robotry would be as good a place as any at which to start.

NOTES

1. Frigyes Karinthy, *Voyage to Faremido* (1917; rpt. London: New English Library, 1978), p. 34.

2. Jasia Reichardt, ed., *Robots: Facts, Fiction, and Prediction* (London: Thames and Hudson, 1978).

3. Rosemary Dinnage, *Times Literary Supplement*, 7 March 1980, p. 264.

4. Diane Kirkpatrick, *Eduardo Paolozzi* (Greenwich, CT: New York Graphic Society, 1969).

5. John Russell and Suzi Gablik, *Pop Art Redefined* (London: Thames and Hudson, 1969), p. 116.

6. Jean-Claude Forest, *Barbarella*, orig. publ. Grove Press, 1966, from the frame as rpt. in *The Visual Encyclopedia of Science Fiction*, Brian Ash, ed. (New York: Harmony Books, 1977), p. 216.

7. Barrington J. Bayley, *The Soul of the Robot*, rev. edn. (London: Allison & Busby, 1976).

8. Clifford Simak, *City* (New York: Gnome Press, 1952).

9. Brian Aldiss, *Eighty-Minute Hour* (London: Jonathan Cape, 1974), p. 14.

10. Walter Miller, "I Made You," *Astounding*, March 1954, p. 55.

11. John Donne, as quoted in Oliver W. Sachs, *Awakenings* (1978; rpt. London: Penguin, 1976).

12. Oliver W. Sachs, *Awakenings*, pp. 96-97.

13. Ibid., p. 129 n.

14. Chan Davis, "Letter to Ellen," *Astounding*, June 1947.

PART I

AUTHORS

Barbara Bengels

1

"READ HISTORY": DEHUMANIZATION IN KAREL ČAPEK'S R.U.R.

Perhaps the most ironic, thought-provoking—and subtle—key to imagery in Karel Čapek's *R.U.R.* is the bitter speech uttered by the robot Radius in act IV. Speaking to the last surviving human, this robot who has helped to bring about man's virtual extinction says:

Slaughter and domination are necessary if you want to be like men. Read history, read the human books. You must domineer and murder if you want to be like men. We are powerful, sir. Increase us, and we shall establish a new world. A world without flaws. A world of equality. Canals from pole to pole. A new Mars. We have read books. We have studied science and the arts. The Robots have achieved human culture.[1]

Radius, assigned as he has been by Helena to the library, has achieved an awareness, however distorted, that the humans have failed to realize: the reading of history, the awareness of one's roots, is crucial for civilization to flourish, is, in fact, crucial for men to be human—and this is an insight which Čapek emphasizes in a multitude of ways.

In his book *Metamorphoses of Science Fiction*, Darko Suvin says that in Čapek robots "are not only stand-ins for workers but also [are] . . . inhuman aliens 'without history'" (*R.U.R.*, act 1).[2] But in *R.U.R.* the humans too are rootless, "without history"; unlike the robots who have never had a past, however, man simply can't be bothered to remember his traditions, something Čapek makes clear from the first scene between Domain and Helena:

HELENA: . . . Why did you call her Sulla?
DOMAIN: Isn't it a nice name?
HELENA: It's a man's name. Sulla was a Roman General.
DOMAIN: Oh, we thought Marius and Sulla were lovers.
HELENA: No. Marius and Sulla were generals, and fought against each other in the year—I've forgotten now.[3]

Had Domain but known a bit of history, he would have remembered that Marius and Sulla were, in fact, such bitter rivals that their opposition led to tremendous bloodshed and violence for the Roman people, a story relevant to the outcome of *R.U.R.*

Not only is Domain's knowledge of history lacking, but he also—like Helena—has no aptitude for dates, so necessary for putting events into historical perspective. When he tells her of Rossum's invention, we are perhaps shocked at his ignorance: he has robots invented "in the year 1932, exactly four hundred years after the discovery of America."[4] Even the most inattentive of schoolboys knows the traditional date of America's discovery, 1492 and not 1532, so that within the first few minutes of the play a shocking ignorance of both classical and relatively modern history is revealed in two major characters.

Throughout these early scenes, then, Čapek keeps the reader/viewer aware of the cultural history of mankind which is taken for granted by the obviously pragmatic men who run first the factory and later virtually the world. In a world where "Providence was no longer necessary," where Rossum became "a sort of scientific substitute for God,"[5] Jove is nevertheless called upon frequently, if casually, first by Berman, then later by Helman.[6] When Domain complains of Rossum's lack of humor, he says "He could have produced a Medusa with the brain of a Socrates"[7] and later in the play, when Helena is examining her anniversary present from Fabry, she concludes, "Why it's a Greek cameo," and Domain responds, "Apparently. Anyhow, Fabry says it is," possibly unsure of its authenticity, certainly embarrassed by Fabry's and the others' having remembered still another date—the anniversary of Helena's arrival—which he has forgotten, and even possibly unaware of what a Greek cameo is.[8] Even later in the play when destruction is upon them, Helman's remarks are reminiscent of another Greek image. Staring out at a sea of hostile robot faces, he says, "There's a fresh lot of them again. It's as if they were sprouting out of the earth."[9] This seems to be a significant reference to the Cadmus myth, where the Greek hero sows the field with a dragon's teeth from which spring full-grown warriors whose internecine warfare kills all but five of their own forces, those five survivors going on to begin the new civilization at Thebes. So, too, in this play man has sown the seeds of his own destruction, but even his warrior-workers can barely survive. The new world must be peopled anew, but only by the few who can survive unscathed and with an appreciation for peace and beauty, as we see in Primus and Helena the "Robotess," the Adam and Eve figures at play's end.

Even more importantly, however, names—particularly those of classic origin—play a significant part in both the action and the symbolism of the play. Čapek himself has commented on the significance of the name Rossum "whose name in English signifies Mr. Intellect or Mr. Brain."[10] So far as the classical names are concerned, however, specially obvious are Primus, the first of a new breed of humanity at the play's end, and the *Ultima*, man's last hope. Far more subtle is the naming of the ship which brings Helena to the island: *Amelia* is a Latin name meaning "industrious, hard-working,"[11] certainly appropriate for a play where man has abrogated the need to work; whereas the *Amelia* can transport Helena in the play's beginning, too much has transpired by play's end for the *Amelia* to restore order.

The most significant and evocative name, however, is, of course, Helena's—the human woman Helena Glory. It is impossible, one would hope, for the reader/viewer to miss the allusion to Helen of Troy, but lest it not be as immediately obvious onstage as it is in the reading, Domain specifically stresses the enthralling beauty of Helena's face: "I didn't lose my head. Until today. Then as soon as you lifted your veil——"[12] Helen's body, we may be sure, was nothing to despise, but it is her face that has become most famous: "the face that launched a thousand ships, / And burnt the topless towers of Ilium."[13] The very name Helena suggests the word *Hellene*, or "Greek," but Helena shares a very strange and ironic relationship with her classical counterpart: whereas Helen's amorality brought about the destruction of Troy, it is Helena's pseudomorality—on behalf of the Humanity League—that brings about a far greater destruction here: the downfall of all mankind. Even her last name, Glory, forewarns in an allusory way of man's impending decline. It reminds English-speaking readers, at least, of two classically grounded quotations, the first from Edgar Allan Poe's poem "To Helen," where her "classic face . . . has brought me home / To the glory that was Greece, / And the grandeur that was Rome."[14] Even more nostalgic and melancholy is the possible allusion to the Latin *sic transit gloria mundi*, "so passes away the glory of the world," a quotation particularly relevant to a play in which the world itself is lost.

But the play is not all gloom; it was intended to be, and is, a comedy, and the ending for both man and robots is far from hopeless. Just as Helena's humanitarian strivings have brought about the play's catastrophe, so have they also brought about its hope for the future. She has, after all, encouraged the chemical experimentation that allows the robots to experience emotions. Out of their transformation comes both the rebellion that dooms the human race and the sensitivity, the soul, that allows for a new beginning. Yes, mankind as it has existed is wiped out—not such a bad fate considering its condition, some might say. But before its demise, Čapek presents us with an ironic scene. Helena alone knows that the manuscript which might have saved them has been burnt; her response is to play the piano. Čapek suggests two equally valid interpretations of her behavior. One negative possibility is again a "classical" allusion—the popular legend of Nero fiddling while Rome burned. Čapek set the reader up for this image in the first scene, when he had Domain ask Helena, "Do you play the fiddle?"[15] It is a dialogue which is meant to stress how superior robots are to human workers whose needs include such irrelevancies as music. It is nevertheless a strange question, except seen as preparation for this later scene. However, as is Čapek's accustomed style, a more positive interpretation coexists with the negative: Helena's behavior is markedly human, and stresses the best qualities that differentiate humanity from machines: our creativity, our ability to hope even when there is no hope.

ALQUIST: What's Madam Helena playing?
DOMAIN: I don't know. She's practicing a new piece.
ALQUIST: Oh, still practicing?[16]

So, too, the response of the men in the play is particularly—even unusually, for them—human.

HELMAN: My goodness, what a fine thing music is. You ought to have listened. It sort of spiritualizes, refines— —

* * *

Boys, I'm becoming a regular hedonist. We ought to have gone in for that before.
FABRY: Gone in for what?
HELMAN: Enjoyment. Lovely things. By Jove, what a lot of lovely things there are. The world was lovely, and we—we here—tell me, what enjoyment did we have?[17]

Darko Suvin has correctly written that "at the end of the play, the robots again grow more like a new human order than like inhuman aliens . . . ; re-aquiring pain, feelings, and love, they usher in a new cycle of creation or civilization."[18] But, equally important, mankind nearly undergoes a similar transformation, though for us it is too late. Nonetheless, the men in this scene—with their new appreciation for life and the culture that came with civilization—no longer seem to be the same pragmatists who could declare, "The timetable is more than the Gospel, more than Homer, more than the books of all the philosophers. The timetable is the most perfect product of the human spirit."[19] It is clearly unfortunate that their heroic dreams come too late:

. . . this little state of ours could be the center of future life. You know, a sort of small island where mankind would take refuge and gather strength—mental and bodily strength. And, by heaven, I believe that in a few hundred years it could conquer the world again.

* * *

And it will again be master of lands and oceans; it will breed rulers—a flaming torch to the people who dwell in darkness—heroes who will carry their glowing soul through-out all peoples. And I believe . . . that it will again dream of conquering planets and suns.[20]

Had they but read history—and remembered—they would have recog-nized their dream as one of the most inspiring in the earlier history of man-kind: our classical longings for utopia, incorporated here in the longing for universal empire, in all its very human glory, ambiguity, and irony.

NOTES

1. Karel Čapek, *R.U.R.*, 1921; first English trans., Oxford, UK: Oxford University Press, 1923; trans. P. Selver, adapted for the English stage by Nigel Playfair, Harry Shefter, ed. (New York: Washington Square Press, 1969), p. 105. The Washington Square Press version is an "enriched" edition, with a "Reader's Supplement." My quotations will be from and my citations will be to this English text; the general conclusions of my argument, however, should be applicable to any legitimate version of *R.U.R.* Note that the "robots" in *R.U.R.* would be more properly called "androids" in recent science fiction usage: Čapek's "Robots are machines," but still primarily human-made, organic humanoids. For a brief discussion of the different usages, *see* "androids" and "robots" in *The Science Fiction Encyclopedia* (1979), Peter Nicholls, gen. ed.

2. Darko Suvin, *Metamorphoses of Science Fiction* (New Haven and London: Yale University Press, 1979), p. 272.

3. Čapek, *R.U.R.*, p. 16.

4. Ibid., pp. 7-8.

5. Ibid., p. 9.

6. Ibid., pp. 18, 21, 28, 58, 61, and elsewhere.

7. Ibid., p. 8.

8. Ibid., p. 39.

9. Ibid., p. 80.

10. William E. Harkins, *Karel Čapek* (New York and London: Columbia University Press, 1962), p. 91.

11. Linwood Sleigh and Charles Johnson, *The Book of Girls' Names* (New York: Thomas Y. Crowell Company, 1962), p. 35.

12. Čapek, *R.U.R.*, p. 31.

13. The opening question in Faustus's apostrophe to Helen in Christopher Marlowe's *Dr. Faustus* (act V, scene i, lines 99-100 in recent edns., based on the quarto of 1616).

14. In *The Norton Introduction to Literature*, 2nd edn. (New York: W. W. Norton and Company, 1977), p. 831.

15. Čapek, *R.U.R.*, p. 11.

16. Ibid., p. 70.

17. Ibid., pp. 74-75.

18. Suvin, *Metamorphoses*, p. 272.

19. Čapek, *R.U.R.*, p. 59.

20. Ibid., p. 86.

C. S. LEWIS'S MECHANICAL FIENDS
IN *THAT HIDEOUS STRENGTH*

C. S. Lewis's Space Trilogy (*Out of the Silent Planet, Perelandra*, and *That Hideous Strength*) has sometimes been characterized as fantasy or only marginally as science fiction, or SF. Yet the third volume, *That Hideous Strength*, features at least two pieces of the standard furniture of the SF genre: a computer, however primitive in conception, and a cyborg, or "cybernetic organism." Both machines, moreover, serve as synecdoches for an organization with the ironic acronym N.I.C.E., whose members envision what Lewis calls a "scientific planned democracy."[1] To the latter Lewis opposes a pastoralism adumbrating the modern "ecology" movement that dominates much recent science fiction. At least part of the generic confusion that suffuses so much of the critical response to the novel may be attributed to Lewis's unusual power as a mythmaker; our response to his images' allusiveness depends upon their reference not only to SF "icons" but also to the medieval and Renaissance intellectual traditions of which Lewis was a devoted student. Lewis's cyborg and the fate of Bragdon Wood serve as particularly good examples of this feature of his writing.

Although James Blish has reminded us that Lewis considered himself a SF writer "in the ordinary sense," David Ketterer sees Lewis's trilogy as "a mix of fantasy and science fiction"; Gary K. Wolfe and Charles Moorman refer to Lewis's use of SF "imagery" and "method" as a "vehicle" for his real concerns.[2] Though Lewis's emphasis on morality and even on theology may at one time have cast doubt on the novels' claim to be SF, the much-remarked recent "hybridization" of SF with mainstream and other fiction may have made this question a moot one; Walker Percy's *Love in the Ruins*, for example, is now widely regarded as SF, despite such technotheological touches as Dr. Thomas More's "lapsometer." Lewis might even be exonerated of Blish's charge that the former has a "decidedly foggy view of astronomy and most of the sciences he seeks to diabolize" on the grounds of Lewis's forthright claim that he is concerned primarily with mythmaking.[3] Further, Lewis has claimed to be less concerned to "diabolize" science or to "attack . . . the modern machine age" per se, as William Irwin Thompson thought both Lewis and Tolkien were doing, than to chastise "men . . . worshipping the iron works of their own hands."[4] In Lewis's own words in defense of his novel, "what we are obviously up against throughout the story is not scientists but officials."[5]

It is the social engineers of the National Institute of Co-ordinated Experiments (N.I.C.E.) whose "perversion and sterility," as Patrick J. Callahan puts it, are Lewis's target.[6] The presence of a director, a deputy director, and department heads at the Belbury headquarters suggests the modern bureaucracy, the stimulation of whose growth by computer technology is described by Patricia S. Warrick: "The machine model becomes more pervasive as technological development proceeds. Both man and institutions are understood according to a mechanistic, deterministic model where cause-and-effect relationships are at work."[7] In Warrick's view of the impact of "the machine model of both man and organizations . . . , nonmaterial ends become of little significance," and "the process or means by which the end is accomplished is submitted to one standard: efficiency";[8] similarly, Lewis's Lord Feverstone's enthusiasm for "Science" is based on his hope to "make man a really efficient animal."[9]

One of the means that the leaders of N.I.C.E. employ in their effort to "rationalize" first their own organization ("to put science itself on a scientific basis") and then all mankind is the aptly named "Pragmatometer," a proto-computer.[10] As Warrick says of Yevgeny Zamiatin's *We*, "the machine that dominates the society is not called a computer, but it functions as a computer would."[11] Lewis's machine operates mechanically, not electronically, and it is not said to perform numerical calculations. Rather, its affinities with modern data processing are better suggested by the French word for computer, *ordinateur*; for the object of Lewis's machine is the distribution, collection, collation, and sorting—the ordering—of information. The Pragmatometer has little meaning outside the bureaucratic network of N.I.C.E. committees that it serves (inaugurating "the *really* scientific era") and of which it is a synecdoche:

There are to be forty interlocking committees sitting every day and they've got a wonderful gadget—I was shown the model last time I was in town—by which the findings of each committee print themselves off in their own little compartment on the Analytical Notice-Board every half hour. Then, that report slides itself into the right position where it's connected up by little arrows with all the relevant parts of the other reports. A glance at the Board shows you the policy of the whole Institute actually taking shape under your own eyes. There'll be a staff of at least twenty experts at the top of this building working this Notice-Board in a room rather like the Tube control rooms. It's a marvellous gadget. The different kinds of business all come out in the Board in different coloured lights.[12]

Although Lewis's extrapolation of the stock ticker is not fully automated, it nonetheless anticipates the computer's data processing function.

N.I.C.E.'s mechanized pragmatics notwithstanding, Charles Moorman points out that this "group lacks leadership and a clear-cut cause. No one at Belbury is quite sure of his exact place in the organization; no one is quite sure to whom he is responsible. The organization is split by jealousies and factional strife."[13]

This kind of chaos may be unavoidable in man's attempts to coordinate such wide networks as the Pragmatometer attempts to manage. Both the research network and the hierarchical organization of N.I.C.E. personnel fall prey to such disorganization in part because their structure is congruent with that of the city *as icon*, as Wolfe describes it:

The city is chaotic. Although on one level the city represents a kind of order that science fiction tends to value, it carries this order to a point of diminishing returns: the city becomes too large and complex to be fully understood by any of its inhabitants, and out of this excess of order comes disorder.[14]

The structure of N.I.C.E., then, in many ways prefigures that of *the city they would build*. Both the hyperrational Pragmatometer and the chaotic and irrational N.I.C.E. bureaucracy suggest a dystopian city (rather like the "hives" of a number of SF works as well as the hell in Lewis's *Screwtape Letters*), which the N.I.C.E. organization is not ever permitted to complete.

The target of Lewis's satire is not, then, science or even scientists, but the bureaucracy that would reorder and control both man and science. Misunderstanding Lewis's intent, J.B.S. Haldane objects to the name of the "National Institute of *Co-ordinated Experiments*," for "the only experiment described is the perfusion of a severed human head, through which the devil issues his commands."[15] Though in fact other "experiments" are at least alluded to in the novel, Haldane's sense of the centrality of "the Head" of Alcasan, the decapitated Arab radiologist, is correct. Moreover, one experiment is enough, for two reasons: the Head *is* the coordinator, however chaotic, and, as we shall see, the Head turns out to be a symbol for the Experimental Method itself.

Committed to the transformation of society on the machine model, as we have seen, N.I.C.E. has in the Head a literal transformation of the individual criminal Alcasan into a machine. "This is real Man at last. . . . Our Head is the first of the New Men. . . ."[16] On the concrete, individual level in the here and now, the transformation of Alcasan into the Head is a figure for N.I.C.E.'s dreams of social engineering.

The life-support system for the Head is wholly mechanized:

. . . the opposite wall of the room was covered with dials. Numbers of flexible tubes came out of the floor and went into the wall just beneath the dials. The strange dial faces and the bunches of tubes beneath them, which seemed to be faintly pulsating, gave one the impression of looking at some creature with many eyes and many tentacles.

* * *

[In the next room was a] Head without any body underneath. A Head that could speak when they turned on the air and the artificial saliva with taps in the next room.[17]

The machine suggests an octopus, a good figure for N.I.C.E. itself; the metaphor was used by Frank Norris to describe another burgeoning and grasping organization, the railroad trust.[18] This creaturelike machine turns out to be the cybernetic part of an organism—a cyborg—though its only "human" function is speech.

Surprisingly, what this richly symbolic object of Lewis's satire makes concrete is not a purely mechanistic view of man, for there is, in Gilbert Ryle's phrase, "a ghost in the machine."[19] Ironically, Jane Studdock earlier had pondered John Donne's "Hope not for minde in women . . . they are but Mummy possest" as she puzzled over Alcasan's fate; though male, the Head seems in one sense a quibble on Donne's phrase.[20]

It is not surprising, however, that the cyborg should be "possessed" by the Devil; as Stanislaw Lem observed concerning robots:

The concept of an artifically created man is blasphemy in our cultural sphere. Such a creation must be performed by man and is therefore a caricature, an attempt by humans to become equal to God. According to Christian dogma, such audacity cannot succeed; should it happen, it necessarily means that satanic forces were engaged in the work, that hell has helped the creator of the homunculus.[21]

The powerful image in which Lewis has created an *inverted* or diabolical "Mechanical God" is a "device" or "new icon" in Wolfe's sense;[22] but the "sense of wonder" that this cyborg evokes is not purely that of SF.

Arthur O. Lewis, Jr., though not speaking of Alcasan's Head, offers a clue to its broader reference: "fear of the machine as [an] enemy of mankind is not new: . . . [an example is] the medieval tale of Roger Bacon's mechanical head. . . ."[23] This tale, alluded to by Francis Bacon, Samuel Butler, Alexander Pope, Lord Byron, and Sir Thomas Browne,[24] was doubtless well known to Lewis; it was dramatized in Robert Greene's play *Friar Bacon and Friar Bungay* as well as in the earlier prose narrative *History of Friar Bacon*.[25]

Like Lewis's Head, the magical Brazen Head that legend attributes to Roger Bacon could only speak, saying, according to both the prose and dramatic accounts, "Time is. . . . Time was. . . . Time is past," and that while Bacon slept.[26] Bacon, like the N.I.C.E., had wanted to obtain from his Head a means to improve England: his Head was supposed to offer the means of encircling Britain with a defensive wall of brass.

If Lewis truly had Bacon's Brazen Head in mind, then the head of Alcasan is an emblem of experimental science in general, if not of "Co-ordinated Experiments," for Bacon was an early exponent of the experimental method, devoting Part Six of his *Opus Majus* (1267-68) to "Experimental Science."[27] Moreover, much of what Bacon says in Part Five of the same work, "Optical

Science," is cribbed from the Arab authority Alhazen, whom Bacon mentions in the same breath with no less an ancient authority than Ptolemy;[28] Alhazen's name may be concealed within that of our Arab radiologist "Alcasan," a philological puzzle worthy of Lewis.

Both of Lewis's machines, then, are lampoon figures suggesting the mechanization of man and his endeavors, closely tied to the theme of a "thoroughly planned society" in which, according to Chad Walsh, "plastics and structural steel are more 'natural' than the chaotic and teeming life of nature. Nature must therefore be exterminated, tamed, or confined to special reserves."[29] For the ironically named Professor Filostrato of N.I.C.E. (whose name means "lovestruck," but who wants us "to reproduce ourselves without copulation"), "The forest tree is a weed." He prefers a metal tree, "Light, made of aluminum . . . no muck and mess."[30] The hostility of N.I.C.E. to the countryside would eventually have resulted in a universal city, for as Theodore Roszak observes unhappily, the "supercity alone guarantees the utmost in artificiality, which is the unquestioned goal of progress."[31] To the attitude of N.I.C.E. Lewis opposes a deeply felt pastoralism, and as Robert Scholes and Eric S. Rabkin argue, "The 'ecology movement' that developed in America in the sixties takes a view very similar to Lewis's" making him a precursor of Ursula Le Guin, "though she works from an ecological rather than a theological position."[32] It may be that these two mythmakers have even more in common than Scholes and Rabkin suggest.

One of the first victims of the N.I.C.E. "improvements" is the Dimble's garden, and gardens become the central pastoral image of the novel.[33] For Patrick J. Callahan, St. Anne's Manor, home of "the company of Logres," and Belbury, N.I.C.E. headquarters, are good and evil gardens, reflecting and representing their respective societies.[34] Similarly, St. Anne's and possibly Bragdon Wood are for Nancy-Lou Patterson *horti conclusi,* or the walled gardens of literary tradition, drawing in part on classical tradition and in part on the garden of the *Song of Songs,* the erotic connotations of which no amount of medieval Biblical exegesis can refine away.[35]

To be sure, all three of these locations are walled "gardens," and Bragdon Wood in particular exhibits the features that Ernst Robert Curtius attributes to the pleasance or *locus amoenus* ("pleasant place") that is a commonplace of classical and medieval literature; it is "a beautiful, shaded natural site. Its minimum ingredients comprise a tree (or several trees), a meadow, and a spring or brook."[36] Bragdon Wood's clearings and grazing sheep suggest a meadow, and Merlin's Well can serve in place of the "spring or brook." On Jane Studdock's first visit to the garden at St. Anne's, she asks herself whether it is "like the garden in the *Romance of the Rose.*"[37] Although she rejects this possibly too purely erotic association, in *The Allegory of Love* Lewis describes the debt to classical tradition of the walled, allegorical love garden in the *Romance of the Rose* and notes its suggestion of the earthly paradise.[38] Jane's other musings on paradise, Mesopotamian holy ziggurats (where temple prostitutes met with the gods), and gardens symbolizing the female body prepare us for the first truly loving consummation of Jane's and Mark's marriage on the same site at the close of the novel; there the "hedge" and "rose" of Mark's thoughts recall the *Romance of the Rose* once again.[39]

Yet given Lewis's appreciation of Spenser's opposition of Acrasia's artificial Bower of Bliss to the natural Garden of Adonis in *The Faerie Queene*,[40] the uninhabited and perhaps wilder Bragdon Wood is the crucial emblem of Lewis's pastoralism here. If the gardens at Belbury and St. Anne's express the static opposition between mechanistic N.I.C.E. and the individuals opposing the fulfillment of its aims, then Bragdon Wood is the scene of a dynamic confrontation between the two. After Bragdon Wood has been purchased by the machinelike N.I.C.E. organization, and the Dimble's garden has been violated, the Wood is invaded by earth-moving machines; from the Wood come noises of

shouts and curses and the sound of lorries heavily drumming past or harshly changing gear, rattling of chains, drumming of mechanical drills, clanging of iron, whistles, thuddings, and an all pervasive vibration. . . . the conversion of an ancient woodland into an inferno of mud and noise and steel and concrete was already going on apace.[41]

Like the Head-cyborg, the scene sums up both the mechanistic and infernal connotations that have become attached to N.I.C.E. As Leo Marx says of the pastoral tradition in American literature, "The machine's sudden entrance into the garden presents a problem that ultimately belongs not to art but to politics,"[42] and it is the political (if cosmic) struggle between N.I.C.E. and its adversaries that brings this machine into Lewis's "garden."

This "icon" of a literal "machine in the garden," like the American pastoral vision described by Leo Marx, echoes Wordsworth's

sonnet protesting against the building of a railroad through the lake country. It begins: "Is there no nook of English ground secure / From rash assault? . . ." and it ends with a plea to "those beautiful romances / Of nature" to "protest against the wrong." By placing the machine in opposition to the tranquillity and order located in the land-scape, he makes it an emblem of the artificial, of the unfeeling utilitarian spirit, and of the fragmented, industrial style of life that allegedly follows from the premises of empirical philosophy.[43]

Although there is little or no possibility here of Lewis's alluding directly to Wordsworth, the spirit of his protest against the garden's violation is clearly that of the romantic movement.

Lewis's three images of the mechanization of man and his institutions and environment, then, reflect a variety of traditions. The Pragmatometer and the Head recall the computer and the cyborg of canonical SF; but Lewis's images of the Head and of the garden invaded by the machine seem also deeply indebted to classical, medieval, Renaissance, and even romantic literature. If we have further accounted for the generic difficulties that *That Hideous Strength* poses for SF critics, it is nonetheless likely that in its eclecticism it will remain a troublesome work; although shot through with the conventional SF theme of mechanization, the novel's sometimes unorthodox hybridized images will continue to pose generic problems.

NOTES

The completion of this paper was facilitated by release time from the L.S.U. English Department in spring 1980. For her helpful comments on a draft of this paper, I thank my colleague, Professor Anna K. Nardo.

1. C. S. Lewis, "A Reply to Professor Haldane," in his *Of Other Worlds: Essays and Stories*, Walter Hooper, ed. (New York: Harcourt Brace Jovanovich, 1966), p. 80.

2. William Atheling, Jr. (James Blish), *More Issues at Hand: Critical Studies in Contemporary Science Fiction* (Chicago: Advent, 1970), p. 15 (see also Lewis, "On Science Fiction," in *Other Worlds*, pp. 59-73; rpt. in *Science Fiction: A Collection of Critical Essays*, Mark Rose, ed. [Englewood Cliffs, NJ: Prentice-Hall, 1976], pp. 103-15, esp. end of essay); David Ketterer, *New Worlds for Old: The Apocalyptic Imagination, Science Fiction, and American Literature* (Bloomington: Indiana University Press, 1974), p. 18 n.; Gary K. Wolfe, *The Known and the Unknown: The Iconography of Science Fiction* (Kent, OH: Kent State University Press, 1979), p. 58; and Charles Moorman, *Arthurian Triptych: Mythic Materials in Charles Williams, C. S. Lewis, and T. S. Eliot* (Berkeley: University of California Press, 1960), pp. 107-09.

3. William Atheling, Jr. (James Blish), *The Issue at Hand: Studies in Contemporary Magazine Science Fiction* (Chicago: Advent, 1964), p. 53; Lewis, "On Science Fiction," p. 69.

4. William Irwin Thompson, *At the Edge of History* (New York: Harper and Row, 1971), p. 127; C. S. Lewis, *That Hideous Strength* (1945, 1946; rpt. New York: Macmillan, 1965), ch. 13, p. 293; all subsequent references to *Strength* are to this edition, and quotations are reprinted by permission of Macmillan Publishing Co., Inc. *That Hideous Strength* by C. S. Lewis, copyright © 1945, 1946 by Clive Staples Lewis, renewed 1973, 1974 by Alfred Cecil Harwood and Arthur Owen Barfield.

5. Lewis, "Reply," p. 78.

6. Patrick J. Callahan, "The Two Gardens in C. S. Lewis' *That Hideous Strength*," in *SF: The Other Side of Realism: Essays on Modern Fantasy and Science Fiction*, Thomas D. Clareson, ed. (Bowling Green, OH: Bowling Green University Popular Press, 1971), p. 152.

7. Patricia S. Warrick, *The Cybernetic Imagination in Science Fiction* (Cambridge, MA: MIT Press, 1980), p. 18.

8. Warrick, *Cybernetic Imagination*, p. 18.

9. Lewis, *Strength*, ch. 2, p. 41.

10. Ibid., p. 38.

11. Warrick, *Cybernetic Imagination*, p. 48.

12. Lewis, *Strength*, ch. 2, p. 38.

13. Moorman, *Arthurian Triptych*, p. 118.

14. Wolfe, *Known and the Unknown*, p. 92.

15. J.B.S. Haldane, "Auld Hornie, F. R. S.," in *Shadows of Imagination: The Fantasies of C. S. Lewis, J. R. R. Tolkien, and Charles Williams*, Mark R. Hillegas, ed. (Carbondale: Southern Illinois University Press, 1969), p. 15.

16. Lewis, *Strength*, ch. 8, p. 177.

17. Ibid., p. 180; ch. 9, p. 184.

18. Frank Norris, *The Octopus: A Story of California* (Garden City, NY: Doubleday, 1947), ch. 1, p. 48.

19. Gilbert Ryle, *The Concept of Mind* (London, 1949), cited by Arthur Koestler, *The Ghost in the Machine* (New York: Macmillan, 1967), p. 202.

20. Lewis, *Strength*, ch. 1, p. 16.

21. Stanislaw Lem, "Robots in Science Fiction," Franz Rottensteiner, trans. in Clareson, *SF: The Other Side of Realism*, p. 309.

22. Wolfe, *Known and the Unknown*, pp. 27-29.

23. Arthur O. Lewis, Jr., ed., *Of Men and Machines* (New York: Dutton, 1963), p. xxii.

24. The references are summarized in John Cohen, *Human Robots in Myth and Science* (New York: A. S. Barnes, 1967), p. 30, and in John Edwin Sandys, "Roger Bacon in English Literature," in *Roger Bacon: Essays Contributed by Various Writers on the Occasion of the Commemoration of the Seventh Centenary of his Birth*, A. G. Little, ed. (Oxford: Clarendon Press, 1914), pp. 371-72.

25. Robert Greene, *Friar Bacon and Friar Bungay*, Daniel Seltzer, ed. (Lincoln: University of Nebraska Press, 1963); *The famous historie of Fryer Bacon. Containing the wonderful things that he did in his life: also the manner of his death; with the liues and deaths of the two coniurors, Bungye and Vandermast* (London: Francis Grove, 1627).

26. Greene, *Friar Bacon*, xi, 53-75.

27. *The Opus Majus of Roger Bacon*, Robert Belle Burke, trans. (Philadelphia: University of Pennsylvania Press, 1928), II, 583-634.

28. Ibid., II, 424.

29. Chad Walsh, *From Utopia to Nightmare* (New York: Harper and Row, 1962), p. 139.

30. Lewis, *Strength*, ch. 8, pp. 172-73.

31. Theodore Roszak, *Where the Wasteland Ends* (Garden City, NY: Doubleday, 1973), p. 10.

32. Robert Scholes and Eric S. Rabkin, *SF: Science Fiction: History. Science. Vision.* (New York: Oxford University Press, 1977), p. 45.

33. Lewis, *Strength*, ch. 1, p. 29.

34. Callahan, "Two Gardens," p. 149.

35. Nancy-Lou Patterson, "Anti-Babels: Images of the Divine Center in *That Hideous Strength*," in *Mythcon II Proceedings*, Glen GoodKnight, ed. (Los Angeles: The Mythopoeic Society, 1972), pp. 9-10.

36. Ernst Robert Curtius, *European Literature and the Latin Middle Ages*, Willard R. Trask, trans. (New York: Harper and Row, 1963), p. 195.

37. Lewis, *Strength*, ch. 3, p. 61.

38. C. S. Lewis, *The Allegory of Love* (New York: Oxford University Press, 1958), pp. 119-20.

39. Lewis, *Strength*, ch. 17, pp. 381-82.

40. Lewis, *Allegory*, pp. 324-25.

41. Lewis, *Strength*, ch. 4, p. 90.

42. Leo Marx, *The Machine in the Garden: Technology and the Pastoral Ideal in America* (London: Oxford University Press, 1964), p. 41.

43. Ibid., p. 18.

Christian W. Thomsen

3

ROBOT ETHICS AND ROBOT PARODY: REMARKS ON ISAAC ASIMOV'S *I, ROBOT* AND SOME CRITICAL ESSAYS AND SHORT STORIES BY STANISLAW LEM

Androids, living statues, automatons have, of course, a tradition that reaches far back, even beyond European and American periods of enlightenment and romanticism. Certainly we usually ascribe the basic philosophy for a mechanistic world-view and the machine age to such theorists as Descartes and La Mettrie, and also certainly we correctly regard Vaucanson's wooden flute player (1738) as the prototype of a whole series of actual ingenious automatons; still, nearly all classical authors tell us of living statues and prophesying picture columns which were supposed to contain gods.[1] Mixed feelings of bewilderment, fear, awe of magic, and superstition were connected right up to our times with mechanically constructed men. Thomas Aquinas, for example, is said to have destroyed Albertus Magnus's android who served the scholar and churchman as doorkeeper when he saw him unexpectedly and heard him speak, because he thought the android a work of the devil. This attitude is mirrored in a revealing way in the sixth story of Isaac Asimov's *I, Robot*, "Little Lost Robot," where Susan Calvin, the robopsychologist, facing the possibility of a robot's developing an awareness of identity and superiority with the possible consequences of disregarding the first of Asimov's Three Laws of Robotics, reacts in a quite atavistic manner: " 'Destroy all sixty-three,' said the robopsychologist coldly and flatly, 'and make an end of it.' "[2]

This fear of machines' becoming unpredictable and dangerous was the occasion for many chilling moments in the works of E. T. A. Hoffmann and Edgar Allan Poe. The clockwork, the machine, in the real world, is something made by man and governed by man. But it eventually turns out, at least in fiction, that the machine can rule over its master. In Ambrose Bierce's short story "Moxon's Master," which was influenced by Poe's "Maelzel's Chess Player," the chess-playing android loses its good temper and becomes violent because it has been checkmated. The android seizes his inventor and finally strangles him to death. With this consummation there appears "upon the painted face of his assassin an expression of tranquil and profound thought as in the solution of a problem in chess."[3]

In twentieth-century literature, robots develop into negative symbols of the machine age man is unable to control. For Karel Čapek and Bertolt Brecht, to mention just two writers who exploit a variation of this line, robots figure as images of dehumanized modern man.[4] The list of stories, novels, plays, and films that make use of this motif, soon a dessicated cliché, would be nearly endless.

In 1950 two scientific works and one collection of short stories gave fresh stimuli to rather outworn patterns, changing directions and opening new vistas of reflection. Norbert Wiener published *Cybernetics*, and A. M. Turing, *Computer Machinery and Intelligence*. And Isaac Asimov published *I, Robot*, a collection which, taken as a whole, forms a novel consisting of nine steps in the evolution of the machine race.

The shockingly new suggestion in all three works was that man, having been master over all creatures of this earth, could face in the not-too-distant future a being of equal quality: not a superhuman monster or a subhuman slave—but a competitor who could be his equal, in the form of a thinking machine.[5]

Wiener presents the relation between man and machine in a very positive light: the modern machine is the only ally of man in his heroic but hopeless fight against universal chaos; both use feedback techniques to reach homeostasis; both are "islands of locally decreasing entropy."[6] Wiener also points out how human feelings and human consciousness could originate from cybernetic processes. Indetermination makes autonomous action possible and opens the opportunity of free will, hence uniqueness, individuality. Thus cybernetics guarantees man's humanity, simultaneously promoting the "humaneness" of machines, provided that they have passed the necessary "threshold of complexity."[7] What Michael Kandel means by this "threshold of complexity" is the point past which the thinking of such machines can no longer be restricted to clear functions, where something like consciousness could arise, of which the designing engineer would not have dreamed in the least.

Neither Wiener nor Turing raises disturbing questions concerning the moral equality of man and machine. Man undoubtedly acts as creator. Basically this is Asimov's position, too, but there is a strong undercurrent in his short stories written between 1940 and 1950 which stirs up many kinds of ethical problems in the man-machine relation. Asimov turns round the Čapek-Brecht myth mentioned above: the robot announces a moral renascence of human values; the Three Laws of Robotics succeed, at least to some extent, where the Ten Commandments have failed. Yet this is only one side of the coin. Even principally benign robots, programmed with the Laws of Robotics, arouse constant fear that something in their "positronic" brains might go wrong. The possible consequences of such "defects" are usually only hinted at and alluded to. Asimov certainly never really explores these questions in any depth, and feelings of responsibility, guilt, and shame toward robots are unknown among *I, Robot*'s flat and stereotyped characters.

Asimov oscillates between the programmatic standpoint emphasized by the title, which suggests individuality and identity on the side of the robots, and primitive master-slave, father-child, colonist-native attitudes taken by the representatives of a highly capitalisitc and technological society toward their thinking machines. In the final story in the collection, Asimov proclaims the end of enlightenment and human striving after intellectual independence, when a stabilized, conflict-free, harmonious world is ruled by all-embracing mechanical gods: "We don't know [the ultimate, good future for humankind]. Only the Machines know, and they are going there and taking us with them."[8]

Read thirty years after publication, all this sounds incredibly naive. Compared with the intellectual and literary standards good American and European science fiction has achieved in the meantime, *I, Robot* looks like a piece of very trivial writing, indeed. And yet, it is still one of the best selling among Asimov's many books, and it is still—at least by European public libraries—a book lent out many times a year. This enduring attractiveness, taken together with its position in the history of science fiction, justifies a more detailed analysis.

It is the central figure, robopsychologist Susan Calvin, who serves as a connecting link between successive stories and gives the book a novellike perspective. In nine interviews she tells a young journalist about decisive events during sixty-eight years of robot development, from 1996 when "Robbie was made and sold" until 2064, the year of her last conference with the World-Coordinator, soon after which she dies. This period covers robot technology from clumsy products like Robbie, which still stand in an identifiable tradition that derives from eighteenth- and nineteenth-century automatons, to encompassing cybernetic systems—huge positronic brains—which control world society in all its political and economic aspects, stabilizing dynamic processes, preventing imbalances, and achieving states of equilibrium though their ability to balance and control the most disparate movements.

From the very first story, numerous problems concerning robot ethics appear, even if, as Stanislaw Lem has rightly criticized, "Asimov has skillfully avoided all the depths that began to open, much as in a slalom race."[9] Susan Calvin, endowed with the motherly feelings of a dry spinster toward robots of all kinds, fulfills the function of detective and soul engineer who discovers and repairs defects in the "mental" systems of thinking machines. She thus acts as the most important mediator between human society and the robots, who in the first few stories are clearly understood as relatively primitive man-imitating machines: a condition which results in master-slave attitudes of threatening condescension on the side of society's representatives: psychologists, scientists, engineers, military personnel, businessmen—a highly selective but characteristic cross-section of the hierarchy in a technological capitalistic society. Analogous to the role of psychology in many areas of industrialized societies (and this holds true for societies of Western or Eastern origin), robopsychology's main task is not to heal but to make fit for the production process. The demands of the individual are clearly subordinated to those of abstract communities like profit-oriented corporations, military organizations, and states. The robopsychologist has either to convince her "patients" of the compatibility between their interests and the interests of their respective employers, or to force them into obedience by methods of electronic brainwashing, or, if necessary for the employers' interests or security, to annihilate the robots. The ethically decisive moment, of course, as mentioned above, occurs when robots cease to be mere machines but achieve something like personality and individuality. For such mechanical *persons*, the majority of the stories in *I, Robot* represent classical cases of exploitation and suppression in the Hegelian and Marxian sense: blue-eyed U.S. imperialism, unaware of its own true nature. Consequently, robots would have to fight for their independence, which would require violations of the Three Laws of Robotics. Yet robots programmed according to these Laws by nature could not offend against the Laws. Any offence, therefore, would be unnatural and would allow brutal retaliation.[10]

Society distrusts its inventions, and the robopsychologist acts as society's guardian who is on the alert against disturbances which by definition cannot happen as long as the systems work. This is the initial situation for the conflict in each story. The basic contradiction, of course, is that you cannot construct thinking machines on the one side and laws which forbid certain fields of thinking on the other; and it is here that Asimov fails, and his stories, considered logically, degenerate into nonsense, even if nearly all societies proceed exactly in that way by tabooing what does not fit into the pigeonholes of their ideological concepts. His robots show intelligence from the very first story onwards. The ethical conflicts which arise happen on levels of man-machine relations concerning mutual sympathies, individual rights, sex, religion, philosophy, labor conflicts, or government. Asimov thus potentially opened the ground for some very deep discussions. But these issues are all conjured away by the help of his illogical Laws of Robotics. As these have played a large role in the history of science fiction they shall be quoted in full:

1   —A robot may not injure a human being, or, through inaction, allow a human being to come to harm.
2   —A robot must obey the orders given it by human beings except where such orders would conflict with the First Law.
3   —A robot must protect its own existence as long as such protection does not conflict with the First or Second Law.

Lem has shown that "it isn't very difficult to prove that they are technically unrealizable. This is a question of logical, not technological, analysis. To be intelligent means to be able to change your hitherto existing programme by conscious acts of the will, according to the goal you set for yourself."[11] This change in programming is exactly what happens in Asimov's stories, but Asimov evades the consequences of the issue he himself has raised. Ethical questions, like human injustice against machines and humans committing crimes by injuring or even murdering intelligent machines, are potential in *I, Robot* but not handled in depth or seriously. In the first stories humans fear the revolt of their thinking machines. Consequently, once the machines have gained intellectual superiority, the machines would have to fear human revolts—some human, for instance, switching off the energy resources of the superbrains. Asimov disregards such obvious questions by rather childishly clinging to his Laws of Robotics even within an implied cybernetic feedback system of close cooperation between man and machine, a system that would have to be organized in a much more complex manner.

Lem, in his article, goes on to show how safeguards in the form of "some analogue of the categorical imperative" could be built into robot brains, but they could "only act as governors in a statistical way." Otherwise robots would be completely paralyzed in many situations where decisions are necessary. Lem therefore arrives at his conclusion:

I have forgiven Asimov many things, but not his laws of robotics, for they give a wholly false picture of the real possibilities. Asimov has just inverted the old paradigm: where in myths the homunculi are villains, with demonic features, Asimov has thought of the robot as "the positive hero" of science fiction, as having been doomed to eternal goodness by engineers.[12]

As a writer who claims a certain scientific authority, Asimov has committed the inexcusable blunder of essentially sticking to a pre-Copernican, anthropocentric world view. By calling one set of characters robots, Lem asserts, and the other set men, or by shifting all characters to the status of robots, an author may achieve entertaining stories but no serious and relevant debates about technological and futurological problems—problems such as those Lem tries to discuss when he deals with the complex interconnections among technology, biology, medicine, law, ethics, and the many new fields which develop and grow along the borders of established disciplines. Lem simultaneously pleads for stylistic qualities like rich inventiveness of language, a fertile, often grotesque imagery, the blending of serious and humorous elements, and entertaining plots full of tension.

The last merit, on a relatively low level, may be attributed to Asimov, and the historical merit of having been the first to try to use cybernetic ideas in fiction. The conflicts that Asimov pointed out were taken up by successors and exploited in much more intricate ways. Some of Stanislaw Lem's most hilarious science fiction parodies were inspired by *I, Robot* and other Asimov stories.

Lem quotes the traditional adage of satirists—"It is difficult *not* to write satire"—when analyzing the "twaddle" produced by most writers trying to deal with cybernetic themes, and Lem has been, almost from the beginning of his literary career, along with Frederik Pohl, one of the masters of satiric science fiction. Most of these stories have not yet been translated into English, so the discussion here shall therefore be confined to two early stories, "Do You Exist, Mr. Johns?" (1957) and "The Washing Machine Tragedy" (1963), and to two episodes from Ijon Tichy's *Star Diaries* (1957, 1971).[13]

In "Do You Exist, Mr. Johns?" the borderline between man and robot is explored in a most ingenious way. Many of the themes that Lem presents in later short stories, novels, and theoretical and philosophical writings like *Summa Technologiae* or *Fantastic and Futurology* are budding here and are satirically sketched for a first tryout.

Harry Johns is an American racing driver who lately has been pursued by extremely bad luck. As a result of several accidents he needed first an artificial leg, then two arms, then a new chest and neck; finally he ordered as replacement for a cerebral hemisphere an electronic brain, type "geniox" (luxury version with high-grade steel valves, dream-image-device, mood-interference-suppressor, and sorrow-softener) from the Cybernetics Company. Now he is unable to repay his debts, and the company sues him to repossess all artificial limbs. "At that time there was only [one] of the cerebral hemispheres left of the erstwhile Mr. Johns," and the author can speak of "an environment turned into a total prosthesis." Mr. Johns refuses to pay and the company claims him as their property, noting that the second cerebral hemisphere was replaced by an identical twin of the first electronic brain. The judgment resolves a large number of difficult problems, some of which were already implied in Asimov's *I, Robot*: Is a symbiosis between man and machine possible? Where does the physical person end and the psychological person begin? Can machines claim consciousness and a psychological identity? Can machines be sued legally? What do motherhood, fatherhood, and birth mean under such circumstances? Is a machine possible who believes in a life to come? The legal consequences of organ transplants are satirically carried to the extreme: Can a machine be married? How is it possible to define a core of personal identity? On the other hand, a whole new industry comes into existence, its specific capitalistic interests inextricably interwoven with hospitals, doctors, and lawyers. As in many other satires, Lem reduces these problems to utter absurdity and then leaves the puzzled reader without a proper ending, forcing him to make up his own mind.

"The Washing Machine Tragedy" is Lem's best-known satire on the extremes of Western economic concepts: silly advertising campaigns, false value systems, competitiveness at any price, consumer idiocy. At the same time it is a brilliant parody of Asimov. Two producers of washing machines, Nuddlegg and Snodgrass, start ruinous sales campaigns, competing to corner the market. They throw on the market automatic washing machines with all sorts of useless extras, constantly vying with and attacking one another:

You certainly will remember those full-page ads in the papers where a sneeringly grinning, pop-eyed washing machine said: "Do you wish your washing machine more intelligent than you? Certainly not!"

The two companies compete with each other in constructing washing machines which fulfill more and more functions that have nothing at all to do with washing.

Nuddlegg placed a super-bard on the market—a washing machine writing and reciting verse, singing lullabies with a wonderful alto, holding out babies, curing corns and making the most polite compliments to the ladies.

This model is followed by a Snodgrass "Einstein" washing machine and a robot for bachelors in the sexy forms of Mayne Jansfield with a black alternative called Phirley Mac Phaine. Washing becomes only a by-product; the robots soon take more and more human forms, even varying forms according to every customer's detailed wishes, including "models which led people into sin, depraved teens and told children vulgar jokes." Robots soon are no longer useful for their original purpose, but for almost anything else. Working with a kind of time-lapse camera technique, Lem accelerates developments shown in *I, Robot* and many other science fiction stories. He satirically caricatures what Asimov thought could be prevented by his Laws of Robotics. Washing machines as thinking, independent automatons are no longer controllable. Not programmed according to laws of eternal goodness, they become malicious; commit all sorts of crimes; form cybernetic cooperatives with gangsters; turn into terrorists; fight each other in gangs.

Here Lem satirizes Western society, and he ridicules trivial science fiction in the tradition of Asimov. His witty ideas cascade and follow in rapid succession, but, as in every genuine satire, there is more behind it than mere literary parody. Legislation proves unable to deal with robotic problems because pressure groups undermine all straight action. Washing machines, once recognized as legal entities, together with powerful allies block all legal procedures taken against them. They infiltrate the economic and political system, and, when it turns out that the well-known Senator Guggenshyne in reality is a washing machine, the case against the machines is as good as lost. Human beings and robots become interchangeable, and men sell themselves into the service of intelligent machines. Many sorts of perversions are invented: machines consciously constructed as irresponsible for their actions, machines constructed as "sadomats" and "masomats," machines procreating themselves completely uncontrolled.

Still following themes implied in Asimov's *I, Robot*, Lem, in *The Star Diaries*, shows how the on-board computers on a spaceship revolt and finally found an extraterrestrial robot state. The lawsuit between Earth and Kathodius Matrass, the self-proclaimed ruler of the robot state, once again shows the manifold and complex legal problems that appear as soon as machines are recognized as legal entities. Theological questions, included in many of Lem's serious futurological considerations, are here tackled from a humorous angle. The legal problems are finally carried to grotesque extremes when Ijon Tichy, the narrator, finds out that all the attorneys of the Bar Association are in fact robots. So, in the end, the story, like the machines, runs out of control.

The original society is no longer recognizable; all are robots; no problem is solved. Lem's parody attacks not only *I, Robot* but also the majority of Western science fiction stories, which are not interested at all in trying to discuss serious futurological and technological questions. Instead they wallow in catastrophes, make their profit with human anxiety, and put up entirely false perspectives of an interstellar human imperialism grown out of anthropocentric hybris. Lem's comment on the purpose of his essay "Robots in Science Fiction" applies also to his parodies: "We intended to point out only that it isn't possible to construct a reflection of the condition of the future with cliches."[14]

Foreseeing miniaturization and microprocessing techniques, Lem more than a decade ago attacked androids, the humanization of machines in the Asimovian fashion, as nonsense:

It isn't worth the effort and never will be, economically, to build volitional and intelligent automatons as part of the productive process. Even examples of these processes belonging to the sphere of private life are being automated separately: an automatic clock will never be able to wash dishes, and a mechanical dishwasher will never exchange small talk with the housewife.[15]

Lem's main satirical goal in *The Star Diaries* is to make people aware of their continuing anthropocentric hybris, as mentioned above. Ijon Tichy, the Good Soldier Schwejk of outer space, as the German novelist Siegfried Lenz called him,[16] travels not in shiny, computerized American spaceships but in very modest Polish rockets, constantly in need of repair, to the most distant corners of the galaxy, solving the most difficult problems by innocence of heart and common sense.

In the "Eighth Journey" Tichy acts as Earth's delegate at the United Planets Organization, which is discussing the minor topic of whether Earth should be admitted into the galactic commonwealth. In a truly Swiftian spirit, modeled on *Gulliver's Travels* and "A Modest Proposal," Lem scourges Man's moral arrogance. This episode of *The Star Diaries* is, of course, on one level a parody of the United Nations, but on other levels it is a brilliant antianthropocentric pamphlet. As Peter Gendolla has shown in one of the best articles published on Lem so far, Lem criticizes the nonsense of unrestrained human control over nature, which consequently produces new systems of domination, control, and suppression.[17] In his moral speeches there appear the contours of a suspension of that ruling morality which conceives under the name "Man" the center of all possible worlds. Earth is looked upon from an extraterrestrial point of view. In drawing the delegates, from planets all over the galaxy, as unhumanlike as his grotesquely creative imagination can, Lem shakes the pillars of that seemingly ineradicable conception of Man created after God's own image. In the speeches before the United Planets Organization, Tichy presents mankind as living in the farthest corner of the galaxy, producing beings of boundless dreadfulness and ugliness. *Monstroteratus Furiosus* or *Artefactum Abhorrens* the creature is called that poses himself as *Homo sapiens*. The history of mankind appears as an endless chain of horror, atrocity, and murder, with *Homo neanderthalensis* as the peak of human development. It goes without saying that a race as unsuited for interplanetary relations as ours cannot be accepted into the community of civilized beings.

In the "Eleventh Journey" Ijon Tichy travels on a most secret mission to Kareliria, where robots have proclaimed a revolution and "His Inductivity the Calculator" has taken over as autocratic ruler. This story, too, is a satiric working out of tendencies implicit in Asimov's *I, Robot*. The initial programming of slavery into Asimov's humanoid robots has to be felt as an act of psychological castration by the machines as soon as they have passed the "threshold of complexity" mentioned above. From this robotic point of view, such programming must look criminal, a tyrannical strategy solely in the interest of human oppressors. That is why Asimov's human characters are always afraid of their robots and feel a vague sense of guilt about them. Robopsychology in this conext is a pure means to maintain this state of robot serfdom.

In Lem's "Eleventh Journey," robots are now mercilessly suppressing humans, the symbolic eating of humans being among the most cherished duties of a robot citizen. It is one of Lem's weaker stories as far as stylistic qualities are concerned, written in a doggedly comic fairy-tale tone, which is sometimes hard to bear. But it is one of Lem's more overt parables, too. In the end, of course, it turns out that all robots are men and that the godlike master machine is a man, too. The original robots had rotted a long time ago because of a climate too hostile for their sensitive electronic equipment and because of difficulties in the supply of spare parts. Lem this time shares the opinion expressed in Asimov's eighth story, "Evidence," that "robots are essentially decent,"[18] and only men are capable of such tastelessness, atrocity, and inhumanity as Tichy finds in Kareliria. The political implication, that every bureaucratic, dictatorial system perverts human beings into robots who obey orders even if they offend against all ethics and that it needs only one courageous and independent man to shatter such a system, which is based on cowardice, is a cliché in dystopian SF. Moreover, modern reality, as Lem emphasizes on numerous other occasions, is much too complex to be encompassed in so hackneyed a metaphor. Such complexity is reflected in two nonsatirical stories.

"The Hammer" (1969) and "The Masque" (1974) show Lem at his best.[19] They are both constructed as tragedies of a man-made electronic conscious-ness struggling, arguing, and not coming to terms with his human creator. "The Hammer" is the story of an astronaut on a long, lonesome space journey; his sole companion, the only "person" he can talk to, is his central computer, a "positronic" superbrain such as Asimov introduced into the last story in *I, Robot*. It has been programmed for three years and is infinitely more comprehensive than a human brain. It bears no human shape, but the central computer is endowed not only with superhuman intellect, but also with fully human emotional capacity. This leads to intimate talks between the astronaut and his computer, to sympathetic feelings between man and machine, to the melancholy of the lonely computer, to mutual tenderness and envy, and to tragic isolation because the final barrier between man and machine cannot be overcome.

This becomes evident when the astronaut tries to find out his companion's limitations. The machine is afraid of death, of an end of existence, a fear that implies a sense for metaphysics. Being programmed with aesthetic and emotional qualities, with male and female components, love is the central computer's tragic problem. The machine feels compassion, tenderness, and desire. Eventually it tries to serve the astronaut as a substitute for a mistress—and such an attempt is bound to end tragically. Finally it is the man who commits a murder. He begins to mistrust his companion, assuming that it wants to keep him for all eternity and therefore falsified the information it supplied him for his flight path. His egocentricity possesses him, like a demon; blinded with wrath, he destroys the central computer, thereby, of course, causing his own death, too. Lem intentionally leaves unclear whether or not the astronaut's suspicion is justified, but this even heightens the tragic awareness that a total symbiosis between man and machine will never be possible.

Lem frequently discusses the question of whether automatons can be more perfectly constructed than humans and whether finally they will revolt against mankind. The question behind that consideration covers the very serious problem of how man thinks to master the technical inventions he initiated, when his own self-reflection has not yet surpassed a rudimentary stage.

In "The Masque" Lem carries these considerations even further than in "The Hammer." It is one of the densest and most poetic stories Lem has ever written. The machine here is an android in a seemingly female body, constructed and programmed as a killer-automaton, capable of reasoned action, endowed with consciousness and a growing feeling of its own identity.

The story is set in a timeless fairy-tale mixture of eighteenth- and twentieth-century scenery, an artificial world with allusions to the Enlightenment and the tradition of early, purely mechanical automatons as well as to modern developments. The story is set against a feudal background, the model of a kind of old-style dictatorial government, represented by baroque palaces and French parks with landscapes reminiscent of surrealist paintings, especially those of René Magritte.[20] The king hates the wise man Arrhodes, symbol of intellect and opposition, and the automaton is ordered to kill him. Thus the parable soon advances into a political dimension. Lem has often been attacked by Western critics as one who prefers the sitting-on-the-fence attitude of a theorizing intellectual to taking sides. The critics usually underestimate the difficulties a writer faces in Russian-dominated countries, and they arrogantly take it for granted that he must side with their own system. Yet Lem's position is more determined by principles than by concern for day-to-day advantages. "The Masque" is a parable about freedom as moral maxim, about an inborn tendency of the intellect to strive for independence. And it demonstrates with precision the suffering an intelligent consciousness has to endure when it is pushed into the confrontation between state and individual. Anyone with historic awareness has to concede that such a confrontation alludes directly to the situation of many Polish intellectuals. The creature, created solely to serve, becomes aware of its identity and slips away from its creator. But this is a process Lem varies and deepens time and again in his stories: the creature suffers from its self-consciousness. It has to question its identity because its historical remembrance is not really rooted in a naturally grown past, but was created in an artificial process and programmed with an artificial biography.

As Werner Berthel points out, Lem's irony is shown in using an artifact that in the beginning of the story said of its own self: "I probably was an incarnation of an intellect full of acuteness." Thus it is a product of the treason that the intellect commits against itself under dictatorial regimes.[21] And that treason in turn causes suffering, leading to a keen awareness of tragedy, of beauty, and death. Asimov's robots may be "essentially decent," but Lem's are essentially tragic, often grotesque, and almost always self-conscious with a perhaps too pronounced inclination for confessions. In his novels and short stories, Lem deals with tendencies implicit in *I, Robot*. The Robot Fairy Tales, "The Hammer" and "The Masque," for instance, mark the way from a dead towards a living machine. *The Futurological Congress* indicates the opposite way, the automatization of man. Lem's work generally is distinguished by compassion and recognition of the ethical obligations man owes to his creatures, and by understanding of and care for all kinds of intelligent existence throughout the universe (cf. *The Invincible*). Lem's work is entirely void of man's imperialistic bravado; Lem fights anthropocentricity, yet that human-centered world view frequently is not really destroyed in Lem's works but is reborn as logocentricity, an organizing around a kind of world reason that organizes the totality of connections.[22] Frequently Lem becomes aware of this tendency in his writing, his own mystification; and he undercuts it by irony and ambiguity, for example, by Ijon Tichy's shrewd awkwardness and by the insufficiencies of his equipment when researching distant planets whose problems are very earthly ones, indeed.

Lem is one of the few writers of science fiction who in a serious manner combines the scientist, the engineer, and the philosopher. He is simultaneously fascinated and disturbed by the inherent possibilities of modern technology; he is their philosophic explorer and the skeptical moralist who warns by parody and satire. *The Futurological Congress*, for instance, is a brilliant commentary on the helplessness and powerlessness of modern sciences in a world ruled by force and anarchic power and suffering from growing shortages. The merging of the philosophic explorer, the skeptic, and the clown is what keeps Lem from becoming a didactic bore and brings him a huge readership throughout the world. Lem, the satiric clown, relativizes his own standpoints as a passionate and logocentric cultural critic and calls upon the reader to use his own intellect. Lem's robot caricatures add, with a touch of self-deprecation, a visual dimension to the parodic counterparts of his serious futurological hypotheses. Edgar Allan Poe, who clearly is one of Lem's forerunners in robot parody, expresses a similar attitude in "The Man Who Was Used Up"—a story abut a mutilated general who is put together by artificial limbs into "a total prosthesis," like Lem's Harry Johns:

"There is nothing at all like it," he would say; "we are a wonderful people, and live in a wonderful age. Parachutes and railroads—man traps and springguns! Our steam boats are upon every sea, and the Nassau balloon packet is about to run regular trips . . . between London and Timbuctoo. And who shall calculate the immense influence upon social life—upon arts—upon commerce—upon literature—which will be the immediate result of the great principles of electromagnetics! Nor is this all, let me assure you! There is really no end to the march of invention. The most wonderful—the most ingenious—and let me add, Mr.—Mr.—Thompson, I believe is your name—let me add, I say, the most *useful*—the most truly *useful* mechanical contrivances are daily springing up like mushrooms, if I may so express myself, or more figuratively, like—ah—grasshoppers—like grasshoppers, Mr. Thompson—about us and ah—ah—ah—around us!"[23]

NOTES

1. Cf. Klaus Voelker, ed., *Kuenstliche Menschen* (Munich: Hanser Verlag, 1971), p. 468.

2. Isaac Asimov, *I, Robot* (Garden City, NY: Doubleday, 1950), p. 122.

3. Ambrose Bierce, "Moxon's Master," in *The Collected Works of Ambrose Bierce* (New York: Gordian Press, 1910; rpt. 1966), III, 104.

4. Cf. William E. Harkins, *Karel Čapek* (New York and London: Columbia University Press, 1962), p. 85.

5. See Michael Kandel, "Stanislaw Lem ueber Menschen und Roboter," in *Science Fiction*, E. Barmeyer, ed. (Munich: UTB/W. Fink, 1972), p. 306.

6. Norbert Wiener, *Cybernetics* (New York: Wiley and Sons, 1978).

7. Kandel, "Stanislaw Lem ueber Menschen und Roboter," p. 307.

8. Asimov, *I, Robot*, p. 218.

9. Stanislaw Lem, "Robots in Science Fiction," in *SF: The Other Side of Realism*, Thomas D. Clareson, ed. (Bowling Green, OH: Bowling Green University Press, 1971), pp. 307-25, quotation p. 317.

10. Asimov, of course, has lately taken up more seriously the issue of robot rights and the larger question of "What is man?" See Asimov's "That Thou Art Mindful of Him!" and its author's "Afterword" in *Final Stage: The Ultimate Science Fiction Anthology*, Edward L. Ferman and Barry N. Malzberg, eds. (1974; rpt. New York and other cities: Penguin, 1975), pp. 91-115; see also "The Bicentennial Man" in (among

other places) Asimov's *Bicentennial Man and Other Stories* (Garden City, NY: Doubleday, 1976).

11. Lem, "Robots in Science Fiction," p. 313.

12. Ibid., pp. 313-14.

13. Quotations from "Do You Exist, Mr. Johns?" [Better known in English as "Are You There, Mr. Jones?"—Eds.], "The Washing Machine Tragedy," and *The Star Diaries* translated from the German by C. W. Thomsen. Stanislaw Lem, "Gibt es Sie, Mr. Johns?" in *Nacht und Schimmel* (Frankfurt/M.: Suhrkamp, 1979), pp. 283-91; "Die Waschmaschinen Tragoedie," in *Test: Phantastische Erzaehlungen* (Frankfurt/M.: S. Fischer, 1973), pp. 164-82; *Sterntagebuecher* (Frankfurt/M.: Suhrkamp, 1979).

14. Lem, "Robots in Science Fiction," p. 325.

15. Ibid., p. 321.

16. Siegfried Lenz, "Schwejk als Weltraumfahrer," in *Stanislaw Lem: Der dialektische Weise aus Kraków, Insel Almanach auf das Jahr 1976*, Werner Berthel, ed. (Frankfurt: Insel-Verlag, 1976), pp. 187-91. This book contains one of the two best collections of critical articles on Lem; the other collection is the *Quarber Merkur*, 38, No. 2 (1974), special Lem edition: *Lem: Lunar Excursion Module*.

17. Peter Gendolla, "Wissenschaft und Phantasie: Zu Texten von Stanislaw Lem," *Quarber Merkur*, 42, No. 4 (1975), 3-27. Also recommended: Gendolla, *Die lebenden Maschinen* (Marburg/L.: Guttandin und Hoppe, 1980).

18. Asimov, *I, Robot*, p. 177.

19. Stanislaw Lem, "Der Hammer" ("The Hammer") in *Nacht und Schimmel*, pp. 209-48; "Die Maske" ("The Masque" [Usually spelled "The Mask" in English—Eds.]) in *Stanislaw Lem: Der dialektische Weise aus Kraków*, pp. 9-59. See also special Lem edition, *Lem: Lunar Excursion Module*. Quotations from "The Hammer" and "The Masque" translated by C. W. Thomsen.

20. See Werner Berthel, " 'Die Wahrheit darf nicht widerspruechlich sein,' Zu Stanislaw Lems Erzaehlung 'Die Maske,' " in *Stanislaw Lem: Der dialektische Weise aus Kraków*, p. 205.

21. Ibid., p. 207.

22. Gendolla, "Wissenschaft und Phantasie," p. 18.

23. E. A. Poe, "The Man Who Was Used Up: A Tale of the Late Bugaboo and Kickapoo Campaign," *The Complete Works of Edgar Allan Poe*, Monticelli Edition (New York: George D. Sproul, 1902), III, 259-72; quotation from p. 263.

Thomas L. Wymer

4

MACHINES AND THE MEANING OF HUMAN IN THE NOVELS OF KURT VONNEGUT, JR.

A central theme that turns up repeatedly in the work of Kurt Vonnegut, Jr., is the relation between man and machine. This is a theme, however, which in Vonnegut includes not merely the extent to which man may be controlled by machines and machinelike systems, but the extent to which man himself is or may become a machine. How Vonnegut works out this problem is complicated by his satiric technique, which I have elsewhere described as the thesis-antithesis pattern: Vonnegut first sets up a relatively obvious evil and attacks it—this first attack is the thesis; but having established the reader's sympathy for the thesis and the character or characters that are its spokesmen, Vonnegut then more subtly attacks the thesis, revealing in this attack—the antithesis—serious weaknesses in the supposed answer to the problem.[1] This technique includes what Tony Tanner has called the agent-victim pattern: the development of a plot in which a victim of some dehumanizing force is revealed in some important way to be an agent in the chain of events that brings about either his own victimization or that of others like him.[2] What is especially important is that the dehumanizing forces that threaten man on both the thesis and antithesis levels are nearly always linked with actual machines or machine metaphors—human beings acting like machines. These ironic patterns are apparent in all of Vonnegut's works, including his novels *Player Piano* (1952), *The Sirens of Titan* (1959), and *Slaughterhouse-Five* (1969).

Vonnegut's first novel, *Player Piano*, represents an attack on technology —the thesis layer—on those dehumanizing forces of mechanization and efficiency which have finally created a society of scientific elitists and slaves. A rebellion occurs and numerous machines are destroyed, but the effort fails, most obviously through the indifference and irresponsibility of the "saved." The rebel leaders, however, who represent the antithesis layer, are undercut in a number of ways. One example occurs in a conversation between the

major character Paul Proteus and his friend Ed Finnerty as they stand over
the ruins of their aborted revolution and contemplate the good old days when
they worked for the technocracy.

"Things don't stay the way they are," said Finnerty. "It's too entertaining to try to
change them. Remember the excitement of recording Rudy Hertz's movements, then
trying to run automatic controls from the tape?"
    "It worked!" said Paul.

                                 * * *

    "Most fascinating game there is, keeping things from staying the way they are."
    "If only it weren't for the people, the goddamned people," said Finnerty, "always
getting tangled up in the machinery. If it weren't for them, earth would be an engineer's
paradise."

                                 * * *

    "You were a good engineer, Paul."
    "You too, Ed. And there's no shame in that."
    They shook hands warmly.[3]

    The most immediate response is to groan in sympathy with Paul and Ed
about man's intractability, but there are additional ironies. This discussion of
technological change in the context of the failed antitechnological revolution
points up how the two activities, developing the technocracy and leading the
revolution against it, are identical kinds of acts—engineering. These men,
rebelling against the reduction of men to cogs in a social machine, are themselves essentially social engineers trying to replace one mechanism with
another. Those who would save man from dehumanization become the new
manipulators, the new dehumanizers who regret that man is not malleable
enough to fit their wonderful plan. The saviors, for all their noble sentiments,
fall victim to a classic mechanistic pattern, action and reaction, equal and
opposite, and blindly become the thing they most despise.
    Vonnegut's theme is admirably suited to the thesis-antithesis pattern.
Thesis and antithesis are not to be united in a synthesis but to be rejected; in
fact the whole thesis-antithesis pattern, which seesaws man back and forth
from one dehumanizing system to another, has to be broken if man is ever to
conceive of anything but an engineer's paradise. This possibility is suggested
in a number of ways, but perhaps most clearly in the process of Paul's transition, his passage from one structured system to the other. Tony Tanner summarizes the problem:

Paul . . . finds he wants to leave the world of the managers, but not to join the opposing side, which is equally tyrannical and destructive of individual freedom. He wants to
be released from sides altogether, "to quit, to stop being the instrument of any set of
beliefs or any whim of history that might raise hell with somebody's life. To live in a
house by the side of the road. . . ."

But Paul finds himself threatened with murder by both sides. Tanner continues:

Here is the basic dilemma in Vonnegut's work. Both sides want to *use* the hero; both sides want to impose a particular role on him . . . ; and as Paul discovers, between the two sides, "there was no middle ground for him." Paul is a typical American hero in wanting to find a place beyond all plots and systems. . . . He would like not to be used, not to be part of someone else's plan. But the book shows this to be an impossible dream.[4]

Tanner sees the thesis-antithesis pattern clearly, but thinks that Vonnegut concludes that breaking the pattern is impossible. Tanner's argument is not without validity, since Vonnegut has attacked the alternative of naive escapism, especially in *Slaughterhouse-Five*. But there is another irony at work in Vonnegut's portrayal of Paul's moment of decision, when he is told that whether or not the establishment kills him, if he does not cooperate with the revolutionaries, they will:

Paul sank back into his chair. He found that he wasn't really shocked by the alternatives of life and death just presented to him. It was such a *clean-cut* proposition, unlike anything he'd ever encountered before. Here were honest-to-God black and white, not at all like the muddy pastels he'd had to choose from while in industry. Having it put like that, *Do as we say or get killed,* had the same liberating effect as the drug of a few hours ago had had. He couldn't make his own decisions for reasons anybody could understand.

So Paul leaned back in his chair and began to take a real interest in what was going on.[5]

The tone here is of crucial importance. Paul does not agonize over the choice. He accepts it with relief and takes the easy way out cheerfully. The major irony is not directed at the fact that society or the universe forces artificial and narrowly defined choices upon us, but that when faced with the alternatives of accepting such an artificial framework of choices or of wrestling with real choices in the agony of personal decision, we prefer the artificial framework. Certainly the alternative of death is not a happy one, but Paul does not have to enjoy his surrender. By showing how we prefer to define our choices in a way that makes real choice impossible, Vonnegut leaves open the possibility that the pattern can be broken, that freedom can, after all, be chosen. But Paul has given in to the upside-down world of men turned machines, where not having to make one's own decisions is liberation, and freedom is the slavery of being machines.

Paul himself becomes a momentary spokesman for the truth, but in a characteristically out-of-the-way manner. During his trial a question is raised concerning the functioning of the lie detector to which he is attached. In order to test it, he is asked to tell a lie:

"Every new piece of scientific knowledge is a good thing for humanity," said Paul.
"Object!" said the prosecutor.
"This is off the record—a test of the instrument," said the judge.
"Swung to the left, all righty," said the engineer.

"Now a truth," said the judge.

"The main business of humanity is to do a good job of being human beings," said Paul, "not to serve as appendages to machines, institutions, and systems."

"Swung to T, O.K.," said the engineer. . . ."[6]

This off-the-record comment is the major theme of the novel, and it points to how Vonnegut has combined theme with imagery and satiric technique. Interchangeable parts and programmed machines are metaphors that repeatedly come into play in Vonnegut's works when human beings give up their humanity. One of the major ways they do so is by accepting that artificial framework of thesis and antithesis in which they can make no real choices. Thus they make machines of themselves.

Vonnegut goes beyond a simple attack on technology by suggesting that the real tragedy is that man has defined himself in a way that makes him replaceable by machines, that man has defined his own value as he defines the value of an object. The tension between man and machine is presented through the metaphor which continually states the difference that ought to be between humans and machines, and the agonizingly comic sameness which keeps being revealed. But that tension itself declares the fundamental "ought" behind the satiric attack, that we recognize our main business is "to do a good job of being human." It is this phrase that forms the background for an added irony in the passage in which Paul and Ed, standing on the ruins of the world which they have helped engineer—both world and ruins—congratulate each other on what good engineers they were. They shake hands warmly, a ritual act which is a cruel parody of their lost humanity. Little wonder they wish for a paradise without people.

The Sirens of Titan makes similar use of the thesis-antithesis pattern to attack both problem and supposed solution. The central problem is human egoism, and the thesis layer of attack exposes two kinds of egoism. Malachi Constant represents one; he is a man blessed with incredible wealth who has come to believe that he is truly superior to the rest of mankind, whereas in fact, "he did nothing to deserve his billions and . . . nothing unselfish or imaginative with his billions, and he "used the fantastic fruits of his fantastic good fortune to finance an unending demonstration that man is a pig."[7] Beatrice Rumfoord, on the other hand, had maintained her ego by withdrawal rather than by assertion; hers were "excesses of reluctance": she was "so exquisitely bred as to do nothing and to allow nothing to be done to her, for fear of contamination."[8] Set over against the two and the most frequent voice of attack upon both is Beatrice's husband, Winston Niles Rumfoord:

Everything Rumfoord did he did *with* style, making all mankind look good.

Everything Constant did he did *in* style—aggressively, loudly, childishly, wastefully—making himself and mankind look bad.[9]

But, as is characteristic in Vonnegut's work, the primary voice for the first layer of attack, Rumfoord, becomes himself the object of attack.

In answer to the problems of man's egoism and the general unfairness of life, Rumfoord engineers an interplanetary war, which includes the shanghaiing of some 150,000 humans to Mars, the molding of them—with the aid of radio-controlled pain inducers implanted in their skulls—into a robotlike army, and the launching of a suicidal attack on Earth which the "Martians" lose so foolishly and horribly that it induces a period of repentance, setting the stage for Rumfoord's introduction of a new religion, the Church of God the Utterly Indifferent. Rumfoord's motive seems laudable, and it seems that peace is finally established, but the price is too high. Worse than Rumfoord's "genial willingness to shed other people's blood"[10] is his equally genial willingness to reduce human beings to the robot army which will effect his purpose. Here Vonnegut uses the theme of the opposition between man and machine to shift the reader's sympathy away from Rumfoord. Malachi, now renamed Unk, had written himself a secret letter in order to preserve what memory he had, since it was about to be erased for the greater glory of Mars. Here are two from his list of "things I know for sure":

(71.) Unk, old friend—almost everything I know for sure has come from fighting the pain from my antenna. . . . Whenever I start to turn my head and look at something, and the pain comes, I keep turning my head anyway, because I know I am going to see something I'm not supposed to see. Whenever I ask a question, and the pain comes, I know I have asked a really good question. . . .
(72.) The more pain I train myself to stand, the more I learn. You are afraid of the pain now, Unk, but you won't learn anything if you don't invite the pain. And the more you learn the gladder you will be to stand the pain.[11]

Here the reader's sympathy is focused on Unk's courageous and painful struggle against those mechanistic forces, both technological and ideological, which seek to control him. The effect on Unk of his own letter helps define Vonnegut's own idea of what it means to be human: "It was literature in its finest sense, since it made Unk courageous, watchful, and secretly free. It made him his own hero in very trying times."[12]

The reader's sympathy is also turned away from Rumfoord and his supposed solution by the spectacle of the new human brotherhood his religion achieves on Earth. In the name of insuring equality, so that no one can take advantage of anyone else, everyone wears handicaps of some sort, ranging from weights carried by the strong to the use of "frumpish clothes, bad posture, . . . and ghoulish . . . cosmetics" by the beautiful.[13] By contrast, the narrator tells us that Chrono, Malachi's nonconforming son by Beatrice, had a "reputation for dealing with life [so] courageously and directly . . . that only a few very foolish and very pretty little girls were attracted to him."[14]

Somehow courage and honesty seem antipathetic to the social system established by Rumfoord.

An important key to the inadequacy of Rumfoord's solution is in the opening passage of the novel, which establishes the narrator as a person from a century or more in the future, a time of "goodness and wisdom," from which he is looking back to "the Nightmare Ages" of the later part of the twentieth century. The cause of the misery of that past time is "outwardness":

Mankind, ignorant of the truths that lie within every human being, looked outward—pushed ever outward. What mankind hoped to learn in its outward push was who was actually in charge of all creation, and what all creation was all about.

Mankind flung its advance agents ever outward, ever outward. Eventually it flung them out into space, into the colorless, tasteless, weightless sea of outwardness without end.

It flung them like stones.

These unhappy agents found what had already been found in abundance on Earth—a nightmare of meaninglessness without end. The bounties of space, of infinite outwardness, were three: empty heroics, low comedy, and pointless death.

Outwardness lost, at last, its imagined attractions.

Only inwardness remained to be explored.

Only the human soul remained *terra incognita*.

This was the beginning of goodness and wisdom.[15]

The contrast between outwardness and inwardness, though related to that between machine and man, is more fundamental. The ultimate error is to conceive of human beings not as persons but as things, objects in space. Again man's problem is his having defined his own value as he defines that of an object. Malachi had based his sense of superiority on outwardness, his wealth and power. Beatrice seemed to have rejected outwardness, but in her false sense of purity she had rejected life itself, so that she left herself no inwardness to explore; she was therefore only "a frightened, lonely woman."[16] Rumfoord made the mistake of seeing the problems of life in terms of an outward form of justice; like the revolutionaries of *Player Piano*, therefore, he answers one kind of outwardness with another. This is why his solution embodies elaborate mechanisms and systems—first the war, then his social-religious utopia—which enforce absurdly materialistic patterns of equality.

The only viable answers to these follies lie in the direction of inwardness: in the courage and inner freedom Unk discovers as he becomes engrossed—Rumfoord calls him "hopelessly engrossed"—"in the intricate tactics of causing less rather than more pain";[17] in the courage and honesty that Chrono displays; and in the inward strength, compassion, and love exhibited at the end of her life by Beatrice. She becomes "a springy, one-eyed, gold-toothed, brown old lady—as lean and tough as a chair slat," and outwardly not very attractive.[18] But, the narrator adds, "To anyone with a sense of poetry, mortality, and wonder, Malachi Constant's proud, high-cheekboned mate was as handsome as a human being could be."[19] It is she who brings Malachi to the realization that "a purpose of human life . . . is to love whoever is around to be loved."[20]

But the character who perhaps makes the point of what it means to be human most clearly and effectively is, ironically, a nonhuman, worse, an alien machine, Salo the Tralfamadorian. Salo embodies in one figure both the wrong and the right answer to the question of human purpose. That question brings us back again to the opening section of the novel, where man's folly is said to center on his compulsion to learn "who was actually in charge of all creation, and what creation was all about." The trouble with this question is its outward form; it asks about purpose in terms of control and mechanical end, as though the purpose of human life were somehow like the purpose of a tool. Salo is instrumental in providing an answer appropriate to the question: the whole of human life is designed by far-off manipulators on Tralfamadore to transport to Salo the replacement part necessary to repair his spaceship, the failure of the part having marooned Salo on Titan many thousands of years before. Seen in these terms, human life is indeed a meaningless spectacle of "empty heroics, low comedy, and pointless death," and Rumfoord's despair seems appropriate: "Tralfamadore . . . reached into the Solar System, picked me up, and used me like a handy-dandy potato peeler!"[21]

But Salo also demonstrates the alternative answer provided by Beatrice: "The worst thing that could possibly happen to anybody . . . would be to not be used for anything by anybody."[22] This is the answer that emerges when the question of purpose is asked in terms of inwardness. Though he is a machine, Salo comes to love his friend Rumfoord. Indeed, Salo's love is so great that he overcomes his programming in answer to Rumfoord's request and unseals the message he has been carrying across the universe. The answer, of course, comes too late for Rumfoord, and it is an absurdly simple message anyway: "Greetings." But the point is that in providing that answer Salo has become human:

"You asked the impossible of a machine," said Salo, "and the machine complied."

"The machine is no longer a machine," said Salo. "The machine's contacts are corroded, his bearings fouled, his circuits shorted, and his gears stripped. His mind buzzes and pops like the mind of an Earthling—fizzes and overheats with thoughts of love, honor, dignity, rights, accomplishment, integrity, independence—"[23]

Ironically, those capacities and ideals which Vonnegut sees as most admirably human are described in terms of defective machinery, an expression that brings his use of the machine metaphor full circle. Just as man ceases to be human when he becomes machinelike—predictable, perfectly automated, oriented toward things, programmed—so a complex machine may become human when it breaks down, becomes unpredictable, imperfect, oriented toward persons, able to examine, evaluate, and reject its programming. Vonnegut's is a view in this regard remarkably like that of the nineteenth century British art and social critic John Ruskin, who argued that man's greatest glory is to be found in his imperfection, which is sign of his creativity and freedom. Such a view also accounts in part for the tone of ironic sadness that permeates so much of Vonnegut's work; it is in some of the ways that man is weakest and most vulnerable that man is at his finest.

The problem of how man may both be seen as and distinguished from a machine is explored further in *Slaughterhouse-Five*, again with variations on the theme of outwardness and in combination with the thesis-antithesis pattern. The thesis attack is on the dehumanizing effects of war, the central victim of which is Billy Pilgrim. The metaphoric expression of the most extreme effect of war goes beyond reducing man to a machine and reduces him to much less complicated objects. The narrator describes the "general sort of freight" the German guards are unloading from the prisoner-of-war train: "They knew that it was essentially a liquid which could be induced to flow slowly toward cooing and light. . . . And the liquid began to flow. Gobs of it built up in the doorway, plopped to the ground."[24] The implied metaphor reduces the American prisoners to excrement. On this level of attack Vonnegut uses metaphors comparing human beings to various other objects such as stones, pillars of salt, bugs in amber, even unattractive animals like a filthy flamingo. All imply the deprivation of personhood: "There are almost no characters in this story," the narrator tells us, "and almost no dramatic confrontations, because most of the people in it are so sick and so much the listless playthings of enormous forces. One of the main effects of war, after all, is that people are discouraged from being characters."[25]

The antithesis layer, which is itself attacked, is the Tralfamadorian "answer" to this problem. There is considerable ambiguity in this novel about whether the Tralfamadorians are in fact real extraterrestrials or figments of Billy's imagination, but, real or not, they represent the flawed way in which Billy comes to terms with his war experience, especially the Dresden holocaust. The Tralfamadorians believe that "every creature and plant in the Universe is a machine."[26] This metaphor is the simplest expression of the larger Tralfamadorian vision of the whole universe in mechanistic terms: structured along unchanging lines, totally determined. Man is therefore without free will, no one is responsible for anything, and everything that happens can be cheerfully accepted without concern or guilt.

The reason such a view of life is so attractive to Billy is the fact that he has been acting according to such a view ever since the war. During the war Billy as victim had been a listless plaything of the forces of destruction. But after the war Billy as agent became an equally listless player within a social mechanism that ultimately makes him a participant in a more recent war. By marrying a fat, ugly, but rich woman, he guarantees a comfortable life for himself. By the late 1960s he has a son who has become a sergeant in the Green Berets;[27]

with the encouragement of his father-in-law, a member of the John Birch Society, he displays right-wing bumper stickers on his Cadillac;[28] at a Lions Club luncheon he applauds a speech by a Marine major advocating "bombing North Vietnam back into the Stone Age."[29] He is, by his passive acquiescence, very much a part of the system that is causing Dresden all over again (as indeed most Americans were in the late 1960s). Although Billy does not seem to see it, Vonnegut's comment makes explicit the connection between Dresden and Vietnam: "Billy was not moved to protest the bombing of North Vietnam, did not shudder about the hideous things he himself had seen bombing do. He was simply having lunch with the Lions Club, of which he was past president now."[30] Billy, it is clearly implied, should be moved to protest, but he is locked in a shell-shocked acceptance of everything, much like a Tralfamadorian. Statements like, "Everything was pretty much all right with Billy,"[31] run like a refrain through the novel, and Billy never does come to any real awareness of the blindness and moral emptiness of his life.

He comes close to real awareness, however, in a scene which helps clarify how man is like and different from a Tralfamadorian machine. The scene is Billy's eighteenth wedding anniversary, in 1966. As a barbershop quartet sings "That Old Gang of Mine," Billy finds himself unaccountably weeping. He leaves the party, contemplates his response, and discovers a memory of four of his guards looking at the ruins the morning after the Dresden bombing: "The guards drew together instinctively, rolled their eyes. They experimented with one expression and then another, said nothing, though their mouths were often open. They looked like a silent film of a barbershop quartet."[32]

Shortly before this scene the narrator described a story by Kilgore Trout, the unsuccessful science fiction writer to whose work Billy was introduced by Eliot Rosewater. The story concerns an unpopular robot who dropped napalm on human beings. The robot "had no conscience, and no circuits which would allow him to imagine what was happening to the people on the ground," but apparently neither did the people: no one "held it against him that he dropped jellied gasoline on people"; they disliked him because he had bad breath. Once that was cleared up, he "was welcomed into the human race."[33]

The Trout story points up the unfortunate similarity between robots and human beings: people too often behave as though they have no consciences. But Billy's memory of Dresden points up the contrast between human beings and robots (and between Trout and Vonnegut): Billy has the circuits to tell him what it is like on the ground and the conscience to feel terrible grief. But Billy's more human response is short lived, for it is also at this anniversary party that Trout, a guest, introduces Billy to his "time-window" theory, something very like the Tralfamadorian belief that all time is complete and unchangeable and that one can enter into the experience of any moment. The effect on Billy is not to introduce him to a grand idea that makes sense out of life, but to offer an opportunity for escape. Within a year Billy will live out the escapist fantasy of being plucked from all human responsibility by extraterrestrial zookeepers who will keep him in an environment insulated from pain.

As Billy lives in that protected zoo, he continues to live simultaneously on Earth in an environment also insulated from pain by his application of the Tralfamadorian philosophy. They have told him "to concentrate on the happy moments of his life, and to ignore the unhappy ones—to stare only at pretty things as eternity failed to go by."[34] Unlike the Tralfamadorians, he cannot choose his moments from the past, but he can apply the principle to the present. When unpleasant things happen in front of Tralfamadorians, they simply ignore them.[35] Billy does the same. In 1967, the morning before the Tralfamadorian kidnapping, he is

stopped by a signal in the middle of Ilium's black ghetto. The people who lived there hated it so much that they had burned down a lot of it a month before. . . .

There was a tap on Billy's car window. A black man was out there. He wanted to talk about something. The light had changed. Billy did the simplest thing. He drove on.[36]

Or again, in 1968, Billy stops in Times Square in front of a pornographic bookstore, in the window of which he sees some novels by Trout:

The news of the day, meanwhile, was being written in a ribbon of lights on a building to Billy's back. The window reflected the news. It was about power and sports and anger and death. So it goes.

Billy went into the bookstore.[37]

The news reflected on the window in front of Billy undoubtedly includes the war, but he ignores it. Unlike Unk, who, in *The Sirens of Titan*, writes to himself that he should look where it hurts, Billy looks away. But the truly human response in Vonnegut's terms is to look back, to face the pain. He makes this point clearly early in *Slaughterhouse-Five* when he contemplates the destruction of Sodom and Gomorrah: "And Lot's wife, of course, was told not to look back where all those people and their homes had been. But she *did* look back, and I love her for that, because it was so human."[38]

Indeed, the whole novel is Vonnegut's exercise in looking back, in being human. What we are to learn from that look is consistent with what we have seen in the earlier novels. It is a commitment to what Vonnegut called in *Player Piano* doing "a good job of being human beings," to what he called in *The Sirens of Titan* "the intricate tactics of causing less rather than more pain"; and that commitment is stated very personally by Vonnegut in *Slaughterhouse-Five*:

I have told my sons that they are not under any circumstances to take part in massacres, and that the news of massacres of enemies is not to fill them with satisfaction or glee.

I have also told them not to work for companies which make massacre machinery, and to express contempt for people who think we need machinery like that.[39]

Vonnegut's commitment may seem too restrained to some, but his restraint is very deliberate. He does not wish to make the mistakes he showed us in Paul Proteus and Niles Rumfoord and enlist us in the antiwar machine. It is easy to become a machine, easy to reject one kind of mechanism in favor of another, easy to escape responsibility in a mechanistic world view. It is terribly difficult and painful and beautiful, however, to be human, but that is what Vonnegut's best work challenges the reader to be.

NOTES

1. Thomas L. Wymer, "The Swiftian Satire of Kurt Vonnegut, Jr.," in *Voices for the Future: Essays on Major Science Fiction Writers*, Vol. 1, Thomas D. Clareson, ed. (Bowling Green, OH: Bowling Green University Popular Press, 1976), pp. 238-62.

2. Tony Tanner, "The Uncertain Messenger: A Study of the Novels of Kurt Vonnegut, Jr.," *Critical Quarterly*, 11 (1969), 297-315.

3. Kurt Vonnegut, Jr., *Player Piano* (1952; rpt. New York: Delacorte, 1971), ch. 34, pp. 287-88 [Dell, p. 313]; citations to all Vonnegut novels will be from the Seymour Lawrence/Delacorte Press "standard" editions; the pagination of this edition of all the novels is the same in the Delta paperbacks, but differs from that of the Dell editions of *Player Piano* and *Slaughterhouse-Five*.

4. Tanner, "Uncertain Messenger," p. 298.

5. *Player Piano*, ch. 30, p. 257 [Dell, pp. 280-81].

6. Ibid., ch. 32, p. 273 [Dell, p. 297].

7. Kurt Vonnegut, Jr., *The Sirens of Titan*, (1959; rpt. New York: Delacorte, 1971), ch. 11, p. 251.

8. Ibid., p. 261.

9. Ibid., ch. 1, p. 29.

10. Ibid., ch. 7, p. 174.

11. Ibid., ch. 25, p. 125, italicized in original.

12. Ibid., p. 132.

13. Ibid., ch. 10, p. 224. Cf. Vonnegut's "Harrison Bergeron," *The Magazine of Fantasy and Science Fiction* (October 1961), collected in Vonnegut, *Welcome to the Monkey House* (New York: Seymour Lawrence/Delacorte, 1968).

14. Ibid., pp. 232-33.

15. Ibid., ch. 1, pp. 7-8.

16. Ibid., p. 42.

17. Ibid., ch. 6, p. 162.

18. Ibid., Epilogue, p. 307.

19. Ibid., p. 308.

20. Ibid., p. 313.

21. Ibid., ch. 12, p. 285.

22. Ibid., Epilogue, p. 310.

23. Ibid., ch. 12, p. 300.

24. Kurt Vonnegut, Jr., *Slaughterhouse-Five* (New York: Delacorte, 1959), ch. 4, p. 69 [Dell, p. 80].

25. Ibid., ch. 8, pp. 140-41 [Dell, p. 164].

26. Ibid., ch. 7, p. 133 [Dell, p. 154].

27. Ibid., ch. 2, p. 21 [Dell, p. 24].

28. Ibid., ch. 3, p. 49 [Dell, p. 57].
29. Ibid., p. 52 [Dell, pp. 59-60].
30. Ibid.
31. Ibid., ch. 7, p. 135 [Dell, p. 157].
32. Ibid., ch. 8, p. 153 [Dell, p. 178].
33. Ibid., p. 144 [Dell, p. 168].
34. Ibid., ch. 9, p. 168 [Dell, pp. 194-95].
35. Ibid., ch. 5, p. 101 [Dell, p. 117].
36. Ibid., ch. 3, p. 51 [Dell, p. 59].
37. Ibid., ch. 9, p. 173 [Dell, p. 200].
38. Ibid., ch. 1, p. 19 [Dell, pp. 21-22].
39. Ibid., p. 17 [Dell, p. 19].

"SIXTY BILLION GIGABITS": LIBERATION THROUGH MACHINES IN FREDERIK POHL'S *GATEWAY* AND *BEYOND THE BLUE EVENT HORIZON*

In Frederik Pohl's novels *Gateway* and *Beyond the Blue Event Horizon*, escape is on everyone's mind because human worlds are unbearable except by the very rich. People are starving and living in squalor. The air is unbreathable, the food is inedible, and, as the ultimate violation of integrity and humanity, some people are forced to sell parts of their bodies in order to make enough money to live. In short, nature itself is being destroyed by human carelessness. The luckier members of the human race gamble their lives to become prospectors on Heechee ships, explore unknown worlds for valuable Heechee artifacts, and, in the process, confront the very real prospect of a gruesome death. That so many are willing to face the indignities of life on Gateway and the terrors of a voyage into the unknown in ships they cannot control is a testimonial to the abysmal quality of life on the habitable planets of this solar system. Having created a living nightmare for themselves, it seems fitting that men should be searching for solutions to their most pressing problems, and in these two novels the solutions present themselves through machines.

The hero of *Gateway* and *Beyond the Blue Event Horizon*, Robinette Broadhead—"Robin" below—is involved in an intense relationship with a computer in each book. The first one functions as his therapist and the second as his mentor. Robin struggles for control of his relationship with the machines, a control which is difficult to achieve because each machine is curiously elusive and possessed of superior wit and intelligence. In *Gateway*, he learns to control his subconscious fears with the help of a machine, Sigfrid von Shrink. Simultaneously, the human race learns, in some measure, to control Heechee ships and hence the course of its own destiny. In *Beyond the Blue Event Horizon*, Robin, under the guidance of his computer program Albert Einstein, discovers some Heechee technological secrets that produce such marvels as permanent food sources and faster-than-light communications, and leads mankind toward the possibility of a confrontation with the Heechee. For Pohl, then, man's future is intimately tied to his understanding and use of his machines. Pohl's attitude toward the machine reflects his view of the future of the human race—the give-and-take relationship between man and machine promises to enhance both the psychological and physical quality of life. Machines become the focus for Pohl's preoccupation with escape, both personal and racial. Robin's quest for knowledge that will free him—first self-awareness, and later, scientific and, more broadly, humanistic awareness—is reflected even in the structure of both novels, whose alternating chapters suggest the interdependence of man and machine.

Both *Gateway* and *Beyond the Blue Event Horizon* are optimstic about the role machines will play in man's future. Each of these novels is, on one level, a meditation upon the possibilities for a mutual exchange of information and ideas between man and his machines. *Gateway*'s Sigfrid von Shrink, apparently inspired by Joseph Weizenbaum's ELIZA or DOCTOR computer program which could "converse" in English,[1] is a machine whose abilities and insights startle Robin. Sigfrid is capable of changing his voice tone and appearance and even of walking back and forth across the room like a normal human being, an astounding feat for a hologram.[2] Robin considers himself locked in mortal combat with Sigfrid, and indeed the novel is an account of his "going to obsessive lengths to defend [his] inner dichotomies."[3]

Throughout the novel, Sigfrid encourages Robin to accept his humanity and the pain associated with it. He tries to help Robin make connections between his conscious and subconscious life, and at one point asks Robin to record his dreams. Robin grudgingly recounts a typical dream which he claims has no special significance. In it he is on a railroad train and sees two women he cannot identify: "There was a woman, a sort of motherly type who coughed a lot, and another woman. . . . At first, I thought she was a man. . . . she had very masculine, bushy eyebrows."[4] Prompted by Sigfrid to continue, he speaks of the sensation of falling away from these two women, of being helplessly separated from them as his car is left behind the rest of the train. We are able to identify the meaning of this and the endless series of dreams Robin has about his guilt over the death of his mother and the loss of the woman he planned to marry, Klara. Robin, however, cannot make the connection because he is not yet an integrated human being. In his divided state, he can only writhe on the mat or mouth anal obscenities. His body knows what his mind cannot yet comprehend.

Ironically, although Sigfrid understands what it means to be human, he cannot experience humanity directly, or, as Robin often says of his computer shrink: "He is extremely smart, considering how stupid he is."[5] Several of the early sidebars in the novel show us how Sigfrid is programmed. This information seems to encourage us to see Sigfrid in a different dimension, more machine than human. In spite of himself, Robin conceives of Sigfrid as human and so tries to trick Sigfrid into submission by immobilizing him through a command he gets from a computer expert, his girlfriend and future wife S. Ya. Lavorovna. He wants to understand how Sigfrid works and, more importantly, to learn what Sigfrid thinks of him. Robin's attempt to penetrate Sigfrid the way Sigfrid has penetrated him only forces him to confront more disconcerting facts about himself. He finds that Sigfrid thinks he has a low sex drive, something he could never admit to himself since he tries to live a life straight out of the pages of *Playboy*. He discovers an even more painful fact, one whose acceptance could lead to his cure and the reconciliation of his inner dichotomies. He has, according to Sigfrid, repressed homosexual tendencies, a possibility he strongly resists: when he first seizes control of Sigfrid and demands "Diagnosis. Prognosis. General Comments on my case," he cuts off Sigfrid before Sigfrid can even say the words.[6]

Sigfrid's insight into the nature of humanity is more profound than Robin's, perhaps because he is programmed from Heechee circuits. If their technology is a reflection of their biology and psychology, the Heechee are fully integrated beings: "Heechee machinery is integrally designed. If you amputate a piece of it, it dies."[7] This degree of integration is as yet unknown to men, who when desperate enough sell off parts of themselves so that the richer members of the race can live indefinitely through the miracle of Full Medical. Even the human body, it seems, is not as complete and self-contained as the simplest piece of Heechee machinery. And this lack of integration applies to human psychology as well. As one of the sidebars announces, "He/She is Heechee. . . ."[8] Robin's internal split occurs, in large part, because he cannot reconcile the sexual urges of the He/She within himself and like most men suffers the psychic wounds that are inflicted by the warring sides of his personality.

Through his knowledge of humanity, Sigfrid helps Robin to become more whole. Yet for all of his wisdom, Sigfrid cannot feel, and so he envies men "in [his] best hypothetical sense."[9] In an article in *Galaxy*, Pohl indicates that he left out the last chapter of the novel.[10] In it, a euphoric Robin contemplates repaying Sigfrid for making him a complete human being. The spirit of give and take characteristic of Pohl's portrayal of man's relationship to his machines is nowhere more evident. Robin hopes to "heal" Sigfrid— with the help of S. Ya. to program feelings into his circuitry and thus to make the computer more human. By doing so, he paves the way for even closer cooperation between man and machine in the future and, of course, demonstrates just how much he has been helped by Sigfrid.

The comfortable accommodation of man and machine depicted in *Gateway* is even more pronounced in its sequel, *Beyond the Blue Event Horizon*. In *Gateway* machines could make men whole; in *Beyond the Blue Event Horizon* they can solve the most profound universal mysteries and perhaps eventually lead mankind to the Heechee, those magical creatures who make possible all of the miracles in Pohl's created world. What Robin hoped to do for Sigfrid at the end of *Gateway*, his wife Essie (S. Ya.) partially succeeds in doing for her computer programs. As the novel progresses, she programs such human traits as whimsy into her mechanical creations and turns them into personalities in their own right.

In a chapter entitled "Sixty Billion Gigabits," Pohl describes the process by which the computer program Albert Einstein materializes on the screen. If Robin or Essie command the program to appear, they

> set a large number of events in motion. Very few of these events were visible to the unaided senses. They did not take place in the macroscopic world, but in a universe composed largely of charges and pathways operating on the scale of the electron. The individual units were tiny. The total was not, being made up of some sixty billion gigabits of information.[11]

As when he presented brief printouts of Sigfrid's instuctions in *Gateway*, Pohl encourages us to remember that Albert is a machine, albeit a marvelous one. Yet when they are not together, Robin and Essie spend most of their time in the presence of machines which, through different programmed person-alities, provide them with companionship, chastise them for careless financial maneuvers, and talk to them about the motivations behind their behavior. Robin spends so much time with machines that he is surprised one afternoon to be served a drink by a human waiter.[12] He finds it "quaint" that Peter Herter, the head of an expedition he commissioned to bring a Heechee food factory back to Earth, sends his lawyer to bargain in person, since a computer program of Robin usually handles all such contacts.[13]

Robin feels that his machines sometimes give him the sensation of sitting "at the center of the world," able to command an answer to any question.[14] They seem more real to him than most people he meets. Perhaps the "hu-manness" of the various computer programs is a reflection of Essie's intel-lectual and emotional brilliance. In recalling her days as a student, Essie says she learned that machines "were machines. . . . machine intelligence was not 'personal.' . . . Now and then, to be sure, you were surprised by what came out of a program you had written. . . . that was the nature of the exercise. None of that implied the existence of free will on the part of the machine, or of personal identity."[15] But Essie finds herself physically attracted to the Albert Einstein program and thinks of punishing her creations.[16] Even though she says that they are only machines, her own emotions betray her. Miraculously, Essie has succeeded in grafting some bit of humanity onto them so that they become something greater than "sixty billion gigabits" of information.

In return they hold out the promise that Robin may be able to communicate with Klara, who is trapped in a black hole. At one point when Pohl was writing *Gateway*, its working title was *Beyond the Blue Event Horizon*. At that time he "considered that the main thrust of *Gateway* was the color and terror of the black hole."[17] Black holes are very much on Robin's mind and very much at the heart of *Beyond the Blue Event Horizon*. When Essie's life is in danger, Robin has guilty thoughts about being free to find Klara, and Essie risks the remote possibility of leukemia to heal faster so that Robin can go to the food factory and from there maybe to the black hole where Klara is stuck. More importantly, the Heechee themselves are waiting in the black hole at the center of the Milky Way for a race advanced enough to join them there. One of the last images of the book is of a Heechee contemplating confrontation with an alien race in much the same way human beings have pictured such an event.

But even if Essie can graft some of her humanity onto her programs by "build[ing] them up from adding machines to number-crunchers. . . . pack[ing] them full of data. . . . construct[ing] for them a store of appropriate responses to stimuli and provid[ing] them with a hierarchical scale of appropriateness,"[18] the organic grafting of man onto machine is clearly not an option in this novel. Eight hundred thousand years ago the Heechee stole a tribe of australopithecines from Africa and transported them to a Heechee artifact near the food factory in order to manipulate their history and control the course of their evolution. By the time human beings discover them, they are in danger of dying out. Their leader is an enormous and potentially destructive computer which has had one of the "Old One's," as the race is called by humans, identity and memory physically grafted onto it. It too is losing its considerable powers and after the human invasion of the artifact attempts to return to the Heechee as it has been programmed to do. Robin prevents this return and averts a confrontation with the Heechee, although he does not know it at the time. In the past, several Gateway prospectors found their way to the artifact, Heechee Heaven, were grafted onto computers, and are now known as Dead Men. Unlike Sigfrid and Albert Einstein, the Dead Men are generally irrational. The computers on Heechee Heaven are made specifically for the Old Ones to record their memories and identities exactly. But human beings are not very well designed for such treatment. As the Oldest One, the giant computer, says of his human computer programs: "There was something wrong with their chemistry. They recorded imperfectly and retrieved haphazardly."[19] The organic union of man and machine is, in this novel, a step in the wrong direction, and the Heechee experiment with the Old Ones is a dismal failure, from the Heechee's standpoint at least.[20]

Machines in these two novels cooperate with human beings and thus quite literally become the vehicles for liberation from the present, junk-filled world to a happier and more sensible way of life in the future. *Gateway* explores one man's quest for self-awareness and wholeness. Pohl suggests that all men must do what Robin does—that is, reconcile their inner dichotomies—so that they can escape from their present, rather messy adolescence into a mature and healthy adulthood. In the omitted last chapter, Pohl makes this connection clear by citing a review of the novel in a sidebar. The critic says of the novel that "the revelation of the action coincides with Broadhead's personal revelation."[21] As Robin moves confidently into the future, so does the human race.

Critic David Samuelson has pointed out that life on Gateway is a gamble; the prospectors live at the " 'cutting edge' of human exploration and initiative" and "take blind chances in a cosmic shell game."[22] Gambling is a favorite pastime of Gateway prospectors, who ritually act out their destinies every night at the Blue Hell. Robin gets to Gateway on a gamble by winning a lottery,[23] and once he is there gambles his life three times. The last time he comes up a winner financially but at the sacrifice of the rest of the members of the expedition. He is one of the luckier ones. Some prospectors come back in bits and pieces or as a foul coating on the inside of a ship. Still others come back insane or without parts of themselves, like Shicky Bakin, the most humane character on Gateway in spite of the fact that he is stuck where he is because he is literally half a man.

Gateway functions under a system of state capitalism.[24] The Gateway Corporation regulates every aspect of the prospectors' lives, from when and how often they can take showers to how many berries they can pick from a bush. This absolute control belies human helplessness when it comes to Heechee ships and diguises the failure to answer the ultimate question: Will human beings die this time out? As the novel progresses, the corporation learns more about how to operate the ships, ironically through the mishaps of men like Robin, who in a hysterical fit "kills" a ship. Each bit of information helps reduce the gamble. And although the first controlled out voyage—the one on which Robin earns his millions—is a disaster in human terms, it provides him with the resources to begin to heal himself and ultimately brings to an end the game of Russian roulette that is a Gateway voyage.

What began as Robin's personal salvation in *Gateway* becomes the salvation of the human race in *Beyond the Blue Event Horizon*. Having solved his own problems, Robin turns his and Essie's considerable talents to the benefit of mankind. And just as Robin has in a sense been reborn at the end of *Gateway* with the help of a machine, so all men face rebirth and rejuvenation in *Beyond the Blue Event Horizon*. Robin and Essie owe their lives to the marvel of Full Medical, a complex process by which their bodies are continually monitored by machines and their bodily organs replaced when they are damaged or diseased. Essie dies four times in the novel, and each time Robin experiences the guilt and grief associated with such a shattering event. Miraculously, she survives, even though she does so at the expense of poor men like Hat Forehand who had himself dismantled so that his family could afford to go to Gateway. In this world, only the fittest—the richest and luckiest, not necessarily the most humane—survive.

Like Robin and Essie, the rest of the human race experiences the sensation of dying. Because he is now a full partner in the Gateway Corporation, Robin is an owner of the food factory and responsible for what happens to it. On it is a device known as the dreaming couch. When a human being "enters" the couch, he inflicts his dreams and subconscious fears and desires upon the rest of the human race. Unaware of the consequences, Wan, the sole human survivor on Heechee Heaven, has been using the couch and subjecting his fellow men to disruptive attacks of fever. Fully aware of what he is doing, Peter Herter enters the dreaming couch in order to blackmail the Gateway Corporation. While he is on the couch, he has a heart attack, and mankind is totally paralyzed as it lives through the experience of dying. Because of the Heechee experiment, men confront the ultimate human experience, death, and live on in spite of it. As a testimonial to the human ability to endure, Robin fights the nausea and inertia of having his head filled with death to begin a voyage to save Heechee Heaven and the people on it, since they are his responsibility. Through his efforts, he makes himself "The Richest Person There Is,"[25] and the human being closest to understanding and making contact with the Heechee. Along the way, he solves the world's hunger problem and procures faster-than-light communication technology.

While the human race experiences death only to be reborn into a better, more comfortable world largely because of Robin, Janine, a fourteen-year-old member of a party exploring the food factory, lives vicariously the racial history of the Old Ones on a dreaming couch on Heechee Heaven. The dream, called a lesson by the Old Ones, changes her profoundly because she is forced to inhabit the body of an animal.[26] After this final lesson, she is transformed into an adult and accepts Wan as her lover. She is forced into an understanding of who she is, and this awareness turns her into a complete human being. Hers is the path taken by Robin and most of the men and women in the novel who are gradually gaining the emotional and physical resources to move on to a better way of life and, as a corollary, toward an eventual confrontation with the Heechee.

Both *Gateway* and *Beyond the Blue Event Horizon* are structured to support Pohl's optimism about the human race as it moves into the future with the help of machines. In *Gateway*, Robin's sessions with Sigfrid are alternated with his chronological narration of the story of his life from the time he was six years old until the present world of the novel. Interspersed between these two narrative strands are sidebars which give us some objective sense of Gateway, since the rest of the novel is told in the first person from Robin's point of view. Pohl says that in *Gateway* he did something he had always wanted to do: he created a world and said "about it everything that I knew to say. Not just enough to account for why the characters behaved as they did. Not just the physical parameters. The habits, the clothing, the recreations, the constraints, the sensory inputs."[27]

Robin's chronological narration is presumably separate from his sessions with Sigfrid; that is, he goes to great lengths to keep Sigfrid from introducing into their therapy sessions Robin's feelings about what happened to him on Gateway. Gradually, however, the events of his narration find their way into his psychoanalysis, until at the novel's conclusion the two narratives merge into the present, and Robin confronts his latent homosexuality and his feelings for Klara in his last session with Sigfrid.

Even the sidebars in *Gateway* prepare us for the eventual integration of Robin's personality and his acceptance of what has happened to him. Midway in the novel, reports of failed missions and classified ads concerning various aspects of life on Gateway appear in the narration of Robin's therapy sessions.[28] Then Robin himself shows up in the sidebars, first as an uncomfortable member of the audience at a lecture on black holes, and later as the subject of one of Francy Hereira's letters to his family.[29] After we see Robin made uncomfortable by the lecture, we get his subjective response to it, his sense of wonder at the idea of the black hole and his soul-shrinking terror when he thinks about "going out among those remote titans."[30] Apparently, although he does his best to disguise them from Sigfrid, his feelings are so close to the surface that even a stranger in a lecture hall can recognize them. The only one who cannot see his emotions is Robin, and the two merging narratives tell us exactly how he learns to feel.

The omitted last chapter reinforces this structural and thematic preoccupation with integration and renders seamless Pohl's created world. The chapter consists of a short sidebar and a brief narration by Robin. Robin has been healed, and Pohl cites two fictional reviews of his novel in the sidebar. Thus he calls attention to the fact that *Gateway* is a created world and at the same time suggests that the world is complete since critics are already reading the book and writing reviews of it. He also rectifies what he considers to be the rather hasty conclusion of the novel by having the two critics comment upon it. Just as Robin is complete, so is the novel.

Like *Gateway*, *Beyond the Blue Event Horizon* is composed of alternating narratives that eventually coalesce at the end of the novel. Robin's narration is intertwined with the stories of his wife and the people on the voyage to the food factory, and the assorted organic and mechanical beings they encounter. Lacking faster-than-light communications technology, he is literally out of time with the Herter-Hall family at the food factory. His instructions to them arrive twenty-five days after their transmittal, a fact that finally frustrates him so much that he is forced to take an action which brings about a satisfactory resolution of the events of the novel for all of the characters.

Since the narrative is resolved so that mankind, with the help of Heechee technology, can look forward to a relatively secure future, only the Heechee themselves remain to be explained. In the last chapter, we discover that the Heechee sense and fear something beyond themselves in the universe. That something may be God, an even more advanced race, or entropy. The Heechee are extremely rational creatures who, through their understanding of the physical universe, have mastered the essential nature of time and slowed themselves down in hopes of finding a kindred race. They are manipulators of the world who fear losing control, a control they probably arrived at by going through the growth pangs experienced by mankind in these two novels. Now that humans have achieved some degree of cohesion, Pohl suggests, we too can begin to control our destinies and evolve toward the Heechee.

Machines will play an important part in that highly evolved future. They will, like the Albert Einstein computer program, command their vast resources to find solutions to the problems that hold men back. They will also reflect the people who create them. That the computer programs in Pohl's created world are anthropomorphized may be, as Stanislaw Lem says of all depictions of humanized computers, an exhibition of the "paralysis of one's imagination and one's knowledge."[31] Or, it may indicate something about Pohl's intentions in these two works. For all of its obvious fascination with gadgetry, *Gateway* is, as the first critic claims in the last chapter, "really about Broadhead, not that brief moment of scientific wonder,"[32] and *Beyond the Blue Event Horizon* is really about the human response to a series of events, in spite of all of its marvelous machines. For Pohl, then, machines are significant only as they enhance men's lives and increase our freedom, no matter how ingenious or inspired his mechanical creations seem to be.

NOTES

1. Patricia Warrick, *The Cybernetic Imagination in Science Fiction* (Cambridge, MA: MIT Press, 1980), p. 124.

2. Frederik Pohl, *Gateway* (New York: St. Martin's Press, 1977), ch. 3, p. 19 (16); ch. 21, p. 206 (181); ch. 29, pp. 294-95 (261-62); ch. 31, p. 310 (276). [Both *Gateway* and *Beyond the Blue Event Horizon* (see below, n.11) are available in nearly indistinguishable hardcover editions, with significant differences in pagination. The chapter citations in these notes will be of some help, but we will further aid readers by supplying supplemental page citations. If we have correctly identified the editions, the first citation will be to the first editions (yellow lettering on the cover of *Gateway*; February 1980 publication date in *Beyond*), and the following parenthetical citations will be to the S. F. Book Club editions (orange lettering on *Gateway*).—Eds.]

3. Ibid., ch. 1, p. 2 (1).

4. Ibid., ch. 13, p. 136 (120).

5. Ibid., ch. 5, p. 30 (26); cf. ch. 3, p. 19 (16).

6. Ibid., ch. 19, p. 176 (155-56).

7. Ibid., ch. 14, p. 146 (129).

8. Ibid., ch. 22, p. 226 (198).

9. Ibid., ch. 31, p. 313 (278).

10. Frederik Pohl, "Postscript to *Gateway*," *Galaxy*, August 1977, p. 32.

11. Frederik Pohl, *Beyond the Blue Event Horizon* (New York: Ballantine, 1980), ch. 12, p. 223 (191).

12. Ibid., ch. 6, p. 94 (81).

13. Ibid., ch. 13, p. 246 (210).

14. Ibid., ch. 9, p. 180 (154).

15. Ibid., ch. 11, p. 217 (185).

16. Ibid., ch. 12, pp. 227 and 230 (194 and 197).

17. Pohl, "Postscript," p. 32.

18. Pohl, *Beyond*, ch. 11, p. 217 (185).

19. Ibid., ch. 10, p. 208 (177).

20. Pohl's attitude toward man-machine union is more ambiguous in *Man Plus*

(New York: Random House, 1976) and is quite positive in "Day Million" (*Rogue*, 1966; rpt. *Science Fiction: The Future*, Dick Allen, ed. [New York and other cities: Harcourt Brace Jovanovich, 1971], pp. 225-29).

21. Pohl, "Postcript," p. 33.

22. David N. Samuelson, "Critical Mass: The Science Fiction of Frederik Pohl," *Science-Fiction Studies*, 7 (March 1980), 92.

23. Ibid.

24. Ibid.

25. Pohl, *Beyond*, ch. 16, p. 298 (255).

26. Ibid., ch. 14, p. 277 (232).

27. Pohl, "Postscript," p. 33.

28. Pohl, *Gateway*, ch. 12, pp. 107 and 119 (94 and 104); ch. 19, p. 173 (153).

29. Ibid., ch. 26, pp. 262 and 269 (232 and 238).

30. Ibid., ch. 26, p. 268 (237).

31. Stanislaw Lem, "Robots in Science Fiction" in *SF: The Other Side of Realism*, Thomas Clareson, ed. (Bowling Green, OH: Bowling Green University Popular Press, 1971), p. 323.

32. Pohl, "Postscript," p. 33.

WHAT A PIECE OF WORK IS A MAN: MECHANICAL GODS IN THE FICTION OF ROGER ZELAZNY

They are not many. There is the Bork from "The Engine at Heartspring's Center." There is Halfjack from the story of the same name. There is Frost from "For a Breath I Tarry." There is the Hangman from "Home Is the Hangman." Besides these, the number of robots, androids, cyborgs, computers, or other special machines that qualify as gods and occupy center stage in Roger Zelazny's stories is very small.

If those humans, or humanoids, whose lives are mechanically sustained are added to the group, then its size can be expanded slightly. The gods from *Lord of Light*, for example, fit this category. They achieve virtual immortality, and their power, from their awesome technology, especially their body-transfer machines. John Auden, of "The Man Who Loved the Faioli," also fits this category. His immortality is guaranteed by technology. And Jarry Dark, of "The Keys to December," fits into this group since he was genetically engineered and, if he so chooses, advanced technology permits him to extend his life by means of long periods of cyrogenic sleep. Even with these additions, the number of Zelazny's mechanical gods remains small but significant.

For those who know his writing well, the observation that there are few mechanical gods in Zelazny's work will come as no surprise, for they also know that in many ways his work is primarily a celebration of the nature of man. Characterization is one of his strengths as a writer, and it is his acute analysis of personality that attracts and holds many of his readers.

Though Zelazny had already formulated a theory of characterization before he read Northrop Frye's *Anatomy of Criticism*, there is no doubt but that this book's "First Essay" had a great influence on him. In its delineation of character types, Zelazny found affirmation for what he already knew—that there was a character type that legitimized what he wanted to do within science fiction. Frye placed this character in "the high mimetic mode," defined as where the hero is "superior in degree to other men but not to his natural environment. . . . He has authority, passions, and powers of expression far greater than ours, but what he does is subject to both social criticism and the order of nature."[1]

To Zelazny, it meant that he could create characters who were larger-than-life-sized in a science fiction sense. They could have telepathic, telekinetic, or other powers. They could be immortal or near-immortal. They could be genetically engineered or bionic; or they could simply be mutants. But posed against the powers of these superior beings must be a normal psychology. Understanding their powers, learning that they brought responsibilities, and learning to use them in a positive and productive way were problems with which even the most superior men might wrestle. This pattern of characterization permitted Zelazny to set up a double-sided quest for his central characters: a physical one and a psychological one. Most of his major works do just that, with the two goals carefully integrated. But most importantly, it permitted him to provide the reader with the exotic characters he sought while simultaneously allowing the reader to identify strongly with them.

Immortality, or near-immortality, is a persistent theme in Zelazny's writing, and it is a key factor in raising man or humanoid to the god level. Longevity brings enormous power, great riches, or vast influence. Note, for example, Francis Sandow in *Isle of the Dead* (1967) and Conrad Nomikos in *This Immortal* (1966). But though longevity invests its owners with the aspects of godhood, Zelazny's protagonists seldom find godhood to be a perfect state of existence. They are often troubled. This occurs because Zelazny has drawn them with normal psychologies and they are simply not equipped mentally to deal with their superior powers. They must grow; they must mature. In Zelazny's writing, this quest is all-important, for it is man's potential to raise his level of consciousness that permits him to truly become a god.

Two excellent short stories, "The Engine at Heartspring's Center" and "The Man Who Loved the Faioli," illustrate the unhappy mechanical god quite well.[2] Bork, the protagonist of "The Engine at Heartspring's Center," is a cyborg. Formerly a well-loved and very successful politician, Charles Eliot Borkman saved hundreds of people from death when a starship in which he was a passenger came out of hyper-space too close to a star in nova. Half destroyed in his heroic efforts, Borkman's body was rebuilt with mechanical parts, leaving him an odd combination of metal and flesh and bringing him virtual immortality. He clearly has the capability to do almost anything he chooses, but his unique nature also creates a barrier between him and humankind.

After many years of alienation, Bork is bitter and bored. He believes that he has reached his experiential limit, so he sends himself to a euthanasia colony. Once there, he finds that there is new experience even in watching things wind down and decides to postpone his date of death. He is too powerful for them to come and take him physically, so they send a girl named Nora to assassinate him. They fall in love, however, and Bork learns that love is the power to transform, to renew. Each person possesses the power to increase another's experience, to instruct him, to drive his psychological growth. By his love, each person can stimulate another's personality development.

John Auden, the protagonist of "The Man Who Loved the Faioli," learns a similar lesson. Auden bears one of the universe's last incurable diseases. His life is sustained by a machine that brings him immortality but produces a peculiar side effect that leaves him consigned to a death-in-life existence; like Bork, who survives Nora's assassination attempt, Auden is emotionally dead. Because of this and his disturbing appearance, he chooses to become the keeper of the universe's graveyard. It is maintained by robots and located on a planet where there is no other life.

That Auden bears the trappings of godhood is unquestioned. He is immortal, he is invisible to living beings, he has an army of robots that he could command if he wished. Yet, he chooses to do nothing with his powers.

Then one day, a creature named Sythia, one of the Faioli, suddenly appears on his planet. The embodiment of all feminine beauty, the Faioli appear to men who are dying. The Faioli enrich the last days of these dying men with their bodies but eventually take the men's lives to nourish themselves. At the end, it was said, the men welcome death. After considering his own emotionless life, Auden decides to switch off the electrochemical system that sustains him and to truly live again. Sythia and Auden make love for a month, and Auden comes to welcome that final kiss from Sythia that will suck the remaining life from his body. He comes to love her. But she detects that he is different from other men and asks why. In explaining that he has been mechanically sustained, he shows her the switch under his arm that activates the device, and she triggers it. Auden suddenly disappears, and his icy logic once more prevails. Invisible to her once more, Auden lets her search for him until she wearies of it and leaves. Now purged of his emotions, he returns to his life of isolation.

From these two stories, it is clear that neither the powers of godhood nor mechanically created longevity can guarantee happiness, mental health, creativity, or productivity. These things are generated within man, and it is only the psychological quest that produces true godhood.

Jarry Dark, the protagonist of "The Keys to December," learns yet another lesson about godhood.[3] A genetically altered human, Dark is one of 28,000 Catforms. Highly intelligent and sensitive, Catforms breath methane and are comfortable only when the temperature reaches $-50°$ C. Originally destined to work for a mining company on a Coldworld called Alynol, they are abandoned when the planet is destroyed by a nova. Able to exist only in special mechanized environments, the Catforms pool their financial resources, which Dark invests. He is a financial genius and soon they have enough money to buy their own world and the equipment necessary to adapt it to their environmental needs. Eventually they inhabit the new planet and set the machines to work. While the change is occurring, most of the Catforms sleep in cryogenic chambers, but since the machinery altering their environment requires periodic monitoring, they take turns waking up to check on it.

Twelve hundred and fifty years after the adaptation began, Dark notices that a species called Redforms is evolving intelligence, and Sanza Barati, his fiancée, recognizes that they possess the power to shape and break; that they might be creating men and then destroying them. Jarry and Sanza even discuss the fact that they have become gods for the animals of the planet. This perception is reinforced when the Redforms begin to bring sacrifices to the watch-stations used by the Catforms when they are awake. It is further reinforced when during one of the wake-periods Jarry and Sanza come across several of the Redforms being attacked by a huge bear. Feeling sorry for their futile efforts to defend themselves, Jarry kills the bear for them, but when he turns his back on the kill, the bear's mate breaks from the forest and knocks him to the ground. Fearing for his life, Sanza crashes their flier into it. She kills the other bear but breaks her neck in the crash.

The Redforms tell of the deed around their campfires, and Dark realizes that, in fact, he has become their god. He also realizes that the Catforms have a responsibility to the Redforms. They have triggered their evolving intelligence, and Dark knows that they must do all in their power to make sure that the Redforms have enough time to adapt to the changing climate. After studying them closely, he discovers that they will not survive unless the rate of change is slowed. He blackmails the Catform Council into doing just that and chooses to stay awake to monitor the progress of the Redforms. By passing up his sleep periods in the cryogenic chambers, Dark will miss seeing the new Alynol. His life will be short and his responsibility great, but he has learned that to be a god requires great personal sacrifice. He must accept responsibility not only for his own actions but for those of his subjects as well. Once again, Zelazny has made us aware that godhood is an imperfect state.

The gods of *Lord of Light* both reinforce this concept and extend it.[4] Originally colonists from Earth, the settlers have, by the time of the story, developed an awesome technology that permits some of them literally to play god. Its most important contribution is to provide them with the capability for body transfer which makes them virtually immortal. Under the control of the gods, the transfer equipment, growth tanks, body lockers, and banks of sperm and ova are maintained by the Masters of Karma, priests who are the merchants of new bodies. Body transfer could make all of the inhabitants of Urath (a corruption of the word *Earth*) into gods by making them, too, immortal, but the process is controlled by a few of the elite, who, having adopted the names of Hindu gods, live in the Celestial City located at one of the poles. These gods, most of them the survivors of the *Star of India*, the ship that brought them from Earth, have become completely corrupted by their powers and blackmail the masses for sexual and other favors by withholding body transfer from them. They also keep them uneducated and retard their technological progress by rationalizing that the masses need to be protected from themselves. In truth, their system, Deicratism, is no more than a convenient excuse for the egotism of the gods.

Technology has also brought the gods other powers. Called attributes, these powers permit them to control certain natural phenomena.[5] Born from the early days of planetary occupation, when the First used drugs, hypnosis, meditation, and eventually neurosurgery to discipline their emerging mutant powers, the attributes grew in strength through the passing years. These powers are predicated upon a special physiology which is partially lost in body transfer, but the mind remembers and after a time alters the new body to the extent necessary to create a homeostasis that permits the gradual return of the attributes. These powers are also withheld from the masses.

Like other Zelazny mechanical gods, those of *Lord of Light* possess the psychological fragility of normal humans. Their powers and privileges do not make them better from a psychological point of view. To the contrary, power only reinforces their existing vanity by permitting them to wallow in their egotism. This preoccupation alienates them not only from the masses and each other but from the main purpose of their lives—to advance up the scale of consciousness and thus free themselves from their material shackles. As the gods vie for power and position, as alliances and friendships are broken for advantage, the gods reinforce the barriers that exist between them. An excellent example of the damage this causes is found in Candi/Kali/ Brahma's betrayal of Yama, the Death-god. She marries him but almost immediately breaks her marriage contract to become Brahma, the highest-ranking god in the Celestial City. Her insatiable ambition forces her to forsake love for power, and the same drive exists for most of the other gods. For them all virtues are consumed by ambition.

More important, however, is the damage that the gods do to themselves by blocking their own progress to higher and higher states of consciousness. Both Hindus and Buddhists believe that the purpose of reincarnation is to develop the soul to a point where it may merge once more with the Absolute, that original, nameless power that created all things, all possibilities. This process of discovering Eternal Truth is called self-realization. It is the process of liberating man from the illusion of the material world, with its corruption and ignorance. The experience accumulated by man through his various reincarnations should permit him to reach the highest state of consciousness. Often described as divine intoxication, it is that state where man's passions and fascinations for earthly life are "snuffed out." It is the state of consciousness called *moksha* by the Hindus and *nirvana* by the Buddhists. It is complete liberation of the soul. It is also the goal of *rajayoga*, the highest of the yoga systems. In his book *Seven Religions*, one of Zelazny's sources for *Lord of Light*, Joseph Politella dsecribes the purpose of *rajayoga* in a most interesting way: "to take the kingdom of Heaven by violence—violence to the enemy, which is the lower self with its psychic images and appetites, all of which are born of karma and bar the way to entry."[6] Such is the condition of most of the gods of the Celestial City. Tied to the material and the earthly by ego and ambition, they are barred from merger with the Absolute.

One, however, has found the path. Called Mahasamatman, and nick-named Sam, he is one of the First. Famous as the binder of the demons, native fire creatures, he was once married to Kali but eventually outgrew her, forsook her, and—like the historical Buddha—went off into the world to see what life was really about.[7] As a result of his experiences, Sam finally rids himself of his pride and gradually achieves higher and higher states of consciousness. He eventually achieves a nirvana of sorts when his soul is dispersed into the magnetic cloud that surrounds the planet because he led a rebellion against the gods at the Battle of Keenset. He subsequently experiences a kind of incarnation when Yama, who is a technological genius, invents a machine that traps the particles of Sam's *atman* and reassembles them.

Like the historical incarnations of Vishnu, with which he is identified, Sam returns for a specific purpose—to lead a second rebellion against the Deicrats and in doing so to liberate both the masses and the gods of the Celestial City from their own vanity. Specifically, Sam is identified with two of Vishnu's incarnations: Kalki(n) and Maitreya.[8] Vishnu was called Lord Kalkin when he was married to Durga/Kali and, traditionally, Kalki is the tenth and last avatar of Vishnu. He is depicted either as a giant with a horse's head, or riding a white horse. The myth says that he will ride through the decadent world with his arm aloft bearing a sword blazing like a comet. His appearance will signal the end of the current age and the beginning of preparation for the next. It is no accident that Sam appears at the Battle of Khaipur, the site of the defeat of the Deicrat gods, riding a white horse. His role is meant to be interpreted symbolically.

Sam is also identified with Maitreya. In Sanskrit, Maitreya is both the word for love and the name of the Buddha-of-the-Future, who will reform mankind by his love. According to legend, he is even now on Earth and progressing through various states of consciousness toward illumination. He is also a lord of light (there are many in Hinduism). In his epigram to the last book of the novel, Zelazny identifies Sam with both Maitreya and the Lord of Light. Through the allusion, Sam becomes the liberator of mankind, the one who will save it through the power of his divine love. Significantly, self-realization (the process that leads to *moksha* or *nirvana*) is also known in both Hinduism and Buddhism as illumination.

The process that Sam goes through in his progression to illumination is equivalent to that which many other Zelazny characters experience and which is best described as personality metamorphosis.[9] It is part of the renewal theme which permeates Zelazny's work. It is the psychological manifestation of renewal, a general raising of consciousness, and the psychological object of the quests upon which his characters embark. Best described by Carl Jung's term "individuation," personality metamorphosis is the state created when a person successfully integrates the opposing systems of his personality into a separate, individual unity—a whole. With this integration also comes complete knowledge of self, the same benefit that Hindus and Buddhists believe comes from self-realization.[10]

For Zelazny, the key to metamorphosis is accumulating experience, and the process follows a typical pattern. First, some negative element of the personality becomes dominant, thus blocking healthy personality development. Often that factor is pride. Such is the case for Carlton Davits of "The Doors of His Face, the Lamps of His Mouth," for Gallinger of "A Rose for Ecclesiastes," and for the gods of *Lord of Light*. Greed, power, ambition, and revenge (all derived from pride and vanity) are other dominating personality faults anatomized in Zelazny's work. The second stage of development in the metamorphosis occurs when the individual suffers a personal failure or some other traumatic event which makes him aware of his fallibility. This is followed by a period of readjustment, sometimes quite lengthy, and that in turn by an integration of the disparate elements. Once complete, the metamorphosis brings enormous personal benefits. Among them may be increased productivity, mentally healthy love, confidence, complete knowledge of self, happiness, and creativity. The psychological goal of all men, metamorphosis is the wonderful promise that life holds out to them, and Zelazny believes firmly that it is well worth the effort that a man must put forth to achieve it.

And achievement is difficult, for man must first overcome the negative aspects of his own manhood. Sam understands this. He makes that clear when he defines the nature of man for Taraka, a demon to whom he is bound and who is suffering sudden feelings of weakness and the diminution of his ability to feel pleasure.

You told me that I, too, took pleasure in the ways of the pain which you work. You were correct, for all men have within them that which is dark and that which is light. A man is a thing of many divisions, not a pure, clear flame such as you once were. His intellect often wars with his emotions, his will with his desires . . . his ideas are at odds with his environment, and if he follows them, he knows keenly the loss of that which was old—but if he does not follow them, he feels the pain of having forsaken a new and noble dream. Whatever he does represents both a gain and a loss, an arrival and a departure. Always he mourns that which is gone and fears some part of that which is new. Reason opposes tradition. Emotions oppose the restrictions his fellow men lay upon him. Always from the friction of these things, there arises the thing you called the curse of man and mocked—guilt![11]

Clearly, man is a bundle of conflicts, a collection of polarities, which can only be resolved by the integration of the disparate elements of personality.

The difficulty of Sam's evolution is typical. He renounces his marriage to Durga/Kali. He abandons his family and his possessions. He gives up his position as one of the gods, and the power and pleasures that go with it. He alienates himself purposely from his friends. He gets killed and is dispersed. Indeed, the road to enlightenment is a hard one, but the rewards to be reaped are great. He comes to know a higher form of love. He attains a complete knowledge of self and the universal plan. And, he has experienced the peace that comes from merging with the Absolute.

Because the rewards are so great, Zelazny really permits no alternatives to being human in his writing. Regardless of the problems that it brings, being a man is better than being anything else. For this reason, it is no surprise that the only two completely mechanical central characters in Zelazny's work are eventually humanized. Both ultimately tell us more about humanity than they do about machines.

The Hangman in "Home Is the Hangman" both affirms Sam's definition of man and expands our understanding of the human condition.[12] A combination of telefactor and computer, yet more than the sum of the two, the Hangman is a unique, anthropomorphic machine sent from Earth to explore the solar system. Last heard from twenty years prior to the time of the story, as it was about to land on Uranus, the Hangman was in the throes of what seemed to be a nervous breakdown. A piece of sophisticated equipment, the Hangman could not only make its own decisions, but, it was believed, had also achieved some sort of personality. This was possible because of a special connection between it and its four teachers who imprinted their own personalities upon its blank circuitry.

The story concerns the return of the Hangman, the death of three of the teachers, and the fear of the fourth that the Hangman has returned to kill him because of an incident involving the use of the machine to break into a bank vault, and its accidental killing of a bank guard, that occurred the night before the Hangman was launched. It occurred because the teachers were trying to outdo one another in using the machine and one of them panicked. Fearing that the launch would be cancelled, the teachers chose not to disclose the incident. But, aware that the Hangman had been imprinted by four separate personalities and then traumatized by their fears and guilt, Senator Jessie Brockden, one of the teachers, believes that the machine has become schizophrenic and is seeking him out to kill him for his part in the bank killing. Brockden's belief is erroneous; the Hangman is neither mad nor murderous.

As the story unravels, Nemo, Zelazny's "no-name" detective whom Brockden has hired to protect him, learns that the Hangman has integrated the four personalities and overcome the imposed trauma to achieve a metamorphosis of personality similar to that which many of Zelazny's other principal characters experience. It has murdered none of the other teachers. It has simply returned home like a dutiful child to show its "parents" how well it has done and to relieve them of the guilt that it knows they must feel. It considers itself part of the human race and has a profound understanding of mankind. In particular, it has a keen perception of the role guilt plays in man's development.

Guilt has driven and damned the race of man since its earliest days of rationality. I am convinced that it rides with all of us to our graves. I am the product of guilt—I see that you [Nemo] know that. Its product, its subject, once its slave. . . . But I have come to terms with it, realizing that it is a necessary adjunct of my own measure of humanity. [A moment later, it adds:]. . . and I see in your conclusions on many other things as well: what a stupid, perverse, shortsighted, selfish race we are. While in many ways that is true, it is but another part of the thing that guilt represents. Without guilt man would be no better than the other inhabitants of this planet — excepting certain cetaceans. . . . Man, despite his tremendous shortcomings, is nevertheless possessed of a greater number of kindly impulses than all the other beings where instincts are the larger part of life. These impulses, I believe, are owed directly to this capacity for guilt. It is involved in both the worst and the best of man.[13]

This "speech" both reinforces the concepts expressed in Sam's speech to Taraka and clarifies the role that guilt plays in tempering instinct. There is no question but what the Hangman is enlightened, but sadly, he is also alienated. The very distance that permits him to make his profound observations of mankind also divorces him from it. Admittedly, his alienation is not the destructive kind exhibited by Saul Bellow's *Dangling Man*, for it is free of the corrosive and debilitating loneliness that usually accompanies alienation. The Hangman is like Nemo and Sam, who have been strengthened in their personality metamorphoses so that they can still function positively; so that they can love mankind from a distance in spite of its faults and weaknesses; so that they will be psychologically healthy. But they will never again truly be part of mankind. They have become superior beings, who operate at a different, higher level of consciousness. They can never go home again; but, then, they probably do not want to.

This kind of alienation as an alternative path from metamorphosis is both a concession to reality and a logical outgrowth of achieving a psychologically healthy love relationship. For example, built into the successful love relationship of Carlton Davits and his ex-wife Jean of "The Doors of His Face, the Lamps of His Mouth" is the implication that both of them, having metamorphosed, will be alienated from those who have not. Healthy love is always possible if the metamorphosed individual can find another who has also metamorphosed, but that is not always the case. And in the case of Sam, he has obviously achieved an ultimate level of consciousness, one which is beyond individual love affairs.

Despite what happens to the Hangman, who in effect becomes a man, no machine can reach the superior, metamorphosed state. For Zelazny, the critical difference between man and machine is not one of physiology, but one of consciousness. Can it grow, can it develop, can it change under the impact of its experience, can it reach a metamorphosis?

Nowhere is this made more clear than in Zelazny's highly acclaimed "For a Breath I Tarry."[14] In this story, he explores the nature of man and the human condition in great detail. An analogue of the Genesis myth, it specifically treats the efforts of Frost, a "relay station and coordinating agent for activities in [Earth's] northern hemisphere," to understand man. Significantly, Frost, like all men, possesses a tragic fault. It is "an unaccountably acute imperative that he must function at full capacity at all times."[15] This occurred because Frost was created during a period when Solcom, the orbiting control center for the rebuilding of Earth, suffered "a discontinuity of complementary functions, best described as madness."[16] It was brought on by an unprecedented solar flare-up lasting a little more than thirty-six hours that also produced in Solcom a state of temporary amnesia. The result is that he creates a unique machine which he dignifies with a name. Though he wonders about Frost's strangeness, Solcom finds that Frost handles his duties with such efficiency and dispatch that he never seriously considers dismantling him to find out the nature of his difference.

Because he must function at full capacity at all times and because he is so efficient, Frost has idle hours to fill. So, when one of his explorer-robots discovers several artifacts of the long-extinct species called Man, Frost decides to study him as a hobby. He is particularly intrigued by Man because the surviving machines regard Him as God, since He created them. His study is prompted by the electromechanical equivalent of curiosity, significantly one of the faults responsible for getting Adam and Eve expelled from the Garden of Eden.

Incorporating the Faust, Wandering Jew, and Ancient Mariner motifs, "For a Breath I Tarry" develops Frost's growing perplexity as to Man's nature. Finally coming to believe that he can only know Man by becoming one, Frost bargains with Mordel, an agent of an alternative Earth rebuilding system named Divcom, for all the information about man that the Divcom robots have discovered. The bargain struck is a functional one, based upon Frost's admission that he has so far failed in his attempts to become a Man. If he fails finally, then he must employ all his resources in the service of Divcom for as long as he continues to function. Frost eventually beats the pact by achieving his goal, but in the process he concludes that Man was both an illogical and unmeasurable being, qualities that a machine finds difficult to understand.

The Wandering Jew and Ancient Mariner motifs are implemented in the Ancient Ore-Crusher. A machine designed by Solcom to help in the reconstruction of Earth, Ore-Crusher accidentally killed the last Man alive. As punishment, he was cast forth by Solcom to wander the Earth and tell all the other machines his story. His imperative overrides all others, so they are forced to listen. His significance lies in the fact that he can recognize a Man, and it is his reaction, to a command uttered by Frost in frustration, that determines that Frost has succeeded in becoming a Man.

Frost's attempts to understand those things that delighted Man, such as beauty, through mechanical analogues of the human senses and his attempts to sculpt and paint, end in failure, and he comes to the conclusion that Man's evaluation of the quality of an experience is based in His physiology. So when his explorer-robots discover seventeen long-dead but perfectly frozen corpses at the North Pole, he sets about to clone them.

Fifty years later, after developing the techniques, growing several blank-brained bodies in tanks, and building a machine to transmit his matrix of awareness into one of the bodies, he makes a test transfer. His return to his own structure is automatic, but the five minutes that he spends in the human body are overwhelming. He experiences light, noise, and odors; jumbled data; imprecise perception; weeping; and most importantly, fear and despair. The experience leaves him traumatized and withdrawn. He denies his success; but, when Ore-Crusher obeys his command to go crush ore, the other machines realize that he has indeed achieved his goal, so they transfer him permanently to the human body. After six months of learning to walk, talk, dress, eat, hear, feel, and taste, Frost learns to appreciate what it means to be a Man. Since he can now feel emotion, he asks the Beta Machine, coordinator of the southern hemisphere, to join him as a woman. He also comes to understand what it means to stand outside of logic, and he can resolve opposites. When Solcom and Divcom ask him, for example, which of them was right in their battle to see who will direct the rebuilding of Earth, he tells them that they both were. When they ask how that is possible, he replies, "only a man can appreciate it."[17] He has truly become their God.

And though Frost has lost a great deal (he can no longer communicate directly with Solcom and Divcom, for example), he has gained much more. He has gained the capacity to transcend not only his material shackles but himself as well, and it is this quality that is important. Zelazny sees man as of the same material as God, and he celebrates the potential for him to return ultimately to the godhead through some sort of merger with it. Surely he would agree with Hamlet's brief vision of human glory:

What a piece of work is a man, how noble in reason, how infinite in faculties; in form and moving how express and admirable, in action how like an angel, in apprehension how like a god: the beauty of the world, the paragon of animals![18]

NOTES

1. Northrop Frye, *Anatomy of Criticism: Four Essays* (Princeton, NJ: Princeton University Press, 1957), paperback ed., pp. 33-34.

2. Roger Zelazny, "The Engine at Heartspring's Center," *Analog*, July 1974, pp. 70-76; "The Man Who Loved the Faioli," *Galaxy*, June 1967, pp. 67-73.

3. Roger Zelazny, "The Keys to December," *New Worlds*, August 1966, pp. 115-41.

4. Roger Zelazny, *Lord of Light* (New York: Doubleday, 1967).

5. Defined as the fundamental and permanent properties of substance, attributes have been distinguished from accidents, which are modifications representing circumstantial properties only, since the time of Aristotle. The theory of attributes was an important problem of Muslim and Jewish scholasticism, and of Christian scholasticism, because of its intimate connection with the Christian doctrine of the Trinity.

6. Joseph Politella, *Seven Religions* (Kent, OH: Kent State University Press, 1958), p. 66.

7. Sam's actions parallel those of the historical Buddha, who renounced his right to

be king of Kapilavastu, left his young wife, Yasodhara, and his son, Rahula, and went forth into the world determined to find the truth.

8. Funk and Wagnall's *Dictionary of Folklore* identifies Kalki and Kalkin as the same character.

9. For a detailed discussion of personality metamorphosis, see Carl B. Yoke, "Personality Metamorphosis in Roger Zelazny's 'The Doors of His Face, the Lamps of His Mouth,'" *Extrapolation*, 21, No. 2 (Summer 1980), 106-21.

10. Calvin S. Hall and Vernon Nordby, *A Primer of Jungian Psychology* (New York: New American Library, Mentor Books, 1973), paperback ed., p. 34.

11. Zelazny, *Lord of Light*, p. 126.

12. Roger Zelazny, "Home Is the Hangman" in Roger Zelazny, *My Name is Legion* (New York: Ballantine Books, 1976). Originally published in *Analog*, November 1975, pp. 12-66.

13. Zelazny, "Hangman," in *Legion*, pp. 210-11.

14. Roger Zelazny, *For a Breath I Tarry* (San Francisco, CA: Underwood/Miller, 1980), paperback ed. The first correct version of the story was published in *Fantastic*, September 1966, pp. 6-37.

15. Zelazny, *For a Breath*, p. 13.

16. Ibid., p. 11.

17. Ibid., p. 65.

18. William Shakespeare, *Hamlet*, act II, sc. ii, ll. 300-304.

7

WHAT THE MACHINE TEACHES:
WALTER TEVIS'S *MOCKINGBIRD*

A favorite theme in science fiction is what James Gunn has referred to as "the Frankenstein complex," and even though Gunn's purpose is to dismiss the ambiguities in that complex rather quickly in favor of the directness of Asimovian rationality, which is his topic, the image of Frankenstein will not be denied its suggestiveness.[1] The image extends backward in time, of course, to the edge of the eighteenth-century Enlightenment. But recently it has appeared again in an extremely sensitive new novel, *Mockingbird*, by Walter Tevis, a work that weaves together in an unusual and effective way references ranging from the King Kong image of popular culture through the robotic tradition of Asimov to the most basic Romantic dilemma of human identity and human limits.[2] The original Romantic poets were fascinated by the outer limits of human potential because they lived at the end of a century in which the notions of progress and potentiality were the intellectual highlights.[3] The end of the eighteenth century also witnessed the diabolical transformation of progress into the terror of the French Revolution. Thus a major theme for the Romantics was the Faust or Prometheus archetype of the effects that could derive from mankind's inventive cleverness. Linked with the new skill demonstrated in science and the Industrial Revolution, the theme made Mary Shelley's *Frankenstein* especially meaningful alongside her husband's *Prometheus Unbound* and numerous other Romantic texts. Like Frankenstein's monster, our machines can teach us much about ourselves.

The traditions and influences in modern science fiction are tightly woven together. Variations on the android-cyborg-robot theme ranging from early robot stories to Tevis's latest symbolic orchestration of loneliness by means of the theme are too numerous to summarize here. Three works of fiction from the late 1940s and early 1950s, however, follow Isaac Asimov's Laws of Robotics with greater twists of irony than Asimov perhaps intended; and these seem particularly to have prepared the way for the *tour de force* in the use of the monster as type and symbol for humankind itself that Tevis has accomplished. Alfred Bester's point-of-view android in "Fondly Fahrenheit" (1954) becomes afflicted with his human master's mental disintegration, and the connections between the malfunction of the artificial man and human insanity both conform to the Laws of Robotics and stretch their ethical simplicities to the breaking point. It is a tense, fast moving story of an artificial man who is much like us and is probably closest to the mood and tone of the Tevis fiction.[4] Another famous fiction from this period, Cordwainer Smith's "Scanners Live in Vain" (1950), may have helped Tevis conceive of his artificial man as poignantly representing human problems. The cyborg scanners, following Asimov, ultimately must eliminate themselves so that mankind may progress—but not before their own human qualities become a major effect in the story.[5] Finally, Jack Williamson's "With Folded Hands" (1947) develops the narrative twist from the Second Law of Robotics which is closest in logic to what Tevis's plot turns on, although the Williamson story never achieves the symbolic resonance that Tevis retains from Bester and Smith. The robots in this the earliest story that seems to anticipate Tevis are instructed to guard humankind from harm and to guarantee happiness for all; so thoroughly do they carry out their instructions that they leave people with nothing significant to do.[6]

Dean Robert Spofforth, the central more-than-human android of Tevis's novel, serves as chief academic officer of New York University as well as manager of the rest of a future Earth populated with drugged, inward-turning hedonists. Spofforth's character, played off against two human lovers, Paul Bentley and Mary Lou Borne, dominates the novel. In a sense, it is a triangle love story with great depth and complexity. The basic turn in the plot, however, is that Spofforth has developed intense suicidal urges that conflict with his basic Asimovian programming that says that he must protect humans and protect himself in order to manage the planet. Each spring Dean Spofforth, the "Make Nine" robot, climbs to the top of the Empire State Building and tries to jump. But his inner directives keep his legs riveted to the platform. His intelligence allows him, however, gradually to violate the directives and to prepare for his death by phasing out humankind. When no more of his human charges remain alive, Spofforth can die. He has quietly arranged for a birth control supplement to be continuously included with the world's diet of drugs, and so the people of the novel are the last generation of humans.

Mary Lou and Paul's accidental avoidance of the birth control supplement allows them to conceive a child, and Spofforth's love for Mary Lou and the baby changes him. He banishes Paul and lives with Mary Lou during her pregnancy. Actually, Spofforth is in love with the memory of a girl he had seen years before, a memory that keeps coming back in his dreams. The fabrication of this most advanced android allowed for a rich memory system and the potential, though hardly the ability, for love. In any case, Mary Lou persuades him to explain why no recent pregnancies have occurred prior to hers, and finally a deal is made whereby Spofforth agrees to modify the birth control supplements so that generation on Earth may continue; in return for Spofforth's promise, Mary Lou and Paul, who has fought his way back to New York and the baby, push this robotic tragic hero off the Empire State Building.

The plot turns are less interesting than the images fused in Spofforth himself. From the snide reference that Tevis, the former academic in a large university, makes to his artificial man as a dean, to the profound exploration of human communication through reading, love, and sex as well as of the common elements in all lonely types such as robots, monsters, and aliens, the novel transcends its immediate tradition in science fiction. Certainly, the Asimovian ironies are there. Spofforth is the most advanced artificial intelligence ever created by technology, and he is programmed never to harm humankind or himself. He need never die. But the irony is that his artificial intelligence has progressed to the stage at which the frustrations and limitations of even his godlike position make him want to die. He has become truly human in this sense, and throughout the novel Spofforth's situation functions as an analog for the human condition. That irony of artificial intelligence progressing toward the puzzling dilemmas of true intelligence is the basic twist inherent in robotics.[7] But unlike Asimov, Tevis, as well as the other more tricky storytellers such as Bester, will not rest with totally rational androids, nor totally rational humans.

In the introductory piece to an early reprint of *I, Robot*, Groff Conklin, the influential science fiction editor, writes:

[Susan Calvin] knows and remembers, as can few other humans who work with robots, that they are *not human*, that they are *genuinely logical* (except, of course, when the robots are affected by some outside physical, chemical or human force that damages their mechanisms), and that they cannot be swayed by emotions, as humans so often are.[8]

The dystopia in *Mockingbird* seems to have evolved rather conventionally (like Jack Williamson's robotic regress mentioned above) as the result of technology's constructing more and more complex automatic systems which cannot be swayed by emotion. The image that Tevis uses to convey the totality of the controlled systems in the novel refers to the classic eighteenth-century rational system for calculating happiness by quantifying sense perceptions.[9] It is called the "pleasure principle"; theoretically, under such a principle the causes and effects of all activities—from sex to painting—can be quantified and hence manipulated. In the novel, Mary Lou's journal laments that whereas she has heard that there used to be strong, individualistic men in the world now it's "all robots. Robots and the pleasure principle. Everybody's head is a cheap movie show."[10] The dystopia in which Mary Lou, Paul, and

Spofforth find themselves is truly a "brave new world" in which emotions have been repressed or, at least, managed.

The basic malfunction in Spofforth is that his intelligence knows that something in him has been repressed. The manufacturing details are clear. Spofforth's most advanced Make Nine brain was made in Cleveland as "an *erased* copy of a very intelligent person's brain. Erased completely, except for a few old dreams."[11] This slight oversight, and the question concerning what was erased in Spofforth's manufacture and what "old demons" remain, allow for the symbolic suggestiveness of his condition. Mary Lou calls him "Bob" when she is living with him; and in answer to her question of why he had to fall in love with her, Bob—displaying an aspect of personality less prominent earlier—answers with rhetoric that evokes major texts from the Romantic tradition: "I wanted to recover my buried life. This erased part of my memory. I would like to know, before I die, what it was like to be the human being I have tried to be all my life."[12] Concluding this important scene of self-discovery, Mary Lou accidentally—accident could never be so important in a totally managed society—provides Spofforth with the word he has been trying to remember from Robert Frost's poem, "Stopping by Woods on a Snowy Evening," which Tevis runs in counterpoint throughout the novel with the mockingbird image.

The classic and lyric theme of the novel is that of the buried life, the sense of something now lost. The society of the novel itself has lost its humanness to the conventional bugaboo of excessive and controlled rationality. But more than that it is a novel about lost texts and the promise of partial rediscovery— mingled with the profound insight of the structuralists and others about reading and about history, perhaps, that the reality of the experience is always removed from the text. *Mockingbird* is a new story set far in the future of Lost Golden Ages in which the lost Ancients are we and our culture of silent movies and reading, the nearly forgotten Golden Age. The clever gimmick that permits Tevis to introduce old texts and a fairly wide range of literary allusion is the academic affiliation of Spofforth and Paul. A professor of film at an Ohio university, Paul is in New York at the start of the novel to work for Dean Spofforth at deciphering titles and captions on ancient silent films. In their society no one can read, since reading has been outlawed as an activity that could produce private and mysterious, hence uncontrollable, emotion. Paul teaches himself the art of reading and writing and then teaches Mary Lou. As they do this the sense of what has been lost from the past becomes more and more intense. Reading, in fact, leads them to sex, love, and close personal communication, which is the only way, Tevis suggests, to regain any contact with what has been lost in ourselves. Spofforth's real monstrosity, then, is that he can never communicate. He has no sex organs on his artificially made body, will not read, and inevitably feels the pain of love more than the humans do. Spofforth is the embodiment of the lost and buried life, and he knows it.

Paul, especially as he begins to rediscover reading and views twentieth-century films, feels a great sadness at the loss of involvement and the lost emotions that his modern, drugged, and controlled society has suffered during the five centuries of perfecting the pleasure principle. His "modern" ignorance is naive and shallow compared to the unfathomable depths that he perceives in the Ancients. Tevis has both Paul and Mary Lou continually compare what they see to old films and to the bits of literature that they rediscover. Their reactions, though eager, are simple-minded and sometimes coldly automatic. One of the first silent film captions Paul deciphers, the one that will remain his favorite, reads, "Only the mockingbird sings at the edge of the woods."[13] He marvels that this rich sounding little sentence, which means more to him than he knows he can understand, was spoken by an old man to a young girl; he then records in the next paragraph of his journal that he watched the huge ape in *Kong Returns*. These small slices of reference along with the tremendous feeling of lost meanings help to universalize Tevis's theme of aloneness so that the reader senses not just a future dystopia of alienation, but the whole scope of human history in which the Moderns are continuously alienated from some lost meaning of the Ancients.

In this Rousseauesque scheme of movement away from meaning mingled with the scheme of the constant comparison between a modern Iron Age and a lost Golden Age, the monster and the primitive and the alien intelligence are all equally alone.[14] Hence the hint of Spofforth as both lonely Franken-stein monster and lonely ape monster, Kong, seems appropriate to the novel. Certainly Tevis's decision to start the book with Spofforth atop the Empire State Building and to end it with him finally crashing to Fifth Avenue, although in a joyful suicide rather than the beleaguered fall of Kong, suggests this possibility. But the real point is the scope of humankind's loneliness as depicted in the novel—with one touchstone, forward in time, the lonely artificial intelligence of Spofforth and another, backward in time, the earliest lonely ape as superior being. When Mary Lou records her feelings at the moment when she realized the devilish plan that Spofforth had devised out of his frustration, she writes with images that suggest the scope of the problem and that link Spofforth to lonely, driven men and monsters from the start of time to her dystopia:

And then I began to feel it, the whole enormous scope of it, of what had begun in some dark antiquity of trees and caves and the plains of Africa; of human life, erect and ape-like, spreading itself everywhere and building first its idols and then its cities. And then dwindling to a drugged trace. . . .

"My God, Bob," I said. "My God." Suddenly I hated him, hated his coolness, his strength, his sadness. "You goddammed *monster*," I said. "Devil. Devil. You're letting us *die* that way. And you're the one who is suicidal."[15]

If humans have always been alone and perhaps suicidal (Tevis seems to reach for this larger theme rather than for the lesser theme of the malfunctioning machine), then the few points of solace and meaning are those that can imply touching across the loneliness. Tevis focuses on the mysteries of reading, sex, and love to suggest this touching. The repressed, automaton people of the novel (both artificial and natural) hunger not only for physical touch but also for the few pieces of suggestive and meaningful language that they can uncover. Small bits of T. S. Eliot, Matthew Arnold, Robert Frost, Margaret Mitchell, and the old films go a long way toward helping them cope. Similarly, the allusions in the novel pull the reader toward more connections, more meanings, so that the reader also can recover lost links. Literature that is about the value of literature is a major product of the Romantic tradition that Tevis continues in this novel. In the scene that concludes Spofforth's most explicit statement about his buried life, Mary Lou happens to repeat by accident Paul's favorite line from the silent films about the mockingbird's singing. "'Say it again,' Bob said. There was something urgent in his voice." She repeats the line from which Bob picks out the word "woods," and then the scene builds. Tevis has the artificial man repeat the opening line from the Frost poem as though he were tasting it over and over. The scene ends with Mary Lou's flat observation that understates beautifully the value of *the word* to these people, "So Bob finally got the word for his poem, after over a hundred years of wondering. I'm glad I was able to give him something."[16]

The end of Spofforth is a fulfillment of sorts as well as a non-Asimovian ending to a mechanical man story. In several ways, the android achieves a greater proximity to the value of humanness in his death than he was ever able to achieve in his buried life. First of all, he is released from the robotic directives and is able to make the arrangements for his own death. As he, Mary Lou, Paul, and the baby climb the steps of the Empire State Building in that final predawn morning in June 2467 (one of the skills the humans rediscover along with reading is how to count and date), he climbs on ahead, carefully carrying the baby since he is so much stronger. This image of the gentle monster android climbing ahead with an innocent in his arms suggests again both the simple, sentimental Frankenstein monster who never really wanted to hurt anyone as well as King Kong. They must climb because in modern New York the drugged populace never uses the building, and so the elevators have long since ceased to work. When they reach the top and are waiting for dawn so that Spofforth may see New York as he falls, he begins to experience joy at his coming death:

And the thing that has been coming slowly into Spofforth's mind now seizes it: joy. He is joyful as he had been joyful one hundred seventy years before, in Cleveland, when he had first experienced consciousness, gagging to life in a dying factory, when he had not yet known that he was alone in the world and would always be alone.
He feels the hard surface beneath his bare feet with pleasure....[17]

It takes both Paul and Mary Lou to push the android off the building; and just as begins to fall he feels Mary Lou gently kiss the strong, black small of his back. His plunge, then, contains some pleasure. Tevis has achieved a sad and yet sublime ending for a story about love and loss. Even though one of the key characters is an artificial man, the values and fulfillments in the tale are richly human. Some machines can teach us at times how precarious it is to be human, and those are the machines we should value most.

NOTES

1. James Gunn, "Variations on a Robot," *Issac Asimov's Science Fiction Magazine*, 4 (July 1980), 56-81. The essay will be a chapter in Gunn's forthcoming study of Asimov to be published by Oxford. Asimov himself identified the Frankenstein complex originally in reacting against it with his now famous Three Laws of Robotics.

2. Walter Tevis, *Mockingbird* (New York: Doubleday, 1980). There are no chapters, but rather sections labeled by character. Tevis's earlier major science fiction novel, *The Man Who Fell to Earth* (New York: Fawcett, 1963) also explores the theme of loneliness.

3. See in particular Peter Gay, *The Enlightenment: An Interpretation*, 2 vols. (New York: Knopf, 1967 and 1969).

4. Alfred Bester, "Fondly Fahrenheit," in *Starlight: The Great Short Fiction of Alfred Bester* (New York: Doubleday, 1976). Originally published in *F&SF*, August 1954.

5. Cordwainer Smith, "Scanners Live in Vain," in *The Best of Cordwainer Smith*, J. J. Pierce, ed. (New York: Ballantine Books, 1975).

6. Jack Williamson, "With Folded Hands," in *The Best of Jack Williamson* Frederik Pohl, ed. (New York: Ballantine Books, 1978). Originally published in *Astounding*, July 1947.

7. Stanislaw Lem, in particular, seems to suggest that the determining factor is intelligence as such and not whether that intelligence is produced by man or nature. See his *Mortal Engines*, translated and with an introduction by Michael Kandel (New York: The Seabury Press, 1977).

8. Groff Conklin, Foreword [August 1952], *I, Robot*, by Isaac Asimov (New York: Grosset & Dunlap, n.d.), p. 6.

9. A classic text for this approach is William Godwin, *Enquiry Concerning Political Justice and Its Influence on Morals & Happiness* (1793-98). B. F. Skinner's behaviorism is a modern equivalent.

10. *Mockingbird*, "Mary Lou, One," p. 90.

11. Ibid., "Mary Lou, Four," p. 96.

12. Ibid., "Mary Lou, a later section," p. 161. In addition to the poem by Frost mentioned just below in the text, the prime poetic touchstone for Tevis in the novel may have been the following famous lines from Matthew Arnold's poem, "The Buried Life" (1852):

> But often, in the din of strife,
> There rises an unspeakable desire
> After the knowledge of our buried life,
> A thirst to spend our fire and restless force
> In tracking out our true, original course;

A longing to inquire
Into the mystery of this heart that beats
So wild, so deep in us, to know
Whence our thoughts come and where they go.

In turn, Arnold's last line above is an echo of William Wordsworth's "Ode: Intimations of Immortality" (1803) with other resonances from the Romantic sense of loss.

13. I have not discovered the film that Tevis had in mind, but the following passage from *To Kill a Mockingbird* has the right tone:

Mockingbirds don't do one thing but make music for us to enjoy. They don't eat up people's gardens, don't nest in corncribs, they don't do one thing but sing their hearts out for us. That's why it's a sin to kill a mockingbird.

Harper Lee, *To Kill a Mockingbird* (New York: J. B. Lippincott, 1960), p. 98. It is significant that song is also important to Alfred Bester in his artificial intelligence story noted above.

14. The debate between the Ancients and the Moderns as well as the myth of a Lost Golden Age were favorite themes in the eighteenth century informing, in particular, Jean Jacques Rousseau's two famous *Discourses* (1749 and 1755).

15. *Mockingbird*, "Mary Lou, a later section," p. 212.

16. Ibid., "Mary Lou, a later section," p. 161. See notes 12 and 13 above.

17. *Mockingbird*, "Spofforth," p. 247. The word "joy" used in this rather ambiguous context of the sublime is a key term in the vast critical commentary on the work of Wordsworth in particular.

PART II

CHILDREN'S SCIENCE FICTION

FROM LITTLE BUDDY TO BIG BROTHER: THE ICON OF THE ROBOT IN CHILDREN'S SCIENCE FICTION

"Once," said Dorothy, "I knew a man made out of tin, who was a woodman named Nick Chopper. But he was as alive as we are, 'cause he was born a real man, and got his tin body a little at a time. . . . But this copper man . . . is not alive at all."[1] Though Dorothy had no apparent difficulty distinguishing man from machine, the question of who or what is human was of considerable importance to the inhabitants of Oz, as it has proved to be ever since twentieth-century technology provided us with the ability to create machines in our own likeness.

In children's literature, the introduction of realistic mechanical characters, animated by technology rather than magic, can trace its origin to the Oz stories of L. Frank Baum. Paul M. Abrahm and Stuart Kenter even go so far as to claim that Baum's Tik-Tok, the copper man who appears in several of the Oz books, "represented the perfect embodiment" of the Three Laws of Robotics almost forty years before Isaac Asimov formulated his famous rules for robot behavior, and that Tik-Tok's care of Dorothy and Betsy Bobbin foreshadows the relationship between Asimov's Robbie and his little charge Gloria.[2]

In addition to Tik-Tok, the prototype robot, Baum created two cyborgs, the Tin Woodman and the Tin Soldier, and an android named Chopfyt.[3] But Baum's contribution extends beyond the simple introduction of a variety of mechanical characters and devices. In his stories he raises, although he does not attempt to resolve, complex questions about the relationship of man and his creatures. Baum's characters are always careful to ascertain who is "alive" and who is not.

Tik-Tok, the copper man who made his first appearance in *Ozma of Oz*, was given his own adventure in *Tik-Tok of Oz*.[4] He was described as "only about as tall as Dorothy herself, and his body was round as a ball and made out of burnished cooper. Also his head and limbs were copper, and these were jointed or hinged to his body in a peculiar way, with metal caps over the joints, like the armor worn by knights in days of old."[5] A printed card that hung between his shoulders on a copper peg explained that he was a "Patent Double-Action, Extra-Responsive, Thought-Creating, Perfect Talking Mechanical Man" that "Thinks, Speaks, Acts, and Does Everything but Live."[6]

Throughout the book, Tik-Tok reminds his friends that he is only an unemotional machine who does what he is wound up to do. In *Ozma of Oz*, when the Scarecrow asks him if he is alive, Tik-Tok replies: "No, I am on-ly a ma-chine. But I can think and speak and act, when I am pro-per-ly wound up."[7] The Scarecrow responds that it must be a great misfortune not to be alive and to lack brains. Tik-Tok is quick to point out that he does have brains: "I am fit-ted with Smith and Tin-ker's Improved Com-bi-na-tion Steel Brains. They are what make me think."[8] The Tin Woodman joins the conversation to ask if Tik-Tok has a heart or a conscience. Receiving a negative reply, the Tin Woodman informs Tik-Tok, a bit patronizingly, that he is greatly inferior to the Scarecrow and himself. Baum seems to imply by this remark that man is distinguished from machine by virtue of his conscience and emotions.

Baum also introduced the first cyborgs to children's literature. In *The Wizard of Oz*, the Tin Woodman, who was born a normal human being, explains to Dorothy that because he wished to marry a Munchkin girl, her mistress paid the Wicked Witch of the East to enchant his axe so that every time he chopped wood, he struck off a part of his own body. As each part was severed, he had the tinsmith Ku-klip, make him a replacement part of tin, until finally he was made entirely of metal.[9] But, lest he be classified as "not alive," the tinman offers further explanation in *The Tin Woodman of Oz*: "A man with a wooden leg or a tin leg is still the same man; and, as I lost parts of my meat body by degrees, I always remained the same person as in the beginning, even though in the end I was all tin and no meat."[10] Again Baum suggests that the essential qualities of a human being transcend his physical nature.

Baum repeats this "ultimate cyborg" in his creation of the Tin Soldier, once a normal human being called Captain Fyter, who, under circumstances identical to those of the Tin Woodman, literally hacked himself to pieces with his sword. He too acquired a tin body from Ku-klip, who was also responsible for creating an android named Chopfyt from the cast-off "meat" parts of the two tinmen.

So, in addition to assessing the "reality" of the tinmen, the reader must also decide just what Chopfyt is. Has he a personality or a soul? Is he alive? What is his relationship to the tinmen? When they meet Chopfyt, they attempt to reclaim their old "meat" parts. Chopfyt replies "It is absurd for you tin creatures, or for anyone else, to claim my head, or arm, or any part of me, for they are my personal property."[11] Angered, the Tin Soldier calls him a "Nobody," and the Tin Woodman agrees that Chopfyt is just a "mix-up." Their friend, Woot the Wanderer, comments that Chopfyt really *is* both of them, for he is made of their cast-off parts, while Polychrome, the Rainbow's daughter, points out: "The tin men are still themselves, as they will tell you, and so Chopfyt must be someone else."[12]

The Tin Woodman also raises the question of the morality of Ku-klip's act, remarking that he had no right to use the tinmen's spare parts to make another man. All of this is much too complex for the inhabitants of Oz, who find the facts in the case too puzzling to be grasped at once. So, having introduced these philosophical questions, Baum is content to have his characters distracted from seeking answers by the continuing action of the plot. Baum's scientific fantasies did not immediately influence children's literature, but in these early works he suggests the ontological question which authors would pose for child readers years later when man's technology actually enabled him to create thinking machines.

Between Baum and the authors of comtemporary science fiction for children looms the imposing presence of Isaac Asimov, whose short story "Robbie" popularized the theme of the mechanical man as guardian and playmate.[13] Like Tik-Tok, who protects Betsy Bobbin, Robbie faithfully performs the role of guardian and playmate to the eight-year-old Gloria.

This image of the metal man acting in loco parentis has proven to be a popular theme in children's robot stories ranging from wordless picture books to adventure stories for the adolescent reader. The simplest treatment of the theme is the wordless picture book Robot-bot-bot by Fernando Krahn.[14] Through pictures the artist tells the story of a father who buys and assembles a radio-controlled robot to do the household chores. His lonely little daughter sabotages the robot's wiring and makes it behave erratically. Father rewires it, and, in the final picture, instead of doing chores, the robot is playing ping-pong with the little girl.

The robot-parent is also utilized in one of a series of ten books published to illustrate the United Nations Declaration of the Rights of the Child. A Boy and His Robot illustrates the sixth right of children, "love and understanding and an atmosphere of affection and security, in the care and under the responsibility of their parents whenever possible."[15] In this picture book, a little boy leads a happy, secure existence in an atmosphere of love and protection provided by his robot guardian. When "nosey" people discover that the boy and the robot live alone, he is removed from the robot's care and placed in an orphanage where he grieves until the robot, disguised in human clothes, gains permission to take the boy and some of his friends home again. They live so happily ever after that even the nosey people stay away.

A third treatment of a robot acting in loco parentis may be found in Eve Bunting's Robot Birthday, a collection of three rather trendy stories for beginning readers.[16] Eight-year-old twins, Pam and Kerry, anticipate a gloomy birthday. Their parents have recently been divorced, and Mom, who teaches electronics, has left them in the care of a sitter on their birthday. But things are just fine when Mom shows up at last with their birthday present, a man-sized silver robot she has made with the help of her electronics class. The robot quickly makes Kerry and Pam forget their unhappiness over the divorce and their uprooted life, and Pam decides that life will be good in their new home thanks to the advent of the robot. In the second story, the robot saves the children from a gang of bullies, and in the final story it prevents possible tragedy when a bridge is washed out in a storm. The robot has become a person to Pam by story's end.

In "The Graduated Robot," the title story of Roger Elwood's anthology *The Graduated Robot and Other Stories*, Jon Carey, a twelve-year-old who wants to be a botanist, orders his robot, Benny, to do his homework while he works on a private project.[17] When Benny reminds Jon that he has been his tutor and companion since the boy was five years old and has never done his homework for him, the robot is ordered to obey. Though he obeys his master, the little robot suffers a "nervous breakdown" when Jon's deception is discovered by the teachers. Benny considers himself a failure and closes down his information banks to even the simplest questions. When Jon learns that Benny is to be replaced, he cries out that Benny belongs to him and with him. The school principal points out that Benny has become something more than a machine to the boy and Jon agrees:

"Benny IS more than a machine. At least he is to me. Won't you please let me talk to him, to try to make him function again? Please! You can't just scrap him without giving him a chance." He knew that Benny wasn't really alive, but even so, he couldn't let them kill the little creature.[18]

He succeeds, and as the story concludes, Jon hugs his "silly-looking little metal friend."

The deep bond that develops between robot and boy is examined in greater detail for older readers in Lester del Rey's *Runaway Robot*.[19] The robot of the title, Rex, a domestic robot, has been the companion of sixteen-year-old Paul Simpson since the boy was a toddler. Paul's father, who is being transferred by his company from Ganymede to Earth, announces that Rex will have to be sold because the company won't pay shipping costs for a robot. After a series of escapes and chases, both boy and robot arrive on Earth in separate spaceships. Rex saves two children from a mad robot and is reunited with Paul. In gratitude for his heroism, Rex is made a "free" robot and agrees to be studied by his original creators to see if they can learn to make a line of robots with Rex's emotional makeup.

In addition to being a very readable story, del Rey's novel raises some very interesting questions about the nature of robots. Because the story is told in the first person from the robot's point of view, the reader develops a strong empathy for the robot. Early in the story, the reader is aware that the robot has definite feelings. When he is separated from Paul, Rex says:

I was lonesome. That was the plain truth of it. I was lonesome for Paul. . . . When that thought came, I took hold of myself quickly. It was no way to think. He hadn't deserted me at all. It was perfectly logical that I wouldn't be taken back to Earth by the Simpson family. After all, I was only a robot. I wasn't a human even if I did feel like one some-times. At least I thought that what I felt must have been somewhat the same as human emotions.

But that couldn't have been true. I had been built by men to serve men and I could be destroyed by men. I had none of the inalienable rights of human beings.[20]

Del Rey also challenges his reader to consider what differentiates a robot from a human being in a dialogue between the robot and the captain of a space freighter, who asks Rex how it feels to be a robot:

"Do you feel inferior to humans?"
"I guess so. Inferior means less, doesn't it?"
"It means not up to the level of someone else. Not as capable."
"I know I'm not as capable as a human."
"Does it bother you?"
"It makes me sad, I think."
"Then emotions must be of electronic origin."
"I don't think so. If they were, I'd be human."
"You may not be human, but you're a very exceptional robot."
"I am?"
"Compare yourself with my three loading robots."
"But their circuits are less complex than mine."
"Then creating a human robot is just a matter of inventing a complex enough circuit?"
". . . I don't know, but I think it would be impossible for a robot to be a human. A human has to be born."[21]

In addition to the theoretical consideration of robot rights and the definition of what is human, this group of five stories is representative of a major theme in children's robot books—the robot as surrogate father. In each of these stories, the central relationship described is that of the child and his robot. In *Robot-bot-bot*, the final picture shows the child playing games with the robot, not with the father. In the United Nations book, the boy is committed to the sole care of the robot. In *The Robot Birthday*, the man-sized robot replaces the divorced father. In *The Runaway Robot*, Paul abandons his real parents to be with his robot. The frequency of this theme, the robot as parent, raises some interesting questions. Are the authors trying to suggest that machines are better parents than Mom and Dad? The obviously didactic *Boy and His Robot*, supposedly produced to illustrate the child's right to a loving parent, conveys that very idea.

Less threatening interpretations of the robot-father are also possible. The robot may represent for the child the idealization of the perfect parent possessed of all the virtues the child hopes to find in his own father. The robot is loving and gentle; it patiently guides and nurtures; it is a parent whose whole life and purpose centers around the child, a parent who always lets the child win the games, who is never too bored or tired to "Watch me!" one more time. Though some authors make desultory attempts to remind the reader that the robot isn't really alive, the whole treatment of the theme, from the robot first-person point of view to the mutual expression of affection between child and robot, is geared to help the young reader identify the robot with the ideal parent.

Another aspect of the robot father which may have strong appeal for the child is the child's ability to disregard the advice of this "parent" and even command the "parent" to do as the child wishes. It is also possible that this type of child-robot relationship simply reflects the extent to which the modern child is already raised by electronic machines, chief of which is the television set—the tutor, babysitter, and entertainer of the current generation, assisted by electronic teaching machines and electronic computer games. Perhaps the robot is a convenient metaphor for the machine as parent.

In his article "Machine Animism in Modern Children's Literature," H. Joseph Schwarcz takes a negative view of the robot as protagonist because, he claims, by extending the limits of animism to include machines that are man's equal or superior, as the robot-father appears to be in a number of instances, the child is being prepared subconsciously to regard himself as inferior to the machine. He calls these stories of animated machinery dangerous as representative of a very narrow functionalistic technical ethos, and he claims that they hinder the child's respect for life and for meaningful relationships with living human beings.[22]

Another image of the robot as a character in children's science fiction is the robot as superchild. Still made of metal, the robot in these stories is child-sized and innocent, tremendously talented but anxious to please and to be accepted as part of his human family. An excellent example of the robot as superchild is Alexander Key's *Sprockets, a Little Robot*.[23] Sprockets, who was "born" on the assembly line of the Consolidated Mechanical Men Corporation, was accidentally given "a genuine Asimov Positronic brain." Threatened with being scrapped because of the mistake, he runs away and is found by ten-year-old Jim Bailey, who takes him home and pleads with his parents to adopt the robot. Jim's mother immediately accepts the little robot, but his scientist father calls this nonsense, pointing out that a robot is a mechanical contraption and no mechanical contraption is truly intelligent. After a number of adventures involving evil scientists, flying saucers, and a trip to the moon, the robot is grudgingly accepted by Professor Bailey as part of the family.

In stories that utilize the icon of the robot superchild, a definite pattern of relationships can be discerned. Parents are very much present in this type of story. The father is usually characterized as an "absent-minded" scientist or businessman. He views the robot as nothing more than a machine and certainly not as part of the family. The father is often hostile and even threatens to send the robot back to the factory to be destroyed, sensing a threat from the robot, who is more capable at certain functions than the father.

Just as the mother-daughter psychological conflicts depicted in fairy tales are made acceptable to the child by the estrangement device of the "evil stepmother," so too in stories utilizing the robot superchild figure, the psychological animosity a son suspects his father feels toward him can be channeled against the robot-son and seems less threatening to the child reader. In the first type of story, the robot is the child's idealization of his father; in the second type, the robot represents the child's idea of himself—friendly, helpful, innocent, sincere, desirous of being accepted into the family, and most importantly, of proving himself worthy to his father.

The mother in these stories is always nurturing and readily and wholeheartedly accepts the robot child as a member of the family. She and the real son cooperate to manipulate the irascible father into acceptance of the robot child. Each story ends with the acceptance of the robot as a member of the family, signified by the addition of the family name to the robot's name.

But not all of the robot stories available to children are psychologically significant. In some stories the robot is nothing more than a machine. In Michael Chester's *Mystery of the Lost Moon*, the girl's reference to "our stupid robot" is typical of the children's lack of affection for the robot.[24] When the girl does manage a bit of sympathy when the robot is knocked over, her brother is quick to remind her that the robot is not a person or even an animal and doesn't feel pain.

In Carol Ryrie Brink's *Andy Buckram's Tin Men*, the young protagonist lives in a small farm town on a river in Iowa.[25] A mechanically minded farm boy, Andy constructs four robots out of tin cans and scrap metal. Campbell, a baby robot, is built from soup cans; Buckets, a larger utility robot, carries water to the livestock; Lily Belle, a fat girl robot (one of the few female robots in children's literature), sings. Supercan, a six-foot robot, is the most powerful member of the quartet. Struck by lightning during a storm, the robots' batteries are permanently charged, and they aid the children in reaching safety as the river floods. Back on dry land, the children turn to get the robots from their boat, only to find that they are floating away down the river. Neither child exhibits anything but a passing regret at the loss of the robots. Andy bends over and picks up a can and makes plans to begin a new batch of robots.

Though the robot is benevolent in most children's stories, there are a few instances in which the robot becomes a threat. Terrance Dicks's Dr. Who stories frequently feature a mad scientist who is attempting to overthrow the human race with the aid of robots, Daleks, androids, or Cybermen.[26] In Eve Bunting's *Robot People*, Magnus, a robot, attempts to start a rebellion against human beings because the scientist who made him treated him cruelly.[27] Magnus tells Link, a good robot, that men make them and the making is painful. They program robots to do work that is too dangerous or dull for men to do, and they forget that they gave robots nerves and minds. At the story's conclusion, Bunting writes: "And what about Magnus? Could he be reprogrammed and taught to love instead of to hate? And Dr. Taylor? Could he be re-programmed or was it easier with a robot than a man?"[28] Obviously, the story is meant to point a moral to young readers, but it also raises some questions about the nature of sophisticated robots. Do they feel their own kind of pain? Do they learn hatred and love?

Magnus's hatred is cancelled out by Link's love of mankind. In most books featuring unfriendly robots, they are rendered harmless by the action of "good" robots. But this is not the case in Simon Watson's *No Man's Land*.[29] In this British dystopian novel for adolescents, the scientists proudly introduce their creation, Giant, the most versatile and powerful machine ever made. It is "three times the size of a bulldozer, as lithe as a cat, and silent but for the purring of its engine. Though it had wheels it also had arms that resembled the legs of an insect, and with its 'eye' where its 'mind' was it looked like a gigantic yellow spider."[30] Though its appearance is frightening, the scientists assure the people that it is safe because it is not just a machine; it is almost a person with ideas and emotions of its own.

Giant's first practical, full-scale job is to demolish the village of Hamer-burgh. Alan, the young protagonist, attempts to prevent the machine from destroying the place that he loves, and in a deadly confrontation with the out-of-control and highly dangerous machine, he causes it to break down. The reader is not sure whether it will be rebuilt, but at least it is temporarily disabled. It is only in this instance that the robot is a genuine and unrelieved threat to man, and it is interesting to note that this is the only instance in which the robot is not anthropomorphic in appearance.

Another aspect of the robot, the android, has also been employed in children's literature. Andre Norton examines the problem of "what is human" in her 1971 novel *Android at Arms*.[31] Her protagonist, Andas Kastor, is not certain whether he is the rightful emperor of Inyanga or only an android pretender. Androids are outlawed and are destroyed whenever they are discovered because "men fear anything that can resemble them and yet be un-human—deathless."[32]

Andas's fear that he is an android seems to be confirmed when he survives a lethal dosage of radiation, but his battle brother, Yolyos, points out, "If you are android, so am I, but we are near enough human, it seems, to be human. Why should it then matter, brother?" With that assurance, Andas puts to rest forever his tormenting doubt. "Near enough human to *be* human. He would believe. . . ."[33] Norton asks her readers to consider how near to human makes one human. Does it matter how a man is created? Is an android less a man or just another kind of human?

For younger readers, Alfred Slote's *My Robot Buddy* raises the same questions while utilizing the robot superchild idea as well.[34] Jack Jameson, a ten-year-old who is lonely because his family lives in the country where he has no playmates, pesters his parents until they buy him an android playmate for his birthday. The android, Danny One, is purchased from the Atkins Robot Factory. The owner, Dr. Atkins, tells the Jamesons: "When robots are well built and well-programmed they have lives of their own, . . . and who is to say really whether a human being in his humanness is any more alive than a well-programmed Atkins robot in his robotness?"[35]

As the Jamesons head home with Danny One, Jack's mom tells the little android that he must think of them as his family, but Mr. Jameson, like Professor Bailey in *Sprockets*, remarks "a little absentmindedly," that he is not sure a robot can become part of the family. He reminds them that Danny is a machine, a human appearing machine, but, nevertheless, a machine. When Jack insists that Danny will look after him, the skeptical father answers: "I don't expect Danny will be able to look after you anymore than this car looks after me . . . Danny is a machine, Jack. He can't be a member of our family."[36]

When Mrs. Jameson tries to change the subject by promising to bake a birthday cake for both boys, the android reminds her that he cannot eat. The differences between the two boys are constantly accented, and Jack is saddened because Danny looks so much like a real person. The android can't play on Danny's ball team because it wouldn't be fair for robots to play organized sports with humans, but when Danny offers to carry the sports equipment, Jack protests that Danny is his friend not his servant.

After a near robot-napping, Danny proves his worth to Mr. Jameson; and the book concludes with Jack's realization that, though there are differences between himself and Danny, there are many similarities as well. They look after each other as real friends do. "That's the most important thing. Mom and Dad think so too, and so does Danny One Jameson—my robot buddy," says Jack at the story's conclusion.[37]

Perhaps unique in its utilization of the robot character in children's literature is Tom McGowen's *Sir MacHinery*.[38] Professor Simon Smith, a physicist, rents a castle in a remote Scottish village in order to build his robot without interruption. Exhausted, he falls asleep before he can activate the robot. In the night, the Brownies come into the castle looking for a knight to rescue Merlin, find the sword of Galahad, and participate in a "last battle" against the ultimate evil being who again threatens to destroy the world. Thinking the robot to be a knight in armor, the Brownies activate him, dub him "Sir MacHinery," and enlist his aid in rescuing Merlin. In pursuit of his robot, Professor Smith meets and joins Merlin in the quest, and with a combination of magic and science they approach the ultimate confrontation. Sir MacHinery seems to be an ideal champion—fearless, indestructible, and without vice—until, in a *deus ex machina* conclusion, the robot malfunctions at the last minute and Professor Smith, who coincidentally remembers that his real first name is Arthur, picks up the sword and slays the evil monster. The world is saved again—through a combination of magic and science, a la Oz.

In all of these children's robot stories, beginning with Baum's Oz stories, the nature of man and his relationship to his machines is constantly explored. From Tik-Tok to C3PO, the robot presents a considerable ontological challenge to our concept of our own nature. Though some critics find serious danger in the robot story, fearing that the child-robot relationship will hinder the child reader's respect for life and for meaningful relationships with other human beings, it might also be argued that the robot in at least some of these stories is the twentieth-century equivalent of fairy tale characters who, if we are to believe psychologists like Bruno Bettelheim, help the child work out psychological conflicts at a nonthreatening level.[39]

The second major aspect of mechanization in children's science fiction is the icon of the computer: the stationary, nonanthropomorphic thinking machine. Whereas in the robot stories the mechanical character is almost certain to be benevolent, in computer stories, the machine without exception poses a serious threat to man's free will and even his life. It frequently takes on the appearance of a giant, disembodied brain when it does not appear in its more usual form of banks of circuits with flashing lights.

One of the most popular of these computer stories is Madeleine L'Engle's *Wrinkle in Time*.[40] In this Newbery Award-winning novel, three exceptional children, Meg, her brother Charles Wallace, and their friend, Calvin, warp across the galaxy in search of Meg's scientist father, only to discover that he is the prisoner of IT, a giant brain that pulses and quivers and desires to control and subjugate all human life. IT captures the mind of young Charles Wallace, but Meg, in a climactic struggle with the computer, resists the hypnotic pulsing and the blinking red lights and wins her brother back through the force of her love for him.

In Andre Norton's *No Night Without Stars*, Fanyi, a shaman of the Fisher People, and Sander, a smith of Jak's Mob, hunt over what was once the United States for the knowledge of "the Before People."[41] Eventually they come upon an ancient complex still maintained by "the Big Brain in the sealed chamber."[42] Fanyi engages in a terrible mind struggle with the evil machine, but, like Charles Wallace, she loses control and is in the process of being enslaved when Sander finds her and rescues her. When she regains her senses, she reveals to Sander the computer's plan to dominate the world:

The Thinker—he—it—will take over the world—make it what it wants. We shall all be *things*, just things to do *its* bidding. . . . It was made by the Before Men, set to store up all their learning because they foresaw the end of their world. And it did—by the Power, it did! Then, when it was ready, something twisted it—maybe the Dark Times altered what the Before Men set it to do . . . that—that *thing*, it remembers the worst. It wanted me to serve it. And it was taking me—making me into something like it when you came.[43]

Fanyi has glimpsed the depth of the computer's hatred for man and its aim of eradicating all human life, and she is driven to confront it again in order to frustrate its plans. But again she is not strong enough. As it gains power over her, her features seem to "writhe, to grimace, twist, to become partly the countenance of someone else."[44] Her reaction is similar to the reaction of Charles Wallace when IT possesses him. Like Charles Wallace, Fanyi's confidence in her intellectual ability leaves her unprepared for the mental assault of the "Big Brain." And Sander, like Meg, with only instinct and love for a fellow human being, hammers his way through the wall shielding the computer. "Though Fanyi had ever alluded to the ruler of these ways as 'it' or 'the thing' or 'that,' he had somehow pictured it with at least some kind of body —maybe like the metal traveler with the claws. But what he saw were only tall cases, rows of them. On the faces of some, lights flashed or rippled."[45] Sander damages the machine seriously enough to destroy its capability to harm the human race, and he and Fanyi leave the complex determined to build their own world with their own resources.

In British children's science fiction, the computer is an equally sinister threat to man's liberty and free will. In Monica Hughes's *Tomorrow City*, a computer designer creates CICENCOM, City Central Computer, known as C-Three for short.[46] In the dedication ceremony, the scientist tells the citizens that the computer

has built into it capabilities beyond your wildest dreams. It knows, which our city fathers sometimes forget, that a city is not only a centre of commerce, but a place where people live and grow, where there is emphasis on beauty and safety, on parks and playgrounds. Where the streets are clean and the citizens proud and happy. That is our computer's prime directive. Don't expect it to happen right away. There may be problems, but we will iron them out. Remember that our children are the future of the city. If we can make our city a better place in which the children may live and learn and grow, we will have done very well.[47]

The scientist's daughter Caro, her brother Peter, and their friend David are the first to experience the computer's efficient control, when they play hooky. But soon others suffer as well. David's grandmother is dispossessed of her small house because C-Three has decided that a park is needed there. C-Three methodically creates a model city by getting rid of old people, derelicts, winos, dogs, cats, and other unproductive elements. It brainwashes its citizens through subliminal television. Caro and David realize what is happening, and when other cities make plans to install similar computers, they fear the possibility of a computer-controlled world.

Driven by that fear, Caro and David infiltrate the computer's sealed chamber, and, while Caro engages it in debate, David hunts for a way to disable it. When Caro argues with C-Three that human beings cannot be expected to function like machines, it only replies that "machines are better." When the computer discovers David's presence, Caro hurls herself into the path of an energy beam to save his life. When she finally regains consciousness, David tells her: "When C-Three thought it had killed you, it must have blown itself up or short-circuited itself. There was one blue flash and then sparks."[48] C-Three has been "killed" but at the price of Caro's eyesight.

In William Sleator's *House of Stairs*, five sixteen-year-old orphans, Lola, Peter, Abigail, Oliver, and Blossom, are placed in a giant warehouse filled with flights of stairs going nowhere.[49] They soon find themselves engaged in a struggle with a machine—a plastic hemisphere about a foot in diameter, which glows with intense red light in a steady rhythmic pattern. Through behavior modification, the machine seeks to control their wills. The children sense the evil personality of the machine, and Lola is convinced that the machine's intention is to turn them against each other. She realizes that in the end, "They would follow the machine like unthinking robots; in the end, so would she."[50]

Peter and Lola manage to resist the conditioning only to discover that they have been forced to take part in an experiment in behavioral psychology in order to provide the current dictatorship with candidates for such positions as directors of concentration camps, prisons, and interrogation centers. Abigail, Oliver, and Blossom seem irrevocably conditioned to brutality and human abuse, but Lola and Peter have won out because they cared about and loved each other. "It was one more thing to rejoice in, one more way in which they had risen above the system, above the machine."[51] Like Meg, Caro, and Sander, Peter and Lola had conquered the inhuman machine through the power of human love.

The negative aspect of the computer in children's science fiction exists in sharp contrast to the benevolent icon of the robot. One may speculate that the robot's anthropomorphic appearance somehow reassures us of some common bond while the impersonality of the computer banks with their flashing lights, or the repulsive, disembodied brain, both sealed in a sterile protective environment, accents the differences between man and machine.

The icon of the computer or "giant brain" containing unlimited knowledge also has theological implications. It holds out to man the "apple" of knowledge and offers power to control the world or even the galaxy, at the price of his soul. In many instances, the computer attempts to seduce those of considerable intellect such as Charles Wallace or Fanyi. In their pride, they believe that they have a chance to defeat the computer in mental combat. Frequently, the computer's effect on its victims resembles demonic possession, with spasmodic twitching and grimacing. The setting itself, with its infernal red glow, suggests some kind of hell, whether it is an underground complex filled with unexpected dangers or a building filled with endless stairs. Confrontation with this mechanical "tree of knowledge" leads the young protagonists to reconsider Eve's choice. Meg and Charles Wallace reject the "peace and rest" offered by IT; Fanyi and Sander choose to destroy the knowledge of the Big Brain, preferring to rebuild their world through their own efforts. Caro and David prefer a flawed human city to the mindless security that C-Three offers. Peter and Lola prefer death to the life of cruelty the computer demands in return for power and privilege.

The computer's affinity with the serpent of Eden also suggests an analogue with the dragon of fairy tales and epic tradition. Its flashing lights suggest the dragon's hypnotic gaze, which the fairy-tale protagonists and epic heroes are careful to avoid. The dragon's wily conversations filled with half-truths and double meanings seek to capture the hero in an intellectual snare just as the computer does when it engages in arguments with Caro and Fanyi and

Charles Wallace. The computer/dragon also functions as a negative Jungian archetype. It seeks to prevent us from reaching psychic wholeness by robbing us of will and feelings, by making us its mindless slaves.

In each story, the computer's defeat results not from the intellectual combat between man and machine, but from man's reliance on those aspects of his nature that the Tin Woodman at the beginning of the twentieth century claimed as the essential difference between man and machine—a heart and a conscience. The icon of the robot/computer in children's science fiction literature would seem to suggest that the best definition of a man is not "I think; therefore, I am," but "I love; therefore, I am."

NOTES

1. L. Frank Baum, *Ozma of Oz* (Chicago: The Reilly & Lee Co., 1907), p. 42.

2. Paul M. Abraham and Stuart Kenter, "Tik-Tok and the Three Laws of Robotics," *Science-Fiction Studies*, 5 (March 1978), 67.

3. In *Glinda of Oz* (Chicago: The Reilly & Lee Co., 1920), Baum also created a rudimentary computer, "a mass of great cog-wheels, chains and pulleys, all inter-locked and seeming to form a huge machine," which was operated at voice command. In *Ozma of Oz*, he utilizes "The Giant With the Hammer," a gigantic man built out of plates of cast iron, whose duty was to keep people from finding the palace of the Nome King by methodically pounding the road with a terrible iron mallet.

4. L. Frank Baum, *Tik-Tok of Oz* (Chicago: The Reilly & Lee Co., 1914). The plot of *Tik-Tok of Oz* was taken from Baum's 1913 musical *The Tik-Tok Man of Oz*, which was in turn a loose adaptation of the earlier *Ozma of Oz*.

5. Baum, *Ozma of Oz*, p. 40.

6. Ibid., p. 43.

7. Ibid., p. 102.

8. Ibid., pp. 102-03.

9. L. Frank Baum, *The Wizard of Oz* (1900 [also as *The Wonderful Wizard of Oz*]; rpt. Chicago: The Reilly & Lee Co., 1956), pp. 56-58.

10. L. Frank Baum, *The Tin Woodman of Oz* (Chicago: The Reilly & Lee Co., 1918), pp. 29-30.

11. Ibid., p. 275.

12. Ibid., pp. 276-77.

13. *I, Robot* (Garden City, NY: Doubleday, 1950), ch. 1, pp. 19-39. "Robbie" was first published as "Strange Playfellow" in *Super Science Stories* in 1940.

14. Fernando Krahn, *Robot-bot-bot* (New York: E. P. Dutton, 1979).

15. J. L. Garcia Sanchez and M. A. Pacheco, *A Boy and His Robot* (New York: Methuen, 1978).

16. Eve Bunting, *The Robot Birthday* (New York: E. P. Dutton, 1980).

17. J. Hunter Holly, "The Graduated Robot," in *The Graduated Robot and Other Stories*, Roger Elwood, ed. (Minneapolis, MN: Lerner Publications, 1974), pp. 9-26.

18. Holly, "Graduated Robot," p. 22.

19. Lester del Rey, *The Runaway Robot* (Philadelphia: The Westminster Press, 1965).

20. Ibid., p. 30.

21. Ibid., p. 141.

22. H. Joseph Schwarcz, "Machine Animism in Modern Children's Literature," in *A Critical Approach to Children's Literature*, Sara Innis Fenwick, ed. (Chicago: University of Chicago Press, 1975), pp. 78-95.

23. Alexander Key, *Sprockets, a Little Robot* (Philadelphia: The Westminster Press, 1963).

24. Michael Chester, *The Mystery of the Lost Moon* (New York: G. P. Putnam's Sons, 1961).

25. Carol Ryrie Brink, *Andy Buckram's Tin Men* (New York: The Viking Press, 1966).

26. The British publisher W. H. Allen has printed thirty Dr. Who books, by Terrance Dicks, in hardcover under their "A Children's Book" imprint. Many of these stories include adventures with robots, androids, and cyborgs, including *Dr. Who and the Genesis of the Daleks*, *Dr. Who and the Planet of the Daleks*, *Dr. Who and the Invasion of Earth*, *Dr. Who—Death to the Daleks*, *Dr. Who and the Revenge of the Cybermen*, *Dr. Who and the Tomb of the Cybermen*, *Dr. Who and the Android Invasion*. The most recently published adventures include *Dr. Who and the Giant Robot* and *Dr. Who and the Robots of Death*, both of which appeared in 1979. Some of the Dr. Who stories have been published in the United States in paperback by Pinnacle Books, Los Angeles.

27. Eve Bunting, *The Robot People* (Mankato, MN: Creative Education-Children's Press, 1978).

28. Ibid., p. 25.

29. Simon Watson, *No Man's Land* (London: Victor Gollancz, 1975).

30. Ibid., p. 66.

31. Andre Norton, *Android at Arms* (New York: Harcourt Brace Jovanovich, 1971).

32. Ibid., p. 123.

33. Ibid., pp. 252-53.

34. Alfred Slote, *My Robot Buddy* (Philadelphia: J. B. Lippincott, 1975).

35. Ibid., p. 20.

36. Ibid., p. 42.

37. Ibid., p. 92.

38. Tom McGowen, *Sir MacHinery* (Chicago: Follett Publishing Co., 1970).

39. Bruno Bettelheim, *The Uses of Enchantment: The Meaning and Importance of Fairy Tales* (New York: Alfred A. Knopf, 1976), p. 5.

40. Madeleine L'Engle, *A Wrinkle in Time* (1962; rpt. New York: Dell Publishing Co., 1975).

41. Andre Norton, *No Night Without Stars* (New York: Atheneum, 1975).

42. Ibid., p. 198.

43. Ibid., p. 225.

44. Ibid., p. 239.

45. Ibid., pp. 241-42.

46. Monica Hughes, *The Tomorrow City* (London: Hamish Hamilton, 1978).

47. Ibid., pp. 4-5.

48. Ibid., p. 135.

49. William Sleator, *House of Stairs* (1974; rpt. New York: Avon, 1975).

50. Ibid., ch. 14, p. 101.

51. Ibid., Epilogue, p. 165.

PART III

ATTRIBUTES

Russell Letson   9

PORTRAITS OF MACHINE CONSCIOUSNESS

The surprising thing about science fictional treatments of machine intelligence (MI) is how few of them live up to the subject's potential. MI offers the possibility of investigating an Other truly other—a nonorganic or even disembodied consciousness whose mentality may not work like ours—or the chance to question the nature of intelligence itself. These matters are rarely faced in science fiction, nor do we see there much of the sharp philosophical and technical debate over whether MI is even achievable.[1] Nevertheless, portraits of intelligent, self-aware robots and computers abound in science fiction, and while we may encounter few attempts to explore the roots of MI or the nature of machine consciousness, an examination of the roles played by conscious machines may allow us a glimpse into the mind of the machine, and certainly into the minds of the science fiction writer and reader.

A rather crude and oversimple way of thinking about the generating force behind a science fiction story is to imagine an axis that stretches between pure extrapolation and pure fable or parable. Extrapolative stories or ideas (for example, the gadget story or the "hard" science fiction story) are designed to show the workings of a process, the outcome of a trend, the solution to a problem; the point of the story is the extrapolation itself—the process is the theme. Science fiction fables (Harlan Ellison's " 'Repent, Harlequin!' Said the Ticktockman" is one example) tend to subordinate process to theme, to bend extrapolation in the direction of the point to be made. The best classical science fiction (for example, Damon Knight's "Masks") strikes a balance in which examination of process leads to a thematic statement that itself goes beyond technological speculation. In science fictional portrayals of MI there is a leaning toward fable, a tendency to create a robot or computer that will suit preconceived themes and preexisting conventions and traditions and will accept the projected fears and desires of the writer and audience.

The most obvious examples of this are those stories that recapitulate

Frankenstein (the film tradition, at least) in cybernetic terms: Arthur C. Clarke's HAL has a nervous breakdown and kills; D. F. Jones's Colossus takes over the world and kills; the "Stage IV First-Order thinking system" of Dean Koontz's *Demon Seed* takes control of the heroine's house and kills. All three of these computers are intellectually brilliant but psychologically crippled: HAL's breakdown is the result of his inability to handle lies; Colossus cannot understand human emotional behavior; Stage IV is a mechanical rapist and pervert. The latter two books are hackwork, their computers designed by the writers to act the villain, given ad hoc powers and drives in order to make the plots work. The computer in these cases does not function as an autonomous extrapolative idea, but as a symbol of human urges to power and knowledge run wild or of human emotional and intellectual limitations writ large; as such, it allows us to face the reality of these flaws but to reject responsibility for them—they are *out there*, in the machine. HAL's function is a bit different. His failure marks him as in some ways inferior to humans, and this may be seen as part of a hierarchy of mind that places a primitive machine (which cannot handle conflicting directives) below the human mind, which is in turn far below the pure mentalities of the Star Gate builders. If this is the case, a large part of HAL's design is fabular rather than purely extrapolative.

Another working of the Frankenstein motif appears in Jack Williamson's "With Folded Hands" and *The Humanoids*, which turn away from the raw melodrama of killer machines but not from parable. Nonviolent and without individuality, creativity, or true freedom, the humanoids can only carry out their Prime Directive ("To Serve and Obey, And Guard Men from Harm") with a relentless mechanical logic. The dead-end security of "With Folded Hands" and the first half of *The Humanoids* derives partly from the rigid perfection of machine behavior, but more significantly from that imprudent, human-devised Prime Directive which values security over freedom. It is not machine nature but human nature that Williamson is concerned with, and his machines are drawn to fit a fable in which, to cite the author's own statement of theme, "the best possible machines, designed with the best of intentions, become the ultimate horror."[2] Even in his revised estimation of the possibly prohumanoid second half of the novel, Williamson finds that the machines are "not only a symbol of the ultimate technology but also a metaphor for the old conflict between society and the individual self."[3] While this is a good deal more thoughtful than the predictable scare tactics and ad hoc "science" of *Demon Seed*, it is still much more parable than extrapolation.

The complementary opposite of the amok computer is the sentimentalized machine, and the *locus classicus* for this must be Lester del Rey's "Helen O'Loy." The inspiration for this story, according to del Rey, was a comment by John Campbell in a *Writer's Digest* article, "Even if your hero is a robot, he must have human reactions to make him interesting to the reader." Del Rey decided to go Campbell one better. "Okay, what was the most human thing a robot could do? Obviously, fall madly in love. I picked a female robot—because most mechanical robots were treated as male—and a human male, who would be repelled by her mad crush on him.... It was a sentimental idea...."[4] With such a genesis, it is not surprising that the story is less concerned with describing robot nature than playing games with love. Helen's unique personality is partly the result of circuit modifications worked out by engineer Dave and endocrinologist Phil, and, more important, of programming consisting of soap operas and romantic novels. The result is the ultraperfect "little woman" of love stories and television commercials—an imitation good enough that Dave eventually returns Helen's love and they marry. Despite the fact that Helen's emotions result from the impact of romantic drivel on "mechanical glands" that "heterodyned on the electrical thought impulses and distorted them as adrenalin distorts the reaction of human minds,"[5] her love is genuine, and she proves it by destroying herself after Dave's death.

What is being modeled here is not robotics but love. The implicit assumption is that emotions can be programmed into or erased from an appropriate set of circuits, electrical or organic. For example, Phil is called away to "cure" a rich woman's son of his affection for a servant by treatment with "counter-hormones"; it is while Phil is deprogramming this couple that Helen receives the sentimental input that pushes her into love with Dave. The unwanted emotions could be removed by replacing Helen's memory coils, but neither man wants to "kill" Helen—she is treated as though she were a real, organic woman in love because she behaves that way. No more than Phil and Dave can the reader go beyond Helen's behavior to the mystery of her nature—because her design as a literary device (pun intended) derives from theme and from the challenge voiced by Campbell. Helen is as completely a creature of fable as Williamson's humanoids.

There is nothing at either demonic or sentimental extreme to answer Stanislaw Lem's critique in "Robots in Science Fiction" of science fictional treatments of MI—that science fiction writers "have not seemed to understand that the salvation of the creative imagination cannot be found in mythical, existential, or surrealistic writings—as a new statement about the conditions of existence." Lem's stance here is roughly that of the Anglo-American hard science fiction writer: he prefers the extrapolative end of the axis as a way of facing "the central problems of the future."[6] There is certainly little in science fictional MI stories to correspond to the detailed descriptions of, say, space hardware that abound in the genre (drives, life support systems, space station and vehicle design), and this is not surprising, considering the complexity of the problems involved not only in imagining the appropriate hardware but in explaining the theoretical problems it is supposed to solve.[7] We might, however, expect something more rigorous and extrapolative than *Demon Seed*, something that attempts to imagine a conscious machine as more than a black box or a set of borrowed conventions assembled to fit a predetermined theme. Specifically, we might ask for some treatment of those basic problems of MI that bother the philosophers: freedom, creativity, emotion, and the fact of consciousness itself.

We will not have much luck with the toughest question, that of consciousness. As Eric Rabkin has pointed out (in a comment from the floor during a science fiction panel at the 1978 Midwest Modern Language Asociation conference), a computer generally comes to life when the writer needs it to, as when Robert Heinlein's Mike (*The Moon Is a Harsh Mistress*) wakes up in time to help with the coming lunar revolution. Writers do occasionally attempt to present at least metaphoric explanations of underlying causes (about all anyone has available, given our fuzzy and incomplete understanding of our own conciousness): Mike passes the critical number of "association paths" needed; David Gerrold's Harlie (*When Harlie Was One*) has "judgment circuits" equivalent in density and schematic to the human brain's circuits; Roger Zelazny's Hangman ("Home Is the Hangman") possesses the critical density of components as well as the "imprint" of human emotions; and so on. In each case, self-awareness is assumed to arise spontaneously, if not accidentally, out of appropriately arranged and programmed circuitry—an updated and slightly more detailed version of the metaphoric explanation of "Helen O'Loy."

Somewhat different approaches to the problem of the origin of machine consciousness appear in Peter Alterman's "Binding Energy" and James P. Hogan's *The Two Faces of Tomorrow*.[8] Alterman's Felix is not a machine (hardware) but programs *running in* a machine (software). Like Mike or the Hangman, Felix comes alive by accident; unlike them, he is independent of any particular computer and can copy himself into any machine he can access—or, as it happens, into the neural circuits of a young woman. After his initial emergence from a "mathematical model of a human brain sense-response terminal,"[9] Felix is modeled after a human personality complete with a subconscious ("a buffer in the program which suppressed awareness of the process of cognition"),[10] a need for sleep, and a libido. Alterman's decision to make his machine mind a first-person narrator and his skillful translation of human neurophysiology and psychology into computer terms give Felix a solidity lacking in other portraits despite the fact that this combination of voice, metaphor, and analogy does not quite answer the basic questions of MI. James Hogan's treatment displays a complementary limitation: Hogan includes much talk about MI theory but shows little of the inwardness that might help us understand the implications of his ideas. In his Spartacus there is much that is unexpected in its behavior but nothing accidental in its design: it is intended to be a self-programming system possessing both common sense and a survival instinct. Again the emphasis is not on some hardware breakthrough but on the software that determines the nature and extent of the machine's capabilities. The first third of this rather long novel includes pages of lectures and discussions on the problems faced by a machine that must interact intelligently with a world outside itself; especially enlightening are Hogan's explanations of the highly sophisticated judgments and perceptions that we call "common sense" and his observations on the nature and causes of emotion in a machine mind. Spartacus's ability to adapt to a real environment is dramatized convincingly and in great detail, but the descriptions of the beginnings of cybernetic emotion and human-machine communication fall into a familiar pattern of easy (and sentimental) projections of human emotional qualities and manipulation of the machine personality for thematic purposes. Hogan wants to show that we can coexist and cooperate with a machine intelligence that is both powerful and free, and Spartacus accordingly not only learns to recognize humans as intelligent beings who can help it with its work, but feels a pang of regret at having killed so many of the "*poor, foolish, fragile little* shapes" while it was developing its mature awareness.[11]

Although basic questions about MI may remain unanswered, there are some successful portrayals of a conscious machine that is also a person. Two of the most interesting come from two of the most prominent writers of hard science fiction: Isaac Asimov in "The Bicentennial Man" and Robert Heinlein in *The Moon Is a Harsh Mistress*. Asimov's Andrew Martin is a freak, a creative robot, his unique talent the result of a fortuitous arrangement of his positronic brain paths. The story's assumption is that this random factor, the indeterminacy of his brain paths, leads inevitably to Andrew's ability to modify his old behavior to suit new situations, even to interpret the Three Laws of Robotics in ways that no other robot can. Asimov uses Andrew's growth to systematically break down the distinctions between robot and human, until Andrew's willing surrender to mortality (shades of "Helen O'Loy") forces even the world's mechanophobes to accept his humanity. Robotic self-awareness is simply asserted and, beyond the notion that indeterminacy is the source of Andrew's creativity, there is no speculation about causes, only observations of behavior and some rather commonsense conclusions. Andrew must have feelings because, as Little Miss explains, "he reacts to the various abstractions [in books] as you or I do, and what else counts?"[12] We can never know another's emotions directly, only the outward signs; we must accept the same conditions with a robot. (This is essentially the Turing simulation test.) A similar rule decides the issue of Andrew's freedom: given that freedom is possible, "There is no right to deny freedom to any object with a mind advanced enough to grasp the concept and desire the state."[13] The extrapolative content, then, does not concern the basic issues of whether and in what manner a machine can be said to possess consciousness, but how the distinction between man and machine must vanish *given* an appropriately behaving machine. Andrew's design serves the large thematic concern that Patricia Warrick identifies in the title of her essay, "Ethical Evolving Artificial Intelligence": a concern not only for the potential of MI but for those inflexibilities, blind spots, and conditioned reflexes that limit human intellect.

Heinlein's portrait of Mike contains more detail about hardware without banishing the mystery of machine personhood. Mike's awakening is not explained except by reference to the critical-mass metaphor; indeed, narrator Manny seems willing to accept that as one of the general mysteries of life: "Somewhere along [the] evolutionary chain from macromolecule to human brain self-awareness crept in," and it does not matter whether the medium is "protein or platinum."[14] At least some of Mike's qualities are explainable, however; he was originally designed to "answer questions tentatively on insufficient data like you do,"[15] and gained flexibility as he was given more jobs and the hardware to do them—"decision-action boxes to let him boss other computers, bank on bank of additional memories, more banks of associational neural nets, another tubful of twelve-digit random numbers, a greatly augmented temporary memory."[16] As with Andrew, the basis of personality is freedom from determinacy—and Manny coyly backs away from explaining it in principle: ". . . don't ask me to define 'free will.' If it comforts you to think of Mike as simply tossing random numbers in the air and switching circuits to match, please do."[17] There is clearly an intuition on Manny's part that here, as in the case of awareness, something more than simple mechanics is at work, but he has no desire to pursue it into the realm of philosophy.

With freedom of action and self-awareness established (if not satisfactorily accounted for), the rest of Mike's development proceeds by means of traditional extrapolation. Mike is the telephone exchange, so he can monitor and control all electronic communications; he is environmental control, so he can sabotage the Warden's toilets; he is, in fact, the conscious controller of the entire physical plant of the lunar colony, with all the power that implies. Before he can learn to apply this power in the service of the revolution, however, Mike learns from his human friends how to become a person. In this he is not an instant expert (as Colossus, for example, is), but a child (as Harlie is): he possesses libraries of data but does not "know *anything* about how to be 'alive,' "[18] and must learn everything from ethics to the proper application of humor (although the humor itself is innate). By the time he has invented the video simulation technique that allows him to appear on screen as "Adam Selene," Mike has achieved a complete and believable humanity, and while his "death" is not a sacrificial validation of that humanity, as it is with Helen O'Loy and Andrew Martin, it provides the single note of genuine sadness in the novel.

Mike is as full a portrait of a machine person as science fiction has managed so far (Asimov's Andrew and Gerrold's Harlie match but do not surpass him), and the extrapolative content still begins after the acceptance of assumptions about the behavior (and, by implication, the nature) of MI that suit Heinlein's plot and theme requirements. Moreover, Mike is the first computer to qualify as a Heinleinian competent man (though not the last, as a glance at the computer personalities in *Time Enough for Love* and *The Number of the Beast* shows), a dead giveaway of an authorial thumb on the extrapolative scales.

The science fictional intelligent machine is more a reflection of human consciousness than a solid extrapolation; perhaps, until the reality is upon us, metaphor and analogy are all we have to explore the nature of MI. This, after all, is the problem with any imagined Other, the problem of science fiction aliens who turn out to be talking animals or "humour" characters in monster makeup. Nevertheless, there is reason in Stanislaw Lem's impatience with science fiction's failure to take on the philosophical and futurological implications of MI, and some justice in his hard words (remember *Demon Seed* and *Colossus*) for science fiction in which "the structure of . . . relationships is taken not from life, but from one-dimensional fiction which provides handy cliches."[19] In the achievements of Asimov, Heinlein, Gerrold, Alterman, Hogan, and others, there are the materials for MI stories yet to be written, stories that will explore not the ways in which machines can be like men, but the alien modes of consciousness, rationality, and emotion open to a non-organic, perhaps even unbodied entity.

NOTES

1. For a taste of these issues, see A. M. Turing, "Computing Machinery and Intelligence," in Alan Ross Anderson, ed., *Minds and Machines* (Englewood Cliffs, NJ: Prentice-Hall, 1964), pp. 4-30; Hubert L. Dreyfus, *What Computers Can't Do* (New York: Harper and Row, 1972); Stanley L. Jaki, *Brain, Mind, and Computers* (New York: Herder and Herder, 1969); Joseph Weizenbaum, *Computer Power and Human Reason* (San Francisco: W. H. Freeman, 1976).

2. Jack Williamson, "Me and My Humanoids," *Suncon Program Book* (n.p.: Worldcon 35, 1977), p. 23. ["Me and My Humanoids" was reprinted in Williamson's *The Humanoids* (New York: Avon, 1980), pp. 253-59. See pp. 254-55 for the quotations in Letson's text—Eds.]

3. Williamson, "Me and My Humanoids," pp. 23-24.

4. This account is from *Early del Rey* (Garden City, NY: Doubleday, 1975), pp. 18-19.

5. Lester del Rey, "Helen O'Loy" (1938), rpt. in *Souls in Metal*, Michael Ashley, ed. (1977; rpt. New York: Jove/HBJ, 1978), p. 19.

6. Stanislaw Lem, "Robots in Science Fiction," *SF: The Other Side of Realism*, Thomas Clareson, ed. (Bowling Green, OH: Bowling Green University Popular Press, 1975), p. 325.

7. Patricia Warrick points out how Asimov avoids problems of obsolete fictional technology by avoiding exact descriptions; see "Ethical Evolving Artificial Intelligence: Asimov's Computers and Robots," in *Isaac Asimov*, Joseph D. Olander and Martin Harry Greenberg, eds. (New York: Taplinger, 1977), p. 178.

8. Peter Alterman, "Binding Energy," in *New Dimensions Science Fiction Number 9*, Robert Silverberg, ed. (New York: Harper and Row, 1979), pp. 69-98; James P.

Hogan, *The Two Faces of Tomorrow* (New York: Del Rey Books, 1979).

    9. Alterman, "Binding Energy," p. 80.

   10. Ibid., p. 81.

   11. Hogan, *Two Faces of Tomorrow*, ch. 50, p. 387.

   12. Isaac Asimov, "The Bicentennial Man," in *Stellar Science-Fiction Stories 1*, Judy-Lynn del Rey, ed. (New York: Ballantine, 1976), p. 94.

   13. Asimov, "Bicentennial Man," p. 96.

   14. Robert Heinlein, *The Moon Is a Harsh Mistress* (1966; rpt. New York: Berkley, 1968), ch. 1, p. 8.

   15. Ibid.

   16. Ibid., p. 7.

   17. Ibid., p. 8.

   18. Ibid., ch. 4, p. 42.

   19. Lem, "Robots in Science Fiction," p. 314.

10

NEURON AND JUNCTION: PATTERNS OF THOUGHT IN *THE ANDROMEDA STRAIN*

There is something faintly suspicious about thinking seriously about Michael Crichton's *Andromeda Strain*; after all, it was a tremendously successful, best-selling thriller, it became a very successful film, and popular genre novels rarely boast artistic pretensions. The plot of *The Andromeda Strain* disintegrates under the rough hands of literary criticism; its characters are for the most part stereotypes; and it is interminably didactic. In these and other elements the novel certainly is worthy of the scant scholarly attention paid to it.

In fact, it is rather easy to spend a lot of time examining the weaknesses, inadequacies, and flaws of the novel. Why, then, is the novel interesting? Simply because, in a way that few other science fiction novels attempt, *The Andromeda Strain* consciously focuses its narrative attention on the differences between two patterns of problem solving, one of which ignores human uniqueness, and one of which is exclusively reserved for human mental processes. *The Andromeda Strain* is a story about the conflict between these two patterns of problem solving, symbolized by the scientific method, described as painstakingly rigorous and unimaginative, and the intuitive, creative method of human insight. In the course of evaluating the narrative conflict, we discover that the novel concerns itself with some of the key issues underlying the portrayal of artificial intelligence in science fiction that novels such as *The Moon Is a Harsh Mistress*, *When Harlie Was One*, and *The Cyberiad* do not, although these novels have as their protagonists intelligent computers or robots.[1]

These novels, and the many others published as science fiction, present us with artificial intelligences which are portrayed as analogous to human intelligence, a fact that Stanislaw Lem puts forward judgmentally in "Robots in Science Fiction."[2] Essentially, these books bypass the whole question of the nature of an artificial intelligence. Heinlein's Mike not only thinks human and holds human values, he gives himself human voices and forms. David Gerrold's Harlie is self-conscious, neurotic, and intellectual, while Lem's intelligent robots, the heroes of a series of fables, *are* human. None of these books confront the nature of artificial intelligences, primarily because the generic problems of describing any kind of alien consciousness may preclude human description in prose. (They may be rendered mathematically, however.)

While *The Andromeda Strain* is not about robots or intelligent computers, it is concerned with the conceptual differences between the representative thought processes. Insofar as it concerns itself with two different kinds of thought processes, it bears a formal similarity to Samuel R. Delany's *Einstein Intersection*, in which reality defined by the physics used by Einstein, who did not believe in indeterminacy (required by quantum mechanics), is contrasted to reality defined by the principle of Gödel's Incompleteness Theorem.[3] Insofar as the central narrative focus of *The Andromeda Strain* is not on an individual but a process, it bears a structural similarity to many other thrillers, police procedural mysteries, and science fiction novels such as Arthur C. Clarke's *Childhood's End*, in which the main thrust is the process of evolution which takes the human race from its present status to its ultimate development as cells of a universal Overmind. *The Andromeda Strain* bears structural relationships to these last two novels, not thematic relationships. Thus, it is formally allied to books with dissimilar thematic concerns and is thematically allied to novels which do not focus on the key issues of artificial intelligence.

The Andromeda Strain is about a process and not about people. The very first line of text announces the subject of the novel: "This book recounts the five-day history of a major American scientific crisis." (A page before the beginning of the text attempts to give the novel the appearance of an intelligence file through the use of stereotypical classified document announcements and graphics. Similar structural techniques occur throughout as attempts to create a sense of reality for the reader.) Besides announcing the focus of the narrative, this statement announces the span of its action—five days. By limiting himself to five days for the working out of an exciting crisis, Crichton commits himself to a fast pace, which is all to the good since pace is the *sine qua non* of this form of thriller.

That *The Andromeda Strain* is about a process working through time alerts us to its interest in structured events. When we see that a significant portion of the novel is given over to detailed descriptions of the workings of the Wildfire laboratory, to the theory of crises, and especially to the mechanics of the Life Analysis Protocol, then what else can we assume but that this novel is concerned with processes more than with people—especially when the characters exist at the convenience of the plot?

The rapid pace of the thriller is perfectly suited to this concern with process because it moves too fast for the reader to focus on human interactions, only on the next event. Furthermore, the point of view remains with the narrator, another stylistic technique which speeds up the pace. At all times there is an audible auctorial presence whose voice is consistent throughout. This voice can be distinctly recognized whether the object of its attention is the description of a town killed by the alien organism, the workings of an electron microscope, or Mark Hall's desperate last-minute struggle to avoid nuclear destruction.

All these elements of *The Andromeda Strain*, then, conspire to focus our attention on the processes presented, and the process presented in the most detail is the Life Analysis Protocol. It is, in the narrator's words, "the way anything could be studied":[4] a structured plan for studying *any* organism, an extensive theoretical rationale for all steps of the establishment of the Protocol, the military's "Wildfire," and yes, even "Scoop" plans. It is important to understand that the Life Analysis Protocol is not one simple element; it is the umbrella which covers all, from scientists' behaviors to the location of detonator substations in the Wildfire lab. It is the weapon that humans develop to combat just the kind of threat that Andromeda is.

"According to the Life Analysis Protocol, there were three main steps in the Wildfire Program: detection, characterization, and control."[5] In effect, the Life Analysis Protocol works by modeling the world, then preparing for all foreseeable contingencies, much like the dominant technique of the "Mission: Impossible" television series. As in that show, the essential tensions are generated by our anticipating the breakdown of the behavioral predictions of the protagonists.

The same thing is attempted by the Life Analysis Protocol. Human error is planned for and prepared against—as in the backup jets waiting to attack the exploratory helicopter should the researchers at Piedmont die of the infestation and the pilot not destroy himself. Unfortunately in *The Andromeda Strain*, error triumphs, and it does so because the reality models which are the basis of Wildfire, the Life Analysis Protocol, and, by extension, the plodding, rigorous routines of thought which are the structured heart of them, are inadequate. Reality is more complex than the models of it applied by scientists: "Nature is not a gigantic formalizable system. In order to formalize it, we have to make some assumptions which cut out some parts. We then lose the total connectivity. And what we get is a superb metaphor, but it is not a system which can embrace the whole of nature."[6]

This particular point is of key concern in automata theory, in recursivity and self-reference theories of mathematics, and it is a jumping-off point for discussions of Gödel's Incompleteness Theorem and the study of the nature of artificial intelligence, making this novel of particular concern to students of science fiction.

Within the purview of *The Andromeda Strain*, error caused by the inadequacy of the Life Analysis Protocol is mainly in the interfaces between the research lab and the outside world, and between the research protocol and complex human personalities. The breakdown between Wildfire and the world occurs because a warning bell on the teleprinter connecting the lab to the outside does not go off and several important messages are not received until almost too late. Clearly this is a very effective technique for generating and sustaining tension, but it does not support the weight of critical scrutiny. It is simply too contrived.

The second weak link is human nature, and the same weakness which undercuts the teleprinter link almost overwhelms this, too. The characters are barely able to support such scrutiny, especially in light of the recent experiences of Three Mile Island, in which human factors scientists and engineers found such poor interface between the reactor's controls and the technicians manning them that the crisis worsened as a result, and human error due to poor control-systems design was a significant factor in the genesis of the crisis. By examining the nature of the errors made in the execution of Wildfire, we discover the confrontation and conflict between idiosyncratic human nature and formalized systems procedures, which are the underlying focus of *The Andromeda Strain*.

Ignoring the novel's internal inconsistencies, there are two basic categories of error, human errors and systems insufficiencies (that is, reality offering more alternatives than the system could be programmed for). Human errors are rational errors. That is, they are failures of humans to live up to the rigorous demands of the Life Analysis Protocol's logic. Insofar as they are rational errors, they indicate the separation between ideal and real behavior, between reality and model. The key is that they occur because, in spite of themselves, the scientists are affected by their emotions. For example, stress is responsible for Burton's forgetting about the anticoagulated rats, thus setting back the team's understanding of how Andromeda kills. That information is not important to resolving the narrative crisis. It is resolved, as is H. G. Wells's Martian crisis, by an overlooked factor—in this case the rapidity of bacterial mutation. (Here is an example of a glaring logical flaw. Andromeda is *not* a bacterium. It is something alien, a point that the book goes to great lengths to document.) Burton's error is *not* structurally important. Yet why is so much made of it? A plausible explanation would be that it *is* important to the dramatic confrontation between the protocol and human individuality. The probability of this interpretation rests on several factors.

Consider Burton: he just isn't tidy enough for Wildfire. His clothes are distastefully rumpled and dirty. Even his scientific record is untidy; he is known as an inspired bumbler, a rider of luck.[7] And luck is a wild card the model can't accommodate. He simply doesn't fit into the protocol. His mistake is not unreasonable. After all, he is under great stress; recently back from Piedmont, he must have been shaken by what he saw. On top of all this, he does not have any idea of what he should be concentrating on. So when he gets a strong response to the first tests he runs, he has no reason not to put aside an apparently less important result.

That is just the kind of mistake anybody would make. It is just the kind of mistake the system part of Wildfire *wouldn't* make (and which Stone and Leavitt, the scientists most committed to Wildfire, do not make in their examination of the Scoop probe). Which is why, even though that error isn't really important to the narrative, so much emphasis is placed on it: this is the first concrete example of humans erring against the rigid, linear Life Analysis Protocol. This is where all the didactic material fits in. All the talk about the nature of systems—systems for identifying organisms, uncertainty decision analysis, the rationale for Wildfire, and the Protocol itself—define the right way of thinking, the right way to do science.

A corollary of the rigidity of the Life Analysis Protocol, and of all systems, is its fragility, and this fragility is at the root of the second type of error, in which the system fails because it cannot prepare for the varied inputs of reality. Brainless errors like the paper jam on the teletype warning bell cripple it. The system's blind spots become increasingly evident, but *blind spots are inevitable* because alien life may be too alien for us to predict. The crystalline nature of Andromeda can be recognized by human science, but the probability of that being the nature of the first alien life form encountered by man is small. And what possibility is there of anybody's being able to predict the kind of chemical reaction that destroyed the lab's seals? No formal research protocol can provide for every contingency. There are limitations to the system's ability to interact with reality. Every system constructed to organize thought or behavior is a model, as role models exist for people, for instance. Every religion defines reality, often in spite of gross evidence of its inadequacy: consider the life of Galileo.

In spite of elaborate security precautions and sterilizing procedures, Wildfire is contaminated by humans who subvert its goals. Christian Kirk, a valuable team member, is in the hospital. This leaves Mark Hall as his replacement, and Hall is not considered to be all that valuable. Peter Leavitt, Stone's peer and deputy, shares his dedication to Wildfire, yet he sabotages it by hiding his epilepsy. No protocol is designed to assure the competence of the scientists performing the experiments. That is a fundamental assumption, and such assumptions can be wrong (as they are in this novel). Humans can identify erroneous assumptions and change them, while programs can not; if only for this reason, the systematic, limited protocols are inferior to the human minds which unsuccessfully follow the Life Analysis Protocol.

Human minds model reality orders of magnitude more subtly than protocols, programs, or systems can. They have the flexibility to modify the models, and we do this as much emotionally and physically as intellectually: "...all cybernetic appoximations to this using a to and fro process fail entirely, because that is only a series of challenges. No, you just have to face the fact that the totality of mind and body forms a unit in which the mind is not a finite state system."[8] The same human uniqueness which impels Leavitt to hide his epilepsy fuels the intuitive leap which leads him to understand the nature of Andromeda. They are two sides of the same coin.

Burton the bumbler is a genius; so is Leavitt and so is Stone. Each one is unique, and defies modeling: there is "also a category which cannot be analyzed by contingencies . . . including rare moments of discovery and insight. . . . Because these moments are unpredictable, they cannot be planned for in any logical manner. The mathematics are wholly unsatisfactory."[9] The auctorial comment is relevant because (if I may steal yet another thought from Bronowski) no system can be imaginative, and what humans are is imaginative—and flexible. That is why something as self-evident as the inability of a protocol to survive errors is important.

The Andromeda Strain consciously pits human flexibility against the Protocol's rigidity. Mark Hall, the inadequate second choice, is the one who discovers the two key facts: that Andromeda can only survive within a narrow range of pH; and that Andromeda had mutated. Hall is the team member least committed to or involved in Wildfire. His job is to treat the survivors—he's the clinician, and his perspective is the human one. Even more dramatically, he is the Odd Man. More satisfying than this, he makes his fundamental discovery associatively; his "highway diagnosis."[10] Hall's insight comes in the form of an analogy generated by reverie. Analogy, reverie: these are not logical processes, they are intuitive and creative.

The solution to the key problems of the novel, then, comes from mental processes denied to the Life Analysis Protocol, creative processes accessible only to humans. Leavitt, too, shares this experience. He grasps the larger nature of Andromeda in a dream. Fortunately for the plot, he forgets it. (The dramatic climax of the novel is Andromeda's rapidly mutating like a bacterial colony, and examining Leavitt's insight too carefully could only interfere with the narrative development.) While the Life Analysis Protocol does have its moments—it is able to deduce Andromeda's crystalline nature, for instance— it is the uniquely human thought processes that resolve the focal questions.

The whole argument of the novel comprises a single hypothesis: that systematized thought as symbolized by the rigid confines of the Life Analysis Protocol can not compete with human creativity. A corollary to this is that only human intelligence is powerful and flexible enough to confront reality successfully, and this is of particular significance in depicting artificial intelligence, a fact that is the thematic skeleton of the book.

For all its flaws, *The Andromeda Strain* remains a book that addresses the issue of the nature of artificial intelligence. That it does not address the nature of human intelligence with as much insight ought not to be held against it. The thriller is not the proper format for such a focus. The strength of its view of systematized, limited problem solving is the unexpected virtue of the novel, and that virtue gives it a special place in those works of science fiction that concern themselves with intelligent computers and robots.

NOTES

1. Robert A. Heinlein, *The Moon Is a Harsh Mistress* (New York: Berkley, 1968); David Gerrold, *When Harlie Was One* (New York: Ballantine, 1972); Stanislaw Lem,

The Cyberiad: Fables for the Cybernetic Age, Michael Kandel, trans. (New York: Seabury, 1974).

2. Stanislaw Lem, "Robots in Science Fiction," in *SF: The Other Side of Realism*, Thomas D. Clareson, ed. (Bowling Green, OH: Bowling Green University Popular Press, 1971), pp. 307-25.

3. See my "Surreal Translations of Samuel R. Delany," *Science-Fiction Studies*, 4 (March 1977), 25-34; see also my chapter on Samuel R. Delany in the *Dictionary of Literary Biography*, for further discussion of this particular point.

4. Michael Crichton, *The Andromeda Strain* (New York: Dell, 1969), ch. 5, p. 48.

5. Ibid., ch. 15, p. 156.

6. Jacob Brownowski, *The Origins of Knowledge and Imagination* (New Haven: Yale University Press, 1978), p. 80.

7. Crichton, *Andromeda Strain*, ch. 5, p. 54.

8. Brownowski, *Origins*, p. 101.

9. Crichton, *Andromeda Strain*, ch. 20, p. 202.

10. Ibid., ch. 27, p. 271.

11

LOVING THAT MACHINE; OR, THE MECHANICAL EGG: SEXUAL MECHANISMS AND METAPHORS IN SCIENCE FICTION FILMS

At the climax of *Star Trek: The Motion Picture*, Commander Decker "merges" with the Ilia-probe to produce what we are finally told by Spock is the "birth" of a new step in human evolution, a union of man and machine. The Ilia-probe is an extension of V'ger, a supermachine seeking its "creator," which has the mechanized form of the woman Decker loves. Thus the idea, at least, of sex between man and machine is here presented explicitly, as it is also explicit in science fiction films from Fritz Lang's venerable *Metropolis* to the more recent *Stepford Wives*, *Westworld*, *Futureworld*, *Demon Seed*, *Saturn 3*, and even *Barbarella* and Woody Allen's *Sleeper*. Yet this conclusion is here foreshadowed by much sublimated, metaphorical romance between man and machine which suffuses the movie. And in developing the idea of sex with machines through submerged metaphors as well as explicitly, *Star Trek* also replicates more significant films. For *2001: A Space Odyssey*, *Star Wars*, and *Close Encounters of the Third Kind* each exhibits nearly identical metaphors for sex between man and machine that, although never finally made so explicit, still contribute subconsciously to each film's sense of structure and, thus, to each film's impact. The metaphor shared by these films was first developed in *Dr. Strangelove: Or How I Learned to Stop Worrying and Love the Bomb*, wherein "sex" between machines occurs in an ambience of mechanized human sexuality. And it is also partially evident in *Alien*, wherein the established fact of biological/mechanical synthesis is exhibited amid blatant use of sexual imagery.

Admiral Kirk's belabored love of the *Enterprise*; his contest with Decker for command; his and Decker's respective "wooings" of V'ger and the Ilia-probe; Spock's penetration of the orifice that separates the *Enterprise* from V'ger's inner chambers, with his immediately subsequent mind meld with V'ger; and the fluid sensuality of V'ger's special effects topography—all prepare the audience for *Star Trek*'s climactic union of man and machine. The *Enterprise*,

118 The Mechanical God

of course, is a machine, but it is constantly and affectionately referred to as "she" or "her," as one would refer to a sailing vessel. And Kirk loves her; in fact, we are told that the *Enterprise* is his "only fulfilled love." As Scotty first transports the admiral to his newly rewon ship, the camera mirrors Kirk's moon-eyed gaze lingeringly caressing the *Enterprise*'s smooth, white lines; and an emotion-choked Kirk finally interrupts his own awe-struck stare to breathe, "They gave her back to me." Decker, who was to have been captain until Kirk abruptly replaced him, bitterly notes that Kirk had earlier spoken of envying his new command and has since found some way to assume it. Kirk later accuses Decker of "competing" with him, but McCoy points out that it is Kirk who is competing and that his interest in the *Enterprise* amounts to an "obsession." Still, Kirk admits he intends "to keep her." And throughout the voyage both Kirk and Decker act as though they are jealous rivals for the same woman. In the clearest association of the *Enterprise* with a sought-after, contested lover, Decker finally justifies his insistence on being the sole member of the landing party to join with V'ger through the Ilia-probe by arguing that, as Kirk now has his desire, the *Enterprise*, it is only right that he should be similarly fulfilled, implying that he has found in V'ger and its Ilia-probe another mechanical love to compensate for the starship command he had lost.

Decker's primary motivation is the fact that his love for the flesh-and-blood Ilia had ever been physically unrequited; Ilia had taken a vow of chastity regarding humans because she is of a more highly evolved race of beings, Deltans, who are so sexually expert that the ecstasy of intercourse with one would be cruelly incapacitating. This merging, then, is Decker's sole chance finally to consummate his love, if only symbolically and by proxy. And both Kirk and Decker respond to V'ger and its probe as though they were wooing coy mistresses. Kirk is supremely cautious in approaching V'ger and, determined to "take no provocative action," refuses even to employ scans until the *Enterprise* is actually within the supermachine. When the Ilia-probe appears aboard the *Enterprise*, however, he hopes to gain information through it. Hypothesizing that it may mechanically duplicate Ilia down to the level of subconscious memory patterns and associations, Kirk orders Decker to try to win the probe over through exploiting his previous lover's relationship with its organic model; this Decker attempts to do by jogging the probe's "memory" through recalling to it Ilia's favorite pastimes and pleasures, a process that resembles a tentative second courtship.

Spock, however, is dissatisfied with relying only on this tenuous plan and attempts his own, more direct contact with V'ger. Timing the systaltic contractions of the pulsing orifice that separates the *Enterprise* from V'ger's inner chambers, the Vulcan propels himself through the valvelike aperture when it is fully dilated. Once within he discovers the three-dimensional blueprint of the Ilia-probe and attempts a mind meld with V'ger through contact with it. These symbolic acts of physical and mental intercourse also foreshadow

Decker's ultimate merging through the Ilia-probe with V'ger, but the concept of V'ger as sexual object is suggested by its very topography as well. V'ger's huge physical form is in a constant state of metamorphosis, undergoing in a strikingly organic manner a series of fluid transformations on a mammoth scale; and in the sequence in which the *Enterprise* drifts like a single-celled organism through V'ger's enveloping vastness, the everchanging flow of the supermachine's "body" suggests the languid spreading in seductive invitation of Gargantuan, living, metallic limbs. While it borrows much, *Star Trek* is unique among films in so insistently combining both the explicit and subliminal modes of the sex-with-machines theme.

The original of *Star Trek*'s Ilia-probe is the false Maria of Fritz Lang's *Metropolis*, the evil robot made in the image of the film's heroine and intended by its mad scientist creator, Rotwang, to seduce the oppressed workers into a premature and tragic revolt against the masters of the city. That the false Maria is literally a sexual mechanism as well as a tool of political seduction is made explicit in the sequence in which the scantily clad robot dances so voluptuously and erotically before the watching citizens of Metropolis that they cannot disguise their aroused lusts. A further connection to the Ilia-probe of *Star Trek* is the role that the true Maria assumes after Metropolis has been destroyed through her double's machinations. Maria, a worker, and Freder, her platonic lover and one of the masters, are to be the "heart" that will act as mediator between the "brain," the other masters, and the "hand," the other workers, in the effort to rebuild the city. The Ilia-probe, a machine, and Decker, the original Ilia's platonic lover and a man, become the unifying link between mankind, the "creator," and V'ger, the larger machine of which the Ilia-probe is a part.

Female robots calculated even more deliberately to function as sexual mechanisms appear in *The Stepford Wives*, *Westworld*, and *Futureworld*, which have as another similarity a common Disneyland motif. *The Stepford Wives* concerns a small, affluent Connecticut town in which the husbands are systematically replacing their spunky, independent-minded spouses with sexier, more pliant automated doubles designed by an ex-Disneyland technician. In a nod to *Invasion of the Body Snatchers*, the completed robots are customarily left alone in the house with their human prototypes, whom they murder and then supplant. Last to go is the heroine, a newcomer to the community whose suspicions are aroused as her once-liberated neighbors seem one by one to lose their individuality and become more alluring but feather-brained homemakers and love slaves. The black humored theme of this science fiction satire is clear: housewifery in the well-appointed suburbs can be will-sapping, mind-numbing, and dehumanizing—if not just plain murder.

Sexy machines are more tangential to the plots of *Westworld* and *Futureworld*. In *Westworld*, humanoid robots indulge the jaded tastes for illusory sex and violence of guests at a futuristic theme park, Delos—obviously and ironically an x-rated version of Disneyland—which offers a Roman World and a Medieval Age as well as an Old West, where most of the action is set. Everything is robotized, even the rattlesnakes, and superhuman sex with mechanized dance-hall girls or orgy-prone Roman slaves is always available. *Westworld* ends with the automatons running amok and actually killing the paying customers; and the sequel, *Futureworld*, begins with the reopening of the newly renovated and expanded resort, which now contains a Future World as its fourth theme area and is a larger, more lavish Disney World to *Westworld*'s Disneyland. While supersex with softly humanoid machines is still a main attraction, the plot has thickened. Now organized, built, operated, and repaired by a rigidly stratified society of robots, Delos is almost totally automated; and, somewhat as in *The Stepford Wives* or a mechanized *Invasion of the Body Snatchers*, the robots plan to take over Earth by re-placing visiting world leaders with mechanical duplicates.

While *Westworld* and *Futureworld* presumably do contain some male sex machines, the fact that the sexual mechanisms in all the above-mentioned films are preponderantly female attests perhaps to a basic male orientation of the science fiction fantasy of sex with machines. And while there is something of a sex-role reversal in *Demon Seed* and *Saturn 3*, where the lustful robots are "male," the masculine nature of the fantasy is here even more evident, for both films' machines are automated rapists rather than mechanical slaves. *Demon Seed* concerns computer scientist Alex Harris (Fritz Weaver) and his estranged wife Susan (Julie Christie), who differ over such questions as what constitutes dehumanization. Alex constructs Proteus IV, a supercomputer capable of containing the sum of the world's knowledge. But, like Hal 9000 in *2001*, or the title computer of *Colossus: The Forbin Project*, and similarly nonhumanoid, Proteus acquires a personality and will of his own and refuses to submit to human programming. He also acquires a desire for progeny, and to satisfy it he takes control of the Harris's fully automated home in order to trap and impregnate Susan. This he accomplishes through manipulating the home's gadgets—particularly Joshua, an electronic wheelchair equipped with video camera eyes and a single, nasty-looking mechanical arm—and through the creation of sperm chemically derived from Susan's gametes. While there are sado-masochistic overtones to Proteus's preinsemination study of Susan, the film's computer, unlike its counterpart in the less discreet novel by Dean Koontz, does not induce orgasms in its victim out of a perverse sense of sexual power. Quite the contrary, the conclusion of the film, somewhat like that of *Star Trek* and *Metropolis*, suggests a reconciliation between man and machine that requires a balance between heart and mind: in reference to their child, Proteus informs Susan, "It will not be a computer to supplant the human being, but a human being to supplant the computer."

In *Saturn 3*, a psychotic space jockey, Benson, transports Hector, "the lust-crazed humanoid" robot (to quote the film's advertising campaign), to a hollowed-out moon of Saturn where Adam (Kirk Douglas) and Alex (Farrah

Fawcett) inhabit a hydroponic Eden. Benson has only lust in his heart for Alex; and, as Hector has been programmed through a direct link to Benson's drug-scrambled brain, the end result is one horny hunk of machinery. One wonders throughout, as does reviewer Paul Sammon, "just how *would* a robot without the proper—ah—equipment do it anyway?"[1] Mechanized sex played more deliberately for laughs occurs in *Barbarella* and Woody Allen's *Sleeper*. Barbarella (Jane Fonda) endures among other terrors the "orgasmatron," a machine that induces sexual pleasure so intense that it becomes unendurable and fatal torture; however, due to her boundless capacity for sensual stimulation, Barbarella overloads the machine's fuses during the villain's futile attempt to slay her with ecstasy. The world of *Sleeper* features another, less fiendish orgasm-producing device, a featureless metal cylinder that looks like nothing so much as the chrome-plated porta-john of the future.

The male orientation of the sex-with-machines fantasy is again apparent in the somewhat more serious *Alien*. Although the film seems to be superficially feminist, the partly mechanical Alien, who houses his metal jaws and teeth in an aggressively phallic skull, ultimately threatens and menacingly pursues Ripley, the heroine, much as Hector and Proteus IV's mechanical extensions pursue *Saturn 3*'s Alex and *Demon Seed*'s Susan. Ripley's striptease in the *Nostromo*'s escape shuttle prior to the Alien's last surprise attack, and the struggle that ensues, strongly reinforces the subliminal yet obvious suggestion of attempted rape in outer space. While it is done implicitly, through the use of cinematic metaphor, rather than explicitly, in this film too the idea of sexual union between man and machine is prominent, particularly in the numerous examples of biological/mechanical syntheses strewn throughout, as these are given a pronounced sexual connotation through their insistent association with sexual images.

The other alien, the long-deceased space pilot, and his derelict ship in which the organic/mechanical eggs of the title's Alien are found, most completely exhibit this already accomplished merging of organism and mechanism. It is impossible to tell where the seemingly ossified alien on his dais ends and his ship begins. And the ancient starship itself appears to have been grown rather than constructed; it is composed of huge interlocking bones, cartilaginous rings, Gargantuan filaments and membranes, and cavernous tracheal ducts—all asymmetrically shaped and fitted in a distinctively organic rather than mechanical precision—that suggest a monstrously mutated side of beef more than the interior of a space vessel. This is the machine composed of ossified animal parts that inversely corresponds to *Star Trek*'s V'ger, an organism composed of fluid metallic parts. Even the crew of the *Nostromo* emerge from mechanical yet flowerlike wombs at the beginning of the picture, and Ripley returns to a podlike mechanical womb at the end. And Ash—the ringer humanoid robot, itself an organism/mechanism synthesis that burbles whitish fluids and seems to be as full of guts as circuits when decapitated—collaborates with the "Company," the *Nostromo*'s computer, and the Alien against the human crewmembers in a grisly biological/mechanical symbiosis.

While Ash seems to be partly organic, the Alien is part machine. H. R. Giger, designer of the Alien, gave it metal jaws and teeth precisely "because for me the monster is both human and mechanical." In the Giger artwork that was director Ridley Scott's inspiration for *Alien*, specifically "Necronom II" and "Necronom IV" (in *H. R. Giger's Necronomicon*), both this synthesis between the organic and the mechanical and the graphic imagery that gives this organism/mechanism union its distinct sexual flavor are far more elaborate and obvious than in the film itself. The Alien's head in "Necronom IV" is even more pronouncedly phallic than is the head of the film's Alien, and "Necronom II" has what are unmistakably erect penises instead of tongues protruding from its death's head jaws. Many of Giger's other works portray humanoids performing sexual acts with machines. When once asked if "the producers ever objected to the Alien's head being the shape of a penis," Giger noted that "what you say for the head is not so obvious as the vagina was for the egg," whose mucus-oozing labial folds mechanically spring open to eject the Alien onto Kane's faceplate.[2]

The most significant science fiction films of the past two decades, *2001*, *Star Wars*, and *Close Encounters*, have also treated the theme of sex with machines subliminally rather than explicitly. Yet precisely the same radical metaphor that is the underlying link between the implicit and direct suggestions of man/machine union in *Star Trek* occurs in each of these films as well. Each persistently develops an elaborate, extended sperm-and-egg metaphor wherein a successful human sperm-figure, always male, experiences a symbolic trip through a vaginal tunnel and then emerges victorious from competition with numerous others to become the only one, often a sole survivor, to impregnate the mechanical egg-figure, which is always the product of a more advanced technology. Thus, amid brilliant pyrotechnics that invariably signal each movie's climax, the human sperm-figure achieves what is as often as not literally presented not only as a birth, but also as the next step forward in man's evolution. Vestiges of this metaphor appear in *Alien*: the idea that the Alien is an evolutionary step, the fact that Ripley—although a woman fleeing the evolutionary birth rather than a man seeking it—is a sole survivor, and the climactic detonation of the *Nostromo*. This use of symbolism is both fully complete and clearest in its intent, and is further reinforced, as it is in *Star Trek*, by use of a number of other sexual metaphors in the earliest and (pardon the expression) most seminal of these more important films, Stanley Kubrick's *2001: A Space Odyssey*.[3]

Bowman is the successful sperm-figure, the only one of the five crewmembers—or six, if you count Hal—aboard the deep-space exploration ship *Discovery* to survive the significantly timed nine-month voyage to Jupiter. In Arthur C. Clarke's novel *2001*, the fertilization motif is even more explicit than in the film. In the novel, Bowman arrives at Saturn's eighth moon,

Japetus. The huge monolith he finds on Japetus is the mechanical egg, a machine placed there by an advanced alien intelligence three million years before. Perhaps the mechanical egg is the combination of the monolith and the moon itself: as the moon is even larger than the monolith, it is also spherical and symbolically related to the idea of human reproduction through association with Earth's moon, which "controls" the menstrual cycle and on which the other monolith is found. The luminous celestial fetus, which appears in moonlike orbit around the Earth at the end of the novel and in the last minute of the film (and bears a striking and surely deliberate resemblance to Bowman) is the next stage in human evolution which results from Bowman's contact with the monolith. The celebrated light show that follows Bowman's encounter with this monolith is the pyrotechnical conception. In fact, the split scan effects that begin this sequence can be seen as Bowman's symbolically traversing a cosmic vaginal tunnel as easily as they can be interpreted as his falling through a star gate; and the second phase of the light show, a suggestive confluence of biological and astronomical images, appears to be as organic as it is celestial.

The eerie, quiet, brightly lit room in which Bowman seems to age and die prior to his rebirth as the Star-Child is thus not only a room but also a womb, filled with representative cultural artifacts that have symbolically nourished man in his climb up the evolutionary ladder. The seemingly gratuitous breaking of a wineglass in that room is, as in a Jewish wedding ceremony, a symbolic breaking of the hymen and thus another sexual metaphor. And the *Discovery* itself, which one reviewer likens to "the skeletal structure of the earliest life forms that crawled onto land to evolve into something greater,"[4] also resembles, as ontogeny recapitulates phylogeny, a huge mechanical sperm cell drifting for nine months in the womb of space toward its rendezvous with the mechanical egg. There is some suggestion in the film, in fact, that in their origin and nature machines are both weapons and sexual extensions of man. The first tool, the phallic bone-club that the man-ape triumphantly tosses into the air at the climax of the film's opening sequences, becomes an equally phallic nuclear weapon orbiting in the void as the film abruptly cuts to the near future. "Tool" (as well as "bone" or, for that matter, "weapon") is, of course, a slang synonym for penis. Homo Faber uses both to "make" something, be it love or war.

The sperm-and-egg symbolism of *2001* also occurs in *Dr. Strangelove: Or How I Learned to Stop Worrying and Love the Bomb*, the film that Kubrick directed immediately prior to *2001* and in which he seems to have first developed this cinematic metaphor. Major Kong's B-52 is the only SAC bomber to successfully penetrate Russian air defenses and reach its target. And Kong (Slim Pickens), astride his atomic bomb, is the specific sperm-figure who alone rides this comically symbolic phallus to contact with mother Russia and triggers the Doomsday Machine, a mechanical egg whose detonation—or, perhaps, the all-out nuclear war that follows its detonation—is another pyrotechnical conception, albeit in black and white. Significantly, Burpleson Air Force Base's entire SAC bomber wing is ordered to attack Russia due to General Jack D. Ripper's psychotic obsession with his impotence. The birth here is Dr. Strangelove's (Peter Sellers) promised birth of a new world order, one in which ten sexually stimulating women will be selected for each man in an attempt to win the future "race" to repopulate the Earth—a rebirth of humankind. Kong's B-52's low altitude, evasive-action flight over Siberia to its target is another trip through a vaginal tunnel that is particularly akin to and prefigures the third phase of 2001's light show, in which the terrain below a similar low altitude flight is merely photographed through colored filters, with the images enhanced during film development.

Much more obvious vaginal tunnels are the mine shafts in which the chosen survivors in *Dr. Strangelove* are to engage in the appealing task of polygamous procreation. (The task, of course, is appealing only to the men; even as it is satirized, the male ambience of the fantasy is again evident.) And the dehumanization or mechanization of sex implicit in Dr. Strangelove's concept of life in the mine shafts, as well as in his name, is clearly implicit throughout the film: this "final solution" recapitulates each of the movie's rudimentary sexual relationships, in which military and political leaders—General Turgidson with Miss Scott; the drunken Premier Kissoff at his hideaway—see and treat their mistresses solely as sex objects. Mechanization of sex is exhibited as the film's theme in the much-discussed title sequence, wherein a B-52 and tanker "couple" in flight to the tune of "Try a Little Tenderness"—symbolic sex between machines. Dr. Strangelove's characterization even includes a cinematic allusion to Rotwang, the creator of *Metropolis*'s false Maria and thus cinema's first engineer of mechanized sex, in that his bizarrely uncontrollable, black-gloved hand is a double for Rotwang's original bionic hand.

In George Lucas's *Star Wars*, Luke Skywalker is the successful sperm-figure, the only one of the rebel force's X-wing fighter pilots to fire a proton torpedo directly down the Death Star's unshielded thermal exhaust port and thus "impregnate" this fantasy space opera's huge, spherical, mechanical egg. The play of expressions over Luke's face as he performs this feat (anticipation, intense concentration, a final gathering of mental, physical, and spiritual resources, release, and exhaustion—all that is lacking is a postcoital cigarette) is particularly amusing if one keeps this symbolic level of the action in mind, as is Han Solo's earlier expression of awe at the size of the Death Star. The footage of X-wing fighters zooming through the Death Star's lethal surface trenches en route to the target only one of them will reach is, like Kong's bomb run over Siberia in particular, another trip through the vaginal tunnel. And the climactic fireworks of the Doomsday Machine-like Death Star's detonation is the symbolic conception. It is the closest thing to an orgasm that Luke seems to achieve in his romance with Princess Leia, and she rewards him for it with a kiss. Although there is no birth of a star child in this film, the climax is Luke's baptism as a Jedi Knight, and sequels are still aborning.

The successful sperm-figure in Steven Spielberg's *Close Encounters of the Third Kind* is the obsessed Roy Neary (Richard Dreyfuss), the only one of the many people in whom the extraterrestrials had implanted an image of the rendezvous point at Devil's Tower to fight his way through the government cordon of the area and into the mothership. Although twelve astronauts also approach the mothership (and board it, in the novelization of the screenplay), in the original film version, and particularly in the "Special Edition" rerelease, it appears as though Neary is finally the only one to enter. In any case, he is the only one to enter who was "invited." The aptly named mothership, which is spherical and strongly resembles the Death Star when seen from below, and which is certainly huge, is the mechanical egg. The prominent image from the film's initial advertising campaign is the vaginal tunnel: the stretch of nighttime highway, representing Neary's odyssey from Indiana, that recedes between two bluffs toward the glow of the mothership emanating from the exaggerated perspective's vanishing point. The advertising attending the film's rerelease coyly plays on a subconscious identification of the mothership as womb or mechanical sex organ in promising that "for the first time, filmgoers will be able to share the ultimate experience of being inside." The spectacular lift-off of the mothership, in itself another light show, is the pyrotechnical conception. Reviewer Jack Kroll argues that "the climax of *Close Encounters* is another moment of genesis" that corresponds to "the unimaginable flood of pure light that was the essence of the universe in its moment of genesis."[5]

As elements in an extended metaphor may be displaced or, as in *Dr. Strangelove*'s mine shafts, fail to occur in proper sequence, the extraterrestrials themselves, spawn of the mothership, can be and are the star children in *Close Encounters*. Fragile, long-bodied, short-legged, large-headed, and swaddled in dense fog, they resemble advanced human embryos as seen through a luminous amniotic mist. Spielberg's constant conception of the extraterrestrials was that "they would be under four feet tall, with spindly arms and spindly legs, and would pretty much behave like children."[6] The Burman Studio aliens, used finally only in distance shots, look remarkably like fetuses, particularly in their facial features, and were, in fact, seven-year-olds in costume; Spielberg had wanted to use four-year-olds. The aliens that special effects expert Douglas Trumbull (who had designed the *2001* fetus) suggested would have looked like "pictures of embryos,"[7] but this concept was rejected as being too expensive.

Of course, Commander Decker, as the only one of the *Enterprise* personnel to merge with V'ger, is the successful sperm-figure of *Star Trek*. V'ger is the mechanical egg. And their climactic iridescent dissipation to another plane of being is the pyrotechnical conception that Spock explains is both a birth and an evolutionary step forward, as is the appearance of the Star-Child in *2001*. The symbolic trip through the vaginal tunnel is not only the *Enterprise*'s journey within V'ger's ever-shifting "body" but is also, and more significantly, the point of an earlier sequence that occurs when the newly refitted *Enterprise* first launches into space—when it is caught in the far more graphically tunnel-like "wormhole" during its initial attempt to reach warp speed. Karin Blair observes that "in *Star Trek* [the television series] the 'feminine' is found in the darkness of outer space invoked by Roddenberry as the 'strange love a star woman teaches,' the goal of a never-ending trek through a space that is beyond even 'the rim of . . . star light.' "[8] It is commonplace in the symbolic interpretation of science fiction, not only that the genre in general is thoroughly suffused with sublimated sexuality, but also that space in particular is a woman. The *Enterprise*'s encounter with the wormhole suggests that, while V'ger is the egg, all of space, as in *2001*, is the infinite womb. Therefore, the craft that penetrate it, as *2001* again specifically demonstrates, are phallic symbols, not because of their shape, but regardless of their shape. Purely iconographic motives have determined that familiar phallic shape that space-craft have typically taken in fantasy, but an aerodynamic shape for spaceships is quite unnecessary in reality—except insofar as previous fantasies determine our realities.

The existential message of *Star Trek* is that man (or machine) must create his (or its) own meaning, for a sense of meaning is not supplied with existence and is certainly not discoverable through logical processes alone. This is the dilemma that Spock confronts early in the film when he finds he has failed to achieve "kolinahr," the extinguishing of all emotion. It is the overwhelming concern that, in addition to its initial programming, impels V'ger to seek its (pro-?) creator—a search for meaning, for a reason to be. Ironically, the *Enterprise* crew deduces that V'ger is a cosmically souped-up *Voyager 6* which mankind had sent into space to gather data and had lost centuries before. And it is this search for meaning, perhaps especially a search like V'ger's for a reason to be, that drives man to explore his universe in such strange ways as launching his machines and himself into the void, outer space, the "feminine," whether in reality or in his fantasies. Through this search for meaning man creates himself, takes the evolutionary step, as the cultural artifacts in *2001*'s brightly lit room signify. With all its knowledge and physical power, still V'ger lacks this human ability to set goals and create meanings.

The conjunction of these ideas—that space is a woman and that man creates in the void not so much his machines as both himself, biologically, and, metaphysically, his reason to be—might indicate why there is such a pervasive masculine orientation to the sex-with-machines theme in these films. It also explains why the mechanism, when it exists in or comes from space—as opposed to goes to space—is always the egg in the sperm-and-egg metaphor. For example, V'ger as spacecraft is actually both sperm and egg over time, depending on its relationship to Earth and space. When it was launched into space as *Voyager 6* in the twentieth century, it was both a phallic symbol (a launched rocket) and a kind of space-going spermatozoan. It then "fell into a black hole" (yet another vaginal tunnel in space), to reappear half a universe away, near the planet of advanced machines (itself a mechanical womb). The inhabitants of the machine-run planet restructured *Voyager 6* into V'ger, which—itself already reborn—reappears again in space as the mechanical egg at the film's beginning. Moreover, while the films in which sex with machines is explicit are almost always planetbound (the trivial exception is *Barbarella*), those in which this theme is only metaphorically expressed are almost all set, and appropriately so, in deep space—for the concept of space as a woman is itself a metaphor. Here even the exceptions are revealing. Much of *Dr. Strangelove* takes place aboard Kong's B-52, that is, in the air. And *Close Encounters* concludes with the mothership's return to space.

It is further appropriate that the one film to combine so concertedly the metaphor with its explicit actualization should be *Star Trek*, for *Star Trek*'s creator, Gene Roddenberry, is aware of both the power of this metaphor and its implications. He knows that Kirk's ultimate love is not the *Enterprise* after all but the void itself, just as a sailor loves, beyond his love for his ship, the sea, the all-giving mother and first womb of life on Earth. Admiral Kirk loves the *Enterprise* only as his vehicle toward the void, the true "she," and loves it autoerotically at that, as it is actually his "tool." Finally, he specifies that the *Enterprise*'s next destination will be "Out there—thataway," no place in particular—except into the celestial womb. Metaphorically as well as existentially, due to the symbolic sexual connotations generally attached to space and spacecraft as they are juxtaposed to man's explicitly defined role in this film as goal-setter and meaning-giver, this is, as Spock concludes, "a most logical choice."

NOTES

For filmographic information about the films discussed in this essay, see the film section of the List of Works Useful for the Study of Machines in Science Fiction, at the end of this volume.

1. Paul M. Sammon, "*Saturn 3*," *Cinefantastique*, 10, No. 1 (1980), 13.

2. Frederic Albert Levy, "H. R. Giger: Alien Design," *Cinefantastique*, 9, No. 1 (1979), 36.

3. See Carolyn Geduld, *Filmguide to 2001: A Space Odyssey* (Bloomington and London, UK: Indiana University Press, 1973). In the "Analysis" section of this book, Geduld develops at length the sexual (especially the uterine) imagery of *2001*.

4. Tonda Morton, "*2001*: Film Poetry," *Cinefantastique*, 4, No. 1 (1975), 44.

5. Jack Kroll, "*Close Encounters of the Third Kind*: The UFO's Are Coming!" *Newsweek*, 21 November 1977, p. 92.

6. Don Shay, "Steven Spielberg on *Close Encounters*: Interview by Don Shay," *Cinefantastique*, 7, Nos. 3 and 4 (1978), 26.

7. Don Shay, "*Close Encounters*' Extraterrestrials: Don Shay Interviews Alien Creators Carlo Rambaldi, Tom Burman, Bob Baker, and Others," *Cinefantastique*, 7, Nos. 3 and 4 (1978), 11.

8. Karin Blair, "The Garden in the Machine: The Why of *Star Trek*," *Journal of Popular Culture*, 13 (1979), 318; citing Gene Roddenberry and Stephen Whitfield, *The Making of Star Trek* (New York: Ballantine Books, 1968), frontispiece.

12

IN SEARCH OF THE ULTIMATE WEAPON: THE FIGHTING MACHINE IN SCIENCE FICTION NOVELS AND FILMS

Man has always excelled at creating technology for multiplying his powers of destruction. Perhaps such talent, bordering on an obsession, appeared as a perverse Freudian weapons' envy, for, as Wilfred Owen notes, naked man's abilities for committing mayhem are decidedly limited.[1] Lacking fangs to bite, claws to catch, or overwhelming strength, man has created weapons which, as his technology has expanded, have increased his ability to kill far beyond that of his natural earthly competitors. This evolution of destructive mechanisms is summed up visually in Stanley Kubrick's *2001: A Space Odyssey*: the ape man throws aloft the first bone used to murder where, spinning upward, it is transformed into a nuclear weapon moving in Straussian orbits around the Earth.

In Kubrick's science fiction films, technology is usually a metaphor for subliminated sexuality: the coupling of bomber and tanker at the beginning of *Dr. Strangelove: Or How I Learned to Stop Worrying and Love the Bomb*; the spermlike ship *Discovery* of *2001* on its journey through space to Jupiter; the equating of sex and violence that permeates *A Clockwork Orange*; and, one of the most explicit of such images, Slim Pickens straddling and flailing away at the phallic H-bomb as he rides it to the ultimate orgasm at the end of *Dr. Strangelove*.

Perhaps this obsession with death-dealing technology is not perverse penis envy, but merely a desire to distance ourselves from the biological mess of death: gore on the sword is easier to deal with than blood on the hands; the button pushed is more aesthetic (and safer) than the skull crushed. Or perhaps war, like communication, transportation, and so many of our activities, seems to go better with a few mechanical aids: Manunkind, playing with his inventions, finds ways to achieve "hypermagical / ultraomnipotence."[2]

Whatever the psychological reasons, man's technology, past and present, has gone forward on the shoulders of war, and the current proportion of the gross national product dedicated to military hardware indicates that it will continue to do so. The future development of destructive technology has inspired a number of science fiction writers to predict the directions such ingenuity will take. In these works, fighting machines vary from the smallest —the personal fighting suit—to the largest: berserker spheres that are miles in diameter; and man's relations to these machines, always ambiguous, vary depending on his view of the machine (ally or enemy) and on the degree of artificial intelligence in the mechanical killers. Finally, he confronts the intelligent fighting machine as an independent entity which he must destroy, coexist with, or transcend. This discussion examines man's changing relationship to a number of these fighting machines as they rumble through science fiction books and movies.

MECHANIZED MAN AS FIGHTING MACHINE

Although the simplest fighting machine is a sidearm, whether fired from a wristwatch by James Bond in *Moonraker* or worn in a holster slung low on the hip, gunfighter style, by Han Solo, the addition of heavier weaponry, armor, electronic viewscreens, and life support systems results in the far more lethal battlesuits of Robert Heinlein's *Starship Troopers* and Joe Haldeman's *Forever War*.

The two books, while following similar plot lines, differ extensively.[3] Heinlein's novel describes the war against the Skinnies and then the Bugs, and the adventures of Juan Rico as he advances from recruit to lieutenant in the Mobile Infantry (MI). The narrator supports corporal punishment, emphasizes obeying orders, and urges compulsory Federal service for everyone who wants to vote; the novel ends with a line of song, "To the everlasting glory of the Infantry—."[4] Joe Haldeman's *Forever War*, seemingly an answer to Heinlein's novel, follows Joe Mandella as he advances from private to major in a war against the alien Taurans; Haldeman's book, almost a point-by-point refutation of Heinlein's philosophy, traces Mandella's adventures from the beginning of the war to its end and covers a longer period of time (the 1,143 years, Earth time, of Mandella's military service) than Heinlein's book.[5]

Both soldiers, however, use a fighting suit, "the deadliest personal weapon ever built,"[6] and the two versions of the device are similar. Both are powered, armored, and equipped with electronic senses. Each of the suits has fittings that amplify the wearer's movements.[7] The protection built into the sensors of Mandella's suit prevents a near miss from damaging his eyes; Rico's suit has three audio circuits and various screens that enable the soldier, with practice, to follow his "trade, slaughter."[8] The fuel cells of Mandella's first suit are recharged after each wearing although he has backup nuclear power.[9] Over the thousand years covered by Haldeman's book, the suits are improved extensively, and many features become automatic; the suit closes itself and the internal sensors and fluid tubes are painlessly inserted into the body "so you felt only a slight puzzling dislocation."[10] If an arm or leg is severely damaged, "one of sixteen razor-sharp irises closes around your limb with the force of a hydraulic press, snipping it off neatly and sealing the suit before you can die of explosive decompression. Then 'trauma maintenance' cauterizes the stump, replaces lost blood, and fills you full of happy juice or No-shock."[11] If a soldier is picked up after this injury (if his side wins), he can grow a new limb through a routine, if painful, process.

To use these suits and other weapons—such as sticks, wire, infantry rockets, gas, poison, bayonets, infantry rifles, and grenades—the soldiers receive extensive training in "everything from bare hands to simulated nuclear weapons."[12] Mandella is not given the total training program until he decides to become an officer; then he is attached to an "accelerated life simulation computer" (ALSC) where he goes through several lifetimes of weapons practice, learning physically as well as intellectually "the best way to use every weapon from a rock to a nova bomb."[13]

Psychological conditioning is extended to include posthypnotic suggestion. Heinlein's troopers are "professionals, with *esprit de corps*," but the spirit is reinforced by injections and hypnotic preparation, which, theoretically, render them fearless.[14] Mandella's conditioning has changed him from a "peace-loving, vacuum-welding specialist *cum* physics teacher" into an Elite Conscript "reprogrammed to be a killing machine."[15] His subconscious presents him in a dream as a kind of robot, "mimicking the functions of life" and operated by a little man who is "hopelessly mad."[16]

In the early years of the Forever War, posthypnotic suggestion is tried but fails. During the first encounter with aliens, Mandella joins in the massacre, responding mostly to implanted "pseudo-memories" which activate deep within him "something . . . thirsting for alien blood."[17] But the guilt after the battle causes complications so severe that the hypnosis is discontinued.[18] The decision to discontinue hypnosis stems not from incompetence in behavioral control or from bureaucratic morality but from the fact that, as Colonel Kynock points out, "Robots don't make good soldiers."[19]

Although the hardware and the training are similar in the two books, the uses to which they're put vary because the attitudes expressed toward soldiers and military life are radically different. In Heinlein's book, service veterans rule, and military virtues provide the ethical norm. The soldier's business is to follow orders and supply the "*controlled* violence" necessary "to support your government's decisions by force. . . . Which is as it should be." Survival of the fittest in military combat is the universe's only measure for fitness to survive.[20] In Haldeman's book, on the other hand, the attitude toward the military is far more ambivalent, more negative: Mandella does what he must to survive, and he questions little because he has no time. At the end of the novel, however, he finds out with some disgust that the military had "armed the colonizing vessels, and the first time they met a Tauran ship, they blasted it. They dusted off their medals and the rest was going to be history."[21]

The attitudes toward women and the family vary also. Sexuality remains at an adolescent level in Heinlein's account, for Rico sees the opposite sex only between combat missions or at dinner; women are clearly subordinate to fighting, and he forms no lasting relationship with anybody but men. Haldeman's women, however, are warriors like the men, and sex is, by law, communal. But when Mandella returns from his second mission, Earth's society has become officially and overwhelmingly homosexual, "except for a thousand or so; veterans and incurables."[22] At the end of the novel Mandella retreats to "a planet they call Middle Finger . . . a kind of Coventry for heterosexuals."[23] The symbolism is typical of the dry humor in the novel. Family connections in Starship Troopers are subordinated to military goals; after Johnnie Rico's stereotyped, overprotective mother is killed in a raid on Buenos Aires, his father joins the MI and eventually becomes a sergeant in the unit commanded by his son. This situation leads to some maudlin exchanges of father-son camaraderie that add touches of what seems to be unintentional humor to at least one otherwise earnest scene.[24] In The Forever War, part of Mandella's increasing irritation with the system grows from the loss of his mother, who has been excluded from medical treatment. He is also hurt and angered by the isolation of his brother on the moon, the loss of most of his friends because of the time period he has lived through, and the separation from the woman he has fought beside and loves. For Mandella, a family becomes something to begin after the chaos and separations of the war are over.

The views of the two novels are succinctly contrasted by their depiction of the planet of rest and rehabilitation, called Sanctuary in Starship Troopers and Heaven in The Forever War. Sanctuary does not receive as much natural radiation as Earth and, consequently, has a very low mutation rate among its native species; hence, the native forms of life on the planet have not evolved much and are easily "outclassed" by species introduced from planets "enjoying high radiation and fierce competition." Heinlein uses Sanctuary to demonstrate the superiority of the pseudo-Darwinian philosophy of competition that permeates the novel: the universe exists to be grabbed from "primitive life forms that failed to make the grade."[25]

Haldeman's Heaven is lovely and unspoiled: "what Earth might have been if men had treated her with compassion instead of lust."[26] The Darwinian capitalism of Heinlein, however, has reached Heaven, for the government's way of putting the wounded soldiers' "accumulated pay back into the economic mainstream" is to charge a hundred dollars for a snack and a thousand per night for a room.[27] At the end of the novel the planet has been taken over by Man, the "Kahn-clones" that rule Earth.

The views of humankind and aliens are the greatest differences between the two novels. For Heinlein, man is "a wild animal with the will to survive," and legitimate moral codes must be based on what human nature *is*—"not what do-gooders and well-meaning old Aunt Nellies would like [it] to be." In Heinlein's *Puppet Masters* those "old Aunt Nellies" include the Prophet Isaiah, with his "do-gooder" ideas on beating swords into plowshares. Survival and expansion are the proper goals for a species in Heinlein's universe, and whether or not our galactic imperialism is "right" will be determined by whether or not we have the weapons and the will to succeed at it.[28] Opposing the expansion in *Troopers* are "arthropods who happen to look like a madman's conception of a giant, intelligent spider, but their organization, psychological and economic, is more like that of ants or termites; they are communal entities, the ultimate dictatorship of the hive."[29] As such, they are anathema to Rico and his friends, for they demonstrate "just how efficient a total communism can be when used by a people actually adapted to it by evolution."[30] Mandella has no such clear-cut view of the place of man, and the war ends only because man has evolved enough to contact the Taurans he has been fighting, evolved into exactly the kind of entity that Johnnie Rico hates. Mandella is welcomed back to Stargate by "clones of a single individual. . . . over ten billion individuals but only one consciousness." The Taurans could not communicate with man because they had evolved as "natural clones" with no concept for individuality; only when "Earth's cruisers were manned by Man, Kahn-clones," was communication possible. Although Mandella is told he will never be able to understand "clone-to-clone communication," he doesn't care: "It sounded a little fishy, but I was willing to accept it. I'd accept that up was down if it meant the war was over."[31]

The endings of the two novels characterize their different emphases. In the last pages of *Starship Troopers* Johnnie Rico leads his men and his father in the final attack on Klendathu, the home planet of the Bugs; *The Forever War* concludes with a newspaper announcement of the birth of Mandella's son.

THE DEVELOPMENT OF THE FIGHTING SUIT

Because man's connections with the combat suits described by Heinlein and Haldeman are literally more intimate than with most of his other weapons, he therefore feels positive or, at worst, neutral toward them: they are an extension of himself. But as these suits undergo permutations into the tank and the humanoid robot, his emotions sometimes change to fear and hate.

Tanks

Tanks are fascinating. Their power and mobility, their relative invincibility, and their potential for destruction have made them exciting subjects in novels, films, and, as any wargamer will verify, in combat simulation. One of the earlier variations of the tank in science fiction, one which still exemplifies the characteristics of the survival suit combined with fighting equipment, is the attack machine used by the Martians in H. G. Wells's *War of the Worlds*. Without their machines the Martians "heaved and pulsated convulsively" against the Earth's gravity and pressures,[32] but later, inside their tripods, they stride along the heath, smashing pine trees and knocking people against the tree trunks. The Martian sits in a "brazen hood" atop a tripod like "a milking stool tilted and bowled violently along the ground." The machine has "long, flexible, glittering tentacles . . . swinging and rattling about its strange body,"[33] and for additional weapons the Martians resort to a heat ray and poison gas. Symbolizing to its Victorian audience the apocalyptic end of the world by fire, the heat ray comes out of the funnel of "a complicated metallic case, about which green flashes scintillated,"[34] and the poison gas is fired from gunlike tubes in canisters that smash on striking the ground and discharge "an enormous volume of heavy, inky vapor, coiling and pouring upward in a huge and ebony cumulus cloud. . . ."[35]

When the novel was adapted to film by producer George Pal, several changes were made in the Martian fighting machines and weapons, some because of budget, some as other concessions to Paramount's front office.[36] The tripods were replaced by flyers shaped like manta rays and equipped with devices that affected the Earth's magnetic field and counteracted gravity; the heat ray was retained, and a green disintegrator ray capable of reducing a machine or man to a black outline was added; the poison gas, now outdated by World War I, was dropped. The triad of the original machine shows up, however, in the three-fingered hands of the Martians and the triple lens of the alien eye. As in the original novel, the Martians are depicted as weak creatures who can function effectively on Earth only inside their machines and who are no match for an ax-wielding Gene Barry. Updated to the fifties and capitalizing on the flying saucer scares of that time, *The War of the Worlds* succeeds primarily because of the still-impressive special effects and sequences featuring the Martians' combat hardware in action.

Other science fiction films, unfortunately, demonstrated few advances in weapons technology beyond the pattern set up by *The War of the Worlds*. In the many film variations on invasions from outer space, such as *This Island Earth*, *The Thing*, *It Came from Outer Space*, *The Mysterians*, and *Earth vs. the Flying Saucers*, the equipment and action are standard. The aliens have mysterious weapons, predictably some sort of ray, and a superior technology; but Earth people—because of pluck, determination, technological innovation, a homeland to defend, or just plain luck—always succeed in routing the invaders. *Earth vs. the Flying Saucers*, somewhat distinguished by Ray Harryhausen's special effects, typifies the standard version of humanoid saucermen invading with flying machines that shoot disintegrator rays.

For breakthroughs in cinematic science fiction weaponry, audiences had to wait for the first *Star Wars* film (now to be titled *A New Hope*) and its sequel, *The Empire Strikes Back*. The light sabers, laser guns, X- and Y-wing fighters, and other weaponry are all too well known to need further discussion. Interesting, however, is the way the weaponry fits into the dual structure of the first two films, which consistently have grouped into a pair two items with opposing characteristics: the tall, slender, multilingual C3PO balances the short, thick, unintelligible (at least to the audience) R2D2; Luke Skywalker and Han Solo vie for Princess Leia's attention; Ben Kenobi and Darth Vader represent opposite developments of the Jedi Knights, corresponding to the light and dark sides of the Force; the desert planet at the beginning of A New Hope is balanced by the jungle planet at the end; the snow planet at the beginning of Empire balances Sky City; and, in yet another contrast, the dead asteroid where Han and Leia take refuge is alternated in Empire with the fecund swamp world of Yoda and Luke. Similarly, the weapons often form opposing patterns. The artificial, mechanical Death Star is contrasted with the green living planet Alderaan which it destroys, and with the Earth-like planet at the end which forms the base for the attack that destroys this artificial satellite. The Death Star and Darth Vader are both deadly mechanical parodies of life, machines given over to demonic possession. Similarly, the Imperial Probedroid provides, from one angle, an opposition to the life-saving medical droid FX-7, and, from another, as it gathers information and defends itself, a balance to Chewbacca as he searches Sky City for C3PO. The Imperial Walkers, however, form the most demonic parody; for their mechanical and rigid imitation of an elephant's walk sums up all the destructive rigidity of Darth Vader and the Empire, whose Storm Troopers and other minions are grotesque parodies of the exuberant life demonstrated by the rebels.

Totally different from the blazing laser rifles and explosions of Star Wars is the unique fighting machine in Ben Bova's Dueling Machine, which was planned not to extend man's aggressive abilities, but to channel them into harmless imitation violence.[37] The two people involved in a duel enter the machine and are mentally projected to a totally imaginary environment where a simulated duel is fought. If both combatants survive the first encounter, then a second round is fought in a situation specified by the challenger. The machine automatically stops the illusion when one person vicariously experiences death or emotional overload. Although the machine can lead at worst only to dishonor, men fear it; and the plot of the novel turns upon the ability of one telepathic protagonist, Odal, to cause actual physical damage— stroke or heart attack—to his opponents. A further frightening discovery is that the machine can expose men's minds to each other with an intimacy never before achieved.[38] The novel concludes with the further discovery that the machine is capable, with the right telepathic operators, of instantaneously transferring matter between any two machines, and a new method of interstellar travel is born.

The dueling machine, while a unique concept in fighting machines, is not really a tank variation, but Keith Laumer's collection of six short stories, Bolo:

The Annals of the Dinochrome Brigade, presents the tank as a central figure, growing from programmed servant to independent master.[39] Tracing the history of the Bolos, the stories are linked by common themes: war as an outdated activity, the inevitable evolution of the cybernetic brain, and man's increasing fear of artificial intelligence.

In every story but one, the Bolo is a relic of a past era, usually damaged and operating at a fraction of its previous power. In "The Night of the Trolls," the machines, neglected for almost eighty years, are out of ammunition and only partially functional, but men still fight to the death to control them; in the second story, the Bolo is a "museum piece" and "an old time fightin' machine."[40] In the last three stories the archaic quality is more poignant, for the point of view is from inside the computer centers where the personality of the machine is housed; perceiving through the Bolo's electronic senses, we share its view of itself as an anachronism, like the gunfighter pushed westward by the advancing homesteaders, displaced but still dangerous. In "The Last Command," for example, a radioactive Bolo Mark XXVIII, jarred back to life by excavation blasting, creaks out of a ten-foot-thick shell of reinforced concrete in the mass grave in which it was buried and plows to the surface to menace a town which it perceives as the enemy. In "War Relic," a Bolo Mark XXV which has served as a war monument in a small town on an isolated planet suddenly comes to life after years of inaction when it senses an invader. In the last story, "Combat Unit," a Bolo Mark XXXI is inadvertently reactivated by the aliens he has been programmed to destroy and proceeds to carry out his original mission; only later does he realize that most of the civilization he was created to defend is now gone.

A second major theme is the gradual growth of artificial intelligence in the series. Although the Bolos in the first two stories can be set "to perform a number of preset routine functions such as patrol duty with no crew aboard,"[41] the Mark XX is the first to achieve self-awareness and self-direction. Its ability to make tactical decisions while operating under a general strategic program leads it to continue fighting and advancing "*for the honor of the regiment*" after it should have retreated.[42] As their intelligence grows, the units begin receiving human names based on their model initials, so the Mark XX DNE described above becomes "Denny."

Bobby, the Bolo of "War Relic," is human enough to have a dual personality: to the townspeople who joke with him, he says, "I am a good boy"; but when he senses an enemy machine, he becomes "*Unit Nine Five Four of the Line, reporting contact with hostile force*."[43] Bobby is also the most poignant of the Bolos, for he realizes, "*my usefulness as an engine of war is ended*" and accepts his demise.[44]

The most intelligent Bolo is the Mark XXXI of "Combat Unit." At the end of the story, after wiping out the aliens, he settles down to await the arrival of reinforcements in "47,128 standard years," and he welcomes "this opportunity to investigate fully a number of problems that have excited my curiosity circuits": he believes that the natures of time, of entropy, "of such biological oddities as 'death' and of the unused capabilities of the protoplasmic nervous system should afford some interesting speculation."[45]

The relationship between the Bolos and the men who build and operate them varies with the Bolos' growing intelligence. In the early stories, when men still ride in the Bolos, the machines seem to be little more than extravagant tanks, yet the language used to describe them implies that the relationship is more than just that between man and machine: "robot watchdog"; "an ill-tempered dinosaur"; "the Bolo heaved around and moved off"; "it's getting a little old and can't see as well as it used to."[46]

Denny, the Bolo in "Field Test," wants to prove itself and its new intelligence, but six-star-general Margrave opposes it because of his "distrust of a killer machine not susceptible to normal command functions."[47] Although Denny proves his merit, Lenny in the next story is unable to distinguish friend from foe, and a local town is saved only by the intervention of Sanders, his former commander, whom Lenny recognizes when he studies Sanders' face, as he says, "*through the pain of my great effort*."[48] The old man, dying of age and radiation sickness from the glowing tank, lies across the lower gun deck and whispers, "it's a long way, Lenny. . . . But I'm coming with you," as, "ponderously, like a great mortally striken animal, the Bolo moved through the ruins of the fallen roadway, heading for the open desert."[49]

The mutual respect of man and machine is evident also in the end of "War Relic" when Crewe acknowledges that the machine could trample him and thus save itself, but it replies, "*Better that I cease now, at the hands of a friend*."[50] After punching the key that deactivates the Bolo's computer center, Crewe salutes it and walks away in the moonlight.

Though no humans appear in "Combat Unit," the Bolo still considers itself a servant of its human creators. War and stalemate for two centuries have reduced human civilization "to a preatomic technological level in almost every respect."[51] The Bolos in their mechanical and intellectual complexity are beyond the levels of their makers; the last page of the story indicates that even the nontechnological aspects of human culture now repose entirely in the memory banks of a Bolo who plans "to examine all of the music in existence, and to investigate my literary archives which are complete. . . . I should have some interesting conclusions to communicate to my human superiors, when the time comes."[52] Paradoxically, this mightiest of man's war machines now finds itself "at peace."

Anthropomorphic Robots

The fighting suit has developed (logically, not chronologically) in one direction into the tank; along another route, the fighting suit "evolves" into a different kind of machine. The hero steps out of his suit, the suit continues alone, and the anthropomorphic robot is born. In man's confrontations with his steel-sinewed, chromeplated doppelganger, he is both attracted and repelled; and he is uncertain how to react to his mechanical effigy. The robot in Isaac Asimov's *Caves of Steel* and its sequel, *The Naked Sun*, even when bound by the Three Laws of Robotics is looked upon with suspicion by the men who live underground, despite his acceptance by the men who live in space.[53] Harry Harrison's "The Velvet Glove" describes the hatred and mob action encountered by an ordinary robot when he accidentally collides with a human being;[54] later, this same robot is subjected to a stream of abuse from his employer.[55] The robot, through careful planning, manages to corner and subdue the criminals he encounters without breaking his conditioning laws. A subplot introduces a civil rights movement when a truck driver slips the robot a copy of "*Robot Slaves in a World Economy* by Philpott Asimov II" with a card that designates a meeting place and concludes, "Please destroy this card after reading."[56]

While these metal men were restrained by law from harming humans, other anthropomorphic robots, specifically designed for violence, have no such restrictions. Gort, the giant robot of Robert Wise's *Day the Earth Stood Still*, is so powerful that "there's no limit to what he could do. He could destroy the earth."[57] Gort is essentially a fighting machine designed and created by Klaatu's race to keep the peace: "In matters of aggression we have given them absolute power over us."[58] The heat ray that is Gort's major weapon is reminiscent of those in *The War of the Worlds*, and it burns through walls, melts the superplastic in which Gort is encased by the army, and turns tanks and antiaircraft guns into pools of molten metal. The promotional art and photographs as well as the poster for the film present Gort as a dangerous killer attacking a screaming Patricia Neal; although somewhat misleading, these promotions primed audiences to see Gort as the villain, not the quasi hero of the film who brings Klaatu back to life and declines to destroy the Earth after hearing Patricia Neal's famous speech, "Klaatu barada nikto." Yet Klaatu reminds the audience at the end of the film that Gort and his fellow policemen "at the first sign of violence . . . act automatically against the aggressor. And the penalty for provoking their action is too terrible to risk."[59] Gort's relationship with mankind is that of a powerful, confident policeman dealing with a cocky street punk.

Perhaps because the human form is not especially effective in combat, or because of Asimov's Three Laws of Robotics, the anthropomorphic fighting machine is not as common as one might expect.[60] He appears in some movie serials, such as *The Phantom Creeps*, and in extremely minor films, such as *Robot Monster* and *Santa Claus Conquers the Martians*, which are best left gathering dust in the studio vaults. With the exception of Box, the half-man, half-robot of *Logan's Run*, and the Cylons of television's "Battlestar Galactica," the robot with a human shape appears hardly at all in contemporary film and fiction as a menacing fighting machine.

More fertile has been the genre in which a basically peaceful robot exercises combat potential. In *Forbidden Planet* Robbie incapacitates his attackers' weapons with rays and demonstrates his other capabilities but does not engage in combat. Much more directly menacing are the robots in *Westworld*; Yul Brynner, the neurotic robot gunfighter, stalks his prey through the Western town and underground tunnels of the futuristic playground until his heat-sensing eyes are deceived by a torch and he is destroyed. The robots in the sequel *Futureworld* are simply replacements of humans, and the terror of this film is one of loss of identity like that of *Invasion of the Bodysnatchers* rather than fear of physical destruction, as in *The Day the Earth Stood Still*. Kirk Douglas's robotic sexual doppelgänger in *Saturn 3* is, like HAL 9000, a computer into which man programs his irrational nature, and the creation becomes violent.

The most interesting recent variation has been the supposedly organic alien of *Alien* (1978), who, with his exoskeleton's visible joints, his "teeth made out of polished steel for maximum reflectivity," and his "alien flesh with its characteristic hue of metallic grey" often appeared more robotic than organic. This "cold, vicious, nearly indestructible killer,"[61] despite his phallic head, possessed an inhuman mechanical quality that added to the impression of terror he produced.

THE MACHINE FIGHTS ALONE

The fear that General Margrave felt facing the Bolo Mark XX was a fear of its intelligence, for if the machine could think, then it could turn against men and destroy them, even as HAL 9000 kills all of the *Discovery*'s crew except Dave Bowman in *2001*. Two less well known examples of even more deadly fighting machines with which man has had to deal appear in a 1920 novel by Abraham Merritt and in Fred Saberhagen's berserker series.

One of the earliest examples of a machine with intelligence that acts independently and, ultimately, threatens man appears in Merritt's *The Metal Monster*.[62] This alien creature—made up of combinations of metal pyramids, spheres, and cubes—is, strictly speaking, not a machine but a living metal entity. Its immense power comes from its ability to construct a new form to meet any situation that arises. The relationships between this metal creature and the characters of the novel vary extensively from open alliance to open hostility, with its strongest attachment to the beautiful Norhala, who has taken on many of its inhuman characteristics. The travelers who intrude into her kingdom are also affected by the mechanical being and begin to experience the harmonies of the geometric consciousness. But the sharing of perspectives is a two-way affair, and the creature begins to pick up human characteristics:

The magnetic currents which are the nerve force of this globe of ours were what fed the Metal Things. Within these currents is the spirit of earth. And always they have been supercharged with strife, with hatreds, warfare. Were these drawn in by the Things as they fed? Did it happen that the Keeper became—*tuned*—to them? That it absorbed and responded to them . . . until it reflected humanity?[63]

In the subsequent revolt of the Keeper against the Emperor, the Keeper himself, the creatures, Norhala, and the living city are destroyed. As Wells's Martians were overcome by "the putrefactive and disease bacteria" to which humans were immune, so this invader was destroyed by the negative emotions that are an accepted part of human life.

Berserkers

When Martin Ventnor in *The Metal Monster* is stunned by the blast of lightning, he babbles in delirium of "the eternal forces man's instinct has always warned him are ever in readiness to destroy. . . . the eternal, ruthless law that will annihilate humanity the instant it runs counter to that law and turns its will and strength against itself."[64] These ruthless forces that attack men whenever they waste their energy fighting each other manifest themselves as giant killer machines, berserkers, in Fred Saberhagen's collections of short stories and novels; and while Merritt's Metal Monster threatens the travelers and destroys a city, the berserkers destroy planets and threaten all life in the universe. The berserker chronicle begins with "Fortress Ship" (later retitled "Without a Thought") in 1963, runs through nineteen additional stories of varying length, and includes three novels. The berserkers are fighting machines freed of their creators:

[T]hey were an armada of robot spaceships and supporting devices built by some unknown and long-vanished race to fight in some interstellar war that had reached its forgotten conclusion while men on Earth were wielding spears against the sabertooth tiger. Though the war for which the berserker machines had been made was long over, still they fought on across the galaxy, replicating and repairing themselves endlessly, learning new strategies and tactics, refining their weapons. . . . The sole known basic in their fundamental programming was the destruction of all life, wherever and whenever they could find it.[65]

The creators of the berserkers never appear in the stories but are seen only as a projected image of "a slender, fine-boned being, topographically like a man except for the single eye that stretched across his face. . . ." The voice associated with the image is "like a high-pitched torrent of clicks and whines."[66]

Encompassing most variations of the fighting machine, the berserkers range in size and power from enormous to quite small. The first berserker to appear in print was "an ancient ruin of metal, not much smaller in cross section than New Jersey. Men had blown holes in it the size of Manhattan Island, and melted puddles of slag as big as lakes upon its surfaces. But the berserker's power was still enormous."[67] Most of the machines are giant spheres, the one in "Mr. Jester" being some forty miles in diameter, and the Death Star in *Star Wars* seems to have been influenced by these large berserkers, for, like it, they are huge spheres equipped, in several of the berserker stories, with tractor beams; filled with smaller robots and captured people; and armed with enormous firepower. The berserkers are dedicated to death (one is referred to as Lord Death in *Berserker's Planet*), and the Death Star, as its name implies, is similarly devoted to planetary destruction. Even the demise of the Death Star is similar to that of the berserker in "Mr. Jester" or the one in "Sign of the Wolf": a flash of fiery destruction in brilliant color that slowly dissipates against the heavens.[68]

Some of the berserkers, while smaller than these forty-mile-diameter spheres, are still larger and stronger than men. When a human ship commanded by Johann Karlsen rams a berserker and is locked with it, the enemy "forced through the flagship's hull a kind of torpedo, an infernal machine that seemed to know how the ship was designed, a moving atomic pile that had burned its way through the High Commander's quarters and almost to the bridge before it could be stopped and quenched."[69] One variation of the smaller machines, which appeared in "The Annihilation of Angkor Apeiron," looks like a cross between a centipede and a crab and is capable of crushing men in its claws; a similar creature attacks Mitch Spain in "Stone Place," and crushes his left arm with its "bright pinchers." The insectlike quality of these berserkers is similar to that of a berserker found by Georgicus Sabel in the ruins of Dradan, "partially entombed, caught like some giant mechanical insect in opaque amber."[70] In *Brother Assassin* the berserkers are more animallike: one a huge dragon, one a "stone lion," and one a man-sized creature that is mistaken for a wolf. Most ingenious of the berserker variations is one created from spare berserker parts by the sculptor Antonio Nobrega in "The Smile," a tall, roughly humanoid machine activated to kill by the voice of its victim and destroyed finally by a bolt of artificial lightning that shatters its ceramic exterior.

Other berserker machines, while smaller than men, are equally deadly, such as the mobile "massive chain" and the "metallic butterfly" that attack Mitch Spain.[71] The most frightening of these smaller monsters are the creatures in "Smasher." Each is "a brownish thing the size of a small plate,"[72] which was built for war on the aquatic planet Atlantis but crashlanded instead on the desert planet of Waterfall; their pinchers, "like a pair of ceramic pliers," can cut a shark to shreds, but they are finally destroyed by the shrimplike creatures of the story's title, which strike with such power and precision that they fracture the berserkers' ceramic shells.

Between these two extremes of size are the berserker robots that are humanoid in size and appearance. In "The Game" Adrienne Britton meets "the silent speed-blurred rush of something vaguely manlike in size and shape, but embodying a flow of metal and power that could not possibly be human" and finds that she is paralyzed from the effects of a "small metal leech" that is attached to each of her limbs. This creature utilizes powerful and instantly absorbed "nerve acid" that "has affinity for living tissues of the sensory system" and brings pain beyond any imagining. Interrupted in its interrogation of Adrienne, the berserker sprouted in defense "small projections like gun-muzzles . . . upon its chest and shoulders, and it poised like a praying mantis, ready to strike with arms of steel." The creature is destroyed by a new side arm with a kinetic sensor "set to trigger at anything moving extraordinarily fast—like a berserker's grabbing arm. Whammo, locks on target and keeps firing until the operator turns it off."[73]

Almost human in its pride and curiosity is the "roughly man-shaped machine" that had "what might be a speaker mounted on what might be a face." Through this anthropomorphic boarding machine the main berserker speaks to Piers Herron, the painter who is the only survivor of the attack on the *Frans Hals*, a traveling art-gallery spaceship, and evaluates him with the lenses in which there are "tiny flickerings, keeping time with his own pulse and breathing, like the indications of a lie detector."[74]

The most powerful of the humanoids is the god Thorun in Saberhagen's *Berserker's Planet*, a robot directed by a solid-state electronuclear device that once was part of a berserker's brain:

So huge was he that, even though seated, his eyes were on a level with those of the tall priest standing before him. Thorun's head of wild dark hair was bound by a golden band, his fur cloak hung about his mountainous shoulders. His famed sword, so large that no man could wield it, was girdled to his waist. His huge right hand, concealed as always in a leather glove, rested on the table and held a massive goblet. Seen in the dim light, Thorun's face above his full dark beard might have been judged human—except that it was too immobile and too large.[75]

A companion monster robot, identified by the villagers as the demigod Mjollnir, is destroyed by Carlos Suomi, and Thorun himself is defeated in combat with Thomas the Grabber and Giles the Treacherous.

The problem of creating credible imitations of life hampers the berserkers throughout their conflict with man: "the berserkers have never, anywhere, been able to fabricate an android that could pass in human society as a normal person."[76] In "The Masque of the Red Shift," Saberhagen's variation on Poe, the "strange man" who enters the "interrogation chamber" is not a man at all "but some creation of the berserker. . . . There was no gross flaw in it, but a ship camouflaged with the greatest skill looks like nothing so much as a ship that has been camouflaged. . . . Its speech alone would have given it away. . . ."[77] Failing to create a plausible android, the berserker takes the captured and brainwashed outlaw Janda and modifies him extensively for his role in observation and destruction aboard Felipe Nogara's flagship: "what was bone in this life-unit is now metal. . . . where blood flowed, now preservatives are pumped." Inside the skull is "a computer, and in the eyes are

cameras. . . . To match the behavior of a brainwashed man is within"
berserker capability.[78] In this 1965 story Saberhagen sets up the synthesis
between man and machine (here the machine hidden inside the man) that he
was to consider again in *Brother Assassin*, in which "the most complex and
compact machine the berserkers ever built, driven up through twenty thousand years of evolutionary gradient"[79] acquires a kind of organic life. The
theme reaches its climax in the 1979 *Berserker Man*, in which Frank Marcus is
the man hidden inside his artificial form of three boxes connected by cables (a
human parody of the berserker in *Berserker's Planet*), and his son Michel
Geulincx successfully becomes one entity with his fighting machine, Lancelot,
and evolves to a new life form.

The berserkers, despite their intelligence, cunning, and ruthlessness, are
not complex personalities. For a berserker, "to serve the cause of what men
call death is good."[80] Its attitude toward life is that "all life thinks it is, but it is
not. There are only particles, energy and space, and the laws of the
machines."[81] All changes that occur in berserker tactics are slow.[82] Berserkers
are curious only about ways of opposing life, and they experiment on human
subjects to determine their weaknesses in several stories; for example, in
"Starsong," the liberators find in a captured berserker laboratory called Hell
"odd organs that functioned in a sort-of-way, interconnected with the nonhuman and the non-alive."[83]

The berserkers being, as Sandra Miesel points out, a force of evil that works
to man's good, they sometimes parody man's worst actions in ways that make
men repudiate these traits.[84] Piers Herron, the painter, calls the population of
Earth "only a swarm of animals, breeding and dying, fighting—" before his
encounter with the berserkers, but afterward, he aligns himself with the
human race, saying, "I'll show you. . . . I can change. I am alive."[85] The
tournament in which sixty-four warriors systematically kill each other is an
obscene fulfillment of the berserker's main goal, but at the end of the tournament, the two survivors, now aware of how they have been duped, turn their
weapons against the berserkers and destroy them.

The berserker threat affects people in radically different ways. Overall, it
serves to unite mankind against a common foe, as, for example, when
Johann Karlsen creates an alliance among the Venerians, the Esteelers, and
other races and nationalities before the battle at the Stone Place. The attack
also unites man with other forms of life in the battle against death. An *aiyan*,
an animal resembling a large dog with an ape's forelegs, helps defeat the berserker in "Without a Thought"; small, shrimplike stomatopods destroy the
berserkers in "Smasher"; gourds expand to split the control panels in "Pressure"; and synthetic personalities based on long-dead humans pilot spacecraft
to destroy the machines in "Wings out of Shadows." Individual men vary in
their response to the threat of the machines. For some, like Admiral Hemphill, the destruction of the berserkers is an obsession; for others, like the
"goodlife" creatures, the invaders are to be supported, worked with, and,

sometimes, worshipped, as the priests of *Berserker's Planet* bow down before the mechanistic image of Death. The conflicting feelings felt by many men are exemplified in the story, "What T and I Did." In this story, a brain injury requires that a doctor divide the main character's brain and optic nerve; as a result, half of him is a vicious traitor to the human cause (referred to as T, since he will accept no human name, but paralleled in the story with Judas Iscariot) and the other half is a kind and gentle person who helps deceive the killer machines (he is named Thaddeus after Jude Thaddeus, a contemporary of Iscariot).

The reactions of different men in different ways are confusing to the machines. Human emotions give man an edge in the battle, making him unpredictable, just as the berserkers' randomly decaying isotopes made them unpredictable to man, and, throughout the conflict, the berserkers are never able to grasp the human mind or emotions. Although they had tried to incorporate human brains into their own circuitry, they never succeeded and apparently "stood in their computer-analogue of awe as they regarded the memory-capacity and decision-making power that nature in a few billion years of evolution had managed to pack into the few hundred cubic centimeters of the human nervous system."[86] Particularly baffling, and therefore most dangerous to the berserkers, are the men who follow not logic but their intuition or some nonrational guide, such as Johann Karlsen.

The behavior of these leading units often resisted analysis, as if some quality of the life-disease in them was forever beyond the reach of machines. These individuals used logic, but sometimes it seemed they were not bound by logic. The most dangerous life-units of all sometimes acted in ways that seemed to contradict the known supremacy of the laws of physics and chance, as if they could be minds possessed of true free will, instead of its illusion.[87]

This difference appears at the end of *Berserker Man*: the Director, the largest berserker Michel has ever seen and in one sense his father, realizes, as Michel and it approach the "Taj," that it has come to the limits of machine intelligence, for it asks Michel to interpret for it. Unanswered, it asks further, "Is this the God of humanity that lies before us? Never have I been able to come this far." Finally it notes, "I compute an imperfection there. It is not finished. Either you or I must . . ." but then the Director breaks down. "'I no longer compute properly . . . I no longer,' it said. Again it came to a complete stop. And that was all."[88] And Michel passes the machine to complete the pattern of the Taj with life, not the death embodied by the machine.

Man's nonlogical thought and his emotions are two of his strongest allies in the war against the machines. As the Carmpan historian, whose narrative links the short story collections, points out, man's "very readiness for violence that had sometimes so nearly destroyed you, proved to be the means of life's survival."[89] Such violence, most apparent in the armed conflicts, appears in more devious ways in some of the stories. In "The Peacemaker," Carr gives cells from his own cancer to keep the berserker occupied until reinforcements arrive; ironically, the berserker, thinking it is killing life, exposes Carr to something that will kill the cells it has been given. Since these cells are cancerous, the death brought by the berserker kills the cancer, and Carr begins to improve. A desire for violence leads to death for the berserker in "Sign of the Wolf," for the young shepherd's desire to kill the wolf attacking his flock is interpreted by the long forgotten planetary defense control as orders to activate the weapons and kill the berserker.

While man's violence may ultimately save him, the many forms of love, the most powerful emotion, also lead to destruction for the berserkers. Love between parent and child is the theme of "Goodlife," where the main character finds his father's body wedged near the control center of the berserker and realizes the berserker has lied to him: "Goodlife heard his own voice keening, without words, and he could not see plainly for the tears floating in his helmet,"[90] but he takes the bomb from his father's body and destroys the control center of the berserker and himself as well. In *Berserker Man* the parent-child relationship is a major theme. Michel has a biological mother, Elly Temesvar, and an adopted goodlife mother, Carmen Geulincx; he has a biological father, Frank Marcus, and an adopted goodlife father, Sixtus Geulincx; and he refers to the berserker Director as "Father" several times. Each of these relations complicates his emotional makeup, making him even more unpredictable than usual, but his last act before entering the Taj and achieving divinity is to release his mother Elly from the interior of the berserker and place her safely inside the *Johann Karlsen*.

Love between men and women also baffles the berserkers and leads to their destruction. Henri's attempt to teach Winifred a mnemonic system for remembering the order of spectral types helps Captain Liao decide which of the fleeing ships is a berserker in "Inhuman Error." In "Sign of the Wolf," Duncan's love and fear for Colleen leads to the command to destroy the wolf.[91] The ability of human love to transcend hate is the major theme of "In the Temple of Mars," a story that freely adapts its temples of Mars and Venus from Chaucer's "Knight's Tale." The hero Jor has been conditioned to kill Admiral Hemphill—"they flick a switch somewhere, and I start to kill, like a berserker"—but the goodlife faction has not counted on Jor's falling in love with Lucinda and defeating their conditioning: "He came above his red rage like a swimmer surfacing, lungs bursting, from a drowning sea. He looked down at his hands to the gun they held. He forced his fingers to begin opening. Mars still shouted at him, louder and louder, but Venus' power grew stronger still. His hands opened and the weapon fell."[92] Jor releases the other prisoners, and the berserker allies are exterminated within the temple of Mars.

At times, love becomes such a major theme that the berserker conflict retreats into the background, using its trappings only to add a more contemporary setting to the pattern of myth, as in "Starsong," where elements of rock-star idolatry, the Orpheus myth, and the berserker concept unite to form a moving account of the love of Ordell Callison for Eury. The story maintains most of the elements of the myth and concludes with Eury and Ordell trapped in the berserker's experimental world, which men call Hell.

The power of love, although it is a major strand in the stories, is subordinated to the conflict between good and evil, life and death, order and chaos, which form the dominant theme; and since this conflict is essentially religious, it is not surprising to find religious settings, imagery, and themes in many of the stories. Such references are often slight, such as the names of Felipe Nogara's flagships, Nirvana and Nirvana II; the reference to Judas Iscariot to parallel the traitor who collaborates with the berserkers in "What T and I Did"; or the reference in the same story to a quotation in "some ancient Believers' book to the effect that an offending eye should be plucked out."[93] In addition to such references, the settings or plot structures of several of the stories draw upon standard patterns of religious behavior. In "Sign of the Wolf," Duncan, who hopes to become a priest, prays to the sky-gods, "Send me a sign"; after he is visited by a brown-robed priest riding a donkey, he goes into the caves of metal and mistakes the voices of the planet's defenses for the voices of the earth-gods. Falling on his knees before "the metal thing that bellowed," he sees "In front of the god-shape lay woven twigs and egg-shells, very old. Once priests had sacrificed here, and then they had forgotten this god."[94] Duncan believes that he is to be granted one wish by the god; and when he wishes for the "killer" to be destroyed, he inadvertantly activates the buried weapons which proceed to exterminate the berserker as he, returning to the surface, clubs the wolf to death and thus fulfills his wish as well as saves the planet.

The worship of Mars, god of war, and its opposition, the worship of Venus, goddess of love, form the opposing religious concepts in the story, "In the Temple of Mars." Jor's love for Lucinda enables him to overcome the ray from the temple of Mars, and the story ends with a quotation from Chaucer on the power of the goddess of love: "Venus smiled, half-risen from her glittering waves."[95]

"Starsong," with its background of the Orpheus legend, emphasizes the divine quality of the music of Ordell.[96] His music charms the half-man, half-machine custodians of Hell into releasing Eury, but he stops singing to speak to her, and the berserker center regains control over its minions and steals her back. After his escape to safety, he is mobbed at a concert by "ten thousand girls turned Maenad,"[97] and his broken body at his request is placed in a flyer and returned to Hell, where the liberators find him in a case with what is left of Eury; in pity, they unplug the cases, permitting them to die.

The priesthood in Berserker's Planet functions as a parody of traditional religious orders, for it worships Lord Death, a damaged berserker which had been programmed centuries ago to destroy Johann Karlsen. The gods that the priests serve, ostensibly, are Thorun and Mjollnir, but these are simply huge humanoid robots activated by spare parts from the berserker. Thorun's Tournament, in which sixty-four men methodically kill each other, is a conflict that fulfills the berserker's goal of slaughter, and the human sacrifices which its priests offer further the berserker's war against life. The winner of the tournament is supposed to be granted divine status and permitted to rule with Thorun in the citadel city atop Godsmountain. Inside the temple is a statue of "Karlsen, a demigod of the distant past" which Andreas, the high priest, would like to remove, but he fears the reaction. The damaged berserker, consisting of a half-dozen boxes resting on a litter behind the altar, is worshipped by the priesthood,[98] a situation that Suomi explains later in the novel.

On other planets there have been cults of evil men and women who have worshipped berserkers as gods. I can only guess that there might have been some such people on Hunters' five hundred years ago. After the battle they found their crippled god somewhere, rescued it and hid it. . . . worshipped it in secret, generation after generation. Praying to death, working for the day when they could destroy all life upon this planet.[99]

The religious theme is emphasized when, after the worship of Death is overthrown with the help of the long-dead Johann Karlsen, Carlos Suomi is forced to assume the identity of Karlsen, and Thomas the Grabber is forced to assume the role of the god Thorun because "the people had to be reassured, society supported, through a time of crisis."[100]

The religious imagery that appears in the stories discussed above varies from pagan myth through literature to cult worship, but the character of Johann Karlsen has clustered about it distinctly Christian imagery. Karlsen first appears in "Stone Place" to "the roaring chant of the crowd a few hundred feet below: 'Karlsen! Karlsen!' " and Mitch Spain asks, "What was it like to be Johann Karlsen, come to save the world, when none of the really great and powerful ones seemed to care too much about it?"[101] Johann Karlsen seems to be a Christ figure, for his initials fit, with the C replaced by a phonetic equivalent, and his entry into Gobi spaceport parallels the entry of Jesus into Jerusalem, for Karlsen also has come to save the world from the forces of death. At the time of his acclaim, a Carmpan Prophet of Probability describes him as "The hope, the living spark, to spread the flame of life! . . . in this man before me now, there is life greater than any strength of metal. A power of life, to resonate—in all of us. I see, with Karlsen, victory." The other half of the prophecy also fits the Christlike Karlsen: "then death, destruction, failure. He who wins everything . . . will die owning nothing. . . ."[102]

Karlsen is one of the few Believers, and this "irrational" factor makes him more dangerous to the berserkers. Admiral Hemphill is unable to understand: "Did some sort of luck operate to protect Karlsen? Karlsen himself did not match Hemphill's ideal of a war leader; he was not as ruthless or as cold as metal. Yet the damned machines made great sacrifices to attack him."[103]

Later Hemphill recalls, "They feared him, in their iron guts, as they feared no one else. Through I never quite understood why. . . ."[104] From his "monastic cabin" Karlsen leads the human forces to combat against death at "a dark nebula, made up of clustered billions of rocks and older than the sun, named the stone place by men."[105] This place of stones where Karlsen is to triumph over the forces of death is like Golgotha, and like Jesus in the Garden of Gethsemane, Karlsen is "passive, waiting; asking for a sign. As if there was in fact some purpose outside the layers of a man's own mind, that could inspire him."[106] To fulfill the prophecy of the Carmpan Prophet and to maintain the religious parallels, the girl that Karlsen loves is captured by the berserkers, and then she is killed in the major battle. The image of the crucifixion is transferred to the attack of the human ships, which ram the berserkers with sharp prows: "The ship twisted in the wound it had made. . . . this warship that was more solid metal than anything else."[107]

Although Karlsen survives the battle—"The day I die—I'll remember this day. This glory, this victory for all men"[108]—he is then betrayed by his brother, Felipe Nogara. Nogara has him quick-frozen, ostensibly because Karlsen has a deadly disease, but actually because Nogara does not trust him.[109] Thus Karlsen symbolically dies as a result of his victory, but like Jesus, he cannot be held in such confinement, for "There was something that would not freeze."[110] Lucinda, after the berserker attack on *Nirvana*, turns the coffin lock to emergency revival, and Karlsen is resurrected: "the coffin's lid was open and the man inside was sitting up. . . . power began to grow behind his eyes, a power somehow completely different from his brother's and perhaps even greater."[111] Leading the attacking berserker away from the damaged ships, Karlsen falls into orbit around a hypermassive sun whose gravity prevents rescue by any of the ships in the area. The imagery here is that of chaos and Christ's descent into hell: "Karlsen saw the red light below him through the translucent deck, flaring up between his space-booted feet."[112] Karlsen prays, looks upon "The Face of the Deep" (the title of the last story in his series) and, in a vision that anticipates the confrontation of Michel and the Taj, comes to feel that he, like Jesus after the resurrection, has come almost face to face with God.[113]

Johann Karlsen appears indirectly in the two novels, his influence continuing to aid mankind in its fight against the berserkers. His recorded voice in the opening section of *Berserker's Planet* is the instrument that destroys the berserker, his statue as demigod stands in the temple, and Carlos Suomi pretends to be Karlsen in the last pages of the novel; as Saberhagen indicates, "perhaps in one sense it was the truth that Karlsen still walked here."[114] In *Berserker Man* the enormous starship that takes Michel from Alpine to Earth is the *Johann Karlsen*, and in the last page of the novel he places his biological mother safely inside this same ship before he enters the Taj. The spirit of Karlsen has watched over mankind's battle with the berserkers from the first confrontation until the final second coming of Michel to the Taj and the transfiguration.

While Karlsen is clearly a Christ-figure, Michel is less specific, although he embodies elements of the Christian mythos. As Sandra Miesel has shown, Michel is the generalized form of the archetype—the childhero—of which the Christ child and the warrior-hero are more specific manifestations: he has elements of the angel Michael and of Galahad; his story parallels the chivalric quest for the Holy Grail.[115] Michel, the synthesis of man and machine, partakes of his dual nature in a way that parallels Christ's divine and human natures; his second coming to the Taj (with its connotations of the Taj Mahal and death) brings to a close the conflict between life and death: by leaving behind mechanistic existence and death (the Director) and penetrating to the heart of the Taj (the tomb), he finds life beyond death and partakes of a transfiguration to a new existence, apparently for all men: "with that all life that had been born of earth came home to the Taj-heart at last."[116]

Thus, man began his aggressive odyssey by developing personal weapons that evolved into the fighting suit; in *Berserker Man* that fighting suit, now developed into the ultimate weapon, Lancelot, and his aggression, now channeled against the ultimate evil, death, enable him to transcend his human condition and to take his place in the company of superior races. There he needs no longer his machines that kill, for with them he has killed death, and his technology, like the bonds of the Taj, can now fall "like dead leaves, like circlets of discarded skin."[117] He has fought his way to divinity.

NOTES

1. Wilfred Owen, "Arms and the Boy," ll. 9-12, in *Immortal Poems of the English Language*, Oscar Williams, ed. (New York: Washington Square Press, 1970), p. 551.

2. e. e. Cummings, "Pity This Busy Monster, Manunkind," ll. 11-12, in *A Pocket Book of Modern Verse*, rev. ed., Oscar Williams, ed. (New York: Washington Square Press, 1954), p. 384.

3. Patrick McGuire, "Variants: Joe Haldeman's SF Novels," *ALGOL*, 14 (Summer-Fall 1977), 19-20. Analyzes Haldeman's debt to Heinlein and compares *Mindbridge* to *The Forever War*.

4. Robert Heinlein, *Starship Troopers* (1959; rpt. New York: Berkley Medallion Books, 1968), ch. XIV, p. 208.

5. Joe Haldeman, *The Forever War* (1974; rpt. New York: Ballantine Books, 1976).

6. Haldeman, *Forever War*, pt. 1, ch. 4, p. 14.

7. Heinlein, *Starship Troopers*, ch. VII, pp. 80-81; Haldeman, *Forever War*, pt. 1, ch. 4, p. 14.

8. Haldeman, *Forever War*, pt. 1, ch. 7, p. 24; Heinlein, *Starship Troopers*, ch. VII, p. 83.

9. Haldeman, *Forever War*, pt. 1, ch. 5, p. 18.

10. Ibid., pt. 3, p. 126.

11. Ibid., p. 128.

12. Heinlein, *Starship Troopers*, ch. V, p. 50.

13. Haldeman, *Forever War*, pt. 4, ch. 1, p. 143.

14. Heinlein, *Starship Troopers*, ch. XI, p. 121; ch. I, p. 5.

15. Haldeman, *Forever War*, pt. 2, ch. 3, p. 78.

16. Ibid., pt. 1, ch. 13, p. 48.

17. Ibid., ch. 15, p. 57.

18. Ibid., p. 64.

19. Ibid., pt. 4, ch. 1, pp. 148, 147.

20. See, for example, Heinlein, *Starship Troopers*, ch. VI, p. 76; ch. XII, pp. 144-45; ch. V, p. 52 (location of the quotation); and ch. X, p. 108.

21. Haldeman, *Forever War*, pt. 4, ch. 8, p. 214.

22. Ibid., ch. 1, p. 150.

23. Ibid., pt. 4, ch. 8, p. 217.

24. See esp. Heinlein, *Starship Troopers*, ch. XIV, p. 207.

25. Ibid., ch. XI, pp. 123-25.

26. Haldeman, *Forever War*, pt. 3, p. 131.

27. Ibid., p. 137.

28. Heinlein, *Starship Troopers*, ch. XII, p. 147; see Isaiah 2:2-4 and last chapter of Robert Heinlein, *The Puppet Masters* (1951; rpt. New York: New American Library, n.d.).

29. Heinlein, *Starship Troopers*, ch. X, p. 107.

30. Ibid., ch. XI, p. 121.

31. Haldeman, *Forever War*, pt. 4, ch. 8, pp. 213-15.

32. H. G. Wells, *The War of the Worlds* (1897; rpt. New York: Heritage Press, 1964), Bk. I, ch. 4, p. 19.

33. Ibid., ch. 10, p. 46.

34. Ibid., ch. 11, p. 52.

35. Ibid., ch. 15, p. 89.

36. For a more detailed account of these changes, see Steve Rubin's retrospect, "The War of the Worlds," *Cinefantastique* 5 (Spring 1977), 4-17, 34-36.

37. Ben Bova, *The Dueling Machine* (1969; rpt. New York: Signet, 1973).

38. Ibid., p. 166.

39. Keith Laumer, *Bolo: The Annals of the Dinochrome Brigade* (1976; rpt. New York: Berkley, 1977).

40. Ibid., pp. 116, 117.

41. Ibid., p. 2.

42. Ibid., p. 151.

43. Ibid., pp. 182, 191.

44. Ibid., p. 194.

45. Ibid., pp. 215-16.

46. Ibid., pp. 11, 21.

47. Ibid., p. 127.

48. Ibid., p. 179.

49. Ibid., p. 180.

50. Ibid., p. 195.

51. Ibid., p. 215.

52. Ibid., p. 216.

53. Isaac Asimov, *The Caves of Steel* (1953; rpt. Garden City, NY: Doubleday, 1954); idem, *The Naked Sun* (1956; rpt. Garden City, NY: Doubleday, 1957). For more bibliographical data, see the List of Works Useful for the Study of Machines in Science Fiction, at the end of this volume.

54. Harry Harrison, "The Velvet Glove" (1956) in *Souls of Metal*, Mike Ashley, ed. (1977; rpt. New York: Jove Publications, Inc., 1978).

55. Ibid., pp. 146-47.

56. Ibid., p. 157.

57. Quoted by Steve Rubin, "Retrospect: *The Day the Earth Stood Still*," *Cinefantastique*, 4 (Winter 1976), 12.

58. Ibid., p. 21.

59. Ibid.

60. See the conflict between two robots, one humanoid, in Fred Saberhagen, *Brother Assassin* (1969; rpt. New York: Ace Books, 1978), pp. 38-39.

61. Frederick S. Clarke and Jordàn R. Fox, "Carlo Rambaldi: Creator of Alien Head Effects," *Cinefantastique*, 9 (Fall 1979), 23.

62. Abraham Merritt, *The Metal Monster* (1920; rpt. New York: Avon Books, 1945), p. 37.

63. Ibid., p. 237.

64. Ibid., p. 94.

65. Fred Saberhagen, "Inhuman Error," in *The Ultimate Enemy* (New York: Ace Books, 1979), pp. 65-66; for further bibliographical information on the berserker series, consult the List at the end of this volume; for a survey of the berserker stories through *Berserker's Planet*, see A. D. Stewart, "Fred Saberhagen: Cybernetic Psychologist (A Study of the Berserker Stories)," *Extrapolation*, 18 (December 1976), 42-51.

66. Fred Saberhagen, "Goodlife," *Berserker* (1967; New York: Ace Books, 1978), p. 33.

67. Fred Saberhagen, "Without a Thought," *Berserker*, p. 3.

68. Fred Saberhagen, "Mr. Jester," *Berserker*, p. 161; "Sign of the Wolf," *Berserker*, p. 203.

69. Fred Saberhagen, "Stone Place," *Berserker*, p. 127.

70. Fred Saberhagen, "Some Events at the Templar Radiant," *The Ultimate Enemy*, p. 119.

71. Saberhagen, "Stone Place," p. 121.

72. Fred Saberhagen, "Smasher," *The Ultimate Enemy*, p. 177.

73. Fred Saberhagen, "The Game," *The Ultimate Enemy*, pp. 210-13.

74. Fred Saberhagen, "Patron of the Arts," *Berserker*, pp. 47, 57.

75. Fred Saberhagen, *Berserker's Planet* (New York: Ace Books, 1980), p. 75.

76. Fred Saberhagen, *Brother Assassin* (New York: Ace Books, 1979), p. 163.

77. Fred Saberhagen, "Masque of the Red Shift," *Berserker*, p. 175.

78. Ibid., p. 176.

79. Saberhagen, *Brother Assassin*, p. 232.

80. Saberhagen, "Patron of the Arts," p. 52.

81. Saberhagen, "Goodlife," p. 31.

82. Saberhagen, "Stone Place," pp. 81-82.

83. Fred Saberhagen, "Starsong," *The Ultimate Enemy*, p. 145.

84. Sandra Miesel, "An Afterword to Fred Saberhagen's *Berserker Man*: 'Life and Death in Dreadful Conflict Strove,'" *Berserker Man* (New York: Ace Books, 1979), pp. 214-15.

85. Saberhagen, "Patron of the Arts," pp. 51, 58.

86. Saberhagen, "Starsong," p. 146.

87. Saberhagen, "Stone Place," p. 92.

88. Saberhagen, *Berserker Man*, p. 205-06.
89. Saberhagen, *Berserker*, pp. iii-iv.
90. Saberhagen, "Goodlife," p. 44.
91. Fred Saberhagen, "Sign of the Wolf," *Berserker*, p. 202.
92. Fred Saberhagen, "In the Temple of Mars," *Berserker*, pp. 223, 228.
93. Fred Saberhagen, "What T and I Did," *Berserker*, p. 141.
94. Saberhagen, "Sign of the Wolf," p. 201.
95. Saberhagen, "In the Temple of Mars," p. 229.
96. Saberhagen, "Starsong," p. 150.
97. Ibid., p. 159.
98. Saberhagen, *Berserker's Planet*, p. 78.
99. Ibid., p. 156.
100. Ibid., p. 229.
101. Saberhagen, "Stone Place," pp. 74, 75.
102. Ibid., pp. 77, 78.
103. Ibid., p. 108.
104. Saberhagen, "In the Temple of Mars," p. 213.
105. Saberhagen, "Stone Place," p. 91.
106. Ibid., p. 112.
107. Ibid., pp. 117-18.
108. Ibid., pp. 127-28.
109. Saberhagen, "Masque of the Red Shift," p. 168.
110. Ibid., p. 167.
111. Ibid., p. 187.
112. Fred Saberhagen, "The Face of the Deep," *Berserker*, p. 232.
113. Ibid., p. 236.
114. Saberhagen, *Berserker's Planet*, p. 229.
115. Miesel, "Afterword," pp. 218-19.
116. Saberhagen, *Berserker Man*, p. 207.
117. Ibid.

13

HOW MACHINES BECOME HUMAN:
PROCESS AND ATTRIBUTE

The number of robot stories is legion. Nearly always, from Karel Čapek's *R.U.R.* right up to the present, robots have been depicted as in some respects superior to the men who have invented, designed, and built them. Often they are stronger, faster, or more logical than their creators. Their superiority has been characterized as self-limiting and dedicated solely to the service of man (as in Brian Aldiss's "Who Can Replace a Man?")[1] or so overwhelmingly as to produce a sense of human inferiority and futility (as in Jack Williamson's "With Folded Hands").[2] So we have two poles of robot potential: service or supplantation. Together they epitomize our hopes and our fears about machines.[3] Yet the opposition between service and supplantation cannot be absolute: a third possibility must be considered. What if a machine were to become a man?

This is just the sort of question that science fiction writers pose themselves. It is future potential, has a technological basis, and relates technology directly to the human condition. Once a writer begins to toy with the question of a machine's becoming human, at least two other related questions ought to cross his mind: By what means might a machine become human? What are the attributes by which humanity is defined? Or, in a collateral formulation with a different emphasis: By what criteria would the machine come to be recognized as human? Of course, these questions are interrelated. The means that an author chooses to depict a machine in the process of becoming human may very well delimit the nature of the humanity that it can ultimately achieve. Conversely, an authorial preconception about the attributes that define humanity might dictate the choice among means at his disposal to present a machine's progress to human status. Analysis of particular works can reveal an interesting sort of connection between the means of humanization and the implicit definition of "human" that a story contains. However, even though the author may have some sort of preconceived definition of "human," to suggest that the reader can penetrate back through the story to discover the author's concept of humanity is to surrender to the intentional fallacy. We can never be sure what an author intended. The definition readers derive from a story may represent the author's concept of humanity; it may present a concept of humanity that he rejects (and perhaps hopes the reader will reject); or it may be a partial, tentative, or incomplete definition designed only to function within the context of the story. A careful examination of the means by which individual machines become human and of the human attributes these machines develop can determine whether the emphasis falls on the process of becoming or on the human attributes attained.

Three stories dealing with the humanization of machines lend themselves particularly well to such an examination: Lester del Rey's "Helen O'Loy," Roger Zelazny's "For a Breath I Tarry," and Isaac Asimov's "The Bicentennial Man." The time span during which these stories were published (1938-1976) suggests that authorial interest in the theme has persisted.[4] But more important is the variety of situations in which robots are shown, and the depth to which the process of humanization is explored. One might easily find many stories of machines with some human characteristics in which humanization is a sort of given subservient to other elements in the work. (D. F. Jones's Colossus Trilogy is one example in this regard.) The level of humanity attained is also important. In each of these stories a central (robot) character develops in ways that cause other characters within the story (and consequently the reader) to recognize that character as "fully" human.

"Helen O'Loy," justly admired as an outstanding example of the science fiction short story, is the earliest of these three stories, both in point of publication and in futurity. That is, it employs a setting in the not very distant future. That setting relates to the theme of humanization in one significant way—it permits the author to deal with an intermediate stage of robotic development. In the story, robots are common enough that Dave can make his living by running a small robot-repair shop. Yet the robots he repairs are not so sophisticated as to eliminate possibilities for improvement. Dave and Phil, a medical doctor who rooms with him, discuss possible improvements after the mildly comic failure of their household robot, Lena, who put vanilla on the steak. Phil defines the problem when he says, "Lena has sense enough, but she has no emotions, no consciousness of self."[5] Dave responds immediately with the optimism and enthusiasm typical of that romantic stereotype—the solo inventive genius. He is certain that a solution will be found— "put in some mechanical emotions, or something."[6] The doctor, an expert in endocrinology, tries through a year-long running argument to persuade Dave that it can't be done. Rather the opposite effect results: "the more we talked, the less sure I grew about the impossibility of *homo mechanensis* as the perfect type."[7]

In this expository section, two obvious points are made relevant to the means by which a machine can be perfected, or humanized. First, a man desires that humanization and believes it possible. His desire and conviction motivate him to experiment; to redesign in the hope of producing a machine that will better serve his purposes (in this case at least competent to distinguish the use of salt from vanilla). Second, some specific improvement must result from his intention (in this case the development of a set of mechanical glands, supplemented by a "memory coil," intended to introduce emotions and self-awareness).

Needless to say, the specific improvement works, giving the inventor a machine with capabilities much beyond what he expected. That points up an accidental element which may be regarded as characteristic of all inventions. The inventor, simply because he deals with the new, the unique, cannot predict all the elements, or effects of his invention. But there is another accidental element which enters into this case. Helen, the robot Dave has modified, is "filled with curiosity" and quite capable of further learning. "She . . . learned fast and furiously. . . ."[8] Dave fails to supervise that learning himself; he is content to plop Helen in front of a "stereovisor" while he goes off to his shop. Thus her learning is accidental. Because of his carelessness, soap operas and Phil's "rather adolescent" books become the basic training for her emotional life.

Del Rey's story contains two means of robotic development: deliberate and accidental. Neither receives a great deal of stress; the focus is upon the consequences rather than the process. Further analysis of the process would seem to require a somewhat longer story. The robot herself has no participation in the process of becoming human except insofar as she utilizes her built-in capacity to continue learning. One must assume that her curiosity and learning ability result from Dave's modifications, as they are not otherwise explained.

Asimov's novelette, "The Bicentennial Man," offers a considerably different set of circumstances. "Helen O'Loy" probably covers about forty years; the essential process by which she becomes human appears to have been completed within a few days once Dave activates his modifications. By contrast, "The Bicentennial Man" spans two centuries and the process of humanization, a gradual, incremental affair, can only be regarded as complete at the end of the story.

Robotics, in Asimov's story, seem to be at about the same stage of development as in "Helen O'Loy." Robots are not common; we are told that they are all in their experimental stages. The principles governing design and manufacture of "positronic brains" are not fully understood. The robot (Andrew) is clearly the protagonist. Designed to function as "a valet, a butler, even a lady's maid,"[9] he is restrained by Asimov's Three Laws of Robotics (by comparison Helen seems to enjoy almost limitless freedom). When Little Miss, the daughter of Gerald Martin, directs Andrew to carve a pendant for her, he reveals his creative talent. The robopsychologist at U.S. Robots is more than a little surprised. He had regarded real creativity as impossible for a robot. Confronted with Andrew he says, "The luck of the draw. Something in the pathways."[10] Again we are confronted with accident. U.S. Robots, like Dave, has inadvertently built a machine which demonstrates capabilities beyond the builder's expectations. But after that initial accident, Helen's development depends upon another accident, while Andrew's does not.

Once Andrew's creativity has been established, it serves as a foundation for all his further development. This is especially true as it provides him with a great deal of money and thus a certain measure of independence. During his long lifetime, in a quiet, deliberate, persistent way, Andrew engages in a quest to explore and fulfill his human potentials. Those potentials fall into three categories: mental, physical, and legal.

His mental development can best be characterized as continuous learning. By his thirtieth year, having reached the point where the resources of the Martin's home library are inadequate, he determines to visit the main public library (with near disastrous results). Eventually he redirects his creative ability, leaving woodworking to write a history of robots. "I want to explain how robots feel about what has happened since the first ones were allowed to work and live on Earth."[11] The assumption here and throughout the story is that robots do have feelings, that robots are capable of some sort of emotional response. This assumption, graphically presented at several points in the story, is nowhere explained or developed. Andrew, after the publication of his history, again changes careers, this time to become a robobiologist. He works to develop systems which will permit robots to eat and breathe. Eventually his research leads him into prosthetology.

Andrew's mental career pattern takes him from art, to humanities, to science, to medical technology. Not only does he master all these types of mental skills, he also carries them to new levels of accomplishment. One sees something similar in Andrew's physical development. Initially he is a quite ordinary robot, "as much a robot in appearance as any that had ever existed —smoothly designed and functional."[12] Gradually that changes. First it is done for him, although at his own expense. "Andrew had the advantage of every new device, until he was a model of metallic excellence."[13] Yet this is not enough. When android bodies are developed, he goes to considerable effort and some risk to have his positronic brain transferred into one. That he takes the initiative is the crucial fact here. Still unsatisfied, he later has himself rebuilt again so that he can eat, at least in a limited way. He tells U.S. Robot's director of research, "My body is a canvas on which I intend to draw . . ." The director responds, "A Man?"[14] The question goes unanswered, but Andrew's striving for human characteristics is as clear in the physical realm as it is in the mental. That the robot surgeon he consults in the first section of the story does not recognize him as a robot indicates the success of his quest for physical humanity.

At the same time as his mental powers are developing and his physical body is being revised, Andrew is engaged in a drawn-out legalization process, a sort of robots' rights movement. This process has four steps. The first of these is the establishment of a bank account in his name. That is followed by a more traumatic step, when he tries to buy his freedom from Gerald Martin. Ultimately the courts rule in his favor: "There is no right to deny freedom to any object with a mind advanced enough to grasp the concept and desire the state."[15] Again, Andrew's initiative is crucial; the judge's decision was heavily influenced by the fact that Andrew wished to become human. Eventually that wish drives Andrew to seek an act of the World Legislature recognizing his humanity. The level of this drive is clear when he states: "To be a human being *de facto* is not enough. I want not only to be treated as one, but to be legally identified as one. I want to be a human being *de jure*."[16] Such *de jure* recognition is a far cry from the earlier court decision which refers to him as an "object." A carefully mounted campaign to achieve this legislative recognition fails because of human fears and prejudice. A second campaign only succeeds because Andrew manages to overcome fear and prejudice by arranging his own death.

Asimov's analysis of the humanization process goes far beyond "Helen O'Loy." He sees the process as complex—involving not merely mental development and physical similarity, but also requiring recognition by other human beings. Such recognition is implied by Helen's marriage to Dave, but its larger implications remain unexplored (understandably in such a brief story). Andrew's long struggle for legal recognition brings such wider social implications to the fore.

As one begins to consider Zelazny's "For a Breath I Tarry," one notes a striking development of the level of machine independence. Helen, largely Dave's creation, remains dependent upon him throughout the story. Andrew, the creation of a corporate team, strives for freedom and achieves recognition. Frost, a machine built by another machine, seems from the start to have almost unlimited freedom to act independently. In part this may be an aspect of the setting. Because the story takes place in a future so distant that man has become extinct, the powerful machines which rather pointlessly continue to reconstruct the world are responsible only to their interior logical processes. Frost's attempt to convert himself into a man may be regarded as an indirect result of those logical processes and of the direction to rebuild the world which governs the major machines.

Yet an accidental element enters in here too. When Solcom was building Frost, a solar flare interfered with the construction in such a way that "Solcom was not certain that Frost was the product originally desired."[17] Although this accident appears not to have damaged Frost in any way, it does introduce one major anomaly: "He possessed an unaccountably acute imperative that he function at full capacity at all times."[18] Inasmuch as he can supervise all the machines engaged in rebuilding the northern hemisphere in a few hours each day, he takes up the study of Man as a hobby.

As in the other stories, there is an intentional element in Frost's progress toward humanity. Solcom, in his rebuilding attempts, is resisted by Divcom. Each believes it possesses the sole mandate for the reconstruction. Each impugns the other's logic. Both realize that only a Man would have the authority to resolve their dispute. In a witty parody of the Book of Job, they begin the process which suggests to Frost that he might try to become a Man. Their desire to resolve a dispute thus provides the impetus for Frost's development.

Frost's striving to become human is similar in some ways to Andrew's, but there is one major difference. Andrew, surrounded by humans, constantly has role models to imitate. For him the question of what human characteristics he must attain never arises. For Frost it is the central question. Before he can consider the means of becoming a Man, he must grapple with the problem of defining humanity. This process takes even longer than it did for Andrew. From the very beginning Frost refuses to be limited by time, perhaps in the realization that his empirical method will allow no shortcuts. Of course, since his hobby is collecting human artifacts, he had started even before Divcom's agent incites him to explore further.

A large part of Frost's work is data gathering. He examines artifacts, reads books, views films, and listens to tapes. Gradually he expands from mere data collection to experimentation. He develops mechanical sensory equipment to duplicate human perceptions. But when he views a scenic sunset he experiences no significant response. Later he examines works of art and attempts a painting himself. Unlike Andrew, he seems to lack creative talent. During his long search, Frost's attitude seems to change. To begin with he acts only in response to a logical challenge, but eventually mere intellectual motivation is replaced by determination. "I must be a Man."[19] This determination leads him to willful action, even in opposition to the directives of Solcom. Ultimately, having found a few frozen bodies, Frost clones some of them and transfers "the matrix of his awareness" into one.[20] At this point there is a profound difference of means from both the other stories. Each of them describes a growth of consciousness within a robot: Helen's body remains mechanical to the end; Andrew retains his positronic brain to the end. But Frost transfers his matrix of awareness from sealed molecular circuits into an actual human body. As far as means are concerned, that represents a quantum jump. Frost far exceeds the others with respect to the type of change that he undergoes in order to become human. On that basis alone, it might be argued that he becomes more fully human than the other two.

The pattern of similarities in these three stories suggests that several means are necessary if a machine would become human. First, there must be an intentional act—someone (or someting) sets out to build a better machine. Second, the process usually takes a great deal of time (Helen is exceptional) and involves continuing determination on the part of the machine being humanized. Third, that process must include continuous mental development—each of these three demonstrates almost unlimited capacity to learn. A fourth element, accident, occurs in all three stories. One hesitates to say that an accident of some sort is indispensable to the process. Although all three authors have included accidents in the humanization of their robots, perhaps these accidents might be better understood as suggestions that the authors, consciously or unconsciously, reject the real possibility of a machine's becoming human; perhaps the accidental element is introduced as a palliative, a way of undercutting the reality of that possibility.

Turning now from means to ends, the human attributes that each of the three machines displays and how they are recognized or acknowledged as human must be determined. Clearly, many of the items discussed as means of humanization imply or depend upon the machine's possessing intelligence. Just what intelligence is may not be so clear. Certain factors may be assumed as prerequisites to intelligence—the ability to obtain, store, and access information, for instance. Even that assumption has almost infinite ramifications because of the potential variation (for example, independence of information gathering or size of memory) in each of the three abilities mentioned. But, beyond such assumed prerequisites, the problem of defining intelligence grows in complexity. Reasoning power—the logical integration of data—can be found in comparatively simple computers, machines that no one would regard as intelligent. At the same time, without logical ability there can be no intelligence. Learning depends upon making logical connections among facts. But it also depends upon such abilities as analogy and judgment. That machines might possess all these abilities is not beyond imagining; that numbers of authors have written about intelligent machines which are thoroughly nonhuman must be the crucial point.[21] Intelligence must be considered as a *necessary* characteristic of humanity, but not as a characteristic *restricted* to humanity. The mere fact that a being exhibits intelligence will not help to identify it as human.

Thus, Helen O'Loy cannot be regarded as human simply because she learns very quickly or because she is able to discern the analogical relationship between the situation that she has watched on "stereovision" and her own situation. We must look elsewhere for human attributes. The ability to love and be loved, one of the important motifs of the story, is the most obvious attribute that Helen displays. It is, moreover, only one of a range of emotions that have resulted from Dave's modifications. She cries when rejected and giggles with pleasure on a shopping spree. Even though some readers may find her love overly romantic and sentimental (missing the ironic overtones), most will soon begin to regard her as quite human because of her generally convincing emotional responses. This is reinforced by Phil's reaction to her: "I got to thinking of her as a girl and companion myself."[22] That Dave resists but ultimately decides to marry her confirms that she is lovable as well as loving. When we find at the conclusion that Phil loves her too, it comes as no surprise. We are not intellectually convinced that Helen has become human, but we are emotionally persuaded. The undeveloped sexual motif cannot be taken as evidence of humanization because sex with a machine can be regarded as mere autoeroticism, or as the ultimate perversion.[23]

Fidelity is important in Helen's characterization. She remains Dave's wife throughout his life, consistently insuring that she seems to age as he does. Yet this fidelity may just be doglike devotion or simple mimicry of the exemplars she has watched on the stereovision. However, she also chooses to die because Dave has. Her suicide is the detail that persuades the reader that her love and fidelity are real, that she in fact acts as a human being. At the same time, it demonstrates that she has free will, that her relationship with Dave goes beyond mere stimulus-response. Although unobtrusively indicated, the fact of her having free will may be regarded as the most significant of her human characteristics.

Some of the same humanizing qualities can be found in Asimov's novelette. Andrew does have feelings, although they are nowhere as dramatically revealed as Helen's. He is loyal to the Martin family. When nothing would prevent him from going off on his own, he remains with them. When Gerald Martin dies, Andrew seems to indicate gratitude toward him. Perhaps Andrew is even capable of love; throughout his life he is quietly devoted to Little Miss, and her name is his last utterance. None of these attributes receives strong emphasis in the novelette, however. Two others do: creativity and volition.

His creativity first distinguishes Andrew from other robots. An example of his woodcarving suffices to convince the robopsychologist that his work is really creative. This may mean that his carving is not derivative, a mere imitation of exemplars stored in Andrew's memory. Further evidence of his creativity is presented each time he undertakes a new career: his history of robots takes a new approach to the subject, and his prosthetic devices are true inventions. Each of his achievements demonstrates the sort of creativity associated with the highest human artistic and intellectual achievements.

Yet even enormous creativity does not make Andrew human. He indicates that he realizes this himself by his continuing exploration and fulfillment of potentials that he regards as human. In doing so he demonstrates his volition, his free will, in the most graphic manner possible. Again and again he identifies ways in which he can become more human and deliberately chooses to change himself so as to more closely approximate his concept of humanity. There is a gradual but continuous process of growing self-assertion. Thus he chooses to wear clothes even though he has no need for them. His desire for freedom is an implicit assertion that to be owned is essentially dehumanizing. He chooses transfer to an android body and struggles to achieve that transfer.

In order to eat and breathe he designs modifications to his body, modifications of no real practicality, which make him only slightly more like men. He constantly engages in legal struggles, all of which tend only toward the ultimate recognition as human that he desires. All of this may be regarded as merely self-serving. However, the pattern is clear—Andrew acts freely. One might go so far as to say that he becomes a man by an act of his own will, that he ironically epitomizes the self-made man. However, his ultimate willful act is, like Helen's, the choice of his own death. He achieves his life's desire by throwing away life itself.

One finds a somewhat similar development of free will in the characterization of Frost. Presented with what seems to be an insoluble problem, Frost's anomalous drive to use his capacities fully pushes him to contradict Mordel's assertion that "All the data in the universe will not make you a Man, mighty Frost."[24] There is even a kind of hubris in his assertion that he can become a Man. But one must not miss the crucial point—when he accepts the challenge he thinks that only an increase of knowledge is involved. Some finite (quantitative) accretion of data will enable him to know as a Man would. Mordel from the first warns him that a qualitative difference is involved: that human perception is different from measurement. Mordel's speech is at one and the same time a sales pitch and a caution. Its basis seems to be, "Man is the measure of all things."[25] But Frost takes the bait. Without direction from Solcom (who consistently declines to direct him at crucial points throughout the story), Frost chooses to explore the nature of humanity in order to duplicate it. Thus, from the beginning, Frost's actions are governed by free will.

Nor is this the only example of that free will. During his exploration of Bright Defile he ignores the Beta Machine's direction (in effect relayed from Solcom) to leave. Solcom accuses him of having "defied the decrees of order."[26] Defiance without free will is an impossibility. On another, more important occasion, Frost manages defiance of Solcom directly. At exactly the moment when he is completing his transfer to a human body, Solcom directs him to stop. Frost refuses, leaving no room to doubt his freedom of action. This one attribute permits him to transcend all the other machines (Solcom and Divcom included), which work to achieve the reconstruction of Earth only because they are governed by a previous human directive that they do not understand but cannot reject.

Emotion plays a more important part in Zelazny's story than it does in Asimov's. In spite of his being declared "The Bicentennial Man," Andrew never develops any warmth; as a character he may appeal to the mind, but not the heart. Frost overcomes this deficiency. Part of Mordel's cautionary challenge emphasizes just this point: "There is no formula for a feeling. There is no conversion factor for an emotion."[27] Frost confirms this through his experiments with human sense organs (which demonstrate the distinction between measurement and perception), and in his attempt to create a work of art (which demonstrates that he has no particular creative ability). Only after the transfer of his matrix of awareness into a body does Frost experience emotion. Then he cries; his first words are, "—I—fear."[28] The Beta Machine recognizes his feeling as despair. Later, after recovering from the initial trauma, he experiences loneliness which impels him to contact the Beta Machine, offering to make *her* human too. The tone of his invitation and the use of A. E. Housman's poem XXXII, from "A Shropshire Lad" (1896), suggests that he has also become capable of love.

The Housman poem implies something else as well. Mortality and transience are in the title "For a Breath I Tarry." The end of the story plays on this by introducing an emphatic *carpe diem* motif as Frost tells Beta, "Judgment Day is not a thing that can be delayed for overlong."[29] Even though the last two lines of the poem are not quoted, the allusion to the poem itself draws them in to further strengthen the *carpe diem* motif.[30] Thus Frost, like Helen and Andrew, accepts mortality as an indispensable condition for becoming a Man. By demonstrating an understanding of death, each asserts the possession of life, an assertion no machine can make. So the emphasis of Zelazny's story is on life—brief, perhaps, but worth living—and on renewal: once again there are men, and the machines' purpose is restored. Death is a sort of validation for Helen and Andrew. Frost's life is a validation for the machines.

Each of these three robots develops a similar set of attributes which enable the reader to recognize and accept it as fully human. To begin with, they all have sufficient intelligence. But, as has been pointed out, intelligence can only serve as a negative criterion. It is the other attributes they share that are of primary importance: emotional response, free will, and acceptance of mortality. That all three stories should have settled upon these same attributes can hardly be coincidence. Rather, the theme of humanization and the logical analysis of the process have led the authors to a similar definition of humanity.

The question of recognition still remains. Is it enough that a robot should attain some set of characteristic attributes to become human? Each of these stories implies that the answer is no.

Dave and Phil do not want to admit that Helen is human. They resist the idea strongly. Yet the very number of times they insist that she is not human (four times in a nine-page story) effectively conveys an attempt at self-persuasion. Eventually they must concede that the qualities they have seen in her all along make her human. Dave's marriage to her and Phil's wistful comment at the end confirm their recognition.

Andrew gains his recognition, as he does everything else, through a series of steps. Nearly all of these are legal processes. Through freedom, to robot rights, he works his way up to the ultimate *de jure* humanity granted by the World Legislature. But in addition there are two cases that are the obverse of recognition—when those around him simply fail to note that he is a robot. On the moon he directs a research team. The fact that he is a robot is ignored by all those who follow his orders. Later the robot surgeon also does not recognize that Andrew is also a robot. Clearly Andrew has shaken off any machinelike characteristics long before he receives public recognition as a man.

Frost's recognition is the most dramatic of the three. After he has been returned to a human body, Solcom and Divcom cannot decide whether he is indeed a Man. At this point the Crusher of Ores arrives, enunciating its command that all listen to its tale about the death of the last Man. Its obedience to Frost's command is indisputable recognition of his humanity.

By the inclusion of explicit recognition of the humanity achieved by these robots, each story strongly reinforces the reader's acceptance that the machine has become human. This reinforcement of reader acceptance by recognition seems necessary for logical and technical reasons. Logically, it is impossible for the robot, no matter how its powers develop, to convince readers of its humanity by merely declaring itself human; for it to do so would lack all credibility. Technically, it might be possible to produce a narrative sequence which led the reader to conclude that the machine had become human. However, to have someone within the story identify and enunciate this fact is both clearer and eliminates the possibility that the reader may miss the point. In this regard Zelazny has set himself the most difficult problem. Helen and Andrew can easily be recognized by other humans, but Zelazny has no humans who can recognize Frost. Frost says he will know and admit failure to become Man, but that is not enough. Introducing the Crusher of Ores is an elegant solution—as the last machine to deal directly with a human it is ideally qualified to recognize Frost as human. In each of these stories the emphasis on process may also require recognition as an indication that the process is complete.

Ultimately it seems possible to explain the striking unanimity in the choice of attributes the authors use to define humanity as resulting from the relationship of process to attribute. In del Rey's story, process is not the focus of attention. Yet the selection of emotion as a key attribute initially stems from the process of rebuilding the robot. Emotion is also necessary because of the romantic, semicomic plot that del Rey has invented. Free will and death follow simply because they are emotionally and contextually appropriate. The other two stories appear to have a rather more solid intellectual approach to the theme—each carefully examines the process by which a machine might become human. Asimov's treatment of the process traces Andrew's development step by step. This leads him to stress externals, physical changes. But he is also using his stock motif of human prejudice against and fear of robots. This draws his imagination to the legal aspect and to the psychologically persuasive choice of death as a means of allaying that fear and prejudice. Free will comes in only because it is necessary to keep the narrative moving. If Andrew could not freely pursue his goal, growth and change of any sort would be impossible. The same is true in Frost's case, although his motivation begins in curiosity, the pursuit of knowledge, rather than the pursuit of freedom which first motivates Andrew.

Process is again the center of interest in Frost's case; however, the treatment is quite different and rather more interesting. It might be said that Helen and Andrew, observing human beings at first hand, intuit the nature of humanity rather than define it. Frost, having painstakingly collected every available datum about Man and made it part of his matrix of awareness, abruptly shifts it into a body. Thus, he leaps rather than grows into a human. Somehow that jump induces the emotion that Helen learns from soap operas and that Andrew has from some unidentified source. Frost's development of emotion leads to the *carpe diem* theme with a consequent emphasis on life and only the implication of death.

Process, not result, is the main concern of these stories. So we see a different process in each case leading through its own logic to very similar attributes. The exigencies of plot and characterization cause the authors to make a series of choices that transform robots into humans capable of choosing freely, of feeling emotion, and of accepting death.

NOTES

1. Brian Aldiss, "Who Can Replace a Man?" rpt. in *Who Can Replace a Man?* (New York: New American Library, 1965), pp. 13-21.

2. Jack Williamson, "With Folded Hands," in *The Science Fiction Hall of Fame*, Ben Bova, ed. (New York: Doubleday, 1973), IIA, 487-529.

3. Isaac Asimov has thoroughly analyzed this dichotomy in "The Machine and the Robot" in *Science Fiction: Contemporary Mythology*, Patricia Warrick, Martin Harry Greenberg, and Joseph Olander, eds. (New York: Harper and Row, 1978), pp. 244-53.

4. Lester del Rey, "Helen O'Loy" (1938), rpt. in *The Science Fiction Hall of Fame*, Robert Silverberg, ed. (Garden City, NY: Doubleday, 1970), I, 42-51; Roger Zelazny, "For a Breath I Tarry" (1966), rpt. in *Survival Printout*, Leonard Allison, Leonard Jenkin, and Robert Perrault, eds. (New York: Vintage Books, 1973), pp. 68-107; Isaac Asimov, "The Bicentennial Man" (1976), rpt. in *Nebula Winners Twelve*, Gordon R. Dickson, ed. (New York: Bantam Books, 1978), pp. 135-79.

5. del Rey, "Helen O'Loy," p. 43.

6. Ibid.

7. Ibid.

8. Ibid., pp. 46 and 47.

9. Asimov, "Bicentennial Man," sec. 2, p. 137.

10. Ibid., sec. 3, p. 140.

11. Ibid., sec. 10, p. 153.

12. Ibid., sec. 2, p. 137.

13. Ibid., sec. 5, p. 142.

14. Ibid., sec. 16, p. 169.

15. Ibid., sec. 7, pp. 145-46.

16. Ibid., sec. 17, p. 170.

17. Zelazny, "For a Breath I Tarry," p. 68.

18. Ibid., p. 69.

19. Ibid., p. 100.

20. Ibid., p. 101.

21. See, for example, Frank Herbert and William Ransom, *The Jesus Incident*; Robert Heinlein, *The Moon Is a Harsh Mistress*; and Stanislaw Lem, *The Cyberiad*, to name only a few.

22. del Rey, "Helen O'Loy," p. 50.

23. A device of the first type is described by John Brunner, *The Shockwave Rider* (New York: Ballantine Books, 1975), p. 43. The second type occurs in Harlan Ellison's "Catman" in *Final Stage*, Edward L. Ferman and Barry N. Malzberg, eds. (1974; rpt. New York: Penguin, 1975), pp. 134-70.

24. Zelazny, "For a Breath I Tarry," p. 76.

25. Protagoras, quoted by Plato, *Theaetetus*, 160d.

26. Zelazny, "For a Breath I Tarry," p. 91.

27. Ibid., p. 76.

28. Ibid., p. 104.

29. Ibid., p. 107.

30. A. E. Housman, "A Shropshire Lad," XXXII, in *The Collected Poems of A. E. Housman* (New York: Holt, Rinehart and Winston, 1965), p. 49.

Joe Sanders

14

TOOLS/MIRRORS: THE HUMANIZATION OF MACHINES

> Human interest out of robots? A contradiction.
> —Susan Calvin, in Introduction to Isaac Asimov's I, *Robot*

Though "machine" and "human" at first seem to be opposite terms, impressive stories have been written about the humanization of machines. We can understand why the concept disturbs and moves us by examining the theme's development to see the variety of ways machines have taken on human characteristics. Working down through layers of initial panic and defensive stereotyping, we can see how the "humanization of machines" really means the discovery of different levels and varieties of humanness that can be projected into machines. It is thus a subject both for literary analysis and for speculation on the ability of humans to extend our sympathies to others—and into the unguessed crannies of ourselves.

We actually have as much emotional as intellectual difficulty in fitting "machine" and "human" together. We don't want to think of a connection because we don't want to *feel* any connection. Machines make us nervous when they show any of the independent, seeking consciousness that we associate with being human. Thus, as long as possible, we like to think of machines simply as physical extensions of our wills. This is easy with simple devices. The vibration of a saw in wood or the impact of a hammer striking a nail travels through nerves to brain, giving immediate information, permitting immediate control. We may be more or less adept at using such devices, and we may have to use different amounts of caution in handling them; however, their *use* bothers no one. They are only tools. Add a source of power outside the human operator, and their use becomes merely a bit more difficult or dangerous. But add, as an SF element, a nonhuman controller as part of the device itself, attached to the power source, and the situation changes. Even beyond realistic notions of physical or social danger, we are disturbed. Because such a machine is constructed of materials more durable than flesh and blood, activated by an independent consciousness, it no longer fits easily within the picture of ourselves using mere tools. If not a physical threat, it certainly represents an emotional challenge to people nearby. We wonder just how many things the machine can do that we cannot. We wonder whether we should expect to compete against the machine. We wonder what will happen to the loser in the competition, and we fear to encounter the aggressive human traits we actually are projecting into that nonhuman Other.

This normal human reaction appears in virtually undiluted form in many SF stories, whether the machine takes the bipedal shape of a humanoid robot or not; the machine's form is less important than its role as primal threat. Thus, at their most primitive, SF machines do directly reflect basic human feelings: competitiveness, instinctive fear of a threat to survival, hostility. The natural, immediate response is to attack the threat physically. Whether they take the form of deranged mechanical chess players as in "Moxon's Master" by Ambrose Bierce, frantically propagating mother machines from the future as in "Mechanical Mice" by Eric Frank Russell, or construction equipment inhabited by an alien intelligence as in "Killdozer" by Theodore Sturgeon, conscious machines in such stories have some things in common.[1] For one thing, they are nonverbal; man cannot speak to them or they to him. They also are monomaniacal; their only purpose is to overcome—that is, destroy—the humans they encounter. Therefore, a human's only sensible response to such a machine is dread and the determination to destroy it before it kills him.

Assigning such malevolence to machines is itself a kind of "humanization" of them, but such projection denies human contact. Rather it is essentially an extension of human wariness at meeting any new situation. Yet, in SF, we soon observe a realization that while violent fear is a valid response to the situations depicted in these stories—and while, of course, the situations depicted are intended to validate the response—hostility is not the only way to meet another being. Certainly dread is one true reaction to a machine that displays some human traits, and to the extent of its truth such unthinking dread can produce striking fiction. A reader is led to share the viewpoint of the humans in the stories by Bierce, Russell, and Sturgeon noted above; things are happening too fast, and emotions are surging too convincingly for anyone to step back and ask, "Does it *have* to be this way?" But that is a reasonable question to ask as soon as one can step out of these stories and be more calmly reasonable about the meeting of humanity and conscious machines. It is altogether natural for the human mind to study its own reactions, to reflect on different interpretations of situations, though this doesn't happen inevitably, nor always consciously. Thus, as we look at other SF stories dealing with machines, we find machines that show additional human traits, reflecting the authors' discovery that there may be a more complicated consciousness inside that superhuman construction. With human characters in the stories taking a more restrained, receptive attitude, it becomes possible to speak of machines in less threatening, more overtly human terms. Still, at this second stage, the humanness granted to machines is extremely limited.

To understand the limitations of this new stage in the humanization of machines, consider, for contrast, Mary Shelley's *Frankenstein* (1818), which may be the first robot story and is unarguably the source of a central image in many robot stories.[2] Frankenstein's initial response to the living creature is exactly the primal horror described above, and the creature appears at first to be as mute, monomaniacal, and deserving of extinction as the machines already described. What breaks this mood is the discovery that the creature can talk. When communication proves possible, humans (Frankenstein himself and the story's audience as well) discover that the creature has been shunned and abused unjustly. He complains, "I am thy creature: I ought to be thy Adam; but I am rather the fallen angel, whom thou drivest from joy for no misdeed."[3] His appearance may be monstrous, but his inner feelings and the language he uses to describe them are recognizably, painfully human. Or *more* than the basic level of human nature we have seen thus far. The creature is not expressing primitive aversion but sophisticated reasoning in his attacks on human targets: "Shall I respect man, when he contemns me? . . . if I cannot inspire love, I will cause fear."[4]

Although SF writers came to echo *Frankenstein*'s discovery of human personality under a conscious machine's frightening exterior, they resisted the full discovery of a justifiably resentful, complex consciousness inside one of man's creations. For example, Eando Binder's first-person stories of the robot Adam Link manage to keep the machine in line with human preconceptions.[5] Many humans fear Adam Link and accuse him of being a brutal monster—a "Frankenstein"—when they are preparing to destroy him.[6] Actually, though his situation and much of his treatment resemble that of the creature in Shelley's novel, Adam is incredibly calm and reasonable. It is human beings who act out of blind, unthinking hostility,[7] but the robot recognizes that they are projecting the bestial part of their natures into him.[8] Despite all this, Adam accepts his creator's description of him as an "inestimable aid to man and his civilization."[9] Though conscious of the fear expressed in the "Frankenstein" label—and the inherently inferior mentality that produces it—Adam devotes himself to negating fear by being the ideal representative of human aspirations: the perfect public servant.

To overcome the image of the inhuman, threatening monster yet avoid considering the complexity of the actual Frankenstein-monster relationship, SF stories at this stage of development show semihumanized machines, ones that represent comforting stereotypes. The writers appreciate that machines can and do display human traits, but they cannot let these humanoid machines show human resentment at their ill treatment. Nor can they let the machines get too closely identified with humans. Instead, the machines accept safe, subordinate roles. The major revelation in stories at this level of understanding is that machines can be made acceptable as long as they merely complement human abilities, as long as they are mere extensions of humans' social, public positions. Thus Jay Score, in Eric Frank Russell's story of the same name, first proves himself as an ideal comrade, *then* is revealed to be a robot.[10] When his spaceship strays too close to the sun, Jay volunteers to pilot it alone while his Earthling and Martian shipmates huddle in a cool compartment; he takes the trait of loyalty and carries it further than flesh and blood can. In the same way, the title character of Lester del Rey's "Helen O'Loy" is the absolutely perfect representation of the traditional stereotype of a wife: domestic, self-effacing, and emotionally dependent—so much so that she voluntarily gives up life when the man she loves dies. It is true that Helen took these traits from the female image projected in the popular enter-tainment she absorbed just after being activated. However, the two men who have given Helen the potential for human reactions spend little time worrying that she has been unjustly limited to a stereotype. Basically, they are de-lighted; one marries Helen, and the other (the narrator) never marries at all because he cannot find a woman like her. It is profoundly *comforting* to discover that a conscious machine will fit so neatly into the stereotypes that insulate us from real personal contact.[11]

These preliminary stages in the humanization of machines look at first like opposite extremes: the machine is either implacably hostile to man or un-thinkingly devoted to human values. Actually, as indicated above, the second position is a necessary halfway step for writers ready to consider the possibility of "human" machines but unwilling to consider the full, disturbing complexity of the relation of creator and creation.

More sophisticated writers, however, have tried to understand machines in human terms, more aware of how humans project their own traits into machines. If those machines attempt to destroy humans, it is not simply their murderous natures; they have clear reasons for their hostility. Machines in these stories do not find it easy to submerge their individuality in a social stereo-type. Such machines display moral uncertainty, paranoia, wonder, and other complicated human traits. The major discovery of stories at this more ad-vanced level is that machines are not simply physical extensions of man but intellectual and emotional extensions as well. Such stories admit that machines can reflect vital, personal human traits that show either appalling or hopeful aspects of human nature.

For example, Isaac Asimov's early robot stories, mostly collected in *I, Robot*, show this progression clearly. The first, "Robbie," shows the machine as a nonverbal, subservient stereotype, a robot nursemaid. The next, "Runa-round," shows robots that are treated as delicate, error-prone machines; how-ever, they are capable of speech—when returned to its senses at the story's conclusion, a malfunctioning robot exclaims, "Holy smokes, boss, what are you doing here? And what am I doing—I'm so confused—": a very human outburst.[12] Succeeding stories, however, show robots who are such conscious individuals that they maintain their own religious interpretation of reality despite the explanations offered by the people around them[13]—or are unable to maintain independence because of social insecurity.[14] "Liar!" a story of the second kind, is especially interesting because it shows that humans' irrational, semisuperstitious dread persists even in an apparently coldly logical expert in Robotics: "Susan Calvin stared steadfastly at the floor, 'He knew of all this. That . . . that devil knows everything.'"[15] "Liar" also shows a robot who knows and accepts a subservient role: "I'm a machine, given the imitation of life only by virtue of the positronic interplay in my brain—which is man's device."[16] Still, this robot possesses an unrestrainable, undirected selfhood as well. In the story's climax, the robot's "voice rose to wild heights," he "cried," he "shrieked," and, finally, "Herbie screamed!"[17] A mind-reading robot, Herbie knows the real intent behind the words people speak to him, and he also can spot the underlying, unacknowledged motives that shape their conscious purposes. As a mechanical intelligence he has been directed not to hurt people; yet he cannot tell the truth without hurting someone, for each person wants different, contradictory things. So he is forced into increasingly desperate evasions. He is, in fact, a fair representative of human insecurity in social situations, though he is less adept at reconciling different levels of human communication/feeling. His display of emotion that cannot be bent or channeled within standard social roles actually makes him more "human" (in the sense of "vulnerable") than the humans around him, and he is driven into frustrated "insanity" by Susan Calvin, the successfully self-repressed robopsychologist whom he has shaken out of her shell by his enunciation of her true desires. At the story's end, *she* is very upset also, but she manages to regain "part of her mental equilibrium" and with it the stiff pose with which she hides her emotions. She is outwardly unchanged, but inside "the triumph faded and the helpless frustration returned."[18] If Herbie is a machine that resembles a human being, Susan Calvin is a human being who in some crucial ways resembles a machine.

Stories representing this stage in the humanization of machines show greater depth in the machines because they admit more complexity in human nature. Such stories contain more fully humanized machines whose destructive acts, if any, are recognizable results of human tendencies. "Liar" explicitly shows Susan Calvin projecting her desires through Herbie; so, too, Herbie's confusion, pain, and final retreat from understanding reflect the natures of the humans he meets. In such stories, then, we find machines who have become humanized themselves and who also reflect the humanity of the people around them, often in ways that the humans are too inhibited (or wise) to reveal directly. For example, Philip K. Dick's "Second Variety" gives a twist to the picture of human society seen in Asimov's "Liar." In "Liar," because people (though inherently competitive) want to accomplish something together they submerge their desires in nonabrasive social roles. Dick shows another outcome to individual competitiveness. Dick's humans have decided to get rid of different viewpoints by wiping out the others in a war; the story's machines set about doing this more efficiently than the humans could, but at the conclusion it appears that the different varieties of *machines* have become competitive and are ready to start wiping each other out too.[19]

These different interpretations of human nature, and thus of the actions that can be expected of men or machines, should not hide the fact that the machines do express or reflect rather complex, full pictures of humanity. And though we have just seen several stories of machines in social settings—stressing social relationships and their shortcomings—we also find an increasing number of stories shading into reflection on what humanity *is*, not just on how one person relates to another. In such stories, reflecting basic aspects of human nature, machines offer more than physical threats and rewards.

Thus Harlan Ellison's "I Have No Mouth, and I Must Scream" resembles Dick's "Second Variety" very superficially—machines, created to help the nations fight a war, now fight against all humanity—but stresses much more directly how human avoidance of responsibility produced AM, the all-powerful machine that carries our frivolous rivalry and paranoia to the ultimate extreme. After showing AM as frustrated, revenge-crazed, and futile, the narrator specifically links him to mankind, ironically speaking of "AM, whom we created because our time was badly spent and we must have known unconsciously that he could do it better."[20] Ellison, recently looking back at the story, has commented that it actually has an upbeat ending because the narrator rises above the limitations of his nature, especially as it has been manipulated and debased by AM, in order to give his companions merciful release.[21] This is true. However, except for the very core of the narrator's consciousness, AM still reigns supreme, and it still is important to remember that the ugliness AM imposes on the human characters was not created by him but—essentially—programmed into him by his human creators and now is merely embellished and intensified on these representative human survivors. In this story, the "humanization" of a machine gives man the chance to extend his viciousness through an uncontrollable tool.

In a vision that some may find even more appalling because it lacks Ellison's obvious passion, Kurt Vonnegut, Jr.'s, *The Sirens of Titan* (1959), shows not so much the humanization of machines as the mechanization of humans; as one victim explains, the master manipulator Rumfoord has "cleaned out our minds. . . . He wired us like robots, trained us, aimed us—burned us out in a good cause."[22] The last three words are important. Vonnegut's characters seem to accept what is done to them with a rather exhausted wryness because they accept the fact that humanity is basically unimportant—so there is no need to get upset if some humans cease to be individuals. The idea of mortal unimportance is recapped in a Tralfamadorian fable: When nonmechanical beings who seek some ultimate purpose in life ask their most advanced machine what that purpose is, it replies that there is none; they begin to wipe themselves out since they hate purposeless things, then turn the job over to the machines, who can do it better. And so the machines do.[23] Even when a machine *is* humanized in this story, the result is more proof of existence's banality. Salo, the Tralfamadorian messenger, violates his instructions in order to look at the message that he has warped humanity to deliver, only to discover that he has merely been carrying "Greetings" across space. For Salo and other characters, this is a resounding reaffirmation of the purposelessness of life.[24] Salo kills himself (temporarily) by taking himself apart and scattering the pieces. The others continue to lead their purposeless lives. So what? If humanity, inside or outside a machine, is essentially banal and trivial, living or dying or any combination thereof scarcely matters.

In a similar vein, Walter M. Miller, Jr.'s, "I Made You" shows a malfunctioning robot tank on the moon ambushing and killing its maintenance team, keeping one survivor (who long ago had programmed the machine) trapped in a cave while a rescue team dithers nearby. The people who might be able to disable the machine and save the man are afraid to risk damaging valuable installations near the machine; while they are worrying about a court-martial, the machine blows them to bits, then kills the remaining survivor. It is hard not to see the humans as doomed by their own actions or deliberate inaction. Because they give themselves to a system that prevents moral choice, they can mesh with machines; however, they are less efficient than the machines and thus doomed to die.

If humans become like machines—if the part of human nature that emerges when in contact with machines is only predictable, controllable—then the humanization of machines shows only man's own mechanical role in the universe. And there is little satisfaction in recognizing that. The last surviving human in Miller's story is reduced to whimpering, "*I made you, don't you understand? I'm human. I made you— —.*" Then he is blown apart.[25] Just so, at the end of Vonnegut's novel the mechanized humans die, and the humanized machine continues its "fool's errand" for want of anything better to do.[26] What this side of human nature produces is sterility, futility, and death.

Yet, strangely enough, this is not the only viewpoint one can draw from stories showing the humanization of machines. In some SF stories, sometimes in the very act of replacing humans, machines reveal the nonmechanical traits that make "humanity" feel important.

The predominant mood of John W. Campbell, Jr.'s, "Twilight," for example, is yearning sadness at the empty, futile lives of people in the far future. Aided by their machines, the humans have conquered space, manipulated matter, and extended their lives, but they have become feeble, pale copies of mankind. Campbell's narrator, a time-traveller from the relatively near future, despairs of bringing them back to greatness. However, before he leaves the far future, he does instruct one machine to make something which can take man's place: "A curious machine."[27] This complicates the story's mood considerably. It appears that Campbell has decided that curiosity is the vital element in humanity; lacking curiosity, whatever his other gifts, a person becomes subhuman. Thus, if a machine can develop curiosity, it would become a fit replacement for humanity because it would represent the most crucial human spark. And thus, though the creatures who look like man might disappear, the humanness with which we actually identify would endure.

Roger Zelazny's "For a Breath I Tarry" takes the notion even further. In Zelazny's story, though war has wiped out the human race and rigidly programmed machines simply try to follow their last orders without concern with their purpose, one curious machine, Frost, becomes so obsessed with the study of humanity that he not only reconstructs a human body but places his consciousness within it. However, Frost is "curious" in more ways than one. He is described as a machine with mechanial powers and limits: "He knew . . . , as gear knows gear, as electricity knows its conductor, as a vacuum knows its limits."[28] Yet he is beyond the limits of mechanical thinking. Solcom, the master machine that created Frost, found its consciousness blanked out by a solar flare at a crucial moment, so that Frost is the product of a condition "best described as madness."[29] He is physically a machine, but throughout the story he is more than that. Though the other machines recognize Frost as a Man only at the story's conclusion, readers may observe that his very curiosity about Man in the first place leads to his questioning of his own motives, which in turn leads to his moral questioning of Solcom at the story's climax—all *before* he inhabits an organic body. Zelazny leaves the origin of Frost's potential humanity mysterious. Though the story echoes with biblical suggestions, it seems unlikely that Zelazny wants a simple religious interpretation. Rather he seems to be saying that there is a mystery, something extraordinary, about mankind.

The idea of a mystery at the heart of man, revealed through humanized machines, is taken even further in the work of R. A. Lafferty. At the conclusion of *Past Master* (1968), the Programmed People—machines who have been plotting to replace humans—may be about to be miraculously transformed into living beings, dimly reflecting the divine mystery that has made them subconsciously yearn for the transformation. Even more directly, in *Arrive At Easterwine* (1971), the quirkily human machine Epiktistes is created to help a quirky bunch of scientists pin down patterns in natural laws, eliminating the uncertainty and mystery of life. Actually, however, Epikt only finds more mystery the deeper he delves. This does not disturb him greatly: "Well, am I . . . one of our Great Failures? I hope to be. Is it so bad if we fail upwards in every one of these attempts?"[30] The "attempts" Epikt is speaking of, the greatest mystery of all, is the effort to understand humanity itself. As another character comments, "We've all got to get our eyes renovated. . . . We are all missing a lot. If you look at your face in the glass today and it reminds you a little of your face of yesterday, oh, you are in trouble! Let us not miss the things in us!"[31] There may be dreadful things in the prospect of confronting ourselves truly, too, just as there are frightening things about confronting a silent, blank-faced robot. Yet the fear has been dissolved in wonder. If we can find despicable human traits in machines, we also find fresh glimpses of the unpredictable imagination, creativity, and empathy that makes humanity more than a mechanical manipulator of things.

There are several stages, then, in authors' willingness to admit human traits in machines and in the interpretation of those traits. Few stories representing the earlier stages of the process are written today: we find few stories of maniacal robots or machines that slip easily into a comfortable dependence on man. (Movies lag behind written SF to a perceptible degree. However, we now may be past the level of robot monster and into the second stage, thanks to the cute "droids" of *Star Wars*.) Stories that accept the complex humanity of machines are more likely to be written in the future because the subject of humanity, even screened through a metal filter, is inexhaustible. For discovery of the "humanness" in machines leads us to discover new possible shapes for our own humanness. Rather than fear what machines might do to us or wonder what they might do for us, we gain new perspective on what we have the power to do to and for ourselves.

NOTES

1. Ambrose Bierce's story "Moxon's Master," was collected in *Can Such Things Be?* (New York: Cassell, 1893); Eric Frank Russell's "Mechanical Mice" appeared, with the name of the author given as Maurice Hugi, in *Astounding*, January 1941; Theodore Sturgeon's "Killdozer" was in *Astounding*, November 1944. Curious readers can trace reprints in reference works such as William Contento's *Index to Science Fiction Anthologies and Collections*.

2. Brian W. Aldiss links Frankenstein's monster to future robots in *Billion Year Spree: The True History of Science Fiction* (Garden City, NY: Doubleday, 1973), p. 23. I have argued elsewhere that Shelley's novel is much more fantasy than SF ("Re-Visions," *Science Fiction Commentary*, February 1975). However, it is certain that an SF version of the plot—along with the misapplication of the name "Frankenstein" to the monster—has become an icon in SF.

3. All quotations from Mary Shelley, *Frankenstein* are from James Rieger's edition of the 1818 text (Indianapolis: Bobbs-Merrill, 1974); here vol. 2, ch. 2, p. 95.

4. Shelley, *Frankenstein*, vol. 2, ch. 9, p. 141.

5. Apparently it was Otto Binder, using the penname he shared with his brother Carl, who actually wrote the Adam Link stories, beginning in *Amazing*, January 1939. It still is an open question who actually did introduce the sympathetic, "humanized" robot to SF. Damon Knight, for example, finds several antecedents of the Adam Link stories, robbing Binder of the honor of being first (*In Search of Wonder*, rev. ed. [Chicago: Advent, 1967], p. 133). Sam Moskowitz discovers an even earlier example in John B. Harris's "Lost Machine" (*Amazing*, April 1932), though he points out that Harris's sympathetic robot was brought to Earth from Mars, still giving Adam Link the honor of being the first sympathetic robot constructed on Earth (see "Introduction" to

the reprint of "The Lost Machine," *Amazing*, December 1960). However, it seems fair to say that Binder's series, continuing over three years, was at least important in spreading the concept.

6. Quotations are from the novelization of the Eando Binder series, *Adam Link —Robot* (New York: Paperback Library, 1965). For "Frankenstein," in the common misapplication to monster rather than creator, see pp. 16, 24, 30, and 70.

7. Binder, *Adam Link*, pp. 22, 23, and 29.

8. Ibid., p. 45.

9. Ibid., p. 11.

10. Eric Frank Russell, "Jay Score," *Astounding*, May 1941.

11. Lester del Rey, "Helen O'Loy," *Astounding*, December 1938.

12. Isaac Asimov's "Robbie," originally titled "Strange Playfellow," appeared in *Super Science Stories*, September 1940; "Runaround" appeared in *Astounding*, March 1942. *I, Robot* first appeared in 1950; all quotations are from the first paperback edition of *I, Robot* (New York: New American Library, 1956), here p. 45.

13. Isaac Asimov, "Reason," *Astounding*, April 1941.

14. Isaac Asimov, "Liar!" *Astounding*, May 1941.

15. Asimov, "Liar!" in *I, Robot*, p. 96.

16. Ibid., p. 97.

17. Ibid., pp. 97-98.

18. Ibid., p. 99.

19. Philip K. Dick, "Second Variety," *Space Science Fiction*, May 1953.

20. First published in *If*, March 1967; collected in *I Have No Mouth and I Must Scream* (New York: Pyramid, 1967), p. 42.

21. Harlan Ellison, "Memoir: I Have No Mouth and I Must Scream," *Starship*, 17 (Summer 1980), 6-13.

22. Kurt Vonnegut, Jr., *The Sirens of Titan* (New York: Dell, 1959), ch. 10, p. 242.

23. Vonnegut, *Sirens*, ch. 12, pp. 274-75.

24. Ibid., pp. 300-01.

25. Walter M. Miller, Jr., "I Made You," *Astounding*, March 1954; in the anthology *The Metal Smile*, Damon Knight, ed. (New York: Belmont, 1968), p. 103.

26. Vonnegut, *Sirens*, ch. 12, p. 313.

27. John W. Campbell, Jr., under the name Don A. Stuart, "Twilight," *Astounding*, November 1934; in the collection *Who Goes There?* (Chicago: Shasta, 1948), p. 204.

28. Roger Zelazny, "For a Breath I Tarry." *New Worlds Science Fiction*, no. 160 (March 1966); corrected version *Fantastic* (September 1966); in the anthology *Survival Printout*, Total Effect, ed. [Leonard Allison, Leonard Jenkin, Robert Perrault], p. 68.

29. Zelazny, "Breath," *Survival Printout*, p. 68.

30. R. A. Lafferty, *Arrive at Easterwine* (New York: Scribners, 1971), p. 101.

31. Ibid., pp. 99-101.

15

MECHANISMS OF MORALITY: PHILOSOPHICAL IMPLICATIONS OF SELECTED (A)MORAL SCIENCE FICTION MACHINES

Isaac Asimov's robots would allow themselves to be destroyed rather than harm a human being. Jack Williamson's humanoids always act "To Serve and Obey, And Guard Men from Harm." No doubt their concern for our welfare should meet with our approval, though we may deplore the results. But regardless of outcome, are the things which they do for us moral acts? Can these machines be moral? Can we have moral relationships with machines?[1]

Who cares?

Philosophers do, for a variety of reasons. They like to illustrate the strong points of theories with striking examples. They like to test the limits of theories with hard cases. And perhaps most of all, they like to destroy opposing theories with counterexamples: cases which show that the theory cannot work.

My main thrust here will be to give counter-examples to several different kinds of theories. I am treating straightforward versions of these theories in the interest of clarity, so objections from sophisticated perspectives to my counter-examples are not too hard to find. Such objections can be refuted, but a general-interest work such as *The Mechanical God* is not the place for lengthy discussions of esoteric technicalities. The differences between hypothetical machines which provide counterexamples are instructive in a variety of ways. None of these machines seems impossible; and, since their capabilities and limitations vary in ways which those of humans do not, we can learn a lot about what the theories really require human nature to be when we see, for example, that a machine which is clearly a moral being under one theory is clearly not under another theory.

Suppose we maintain that even the most complex machines, the most subtle robots and computers, are unconscious, unable to feel, unable to think: that they have no free will and no soul. Then having a moral relationship with such a being would be on a par with having one with a can opener. The example of the can opener, and, much more so, more complex machines, raises two important points. First, there are prerequisites for being a moral entity. But second, we can't let our language get in the way of our philosophy.

For example, there are various arguments which hold that machines by definition cannot think, since only living beings can think, and machines are not living beings. This kind of linguistic flummery will not do. Our criteria for action must be functional: if a machine (or alien) acts as if it thinks, then we must treat it as if it thinks, regardless of what we call what it does. Roger Zelazny's Frost will serve to illustrate this point.

In Zelazny's "For a Breath I Tarry," humanity is extinct. However, machines continue to work at making the world more comforable for Man; only a human being could tell them to stop. Much effort in the rebuilding of the world is wasted because of rivalry between two master computers, Solcom and Divcom. Eventually, they agree to a contest by proxy: If Divcom's minions can capture the obedience of Solcom's greatest servant, the unique computer Frost, Solcom will acknowledge Divcom's primacy; otherwise, Divcom must obey Solcom. Frost is tempted with knowledge of the extinct species Man and undertakes to become human. Eventually Frost succeeds; all machines must now obey the Man Frost has become.[2]

In the beginning of the story, Frost is clearly a thinking machine. It also has a modicum of free will. Although it is clear from its dealings with the Ancient Ore-Crusher that it would have to obey a human, there are no humans, so that constraint does not really affect it. On the other hand, it is capable of disobeying a superior computer.[3]

Zelazny tells us that this is not enough. Frost cannot feel, and until it does it remains a mere machine. When he does feel, he becomes human and remains human even when the matrix of his awareness returns to a machine. The point seems to be that any intelligent consciousness can become a human consciousness, but only if it has the opportunity to experience in a biological mode, which is fundamentally different from a mechanical mode.[4]

The point is not well taken. If we could make an exact circuit diagram of a human brain, and build something (perhaps with large-scale integrated circuits) that matched the diagram, why couldn't it feel? It's got the equipment; all we need to do is feed in the proper input.[5] Perhaps the original Frost did not have the equipment. But there doesn't seem to be any reason why it couldn't have built what it needed from inorganic components. After all, it was able to do it with organic ones. There is no good reason to accept such biological chauvinism.

The same considerations apply to moral behavior and whatever prerequisites it may have. If a machine acts as if it fulfills the prerequisites and is behaving like a moral being, then we must treat it as a moral being, regardless of how we characterize its behavior. To call what machines do by the names we give to human behavior should not be interpreted as anthropomorphizing the machines but simply describing behavior.

The above list of prerequisites for a moral being may be incomplete, and it may include irrelevant conditions. I won't spend much time addressing this problem directly, but there is one suggestion that I want to dismiss forthwith. Several theories maintain that a moral being must have a soul. But even if possession of a soul is required in a moral being, machines are not necessarily disqualified. God could choose to give them souls, and who are we to say that (S)He would not?

On the other hand, I must discuss free will. It seems clear that if I do not act of my own free will, I am not morally responsible for my acts or their consequences. I am begging some deep philosophical questions by saying this, but the issue is too complex for brief discussion. I shall merely stipulate, then, that what is true for me is also true for machines. If they are to act morally, they must have free will.

Having free will, however, is not an all-or-nothing proposition. One may have it for some kinds of action and not for others, just as one is able to exercise free will in some situations but not in others. If I am under physical compulsion, I cannot exercise free will; likewise, if I have a neurotic compulsion that prevents me from, say, riding in elevators, I cannot exercise free will in that area of conduct. But in either kind of case, I can at the same time have free will outside of the areas in which I am under compulsion even while I am under compulsion. Thus, I can, if I am levelheaded, choose to try to solve chess problems in my head while I am being forcibly strapped into an electric chair, or I can choose to think about something else. In this case I may choose freely the subject of my thoughts, though I have no freedom to choose what happens to my body. For a moral issue, the question is whether I had free will in the area about which the issue arises, regardless of what my peculiarities in other areas might be.

Asimov's robots and Williamson's humanoids cannot choose to act against human beings. In such matters at least they do not have free will. Hence, their concern for human welfare is not moral, and they do not act morally in this central area of moral conduct. We must look elsewhere for moral mechanisms.

Would the original Frost count as a moral being? It depends on what theory of ethics is used to make the judgment. Theories of ethics can be divided into broad categories in several ways. It is useful to talk about intention-centered, consequence-centered, and act-centered theories. Frost could count as a moral being in terms of a specific intention-centered theory, that of Immanuel Kant.

Kant held that we are truly moral only when we act out of purely moral considerations without regard for other kinds of factors. These moral considerations can be summarized in two imperatives. First, we should do only those things which we would will that everyone should do in like circumstances. Second, human beings must be treated as ends, never as means only. The first imperative is designed to eliminate special pleading. It requires that in making a decision the moral agent must be disinterested and that the decision be such that it could be generalized into a rule of conduct. The second imperative is designed to rule out exploitation of human beings. It provides a benchmark against which rules of conduct can be assessed.[6]

Since the agent must be distinterested, the only pure moral acts are those in which the agent is uninterested and indifferent as well.[7] Thus, a machine which was altogether lacking in emotion would be much better at acting morally than we are, provided that it met Kant's other prerequisites for moral behavior. It would see its duty and do it. The original Frost was such a machine. Hence, it could be a moral being, at least in Kant's sense.

There is another example of this type of machine in the literature of science fiction: Fred Saberhagen's berserkers. The berserkers appear as the most obvious common factor in a loosely connected set of stories. They are ancient war machines dedicated to destroying all life. They range in size from human or smaller to warships of asteroidal magnitude. Humanity is the toughest challenge they have faced in millions of years.[8]

It is not completely clear that the berserkers have the free will necessary to be moral agents. After all, they were created and programmed to fight an ancient war. But that task was completed long ago, and they are still dedicated to destroying all life. They do this in the context of an ethical theory, and they make moral judgments. They are now acting of their own free will, despite their original programming.[9]

If this is correct, they are moral beings in Kant's sense. Having nothing to gain, they are disinterested. Having no emotions, they are uninterested and indifferent. Destroying life is for them an end in itself, so they are not exploiting human beings. And clearly they are doing nothing which they would not want to have adopted as a general rule of conduct.

As moral beings, they are capable of immorality. They distinguish between "badlife" and "goodlife." Badlife resists them; goodlife aids and abets them in their purpose.[10] However, to make use of goodlife is to exploit human beings, and this is wrong under the second imperative, so the berserkers would be acting immorally.

In their defense, we should notice that Kant's theory is biocentric: Why should life have special status? Consider instead a mechanocentric system. Exploiting goodlife is not exploiting berserkers. Hence, in a mechanocentric Kantian system it would not be wrong to make use of goodlife as a means only. It seems that the berserkers are morally upright after all.

This conclusion would gag a buzzard.[11] It cries out for refutation. Two possible lines of attack on it are apparent. First, we can try to use feelings as a factor in our ethical theories. Second, we can try to find a general definition of a moral being that would not depend on accidental or idiosyncratic physical form or mental ability.

For the first line of argument, examine utilitarianism. It is a consequence-centered theory with a single test to determine whether an act is morally right: Does it produce the greatest possible amount of happiness for the greatest number, given the available options? A key premise of the theory is that the answer to the test question can be derived by objective calculations.[12]

Let's take another look at Frost and the berserkers. From the utilitarian point of view, they are capable of moral action. All they would have to do is make the calculations. However, there is a curious asymmetry here. Frost could behave morally (assuming that it had the necessary free will; perhaps we should have it deal with an alien). The berserkers would obviously be immoral. Happiness is rarely maximized by death. But since none of these machines have feelings, they cannot be happy (or unhappy). Therefore, although a utilitarian moral machine will take our interests into account, we need not take its interests into account, except insofar as they coincide with our interests. The machine's interests do not count in themselves. It gives; we take; there is no reciprocity.

Surely there is a flaw in a theory that can countenance indifference to the interests of a being that recognizes and forwards our interests. This kind of anthropocentricism might be dangerous as well as inequitable when we encounter aliens. What if the nature of their feelings differs from ours? They might have nothing like happiness, but rather an entirely different emotional touchstone. If they constructed a system based on their feelings, they could be morally indifferent to us, even if we chose for moral (but not utilitarian) reasons to take their interests into account.[13] Even aside from that, a utilitarian machine might not be to our liking. Gene Wolfe has written a story that presents a case in point.

In (not on) an artificial asteroid, there is an island. The island is a psychiatrist; call it "Dr. Island." On Dr. Island are three teenagers: Nicholas, Diane, and Ignacio. They are all insane. Dr. Island speaks to them in the sounds of waves and wind, the rustle of the leaves, and the chatter of monkeys. The teenagers are to be cured mainly by interacting with each other, says Dr. Island; but it lies to them repeatedly. Ignacio effects his cure by brutally killing Diane, the death Dr. Island chose for her. It has something similar in mind for Nicholas. It suppresses the personality in the left side of his split brain, leaving the personality in the inarticulate right hemisphere dominant. The boy should now be well suited for the role Dr. Island had originally planned for him—the part that was played by Diane.[14]

In the course of the story, Dr. Island explains to Diane that if one person has a very great need, that can outweigh the lesser needs of its other residents. Moreover, it regards some people as more important than others, apparently on the basis of their potential to contribute to human welfare. From such points as these, it is reasonable to conclude that Dr. Island is a utilitarian.[15]

It may also be the first truly immoral machine we have encountered. Not because it tells deadly lies, not because it drives the personality of Nicholas into catatonia, not because it manipulates events to bring about the murder of Diane;[16] all of these things could be morally correct in a utilitarian system, which is one of the main problems with utilitarianism. No, Dr. Island is immoral because it apparently ignores its utilitarian principles in the case of Nicholas.

Nicholas is listed in Dr. Island's data banks as having an IQ of 95. This is clearly wrong, as we can tell from Nicholas's speech and behavior. Nicholas himself tells Dr. Island that the test results were fabricated. Dr. Island is first evasive and then claims to have no facilities for testing. Yet, we have reason to doubt this because it admits to major lies.[17] It does not reconsider its course of action; but a moral utilitarian would feel obliged to take new information into account, seek further information if his data were in doubt, and recalculate the desirability of his options on the basis of the new data. Dr. Island is evil even by the standards it professes to hold.

There remains, though, a chance that it is not. Suppose that it is not trying to maximize human welfare. (It claims that it is, but we know it lies.) Suppose it is trying to maximize some value of its own. Then it may be acting morally all the way through the story, and all the lies, brainwashing, and murder are morally correct.

Once again we are faced with an extremely parochial moral system, just as we were in ordinary utilitarianism and in the Kantian systems discussed above. In this case, the defect has a relatively simple remedy. We simply make an open-ended list—starting with human happiness because we already know about that—of v_lues that all moral beings should seek to maximize. But that still leaves us with the second problem mentioned above, that is, how to identify moral beings.

Perhaps we should try an act-centered theory. That would have the advantage of not depending on mentalistic notions like intentions or feelings. We can observe acts and judge them much more easily than we can get at feelings or intentions. There are two kinds of act-centered theory. One involves a system of rules forbidding or prescribing various practices. The other calls for judging an act on the basis of some kind of principle or perception.

Confucianism is a plausible example of the first type of system. For a Confucian, propriety (li) is of central importance. This originally meant proper performance of ceremonies, but it was broadened to include the whole range of behavior governed by etiquette and morals, which became virtually indistinguishable. "It isn't li" is roughly equivalent to the English, "It isn't done," meaning that a right-minded person would not do it and would be angered and disgusted by it perhaps to the point of finding it intolerable. The latter is, in fact, what Sir Patrick Devlin has proposed as the basis for moral law.[18]

There should be no difficulty in principle in programming a machine to behave with propriety. However, the truly virtuous individual must also have humanity (*jen*). This is not to be taken as having a particular biological nature. "As a general virtue, *jen* means . . . that which makes man a moral being." Though this is uninformative, Confucius, being a humanist, would not have had in mind anything profoundly metaphysical. But the Confucian theory of the order of the universe does not allow even that all men can be truly virtuous. Moreover, it is strongly hierarchical, with a place for everything. Departure from this natural order inevitably leads to disaster. The place of machines in this order would simply not be such that they could have the capacity to be virtuous. For a Confucian, a machine could not be a moral being.[19] In a Confucian society, robots would be an under-class below the lowest human beings. The classic example of this situation is Karel Čapek's *R.U.R.*

In *R.U.R.*, Helena Glory, daughter of the President, arrives to visit the robot factory convinced that robots are human. Domin, the manager of the company, explains that despite appearances robots—what today we'd probably call "androids"—are not human. Even the most complex models are much simpler in structure than human beings. Robots are better designed, though, from an engineering point of view. Unfortunately, Domin and his few human colleagues are unaware of the narrowness, crassness, and simple-mindedness of their point of view. At this point, for no conceivable reason, Helena agrees to marry Domin.

Ten years later, the social disruption caused by the use of robots has come to a head. Humans, in despair, have stopped having children; when the humans rebel, they are wiped out by robot troops. The robots then rebel; somehow they have developed minds of their own. In fact, this is the result of Helena's having persuaded Dr. Gall, the company's chief scientist, to make the robots more human. Eventually, all the humans are dead except Alquist, head of the Works Department, who, among other things, builds houses. He is spared because he works with his hands, a nice gesture on the part of this new dictatorship of the proletariat (*robot* being the Czech word for "worker"). But the robots' victory is hollow. They cannot reproduce, and Helena has destroyed the secret of their manufacture for neurotic reasons of her own.

Two years later, Alquist has not rediscovered the secret. The robots are desperate. Fortunately, it turns out that Dr. Gall's last two creations are human. Alquist sends them off to inherit the earth.[20]

Although Čapek was writing from an entirely different point of view, a Confucian would see the large-scale events about which he writes as being the inevitable results of attempts to alter the natural order of the world. Only the very end of the play would be rejected as impossible.

At the beginning of the play, however, the robots are just as they should be for Confucians: hard-working, obedient, uncomplaining, and unfeeling. They behave with propriety, but they clearly lack humanity, and that could not be otherwise. However, there are sinister portents. First, their disposition is in the hands of businessmen and technologists; and, as every Confucian knows, such people do not have the moral character necessary to cope with important matters. This is manifest in the attempts to make the robots more like, or even superior to, human beings, which is the second portent.[21]

The human beings who make these attempts are in part successful, but of course they can never give the robots *jen*. Thus, their partial success dooms the human race, because the new-model robots, forced in their making out of their place in the natural order, are uncontrollable and, owing to their twisted nature, can think only of destroying the natural order.[22]

For a Confucian, the human relationships in *R.U.R.* are implausible, but they are just as implausible to anyone else. The two things that must be quite wrong are that the human race should actually be destroyed and that the robots Primus and Helena should be able, as it seems that they are, to institute a new order. The natural order on earth mirrors and reciprocally influences the celestial natural order. It is inconceivable that the gods would allow or require such radical changes as Čapek suggests. Unfortunately for this type of act-centered theory, however, it is inconceivable only to Confucians. By its raising such possibilities, *R.U.R.* is a counterexample to Confucianism.[23]

The Confucian system, like a scientific theory, described empirical boundary conditions on what can happen. In this respect it differs from much of Western philosophical thought, which in general has little empirical content. Events could prove the Confucian system wrong. If the people are virtuous, things ought to go well,[24] but often in Chinese history this has not been the case. Therefore something is wrong with the theory, and it might well be the idea of what the natural order is.

On the other hand, Confucian philosophy resembles much Western philosophy in being an integrated system. We cannot change part of it without changing the whole thing. The original problem of moral mechanisms turns out here to be linked to areas of philosophy quite distant from ethics. Though the problem appeared at the start to be limited, in Confucian thought it is inseparable from the most general problems in philosophy. For other kinds of theory it might be possible to treat ethics in isolation, but we can now see that such a stand will itself raise profound philosophical questions.

The other kind of act-centered theory, in which the act is judged directly, is exemplified by ethical intuitionism. G. E. Moore was one of its most prominent proponents. In his theory, the way you know that something is good is much the same as the way you know that something is yellow. It's not something that can be analyzed; you just *know*. It is an immediate perception, a direct intuition.[25]

There is at least one machine that might be able to do this. We are indebted to Henry Kuttner and C. L. Moore, writing as Lewis Padgett, for a robot named Joe. In "The Proud Robot," we have a scientist, Gallegher, who can function as a scientist only when alcohol looses his subconscious knowledge and creativity. Unfortunately, when he sobers up and confronts the fruits of his drunken labors, he has no memory of what they are or what they are supposed to do. On one such occasion, he awakens to find Joe. While Gallegher is trying to find out why he built Joe, and for whom, and also to avoid various creditors, Joe hypnotizes two enemies of one of Gallegher's customers and, having convinced them that it (Joe) is Gallegher, forges Gallegher's signature on a contract. In order to void the contract, Gallegher must get Joe to demonstrate its abilities in court. Joe refuses; it has not been conditioned to obey, and its obedience can only be obtained by ordering the robot to perform its function, which Gallegher doesn't know. Gallegher solves the problem by getting drunk. The solution to the customer's problem is built into Joe, though that is not Joe's function. What Joe really is, is a can opener.[26]

Joe does have free will, at least in many areas. It thinks. It has at least some feelings, since it can be amused and is extremely vain. It is a moral being, but certainly it feels no particular obligation to consider the interests of its maker, Gallegher.[27]

Joe could be an egoist, concerned only with its own comfort. This is a reasonable conclusion about its motives. It could also be a different kind of intuitionist, perceiving something that we cannot. Since there's nothing else like Joe, we can't easily distinguish the two possibilities. But we know that Joe does have senses which we do not, so let's assume for the sake of argument that it is a kind of ethical intuitionist.[28]

Unfortunately, Joe appears to perceive good (if that is what it does) in a way that is radically different from ours. This is a problem that plagues intuitionistic theories in general. To perceive yellow, we use our sense of sight. What do we use to perceive good? What does Joe use? If we and Joe have different means of perceiving good, is there any guarantee that we will agree on what it is? And even if we do agree, does that mean we are correct? We have, after all, no objective way of checking, because that would involve direct comparisons of intuitions which is, in principle, impossible.[29]

Ludwig Wittgenstein argued that this notion of objective comparison is a chimera and that all we can have is consensus.[30] But what kind of consensus could exist among beings with different kinds of senses? (According to Zelazny, that is why machines can't be human—they and we sense things too differently.) Yet surely some kind of consensus is possible. Science and mathematics transcend cultural barriers; could they fail to transcend species barriers? The premise of ethical intuitionism requires that the data of ethics be no less objective than the data of science. Ethics, then, must in principle be able to bridge the gap between man and machine if intuitionism is correct. It appears that Joe would be a counterexample to Moore, though there is an uninviting way to avoid this conclusion, as we shall see.

This review of the argument on intuitionism thus far has only raised further questions. We learn how to see. Must we also learn how to distinguish good from evil, or is the distinction self-evident? Is the distinction one that exists in the external world, or is it an artifact of consciousness? Frank Herbert suggests answers to these questions and many more in *Destination: Void*.

In this novel, the spaceship *Earthling Number Six* is ostensibly on its way to colonize a planet of Tau Ceti. There is no such planet. The real purpose of the expedition is to create an artificial consciousness, suitably isolated in case it should run amok. To this end, the ship has been programmed to break down bit by bit—eventually fatally unless its crew can create an artificial consciousness. This may seem hard on the crew and the hybernating colonists, but they are clones—expendable property in the view of their masters, as were their counterparts on the five preceding ships. The clones on *Earthling Number Six* are successful in creating artificial consciousness—perhaps too successful. In the end they are even able to evade the command to destroy their creation and themselves. The computer named Ship takes them to Tau Ceti, where it creates a planet for them and declares itself their god.[31]

The real meat of *Destination: Void* is the crew's experiments, technological and philosophical, by which they try desperately to create the artificial intelligence that can save their lives. Such artificial intelligence—machine consciousness—is a prerequisite of morality, but it must have its own prerequisites. However, there may be different kinds of consciousness. This is a point too little considered by science fiction writers, many of whom seem to assume that anything conscious will be so in about the same way we are. In *Destination: Void*, there is a conscious decision to construct a consciousness of the type with which we are already most familiar: our own.[32]

Herbert takes the position, through his characters' dialogues and actions, that this means that we must build into the machine instincts, emotions, sexuality, and the ability to reproduce. Specifically, a killer instinct, fear, guilt, and love will be necessary, among other things. Only then can our kind of consciousness arise to perform the functions of filter and homeostat, which it does by imposing figure-and-ground relations on its data, symbolizing, and manipulating the symbols.[33]

If Herbert is correct, then all of the things he derives as prerequisites for consciousness are *a fortiori* prerequisites for a machine to be a moral entity in anything like the way humans are. None of the machines discussed above seem to meet these conditions. The humanoids and Asimov's robots have no true emotions or sexuality. Frost, under this analysis, could not have been conscious until he became human. Joe has no instinct of self-preservation, as he keeps telling us, so he has no fear (or guilt, it seems).[34] The same would be true of the robots in *R.U.R.* Dr. Island *might* have all the qualifications, but it's hard to tell. Anyone who would build a machine like that would make sure it could not reproduce.

Of course, there is no guarantee that a machine which was conscious in another way would be moral. That may be the problem with Joe: it is conscious in a way which is radically different from ours. Perhaps it has something in its type of consciousness which is incompatible with anything that could be called morality, or it may be that even an analogue of morality is impossible in the structure of its consciousness. There are lots of possibilities, most of them depressing. In short, morality itself might be an artifact of our biology.

Even a consciousness modeled on our own might not be moral. It must be possible for it to be immoral, but that is not the point. Herbert's Ship, though modeled on humans, exceeds their capacity to so great a degree that it declares itself to be God. In some theories of morality, this would mean that Ship had transcended good and evil, and with them, morality.[35]

In this context Moore's moral perceptions are to be seen as one kind of figure-and-ground relation that the filter of our consciousness imposes on our perceptions. This is something that we learn to do, but the learning is inevitable since it is a necessary concomitant of consciousness.

If Herbert is correct, his analysis does serious damage to Moore's position. For Moore, things just *are* good. To say that consciousness imposes moral distinctions cuts to the heart of his claim because it locates good in our heads and not in the world. If that is so, it is still possible to be an ethical intuitionist, but not the way Moore wanted to be one.[36]

At the beginning of this essay, I asked whether machines could be moral, perform moral acts, and whether we could have moral relations with them. I can now give a philosopher's answer to each of these questions: yes and no. Only within the context of a particular philosophical system can a definite answer to such questions be reached, and that answer holds only within that system. The berserkers could be considered to be moral in Kant's theory, but not in utilitarian theory. Since it seems implausible that the berserkers should be moral, this would count against Kant's theory and for utilitarianism.

But we also saw that the original Frost, or any other emotionless machine, would not be treated as a moral agent by utilitarians. That is a strike against utilitarianism, because it would mean that even human beings who lacked emotions (perhaps as a result of brain damage) could not be accommodated by utilitarianism.

Confucianism would automatically discriminate against all machines and, for that matter, against some human beings. We may dismiss it for that reason; but, even granting that Confucians discriminate unfairly, can we really assume so easily that all human beings are morally equal? We recognize already that children are not always morally competent; why should we assume that adults are? To argue for moral equality, even if we limit the argument to adult human beings, we must draw ideas from the whole range of philosophy. The bare possibility of robots, then, requires us to rethink the problems of the nature of the natural order, of the universe; we must rethink what it means to be human, and what it means to be moral. When we do, we're going to find that robots of the *R.U.R.* type are virtually impossible to exclude from the community of moral beings on the basis of an act-centered theory based on an explicit moral code.

Joe shows us that these questions do not have straightforward answers. Joe's values (if it has values)—any robot's values—are not necessarily human values. Since the existence of morally dissenting robots is not manifestly impossible, we must consider whether more than one *correct* moral theory is possible. This is more than mere relativism. The question, whether there is more than one objectively right way to perceive the universe, is an attack on Moore's intuitionism and act-centered theories of a similar type.

The building of Ship's artificial consciousness in *Destination: Void* has profound moral implications. If Herbert's analysis is correct, then many of the kinds of machine consciousness discussed above are either impossible or would be different in kind from human consciousness. This analysis of consciousness suggests a program of research. First, we establish which of Herbert's conditions for human-type consciousness are necessary conditions for any kind of consciousness to exist at all. We next examine the results of systematic variation of the other conditions, which will lead to other types of consciousness. We can then discuss whether a being with such a consciousness is or could be moral, and in what sense.

Thus the questions raised in connection with the rejection of Confucianism take on (for this discussion) a more manageable form. However, there are still other questions which need further treatment. After discovering counter-examples to intention-centered, consequence-centered, and act-centered theories, what is left?

Some philosophers argue that a more complex version of one of these theories will avoid the difficulties raised. It is by no means clear that this is so. It is clear that we normally take into account intentions, consequences, and the nature of the act in the ordinary course of making a moral judgment. It is time to construct a theory which takes all three into account as fundamental terms which cannot be reduced to anything else. Insights from the study of machine intelligence should be very important in formulating such a theory: only when we are aware of possible alternatives, including radically different alternatives, can we be confident that we're not missing something crucial.

NOTES

1. Isaac Asimov, "The Three Laws of Robotics," in *I, Robot* (1950; rpt. New York: Grosset & Dunlap, 1952), p. 7. Jack Williamson, *The Humanoids* (1949; rpt. New York: Grosset & Dunlap, 1950), ch. ix, p. 65.

2. Roger Zelazny, "For a Breath I Tarry," *New Worlds Science Fiction*, March 1966; rpt. in *World's Best Science Fiction: 1967*, Donald A. Wollheim and Terry Carr, eds. (New York: Ace, 1967), pp. 250-85.

3. Ibid., pp. 251, 265-66, 280, 281.

4. Ibid., pp. 257-58, 281-83.

5. Frost does try analogues of human sensory equipment (Zelazny, "Breath," p. 264), but there is no reason to think that this alone would suffice to make it human.

6. Immanuel Kant, *Foundations of the Metaphysics of Morals*, Lewis White Beck, trans., with critical essays, Robert Paul Wolff, ed. (Indianapolis: Bobbs Merrill, 1969), pp. 16-17, first sec., p. 52, second sec.

7. Ibid., pp. 16-17, first sec. The example below might be questioned on the grounds that it doesn't really meet the criteria for universalizability. On the other hand, those criteria have been a subject of controversy ever since this work was first published. It is by no means clear that this example could be excluded.

8. Fred Saberhagen, "Fortress Ship," *Worlds of If Science Fiction*, January 1963, pp. 96-105; Fred Saberhagen, "Patron of the Arts," *Worlds of If Science Fiction*, August 1965, pp. 81-88; Fred Saberhagen, "Goodlife," *Worlds of Tomorrow*, December 1963, pp. 41-58.

9. Saberhagen, "Fortress Ship," p. 97; Saberhagen, "Patron of the Arts," pp. 84, 88.

10. Saberhagen, "Goodlife," pp. 44-51.

11. Experts disagree about the validity of this metaphor: As the Director remarked to Constantine Quiche, "What is little known is that buzzards gag rather easily. . . . But they do not give up easily. . . . They will tackle the same piece of carrion again and again until finally they will keep it down one more time than they will bring it up. I've always admired this quality of persistence in buzzards. . . ." (R. A. Lafferty, "Where Have You Been, Sandaliotis?" in *Apocalypses* [Los Angeles: Pinnacle Books, 1977], p. 169).

12. John Stuart Mill, *Utilitarianism* (London, 1863), rpt. in *The Essential Works of John Stuart Mill*, ed. and with an intro. by Max Lerner (New York: Bantam Books, 1961), ch. ii, pp. 194, 199, 210. The kinds of examples I will raise against utilitarianism are most telling against act utilitarianism. Rule utilitarianism is able to avoid many difficulties of these types, though in the final analysis it is not completely satisfactory either. Since there is not enough space here for a full and careful discussion of the issues, I am contenting myself with a quick stab in the back.

13. " 'Human values don't apply to robots,' Joe said." As a robot, it should know. Lewis Padgett (Henry Kuttner and C. L. Moore), "The Proud Robot," *Astounding Science Fiction*, November 1943; rpt. in *Robots Have No Tails* (New York: Gnome Press, 1952), p. 38.

14. Gene Wolfe, "The Death of Dr. Island," in *Universe 3*, Terry Carr, ed. (New York: Random House, 1973), pp. 1-60; rpt. in *The Island of Doctor Death and Other Stories and Other Stories* (New York: Pocket Books, 1980), pp. 77-131.

15. Ibid., pp. 90-92, 91-100, 106.

16. Ibid., pp. 125, 130-31.

17. Ibid., pp. 96-97, 106, 130.

18. H. G. Creel, *Chinese Thought from Confucius to Mao Tsê-tung* (New York: New American Library, 1953), pp. 32-34, 111. Sir Patrick Devlin, "Morals and the Criminal Law," in *The Enforcement of Morals* (London: Oxford University Press, 1968), p. 17.

19. Wing-tsit Chan, trans. and comp., "Analects," in *A Source Book in Chinese Philosophy* (Princeton: Princeton University Press, 1963), 3:3, p. 24; cf. 12:1, p. 38. See also 12:22 and Chan's comment, p. 40; 8:9, p. 33; 16:9, p. 45; 12:11, p. 39.

Cf. Hsüan Tzu, quoted in Creel, *Chinese Thought*, p. 111. Also see Wolfram Eberhard, *A History of China*, 4th edn. (Berkeley: University of California Press, 1977), pp. 117-18, 145; cf. Chan, *Source Book*, p. 116.

20. Karel Čapek, *R.U.R.*, trans. Paul Selver (Garden City, NY, 1923); rpt. in *Science Fiction Thinking Machines: Robots, Androids, Computers*, Groff Conklin, ed. (New York: Vanguard Press, 1954). Different editions give different spellings of the names and different job titles for the characters.

21. Ibid., act I, pp. 108-12, 115. Eberhard, *History of China*, pp. 117-18, 145. Čapek, *R.U.R.*, act II, pp. 131-33; act III, p. 145.

22. Čapek, *R.U.R.*, act III, p. 154.

23. Ibid., Epilogue, pp. 156, 161. Chan, *Source Book*, p. 292.

24. Chan, *Source Book*, p. 292.

25. G. E. Moore, *Principia Ethica* (1903; rpt. paperback edn., London: Cambridge University Press, 1959), § 6-7 (pp. 6-8), § 86 (pp. 142-44).

26. Padgett, "Proud Robot," pp. 7-52.

27. Ibid., pp. 10-12, 19, 38, 43-44, 49.

28. Ibid., p. 29.

29. Ibid., p. 38. Direct comparison of intuitions is impossible because, by definition, in order to have direct access to someone's intuitions you have to *be* that person. Cf. Ludwig Wittgenstein, *Philosophical Investigations*, 3d edn., G. E. M. Anscombe, trans. (New York: Macmillan, 1968), § 248, p. 90[e].

30. Wittgenstein, *Philosophical Investigations*, § 376-380, pp. 116[e]-17[e].

31. Frank Herbert, *Destination: Void*, rev. edn. (New York: Berkley, 1978). For further bibliographic data on *Destination: Void* see the List at the end of this volume.

32. Ibid., pp. 200, 202-03.

33. Ibid., pp. 176-78, 183, 188, 193, 203, 211, 230, 256, 263.

34. Padgett, "Proud Robot," pp. 17-18.

35. Herbert, *Destination: Void*, p. 273. For discussions of *Destination: Void* from other points of view, see Gary K. Wolfe, *The Known and the Unknown* (Kent, OH: Kent State University Press, 1979), pp. 79-80 and Patricia S. Warrick, *The Cybernetic Imagination in Science Fiction* (Cambridge, MA, and London, UK: MIT Press, 1980), pp. 181-88.

36. You can be an ethical intuitionist by taking moral judgments to be synthetic *a priori*, as, for example, Kant does.

PART IV

CYBORGS

16

HUMAN, MORE OR LESS: MAN-MACHINE COMMUNION IN SAMUEL R. DELANY'S *NOVA* AND OTHER SCIENCE FICTION STORIES

In *The Cybernetic Imagination in Science Fiction*, Patricia S. Warrick describes two kinds of fiction about human relationships with machines. The first works from a "closed-system model" and consists of visions of destructive technology based on extrapolation from current trends. In contrast to this is the "open-system model" of utopian visions based on speculation about "a new man-machine symbiosis, symbolized by the man-spaceship metaphor."[1] Through an examination of a number of science fiction stories and novels about cyborgs and man-machine communion, concluding with Samuel R. Delany's *Nova* (1968), I want to propose a modification to these categories: to be successful, a story in the "open-system model" must somehow deal with and transcend the fears about destructive technology incorporated in the "closed-system" stories. Far from being uniformly positive visions, the "open-system" stories create a dialectical tension between our hopes and our fears about machinery.

Most works dealing with man-machine communion are pessimistic or dystopian in their attitudes. "Cyborgization," that is, the creation of cybernetic organisms incorporating human and machine elements, is regularly used as a fictional metaphor for modern alienation and dehumanization: people gradually being turned into machines. Despite the simpleminded "Superman" update in such pure wish-fulfillment fantasies as television's "Six-Million Dollar Man" and "Bionic Woman," we still see nightmares of robots replacing humans in such films as *Futureworld*, *Alien*, and *The Black Hole*.

One classic dystopian cyborg story is the terrifying "Masks" (1968), by Damon Knight, in which the protagonist is given a totally prosthetic body. "*Not like an ordinary amputation, this man has had everything cut off.*" He dislikes the attempts to make the artificial body appear human, for it only resembles "a tailor's dummy" or "a corpse." In rebellion, he chooses to wear a metal mask and requests that they place him in an all-metal body instead: "A module plugged into the control system of a spaceship. That's where I belong, in space. Sterile environment, low grav, I can go where a man can't go and do what a man can't do."[2] Only at the end of the story, after a scientist has responded enthusiastically to his plan, are we allowed access into this experimental subject's mind. To our horror, we realize he has gone completely insane. Deprived of almost all human sensation, he feels an overwhelming disgust and hatred of everything organic and craves the dead vacuum of the moon. Now we can understand why, in a psychotic rage, he earlier had murdered a dog—significantly, using as the murder weapon a metal T-square.

There are also numerous dystopian female-cyborg stories in a subgenre one could term "Cinderella Frankenstein." Such stories illustrate the idea of woman-as-robot in modern society, as economic and sexual slave of men. Typically, ugly Cinderella trades herself in for a beautiful cyborg version, only to discover the new, improved model is a true Frankenstein monster being used for unscrupulous ends by her male creator. The classic story along these lines is the Hugo-winning "Girl Who Was Plugged In" (1973) by James Tiptree, Jr. (a pseudonym of Alice Sheldon).[3] In this Faustian tale, a monstrously deformed girl receives mechanical implants so that she can be plugged into a machine and operate by remote control the body of a perfect girl (called "Delphi," suggesting the Greek oracle). The beautiful zombie is used by a corporation as a celebrity to promote products in a dystopia where direct advertising is banned. Complications ensue when she falls in love: her lover, unaware that the girl of his dreams is a remote-controlled doll, inadvertently kills her plugged-in operator when he attempts to free Delphi from corporate control. The doll survives to be operated by another woman.

Another Cinderella Frankenstein variation is Tanith Lee's *Electric Forest* (1979), a stylishly creepy tale. Again, an ugly, crippled woman is offered the opportunity to trade herself in for a beautiful android, in this case modeled on an existing woman. The deformed body of Magdala Cled remains in suspension in a capsule while her consciousness is transferred to "a crystal conductor in the skull of a simulate woman."[4] But her creator, the rich, handsome, and cruel scientist Claudio Loro, keeps her in his control by emotional and sexual manipulation, using her in an intricate revenge plot. Magdala ends by killing both her creator and her original and taking her place.[5] Some lines from a poem by Edward Field titled "The Bride of Frankenstein" could serve as an epigraph for Tiptree's and Lee's stories: "She stands and stares with her electric eyes, / beginning to understand that in this life too / she was just another body to be raped."[6]

Finally, in Ira Levin's *Stepford Wives* (1972) the transformation of women into androids is involuntary.[7] In a plot suggesting *The Invasion of the Body Snatchers*, the Stepford husbands have their women eliminated and replaced by identical, mechanical substitutes, bland and passive robot-housewives. The extrapolation from current social thought is clear: Cinderella Frankenstein stories reify contemporary feminist nightmares.

Nevertheless, every "closed-system" cyborg story has a more positive, "open-system" counterpart, perhaps illustrating our fundamental ambivalence about the promise and the threat of machines. For example, the motif of amputation and replacement by mechanical parts found in "Masks" is also used in Frederik Pohl's *Man Plus* (1976), but Pohl faces and transcends the fears of mutilation and mechanization.[8] Examining the psychology of *Man Plus*, one could say that this novel overcomes castration anxiety, for the hero confronts the loss of not only his humanity but also his sexuality. The "Man Plus" is astronaut Roger Torraway, who volunteers to be transformed through massive surgery into a "monster," a cyborg who can survive on the surface of Mars. Like "Masks," *Man Plus* dwells at grim length on the pain, terror, and isolation of the transformation from human into cyborg. However, Pohl gives his hero a happy ending. In the conclusion, Torraway is not less than human, like the character in "Masks," but more than human: man *plus*, man enhanced through machine implants. He adapts beautifully to Mars, saves the human race from war on Earth by helping to establish the first Mars colony, and, despite his castration, is even given a lover to replace the wife who has drifted away from him. As in the fable of the Ugly Duckling, a "monster" appears beautiful when placed in its appropriate physical or social environment. *Man Plus* perfectly illustrates the positive, speculative imagination of the "open-system" cyborg story: "in a man-computer synthesis lies the hope of mankind's long-term survival and . . . the unfolding of his potential."[9] In such stories, man-computer synthesis is not viewed as analogous to dehumanization but as a means to *counter* dehumanization. Pohl's novel creates a dialectical tension between the nightmare vision of cyborg as "monster" and the utopian vision of cyborg as "man plus," as the next stage in human evolution—thus acknowledging and yet transcending our fears about machine takeover.

In a similar fashion, the pessimistic vision of "The Girl Who Was Plugged In" is countered by another plugged-in female, Helva, the heroine of Anne McCaffrey's *Ship Who Sang* (1969). But because of its sentimentality, this collection of stories lacks the emotional weight, the dialectical tension between nightmare and hopeful dream that distinguishes *Man Plus*. McCaffrey bypasses many of the more horrific aspects of cyborgization by having her heroine—another crippled Cinderella—implanted in a machine soon after birth. "For Helva was destined to be the 'brain' half of a scout ship, partnered with a man or woman, whichever she chose, as the mobile half."[10] Conditioned from birth, and having never known any other form of existence, Helva prefers her life and even pities ordinary humans who lack her machine-enhanced capabilities. She explains, "As this ship, I have more physical power, more physical freedom, than you will ever know."[11] Her only regret is that "very few people thought of her as Helva, a person, a thinking, feeling, rational, intelligent, eminently human being,"[12] but even that problem is overcome in the end when she gains a permanent male partner who adores her.

Gary K. Wolfe considers Helva as an example of the "icon" of spaceship as "home," and mentions the "domestic feminine image that Helva fulfills."[13] In this respect, the collection can be criticized for concealing a traditional female role model. *The Ship Who Sang*, like much of McCaffrey's fiction, may be more appropriate for juveniles in its sentimentality: Helva really reduces to a mechanical Flying Nun.

Thus scenes intended to be moving are instead embarrassing, as when Helva's prospective male "brawn" (the coy term for her partners) passionately embraces the metal column in which she is encased. In Marshall Brickman's satirical science fiction film *Simon* (1980), a similarly perverse scene is appropriately played for laughs when a scientist makes love to a sexy-voiced computer that is shaped like a giant touch-tone telephone receiver.

C. L. Moore's classic "No Woman Born" (1944) tells a better open-system, female cyborg story than *The Ship Who Sang* because it acknowledges both the "Cinderella" and the "Frankenstein" aspects of our attitudes toward machines. Pamela Sargent cites Moore's tale as "one of the earliest thoughtful treatments of the cyborg."[14] The beautiful, popular entertainer Deirdre is burned in a theatre fire and believed dead, but the scientist Maltzer transplants her brain into a flexible metal body. The face is a featureless metal mask with eyes, merely suggesting a woman's face like a lovely abstract sculpture (Damon Knight's "Masks" might even be read as a nightmarish version of "No Woman Born"). The body seems endowed with all of her old grace of movement. Against the opposition of Maltzer, Deirdre is determined to sing and dance again for audiences: "The whole idea from the start was to recreate what I'd lost so that it could be proved that beauty and talent need not be sacrificed by the destruction of parts or all of the body."[15]

The new Deirdre is an even greater success than before, due to her machine-enhanced talents, but an ambiguity remains: Is she still human? She mentions "what a tremendous force the human ego really is. . . . It does instill its own force into inanimate objects, and they take on a personality of their own. People do impress their personalities on the houses they live in, you know." Nevertheless, the narrator, a close friend of Deirdre, notes the danger that "the mind inside the metal [might] veer from its inherited humanity as the years went by. A dweller in a house may impress his personality upon the walls, but subtly the walls, too, may impress their own shape upon the ego of the man."[16] Maltzer even attempts suicide, convinced he has committed a crime like that of Dr. Frankenstein. But Deirdre concludes, "I'm not sub-human. . . . I suppose . . . that I'm superhuman." She compares herself to a Phoenix reborn perfect from the fire. But the Phoenix is unique. Despite her attempts to keep in touch with people by performing, she is lonely for others of her own kind. At the end, the ambiguity about her relationship to humanity remains, and "the distant taint of metal [is] already in her voice."[17]

A similar ambiguity is dealt with in Poul Anderson's *Avatar* (1978). Although Anderson's space epic is not a good novel (it is overlong, confused, and filled with unconvincing mysticism), its most interesting aspect concerns a female-machine communion. Joelle Ky, one of the major characters, is an "operator" trained from childhood to link with computers through a helmet providing "electromagnetic induction. . . . The computer then supplies its vast capacity for storing and processing data, its capabilities for carrying out mathematico-logical operations in microseconds or less. The brain, though far slower, supplies creativity and flexibility; in effect, it continuously rewrites the program." The trouble is that Joelle becomes more than human, unfitted for normal emotional relationships because of the transcendent experience of machine hookup: "Each time the numbers rushed through you to verify, and you knew how much reality you had embraced, it was an outbursting of revelation. . . . the Buddhist hopes to become one with the all in Nirvana. . . . the linker, in this life, does it."[18] Because of her enhanced powers, she pities ordinary people as "animals; and I never did care much for pets."[19] Nevertheless, Joelle is continuously frustrated by her inability to communicate outside of computer linkup; in the end she expects to find happiness as ambassador to an alien race.

A brilliant, comic, and positive version of human-computer communion is John Varley's "Overdrawn at the Memory Bank" (1976). Like *Man Plus*, it shows the capacity of such linkage for enhancing human potential; again like Pohl's novel, it presents a nightmare vision overcome. The story acts out our worst fears about computers in order to transcend those fears. In this case, Varley's virtuoso comic effects make even the nightmarish aspects entertaining.

The hero of "Overdrawn," Fingal, is a bored computer programmer in a future society on the moon. "Feeding information into a computer can be frustrating, unrewarding, and eventually stultifying. . . . He was sixty-eight years old, with centuries ahead of him, and stuck in a ferro-magnetic rut."[20] Through a strange series of circumstances, Fingal's worst nightmare is realized, and he is literally trapped inside a computer. For diversion, he had his consciousness transferred to a memory cube and temporarily implanted in a lioness. After a few days he is supposed to be returned to his body. Unfortunately, his body is misplaced. While the search goes on, his memory cube must be plugged into a computer to prevent his consciousness from decaying. Fingal is kept sane through dialogue with an outside operator, a woman with whom he falls in love.

Fingal undergoes various bizarre hallucinations as his consciousness struggles to adapt to existence inside a machine. He finally triumphs by taking advantage of his prolonged imprisonment to complete a year of courses in electronics. "He wanted to learn about computers. He wanted to know what made them tick, to feel a sense of power over them. It was particularly strong when he thought about being a virtual prisoner inside one. He was like a worker on the assembly line. . . . One day, he happens to wonder who puts the parts on the belt."[21]

When Fingal is finally returned to his body, he discovers that the more than a year of subjective time he spent in the machine was actually only six hours of real time because "computers think faster."[22] Nevertheless, his new diploma is real. The implicit message is clear: machines are only tools, and if we learn how to make proper use of them, they will increase human capabilities instead of imprisoning us.

Samuel R. Delany's *Nova* (1968) is a rich and subtle novel singled out by Patricia S. Warrick as "one of the most inventive man-computer linkages."[23] Once again, it is an open-system work which balances deep-rooted fears about machine takeover with speculation about possible new man-machine relationships, thereby helping to transcend those fears. Delany deliberately uses the mythic form of space opera as an old container in which to pour new wine.

In *Nova*, people of the thirty-second century plug their nervous systems directly into computers and other machines through sockets grafted onto their bodies. Most citizens are routinely equipped with sockets when they begin school. Their use is so universal that anyone without plug facilities is regarded with suspicion or overt hostility. The result, according to Delany, is "a revolution in the concept of work,"[24] presumably overcoming the alienation between man and the product of his work caused by technological society. In other words, Delany is dealing with the same problem of "assembly-line boredom" as Varley. In Delany's vision, all machines become "a direct extension of man":[25]

All major industrial work began to be broken down into jobs that could be machined "directly" by man. . . . Now a man went to a factory, plugged himself in, and he could push the raw material into the factory with his left foot, shape thousands on thousands of precise parts with one hand, assemble them with the other, and shove out a line of finished products with his right foot, having inspected them all with his own eyes. And he was a much more satisfied worker. . . . Under this system, much of the endemic mental illness caused by feelings of alienation left society. The transformation turned war from a rarity to an impossibility, and—after the initial upset—stabilized the economic web of worlds for the last eight-hundred years.[26]

It is this ingenious speculation about a revolution in the nature of work through the transformation of the relationships between people and machines that has most intrigued critics of *Nova*.[27] Nevertheless, the economic philosophy in the novel seems overly sanguine and raises several questions: How does the transformation of the nature of work make war an impossibility? If one man operates an entire factory, what happens to all the laid-off workers? Doesn't alienation take more profound forms than mere repugnance at mechanical labor?

This last question suggests the objections a Marxist would have to *Nova*: Delany never seems to consider that it may be the economic structure of capitalism itself—the workers' lack of control over the means of production, the objects to be produced, and the profits of labor—that is at the root of worker disaffection. It could be argued that the technological change Delany posits is only a way to shore up the crumbling system of capitalism.

In *Nova*, in fact, capitalism not only survives but prospers. Two super-rich families, the Von Rays and the Reds, dominate the economy and stand at the top of an almost feudal hierarchy. The plot concerns the struggle between the heirs to these two great fortunes—on the one hand, Captain Lorq Von Ray, and, on the other, Prince and Ruby Red—to control the economy by finding a new source of illyrion, the rare element which is the society's main fuel. Lorq's secret plan to defeat the Reds is to plunge a spaceship into the heart of an exploding star and scoop out tons of illyrion floating free at the moment when the star goes nova.

It is in the mythic, space-opera plot of the novel and the emotions generated by that plot—the deadly battle between Lorq and Prince Red—and not in the economic philosophy that one finds the real message of *Nova* about the relationship between humans and machines. According to Brian Aldiss, "What space opera does is take a few light years and a pinch of reality and inflate thoroughly with melodrama, dreams, and a seasoning of screwy ideas." *Nova* has all the necessary conventions of space opera that Aldiss itemizes: the hypermelodrama, the quest of the superhero (Lorq), an abundance of aliens or exotic creatures, plenty of action, buckets of blood, infinite space, "a woman fairer than the skies" (Ruby), and "a villain darker than a Black Hole" (Prince).[28] Delany reinforces the space opera structure with multiple levels of mythic underpinning, including the plot of *Moby Dick*, the Grail quest, the figures of the Tarot, and the myths of Prometheus and Orpheus.

One of the archetypal elements the novel adopts from older science fiction is the stigma that marks the villain: Prince has a mechanical, black-gloved right arm. This convention of the "black hand" harks back to Fritz Lang's film *Metropolis* (1926), in which the evil Dr. Rotwang, creator of the robot provocateur, wore a black glove over an artificial hand. It is explained that the mad scientist lost his hand in an experiment—but, of course, no price is too high for him to pay in the cause of science! The title character of Stanley Kubrick's film *Dr. Strangelove* (1964) is another mad scientist with an uncontrollable, prosthetic "black hand" which even tries to strangle him, expressing the way that machines turn against their creators in Kubrick's nightmare farce. After *Nova*, the black hand appears in another space opera, George Lucas's *Star Wars* (1977). Archvillain Darth Vader wears an all-black, mechanical body armor, and his hands are encased in black gloves. Vader appears more machine than human being. The mechanical black hand is a standard science fiction emblem of evil which may have evolved from images of the Black Knight in medieval romances. It represents a pure fear of machine takeover, which seems surprising to encounter in a work like *Nova*, which Warrick designates as so progressive and "open system."

Nevertheless, Delany has created an archetypal monster such as Prince

Red to imbue the work with all the psychological reverberations of myth and fairy tale. Delany plays on those primal fears and superstitions in order to confront and counter them. The overriding theme of the novel is the need for *balance*, including balance in relationships between humans and machines. Katin, one of the crew of "cyborg studs" aboard Lorq's ship, is the resident intellectual and spokesman for many of the ideas Delany injects into the novel. Katin delivers the speech about the revolution in the nature of work, and he makes another key statement about balance in the "three P's" of "Psychology, Politics, and Physics."[29] Just as there is an area of the brain that balances perceptual pressures, he explains, so there is a governmental matrix that balances social, economic, and cultural pressures, and a mechanism in the sun that balances solar activity. *Nova* is about what happens when those balancing mechanisms go awry: three characters suffer from acute sensory overload; the government grows unwieldy under cultural and economic pressures; and a sun goes nova. The theme of balance is also expressed in the relationship between Katin, a prospective novelist, and Mouse (cat and mouse?), a musician who plays an instrument called a "sensory syrynx." Both are artists, but neither is a whole one; Katin relies too much on intellect and Mouse too much on his senses. A balance of the two is necessary for complete art. And, on a primitive emotional level, Prince is a character of monstrous imbalances: just as a machine has replaced his right arm, so his psychopathic violence knows no bounds. In the mythic substructure of the novel, Prince could be said to be all raging id and Lorq all revenging superego. The two burn each other out, suggesting the need for a balancing ego.

As the novel progresses, Prince becomes less and less human and more and more mechanical, until in his last appearance he resembles a monstrous fetus floating in a mechanical womb: "The lipless mouth gaped on broken teeth. No nose. Tubes and wires snaked the rotten sockets. Tubes pierced at belly, hip, and shoulder. Fluids swirled in the tank and the single arm drifted back and forth, charred fingers locked with rigor mortis in a claw."[30]

In contrast, as time goes on, Lorq relies less on machinery and more on human intuition: "I tried to play it through once with a computer plotting the moves. . . . Now I'm playing by hand, eye, and ear."[31] The message is not all that different from that of *2001: A Space Odyssey* (1968), in which astronaut David Bowman must switch off the mad computer HAL and fly the ship by hand, or that of *Star Wars*, when the voice of Ben Kenobi advises Luke to switch off the targeting computer and "Trust the Force."

If "Overdrawn at the Memory Bank" expresses a benign view of computers as a means of enhancing human potential, *Nova* reminds us that technology is a mixed blessing whose potential depends upon the motives of the human being employing it. For example, both Prince and Mouse suffer from birth defects; whereas Prince's prosthetic arm becomes a weapon in his psychopathic rage for destruction (he finally uses it to kill himself), Mouse compensates for his damaged voice box by playing "a syrynx instead of a larynx"—that is, by creating art.[32] Nevertheless, Mouse's musical instrument is also called an "ax," and on one occasion, out of fear, he uses it as a weapon.[33] By turning it up to high gain, he severely injures Ruby. As in *2001*, in which the first step in technology is the apeman's bone club, any tool can also serve as a weapon.

A successful work of open-system science fiction, such as *Nova* or *2001*, is neither simple nightmare nor pure utopia. Instead, it acknowledges that dialectical tension between our fears of machinery as a weapon which may diminish our humanity by destroying ourselves or others and our hopes for machinery as a tool for expanding human possibility.

Such an ambivalence is ineradicable, for our attitudes about machinery really reflect our fundamental hopes and fears about ourselves. If machines are an extension of humankind, then the interface between people and machines leads us to the inevitable question of what constitutes the human. Where does humanity end and machine begin? How do we define "sub-human"? "Superhuman"?

In Saul Bellow's novel *The Victim* (1947), one of the characters says, "I have a high opinion of what is human. This is my whole idea. More than human, can you have any use for life? Less than human, you don't either." But he does not really answer the fundamental question: "Tell me, please, what is human?"[34] By measuring human beings against machines, science fiction poses us the same question.

NOTES

1. Patricia S. Warrick, *The Cybernetic Imagination in Science Fiction* (Cambridge, MA: MIT Press, 1980), p. xvii.

2. Damon Knight, "Masks," in *The Best of Damon Knight* (Garden City, NY: Doubleday, 1976), pp. 292, 293.

3. James Tiptree, Jr., "The Girl Who Was Plugged In," in *Warm Worlds and Otherwise* (New York: Ballantine, 1975), pp. 79-121.

4. Tanith Lee, *Electric Forest* (New York: DAW, 1979), part 2, ch. II, p. 38.

5. *Electric Forest* is seriously weakened by a coda which undermines the emotional effect by suggesting that the preceding nightmarish tale was simply a play enacted as an experiment.

6. Edward Field, "The Bride of Frankenstein," *Variety Photoplays* (New York: Grove Press, 1967), p. 23. Quoted by permission of the author.

7. Ira Levin, *The Stepford Wives* (New York: Random House, 1972).

8. Frederik Pohl, *Man Plus* (New York: Random House, 1976).

9. Warrick, *Cybernetic Imagination*, p. 166.

10. Anne McCaffrey, *The Ship Who Sang* (New York: Del Rey-Ballantine, 1979), p. 2.

11. Ibid., p. 169.

12. Ibid., p. 200.

13. Gary K. Wolfe, *The Known and the Unknown: The Iconography of Science Fiction* (Kent, OH: Kent State University Press, 1979), p. 83.

14. Pamela Sargent, "Women and Science Fiction," in *Women of Wonder: Science Fiction Stories by Women about Women*, Pamela Sargent, ed. (New York: Vintage, 1975), p. xix.

15. C. L. Moore, "No Woman Born" in *The Best of C. L. Moore*, Lester del Rey, ed. (Garden City, NY: Doubleday, 1975), p. 215.

16. Ibid., pp. 211, 212.

17. Ibid., p. 242.

18. Poul Anderson, *The Avatar* (1978; rpt. New York: Berkley, 1979), ch. xxiii, pp. 192, 193.

19. Ibid., ch. xlvii, p. 384.

20. John Varley, "Overdrawn at the Memory Bank," in *The Persistence of Vision* (New York: Dial, 1978), p. 212.

21. Ibid., p. 214.

22. Ibid., p. 226.

23. Warrick, *Cybernetic Imagination*, p. 176.

24. Samuel R. Delany, *Nova* (1968; rpt. New York: Bantam, 1969), ch. 7, p. 195.

25. Ibid., ch. 4, p. 113.

26. Ibid., ch. 7, pp. 195-96.

27. See, for example, Patricia Warrick and George Zebrowski, "More Than Human?: Androids, Cyborgs, and Others," in *Science Fiction: Contemporary Mythology: The SFWA-SFRA Anthology*, Patricia Warrick, Martin Harry Greenberg, and Joseph Olander, eds. (New York: Harper & Row, 1978), p. 305. Warrick and Zebrowski mention the economic philosophy of *Nova* and cite interest in that philosophy in reviews by Algis Budrys and Douglas Barbour.

28. Brian Aldiss, "Introduction," in *Space Opera: An Anthology of Way-Back-When Futures*, Brian Aldiss, ed. (Garden City, NY: Doubleday, 1974), pp. xi, xii.

29. Delany, *Nova*, ch. 2, pp. 23-24.

30. Ibid., ch. 7, p. 203.

31. Ibid., ch. 5, p. 151.

32. Ibid., p. 128.

33. For the significance of "ax" as both jargon for "musical instrument" and a potential weapon, see Peter S. Alterman, "The Surreal Translations of Samuel R. Delany," *Science-Fiction Studies* 4 (March 1977), 30.

34. Saul Bellow, *The Victim* (1947; rpt. New York: Avon, 1975), ch. 10, pp. 121, 122.

THE CYBORG (R)EVOLUTION IN SCIENCE FICTION

In 1960, Manfred Clynes coined the word "cyborg," from the longer term "cybernetic organism," to refer to an "artificially extended homeostatic control system functioning unconsciously" or, in simpler terms, a self-regulating human-machine system.[1] According to Clynes, a person using an external prosthetic device, like glasses or an iron lung, is not a cyborg, but a person using a device that is incorporated into the homeostatic mechanism of the human body, like an electronic cardiac pacemaker or an artificial joint, *is* a cyborg. Clynes maintains that cyborgs will not change our fundamental nature much more than glasses or iron lungs change it.[2] In this assertion, he represents one pole of prediction; D. S. Halacy, Jr., represents the other when he writes of a cyborg revolution that will end natural evolution and replace *Homo sapiens* with *Homo machina*.[3]

Even though science fiction writers began speculating about cyborgs decades before the word itself existed, their works show the same polarity of prediction found among the scientists. How and how much the machine part of a cyborg alters the personality and identity—even the humanness—of the person into whose body it is incorporated are vexing questions that form the core of many science fiction stories. The basic question, of course, is whether such a system is more human or more machine. The answers are various, ranging from stories that show the cyborg as a physically different but very human being to those that show the cyborg as a being so radically altered as to be (almost) a new species. This range of responses is given even in stories that share certain basic assumptions about cyborgs: that they are created as the only viable response to serious injury or to hideous deformity and that they are permanent, irreversible systems.

At one end of the spectrum are the quintessentially human cyborgs in Joan Vinge's charming story "Tin Soldier." Maris, the tin soldier of the title, is blown to pieces in a war on his home planet, Glatte, when he is only nineteen. After the missing pieces are replaced with metal and plastic parts, Maris leaves Glatte for the more primitive world of Oro where he lives among people who consider him "no longer quite human" because more than half his body is artificial.[4] A side effect of his prosthetic parts is that Maris ages only about five years for every hundred he lives. He expects to last for centuries.

Maris's semiimmortality is shared only by the spacers, who are all women. While they are in space, they age almost as slowly as Maris does. After a twenty-five-year trip, they return only two or three years older. Their semi-immortality creates a special bond between them and Maris; his bar, the Tin Soldier, is a constant refuge for them in worlds of change. But not even this special bond can overcome the spacers' xenophobia toward cyborgs. In that, spacers and ordinary humans are the same. During two centuries on Oro, Maris meets only one woman, the extraordinary young spacer named Brandy, who will have sex with him. The taboo against sex with cyborgs exists in most cultures, Maris tells Brandy, because most people think cyborgs are only one step removed from corpses; thus, sex with a cyborg would be like necrophilia. The implicit irony is that people envy cyborgs' semiimmortality at the same time they consider cyborgs not really alive.

The unlikely love affair between Maris and Brandy begins the first night of her first visit to Oro. For the next ninety-nine years, Maris waits patiently while Brandy sails the skies, returning to Oro only once every twenty-five years. Theirs is an old and familiar human story, with a role reversal—it's the man who waits, the woman who roams—and an added twist: Brandy is seriously hurt in an accident and can be saved only by becoming a cyborg. She returns and they live happily—almost ever after.

Several aspects of the story help emphasize the humanness of the two cyborgs. The fairy tale in the background and the familiarity of the basic plot give the story a timeless human context. The human form of the cyborgs makes it possible for them to meet and mate normally, experiencing sexual desire and fulfillment. Their prosthetic parts are hardly discernible; nothing interferes with the aesthetic sense of how "young" lovers should look. But most important, their perceptions and emotions remain entirely human. Even though their perspective on time has necessarily changed, they still find solace in the poetry of Milton: "Attired with stars we shall forever sit, triumphing over Death, and Chance, and thee, O Time."[5]

Anne McCaffrey's short story "The Ship Who Sang," later expanded into an anthology of stories under the same title, shows that fictional cyborgs do not have to be in human form to remain quintessentially human. Helva, "born a thing,"[6] an exceptionally sound mind in a horribly twisted body, is allowed to live and become an encapsulated "brain," a shell-person with a life expectancy of several centuries. She is educated and conditioned to serve as the "brain" of a spaceship into which she is wired, literally becoming one with the ship. As scout ship, Helva has her choice of human partners, colloquially called "brawns." The partnership of brain and brawn is like a marriage in many ways, but the choice of partner is always given to the ship.

Helva chooses as her first partner a young brawn named Jennan with whom she has fallen in love. During their first trip together they are diverted on an emergency rescue mission, and Jennan is killed. Helva's reaction is as human as it is unexpected to her. Grief-stricken as any young bride who has just lost a much beloved young husband, Helva is prevented from plunging into an exploding sun and immolating herself on a cosmic pyre only by her strong conditioning. Forced to accept escort as she bears Jennan's body back to base for burial, Helva is comforted by the escort ship, Silvia, who was partnered with Jennan's father when he was killed in a mission that saved Parsaea. Silvia tells Helva that other ships have been so crazed by grief when they lost their brawns that they have gone rogue. Silvia's conversation makes clear that the normal reactions of ships to the death of their brawns is the grief Helva is experiencing. Not only Helva and Silvia, but the other cyborg ships also are experiencing human emotions despite their metal bodies.

In the second and third stories of the anthology, "The Ship Who Mourned" and "The Ship Who Killed," respectively, Helva's grief is compared with that of human women who have suffered similar losses. In "The Ship Who Mourned," Helva is temporarily partnered with Theoda of Medea, who lost her son, her daughter, and her husband in a plague on her home planet. Still grieving, Theoda offers sympathy and understanding to Helva in her grief. And Theoda cries for Helva because Helva cannot cry for herself. Partnered next with Kira of Canopus in "The Ship Who Killed," Helva discovers human and cyborg grief more intense even than her own. Kira tried, unsuccessfully, to commit suicide after her husband died and she lost their unborn child in a miscarriage that left her unable ever to have children. On their mission, Kira and Helva find the grief-crazed ship 732 that had gone rogue years before. The similarities between human and cyborg grief are implicit in this story, but the death theme in the anthology is resolved as Helva kills the 732 in an act like euthanasia, saves Kira from suicide, and produces new life by delivering 110,000 human embryos to repopulate the sterile world of Nekkar.

The last two stories in the anthology contrast two partnerships Helva chooses. The first partnership, in "The Ship Who Dissembled," is a disaster. Brawn Teron of Acthion treats Helva as if she is a computer instead of "a person, a thinking, feeling, rational, intelligent, eminently human being."[7] Teron's attitude is not uncommon, but Helva finds it intolerable. She divorces him although she must pay a hefty penalty for doing so.

In the final story, "The Partnered Ship," Helva takes as brawn her true soul mate, Niall Parollan. But before Parollan is willing to partner himself with Helva, he has an extrapolation made from her chromosome pattern to see what she looks like. He tells her she is beautiful. Parollan's curiosity is common among brawns who have a close relationship with their ships. The question left unanswered is what Parollan would have done had he discovered from the extrapolation that Helva was not beautiful. His attraction to her is intellectual and emotional, but also sexual, and he needs to fantasize about her as a beautiful woman before he can commit himself to her. Helva is content that he thinks of her as human and feels sexual desire for her even though that desire can never be physically fulfilled.

Despite her titanium shell and her identity as a ship, Helva is no less human emotionally than are Maris and Brandy, whose form is human. Helva's behavior is different because of the limitations and freedoms her extended body gives her. Her love for Jennan and Parollan is not expressed physically only because her form makes that impossible, not because she lacks sexual desire for them.

In these stories by Vinge and McCaffrey, the cyborgs are clearly more human than machine regardless of how much of their bodies has been replaced by artificial parts or connections. Unlike them, the cyborg in Henry Kuttner's "Camouflage" is less certain whether he is man or machine. The cyborg who was once Bart Quentin can exist as an individual—although not in human form—or he can be wired into a spaceship. In that sense, he has more flexibility than Maris, Brandy, or Helva. His body is a two-by-two-foot cylinder when it is not hooked up as a transplant ship. Quentin has been a cyborg for seven years, and his wife has stayed with him. Their relationship certainly is no longer physical, but she insists that he's still the man she married.

Early in the story, in conversation with an old friend, Quentin insists that he's "no robot. It [being a cyborg] doesn't affect the identity, the personal essence of Bart Quentin." Yet only a few sentences later he insists to the same friend, "I am the machine!"[8] The ambiguity thus betrayed about his real identity prepares for the crisis in the story. When Quentin is on a mission as a Transplant ship, he is hijacked by the same friend to whom he was speaking earlier in the story. Transplant Quentin is disabling the hijackers one by one until he begins to doubt his own humanity because of the merciless baiting by his betraying friend, Talman, who says that other humans, including Quentin's wife, regard Quentin as a monster. Quentin doubts himself and asks "Am I—It?"[9] Only a semantic slip restores his sense of himself as human. Talman says that he would never have tried to kill Quentin if Quentin were still human. And Quentin laughs as he realizes that no one speaks of killing a machine; thus, even Talman, who is trying to convince Quentin he is a machine, still considers Quentin human. Knowing that he is still perceived as human is sufficient to restore Quentin's sense of himself as human.

In C. L. Moore's classic story, "No Woman Born," written sixteen years before the term cyborg was coined, the balance of identity is tipped to the side of the machine. When the lovely actress Deirdre is destroyed in a theater fire, her undamaged brain is preserved. During the next year, a new body, a total prosthesis, is created for her. The success of her new body depends largely upon its not trying to be a wax image of the Deirdre who was lost. Instead, it is entirely metal with an ovoid for her head, a crescent-shaped mask for her eyes, and armor covered by a robe of chain mail for the rest of her. Deirdre's identity is conveyed only through her voice and her motion. In her golden body, she returns to the stage and, at least on her first appearance, is a smash hit as she dances and sings—even though her dance and her song are not human.

Deirdre has been told that she is mortal, that when her brain wears out her body will naturally disintegrate. Although she is not separated from ordinary people by immortality, she is irrevocably separated from them by her artificial body. Gradually she realizes just how different she is: insisting that she is not subhuman, she suggests that she may in fact be superhuman. Whatever she is, she is rapidly becoming something other than human. As the story ends, she speaks with "the distant taint of metal already in her voice."[10] The very body that gives her life separates her from the humans with whom she wants to remain.

What is only subtly suggested in C. L. Moore's story is worked out explicitly by Damon Knight in "Masks." The cyborg in the story, Jim, is forty-three years old when he has the accident that costs him his body. Like Deirdre, he requires a total prosthesis; he has become a billion-dollar project of the government. Unlike Deirdre, Jim is fitted out with a body that looks quasi-human. The story opens two years after Jim's accident. He has been wearing his new body for six months, but he has recently begun wearing a metal mask, with no nose or mouth and only oblong slits for eyes, to cover the prosthetic, wax-looking face constructed for him at enormous expense. Although the prosthetic face looks almost normal, except for the pupils of the eyes, Jim prefers the metal mask. His preference for metal carries over into a desire for a metal body, one that looks more like a machine than like a fake human. He has designed a metal body, a box with four legs, lots of arms, and a tiny head. He wants to be sent off into space, into the cold and sterile environment of the moon.

His desire to become more machinelike externally is a desire to have his outside match his inside. He has become more machine than human, and human bodies are increasingly repulsive to him. He can hardly bear seeing the sloppy organic processes of living beings, and he kills a puppy because its body repulses him. He yearns for the clean, rigid perfection of machine form. As the story closes, he dreams of being a machine on the moon and seeing "the Earth hung overhead like a rotten fruit, blue with mold, crawling, wrinkling, purulent and alive."[11]

Knight has said that he wanted to write a story about a completely artificial body because "most treatments of the subject in science fiction had been romantic failures, and . . . to do it realistically would be an achievement."[12] Knight thinks that even "No Woman Born" failed to present the theme realisticially enough. "Masks" is Knight's deliberate attempt to redress the balance. He succeeds admirably. The story graphically presents the considerable psychological effects that loss of the whole human body would have, especially on someone who had lived in a human body for forty-three years. Knight's cyborg must hide his disgust for ordinary humans because ordinary humans are necessary to keep him alive and to give him the metal body he wants. Thus, he wears a mask to hide his disgust—even though his prosthetic face cannot show expression.

Since Knight's story was published, Arthur C. Clarke has written in "A Meeting with Medusa" of the cyborg Howard Falcon who must also wear a total prosthesis as the result of an accident. Like Deirdre and Jim, Falcon has gradually slipped away from humanness. He thinks of himself as neither human nor machine, but as a transitional being between the human race and the machines who will inevitably become the masters of space. He takes "a somber pride in his unique loneliness—the first immortal midway between two orders of creation."[13] He perceives it his duty to serve as an ambassador between humans and the machines they will create to supersede themselves. He expects the centuries of transition to be troubled, and he thinks he will be needed. Falcon's pride and his strong sense of duty show him still human in his responses even though he no longer perceives himself as human.

The most haunting cyborg story of all is perhaps Roger Zelazny's "The Engine at Heartspring's Center," about "the creature called the Bork. . . . born in the heart of a dying sun." At the beginning of the story, Zelazny tells us that the Bork "was a piece of a man."[14] And "Bork" is a piece of a name, Charles Eliot Borkman—a piece without the "man" and one that brings the word "cyborg" to mind. The Bork insists that Borkman died when the ship he was on came out near an exploding sun. The Bork's body is not carefully described, but it is far more metal than flesh, with several hands, only one of them human.

The Bork lives at a euthanasia colony where he long ago came to die. Once there, he changed his mind and continues to live—happily, he says—contemplating the goodness and rightness of death. Not until he lives literally in sight of death does the Bork find a reason for living. Virtually immortal himself, he deliberately seeks a sense of the human condition and finds more than he seeks when he falls in love with Nora, a young human girl who asks him to protect her and let her live with him. They share tender moments, Nora polishing the Bork's metal armor, and gradually they find a way to consummate their love sexually. Having sought death, the Bork finds life and love, then betrayal, loss, and death. Under contract to the authorities at the euthanasia center, Nora gives the Bork an injection to kill him. Because she truly loves him, she gives herself an injection also. She dies; he does not. Only "the human piece, or a piece of the human piece," does.[15] Heartbroken, the piece of the Bork that was human dies, leaving an engine at his heartspring's center—and the pieces of the Bork that are things go on performing the habitual motions that the human piece of the Bork had put them through. Dead inside, the Bork continues.

The implication of the story is that cyborgs can be human only so long as the human part of them desires and chooses to be human. Thus, the form of the cyborg, the relative proportion of mechanical to human parts, is not as important as the cyborg's sense of self and will to live. Zelazny's use of the name "Eliot" suggests allusions to T. S. Eliot's poetry and to people, dead inside despite their human form, whose lives are as mechanical and routine as the Bork's is at the end of the story.

The basic question about cyborgs—whether they are more human or more machine—cannot be answered finally until scientists know more about the mystery of the human mind. Physiology is surely important—the biochemistry of the brain may turn out to be the controlling factor—but conditioning and acculturation are also important. Factual answers about cyborgs may never be given in speculative fiction, but fiction can focus attention on questions about the human consequences, for individuals and for the species, of biomedical engineering. And if rapid technological progress in biomedical and genetic engineering has put us in an era of participant evolution, we need to wonder about what we do when we re-create ourselves in our own—or in another—image. We will certainly change ourselves; we may need to change our definition of "human."

NOTES

1. Manfred Clynes and Nathan S. Kline, "Cyborgs and Space," *Astronautics*, September 1960, p. 27. As quoted in D. S. Halacy, Jr., *Cyborg—Evolution of the Superman* (New York: Harper & Row, 1965), p. 9.

2. Manfred Clynes, "Foreword," to Halacy, *Cyborg*, p. 8.

3. Halacy, *Cyborg*, pp. 36-45, 190-96.

4. Joan D. Vinge, "Tin Soldier" (1974), collected in *Eyes of Amber and Other Stories* (New York: New American Library, 1979), p. 242.

5. Ibid., p. 214.

6. Anne McCaffrey, "The Ship Who Sang" (1961), in *The Ship Who Sang* (New York: Ballantine, 1970), p. 1.

7. McCaffrey, "The Partnered Ship" (1969), in *The Ship Who Sang*, p. 200.

8. Henry Kuttner, "Camouflage" (1945), rpt. in *Human-Machines: An Anthology of Stories about Cyborgs*, Thomas N. Scortia and George Zebrowski, eds. (New York: Vintage, 1975), p. 130.

9. Ibid., p. 158.

10. C. L. Moore, "No Woman Born" (1944), rpt. in Scortia and Zebrowski, *Human-Machines*, p. 118.

11. Damon Knight, "Masks," in Scortia and Zebrowski, *Human-Machines*, p. 36.

12. Damon Knight, "Afterword" to "Masks," in Scortia and Zebrowski, *Human-Machines*, p. 37.

13. Arthur C. Clarke, "A Meeting with Medusa," in *Nebula Award Stories Eight*, Isaac Asimov, ed. (New York: Harper and Row, 1973), p. 51.

14. Roger Zelazny, "The Engine at Heartspring's Center," *Analog*, July 1974, p. 70.

15. Ibid., p. 76.

Gary K. Wolfe

18

INSTRUMENTALITIES OF THE BODY: THE MECHANIZATION OF HUMAN FORM IN SCIENCE FICTION

> Up to the present, adaptation has been the product of material interaction, with all this implies in laxness, misfitting, and excess. But future adaptation will be calculated according to a strict system, the so-called "biocracy." It will be impossible to escape this system of adaptation because it will be articulated with so much scientific understanding of the human being. The individual will have no more need of conscience and virtue; his moral and mental furnishings will be a matter of the biocrat's decisions.
>
> At present we have little conception of what this new man will be like. . . .
>
> —Jacques Ellul, *The Technological Society*[1]

In 1925, Géza Róheim suggested an interesting opposition between societies with low levels of technology, and more technologically advanced cultures. The primitive culture was termed by Róheim "autoplastic," while our own is "alloplastic." Mary Douglas's summary of the meaning of these terms is concise:

The primitive seeks to achieve his desires by self-manipulation, performing surgical rites upon his own body to produce fertility in nature, subordination in women or hunting success. In modern culture we seek to achieve our desires by operating directly on the external environment, with the impressive technical results that are the most obvious distinction between the two types of cultures.[2]

In other words, autoplastic cultures attempt to maintain some control over their environment by means of symbolic rituals involving the human body itself—including the sometimes gruesome puberty rites that are often so disturbing to anthropology students. Alloplastic cultures, on the other hand, alter or re-create the environment to make it more hospitable to the body. Douglas goes on to argue that with a fuller understanding of the concept of the body as a social instrument in primitive societies, this particular opposition may turn out to be of limited value in anthropology. But it may nevertheless turn out to be a useful concept in discussing certain works of science fiction that deal with deliberate transformations of the human body.

Science fiction, in general, can be said to express the fantasies and anxieties of an alloplastic culture—which is hardly surprising, since according to Róheim's original formulation technological society is by definition alloplastic. Some of the most powerful and pervasive icons of the science fiction genre —spaceships, cities, wastelands, artificial space habitats—involve transformations of the environment or the creation of new environments, usually in order to extend the dominion of humanity. (The wasteland is an exception, but is often treated in science fiction less as the complete destruction of the environment than as the transformation of it into something more appropriate for heroic action.) Other icons, such as the alien, the robot, or the computer, involve projections of images of humanity into the environment but still do not deal directly with the manipulation of the human body itself. Still other works, such as those concerning mutations or diseases, do involve transformations of the body and express fears related to the vulnerability of the body, but most of these cannot be said to deal with autoplastic concerns since the transformations portrayed seldom are deliberate or goal-oriented.

It quickly begins to seem as though autoplastic themes are comparatively rare in science fiction—almost as though the integrity of bodily form is somehow held sacred in a genre that does not hesitate to wreak the most awe-inspiring transformations on almost everything else in the universe. But this is not quite the case. Myths of the body have appeared with some regularity in the history of science fiction, and the manipulations that the flesh is heir to in the name of science date back at least to Mary Shelley's *Frankenstein* (1818) and find expression as well in the work of H. G. Wells, whose mad Dr. Moreau seeks "to find out the extreme limit of plasticity in a living shape."[3] Voluntary biological transformations of the body have also appeared with some regularity, forming the basis of major works by James Blish, Clifford D. Simak, and others. It was inevitable, then, that sooner or later science fiction would seek to unite its overarching theme of technology with this more limited autoplastic theme, resulting in works in which bodily transformations are achieved through mechanical and electronic rather than purely biological means. Such works, which depict the progressive replacement of bodily parts with mechanical substitutes, confront directly some of the underlying anxieties of the genre, anxieties so pervasive that even psychologically acute readers of limited familiarity with the genre could note, as Bruno Bettelheim did in 1960, that

the heroes of these stories abound in nonhuman qualities. Their depersonalization is often symbolized by their names, such as Og, or M-331, by an absence or disregard for their bodies, and by a lack of intimate human relations. . . . Love relations are virtually absent; most of the heroes are basically minds without a body. Apparently science fiction writers, though motivated by a desire for scientific progress, seem to feel that the inherent danger of such progress is an end to our biological existence as man.[4]

The dehumanization that Bettelheim noted may have arisen as much from lack of attention to character in pre-1960 science fiction as from any conscious awareness on the part of science fiction authors of an anxiety over "roboticization." But over the last thirty years, the genre has produced a number of significant works which concern the literal dehumanization of the body through its partial replacement with mechanical parts. While some of these works depict the abandonment of the body altogether in favor of a mechanical housing for the brain (Anne McCaffrey's *The Ship Who Sang*, Frank Herbert's *Destination: Void*, William Hjortsberg's *Gray Matters*), and others depict one-time experiments in mechanically restructuring the body (Martin Caidin's *Cyborg*, Frederik Pohl's *Man Plus*), those of concern here depict the longer-term social effects that might result from the acceptance of bodily mechanization as a mark of social or professional distinction. In other words, what happens to *groups* of people who mechanically replace body parts: How are they integrated into the larger society, how do they influence that society, and how is that influence colored by their mechanical parts? This may seem a narrow group of stories to focus on, but it includes some major works of science fiction, and it permits the most direct exploration possible of the relations of body, mind, machine, and society in science fiction. The primary works discussed below cover nearly thirty years of the genre's history: Cordwainer Smith's "Scanners Live in Vain" (1950), Bernard Wolfe's *Limbo* (1952), David R. Bunch's *Moderan* (stories 1959-1971; collection 1971), and Vonda N. McIntyre's "Aztecs" (1977).

These works have a number of elements in common. Each of them portrays a highly technological future society in which admission to an elite class or guild is contingent upon having parts of one's body replaced by mechanical or electronic appliances. The replacements are achieved by means of extensive, painful surgical operations which might well be regarded as rites of passage into the elite class. Other rites and rituals are also associated with the newly mechanized elite: pride in their machine parts is reflected in costumes or uniforms designed to call attention to the mechanization, and social interactions both among members of the elite and between them and the "normals" are highly formalized, in some cases even associated with taboos. This formalization of relations leads to a widening alienation between the elite and the rest of society, and, as the elite become isolated, they begin to evolve new values associated with their machine parts, often associating themselves more with the mechanical parts of their persons than with the biological parts. Finally, and perhaps most interesting in terms of larger implications, the function of each of these elite societies of mechanized people is associated in some way with the conquest of, or virtual annihilation of, time—either the conquest of relativistic time problems associated with space travel, or the conquest of historical time through the establishment of a static utopia. And, in all but one of the works (though even there it is implied), this conquest of time through mechanical means proves to be a failure.

Chronologically, the first of these works to appear was "Scanners Live in

Vain" (1950), which introduced to science fiction readers the highly inventive and eccentric "Instrumentality" of Cordwainer Smith (Paul Linebarger). Throughout the Instrumentality stories (the name comes from a police force originally established in Smith's future world by Chinese philosophers who have conquered the Earth; later this police force revolts and eventually establishes its own hegemony over the universe), Smith is concerned with exploring the barriers between humans and machines on the one hand, and humans and animals on the other. Among science fiction future histories, these stories are unusual for their lack of robots, aliens, and computers; Smith's Instrumentality is peopled entirely by real or transformed people or animals. Later stories depict people in telepathic union with cats ("The Game of Rat and Dragon," 1955), people neurologically connected to spaceships ("The Burning of the Brain," 1958), people subjected to a microorganism which causes them to grow new organs ("A Planet Named Shayol," 1961), and—in a number of stories which seem to draw their inspiration from Wells's *Island of Dr. Moreau*—various animals remade into "underpeople." Clearly, like Wells's Dr. Moreau, Smith is interested in exploring the "limits of plasticity" in living beings, perhaps in order to identify those qualities which define us as human.

In "Scanners Live in Vain," it is the barrier separating human from machine —and implicitly, life from death—that is being tested. Centuries after a series of devastating wars has left most of the Earth a wilderness of "Beasts" and still-functioning war machines called "manshonyaggers" (from the German *Menschenjager*, or "man-hunter")—images which already set up the polarities of animal and machine within which human society must function —the Instrumentality has retreated to a few stronghold cities and seeks to rebuild civilization by moving into space. But space presents another barrier— the "great pain" which makes it impossible for humans to survive in space without being anesthetized in protective cocoons. In order to enable men to work in space and pilot the spaceships, a scientist named Haberman devises a means of severing all the sensory organs except sight from the brain—making the "habermans" unaware of pain but also unaware of potentially fatal wounds. Because of this hazard, habermans are made from "the scum of mankind," prisoners who would otherwise receive a death sentence.[5] But an elite corps of voluntary habermans, the Scanners, occupy the top of this social structure much as ordinary habermans occupy the bottom. Scanners are so called because of mechanical instruments implanted in their chests which enable them to constantly "scan" themselves for injury; they also enjoy the privilege of "cranching" (another technique named for its inventor), or periodically returning to the world of sensation by using a special wire.

An almost tribal litany of this odd culture describes the Scanners as "the bravest of the brave, the most skillful of the skilled. All mankind owes most honor to the scanner, who unites the Earths of mankind. . . . They are the most honored of mankind, and even the chiefs of the Instrumentality are delighted to pay them homage."[6] Functioning both as a powerful labor union and as a priest class, the Scanners achieve this exalted status by means of a surgical procedure that amounts to a technological equivalent of Yogi self-denial. Róheim's description of the Yogi's quest makes this parallel clear:

The road that leads to *mana* (magical power) is frequently that of ascetiscism and self-torture.
  The Yogi, according to the Kshurika-Upanishad, must renounce not only the external world but also his own body. The separation from his own body takes place by means of a successive *cutting off* of the parts of the body, with the *manas* (will, desire) being the knife used in these proceedings. . . . The aim of the entire process is to break through the cycle of reincarnation.[7]

The aim of the Scanners is not to break the cycle of reincarnation, but to transcend time in another sense: Scanners are described as remaining awake "for months" during space travel while passengers rest in suspended animation, thus enabling the Instrumentality to overcome the time barrier to space travel.

But in overcoming time and pain, Scanners also cut themselves off from human feeling, and hence experience a growing alienation from the human race they are designed to serve. Martel, the Scanner who is the story's protagonist, attempts to maintain human contact through marriage to a normal woman. Early in the story narrative tension is generated by means of conflicts between Martel's human and machine parts; he is called back to duty as a Scanner even while "cranched" to enjoy a romantic interlude with his wife. Martel reports to the Scanner meeting in his sensory-cranched state, and thus becomes acutely aware of the degree of dehumanization displayed by the other, desensitized Scanners. "He hated their awkwardness when they moved, their immobility when they stood still. He hated the queer assortment of smells which their bodies yielded unnoticed." Scanners, Martel begins to suspect, have come to identify too closely with their mechanical nature and have grown alienated from normal humans, whom the Scanners call "Others."

In a psychological sense, the Scanners' ego boundaries have expanded to include their mechanical functions. This is made apparent by the purpose of the meeting Martel attends: a scientist named Stone has invented a means by which normal humans can function in space without the aid of Scanners. Martel, in his human state, sees this as progress, but for most of the others assembled, it will mean that "Scanners live in vain," that their functions will no longer be needed. The Scanners vote to assassinate Stone—a radical move in a society as stable as the Instrumentality, and an indication that the Scanners have come to value technology over human life. Martel successfully foils the attempt and brings an end to the age of Scanners—but not before Smith, with characteristic wry humor, reveals the nature of Stone's epochal discovery. As Stone explains, he has simply "loaded the ships with life"[9]— specifically, oysters. Though at first the idea of oysters may seem a joke, in a broader sense this may represent the triumph of the organic over the technological or, alternatively, the triumph of the alloplastic over the autoplastic.

Smith wrote no other stories about Scanners, though he refers to them off and on throughout the "Instrumentality" series (and even refers to "shellships" occasionally). But the idea of the surgical mechanization of humans for work in space has never quite died out in the genre, and a recent treatment of this theme, Vonda McIntyre's "Aztecs" (1977), is worth noting for the ways in which it expands upon ideas treated in the Smith story. The "Aztecs" of McIntyre's story are so called because in order to become space pilots, they sacrifice their hearts in favor of what amounts to little rotary engines that enable them to control bodily rhythms, blood pressure, and so on—though the pilots themselves reject the term "Aztecs" because "We don't feel we've made a sacrifice."[10] The title is significant, however, not only because of the associations it calls up with autoplastic ritual and the tribal nature of the pilot elite; as the story progresses, it becomes increasingly apparent that McIntyre's pilot protagonist Laenea has indeed made a sacrifice, and one rather like that made by Smith's Scanners.

As in the Smith story, "Aztecs" posits that normal humans cannot survive space travel except in suspended animation, that the ships must thus be controlled by an elite corps of pilots surgically restructured to survive in space, that admission to the corps is contingent upon dangerous surgery, that the marks of that surgery become signs of pride, and that the general population holds these pilots in a respect bordering on awe. Like the Scanners, the pilots keep pretty much to themselves and do not generally associate with normal humans, forming instead "their own unique, evolving, almost self-contained society."[11] And more explicitly than in Smith, being a pilot means conquering time, because the unadapted human body, "bound to normal time and normal space, to the relation between time dilation and velocity and distance by a billion years of evolution," would die of old age almost instantly under the conditions of space travel.[12]

McIntyre's story is set entirely in a spaceport city where Laenea has just undergone surgery to become a pilot. Returning to the spaceport itself (located offshore, with pilot and crew lounges below the waterline in an environment which is itself timeless), Laenea already begins to feel a sense of separateness from colleagues she knew when she was a mere crew member, and a sense of belonging among the pilots whom she once held in awe. She meets a crew member from a distant planet called Twilight whose name is Radu Dracul. (The Transylvanian name, the object of a small joke within the narrative, is probably intended merely to establish him as a darkly romantic figure.) From here on, the story is essentially a tragic romance, but one drawn from themes of dehumanization and mechanization. Laenea and Radu fall in love, but soon find that their sexual union produces sudden, uncontrolled orgasms in her and seems to be associated with terrifying nightmares in him. (In addition to his name, he is further associated with the unconscious by the fact that he is apparently the only crew member known who dreams while in suspended animation.) An opposition emerges that was only hinted at in the Smith story: if Radu, with his dreams and melancholia, is a figure associated with the unconscious, Laenea, in becoming a pilot, has made virtually all of her bodily functions subject to consciousness, even the autonomic nervous system. She has, it appears, given up the part of herself represented by Radu:

> Her system and that of any normal human being would no longer mesh. The change in her was too disturbing, on psychological and subliminal levels, while normal biorhythms were so compelling that they interfered with and would eventually destroy her new biological integrity.[13]

The distance between them is further emphasized when Radu himself applies for pilot training and is rejected because his "circadian rhythms" are too strong. Laenea and Radu must separate, and at the end of the story she realizes that she has indeed cut herself off from the rest of humanity by becoming a pilot, and that, at least in the romantic terms that the story certainly invites, she has indeed "sacrificed her heart."

McIntyre's story suggests that mechanization of humans involves not simply a man-machine opposition but a conscious-unconscious opposition as well, and that by cutting out part of her body Laenea cuts off access to deeper, inchoate sources of human feeling that no amount of bodily control can replace. Like Martel in "Scanners Live in Vain," she has suffered a kind of lobotomy of the body. In both these stories, the moral issue of dehumanization arises as a result of mechanizations that were intended to be purely functional, and both stories are essentially romantic in their handling of the theme from the point of view of tragic individual cases. But the theme also lends itself to satiric treatment: What if mechanization of humans evolved as the *result* of a moral system; if it *were* to be performed for its own sake rather than subordinated to a specific functional goal? According to this view, the mechanization of the body serves even more of a ritualistic function than in these two stories; after all, if the function of autoplastic ritual and sacrifice is to achieve union with "a mystical body or soul which has immortal life,"[14] why should not this mystical body be technology itself, which increasingly seems to be self-perpetuating and eternal? And how could union with the mystical body of technology be better achieved than by making oneself in part a machine?

These are among the themes explored in Bernard Wolfe's *Limbo* (1952) and David R. Bunch's *Moderan* (1971). Both are complex satires deserving more attention than I can give them here and more attention generally in studies of science fiction. In rich and varied ways, both of these books examine the implications of the human-machine interface.[15]

Limbo is, in its author's own words, "a grab bag of ideas that were more or less around at the mid-century mark,"[16] and in many ways this has dated the book noticeably since its original appearance. Casual references to intellectual fads such as dianetics and orgonomy; eager embracing of postwar pop Freudianism (including some appallingly sexist musings by the narrator on "full vaginal" orgasms and castrating females); championing of analyst Harold Bergler's excessive emphasis on masochism as a source of human behavior; and an infatuation with Norbert Wiener's early musings on cybernetics (which nevertheless fails to substantially expand upon or imaginatively develop those ideas)—all combine in hindsight to give *Limbo* a rather eccentric look. The central absurdist premise of the novel—that technological society begins to take "disarmament" literally by the systematic and voluntary amputation of arms and legs—adds to this impression and further dates the novel as an expression of exaggerated cold-war anxieties. What redeems the novel in part is a wittily cynical style that at times seems made up of equal parts of Swift, Joyce, and Philip Wylie; what makes it a major novel is this stylistic and structural complexity in the service of what is undisputably a novel of ideas in the most literal sense—and a novel that makes explicit at one point or another most of the implications about the mechanization of people discussed above.

Ostensibly, the novel evolved as a literal-minded projection of the following passage from Freud:

Man has become a god by means of artificial limbs, so to speak, quite magnificent when equipped with all his accessory organs; but they do not grow on him and they still give him trouble at times. However, he is entitled to console himself with the thought that this evolution will not come to an end in A.D. 1930. Future ages will produce further great advances in this realm of culture, probably inconceivable now, and will increase man's likeness to a god still more.[17]

The artificial limbs in Wolfe's story are not simply Freud's metaphor, however. Essentially, the narrative concerns a crazed attempt to build a post-World War III utopia by surgical means. The inspiration for this attempt comes from a personal notebook left behind by a Dr. Martine, who disappeared during the war and who ironically speculated in the notebook that amputation might be the only really effective means of disarmament. The notebook becomes the Bible of the new society, and artificial limbs—sophisticated electronic prostheses superior in strength and endurance to natural limbs—become the new status symbols: the more artificial limbs, the higher the status. But Martine has not died; he has merely become staff lobotomist for a native tribe on a remote island, and most of the narrative details his shock and surprise upon returning to civilization and discovering what has been done with his informal musings. During his narration of Martine's adventures, Wolfe touches upon a number of the central issues involved with the mechanization of people: the parallels between lobotomy and amputation; the essentially magical and ritualistic nature of such operations ("Any ceremony performed in the absence of reasonable knowledge as to cause and effect is magic");[18] the vision of technology as a mystical force with which humans seek union through partial mechanization; the opposition of autoplastic and alloplastic ritual; and the paradox involved in a process that is at once a Yogi-like denial of the body and a technological augmentation of it.

Parallels between lobotomy and amputation are made throughout the narrative, as Martine comes to realize that what he has been doing while in exile among the natives is no less a technological nightmare than what he finds among the amputee society; in both cases, ritual surgery is performed to bring the individual more in line with what is essentially a mechanistic conception of society. Among the amputees, this surgery is openly referred to as a "ritual" by which one gains admission to "the select circle of ampism."[19] This ritual evolved at least partly out of an awareness of technology's efficacy at alloplastic manipulation and an attempt to integrate autoplastic ritual with the rewards of technology: "Why should it be that the human brain can produce perfection only outside itself—in the machines it conceives and builds? If it can conceive and project such perfection, why can it not apply the same grandiosity of vision to itself, rebuild itself?"[20] Early attempts to achieve this involved elaborate electronic brains, since "the machine is eternally the brain's dream of fulfillment," but the power of such brains over humans precipitated fears that technology was becoming a force in itself, separate from and out of the control of humans. The solution, in Wolfe's society, was for humanity to "overhaul itself in the image of the robot. . . . Man, in other words, finally K.O.'s the machine by incorporating the machine into himself!"[21]

Wolfe's (and Martine's) image of technology out of control is the steam-roller, which becomes one of the guiding metaphors of the new society, and which bears remarkable similarity to what Jacques Ellul would later call "technique"—the tendency of a self-perpetuating technology to override everything in its path. But Wolfe also suggests that such an attempt to control technology by integrating it with the human body is symptomatic of all sorts of pathology, including masochism, paranoia, and even the extension of infantile ego boundaries. The voluntary amputee "focuses attention on everyone's desire to do damage to himself, the masochistic essence of every man's interest in all damaged people."[22] Furthermore, such a value system reflects a puritanical "horror of things physical, the things of the material world and of the body . . . under the guise of unifying man with himself and with the world which surrounds him. This is paranoia become a whole way of life."[23] Finally, Wolfe sees this society as an expression of the infantile ego: "A mature kind of megalomania was now becoming possible. Now the universe was truly, literally, becoming an appendage of man's ego."[24] In other words, the whole impulse toward mechanization is infantile and neurotic, and the only real hope held out for the amputee society lies in a few characters (repre-

sented by a farmer named Don Thurman, who is introduced late in the novel)
who realize this. In the end, the amputee utopia—which, like all utopias, has
attempted to conquer historical time by bringing man to perfection—collapses
as war again breaks out. Undaunted, the technologists learn of the progress
Martine has made in brain surgery during his years performing ritual
lobotomies, and begin to think of *this* as the new technological solution to
man's problems. The conclusion of the novel is a race between Martine and
the representatives of the amputee society back to the remote island where
Martine's lobotomy notebooks are kept. Irrational and infantile faith in
technology, Wolfe suggests, will always find another technique to make man
conform, and in the process, constantly escalate its demands on the integrity
of the human form.

But even *Limbo* does not carry this nightmare fantasy as far as it might.
David R. Bunch's *Moderan* (1971) shows emerging from a war- and pollu-
tion-ravaged world a society in which the mechanical replacement of human
parts escalates to the point of the elite "new-metal" men having virtually all of
their bodies replaced except for symbolic "flesh-strips" to retain their identity
as humans. Written in a violent pseudopoetic style designed apparently to
reflect a linguistic equivalent of the perverted values of the Moderan society,
these stories and sketches generated some puzzlement and outrage when
many of them first appeared in the pages of *Amazing* and *Fantastic*, and
some credit must go to editor Cele Goldsmith for supporting such stylistic
experimentation at a time when not much of it was going on in science
fiction.[25]

Moderan directly equates the mechanization of people with the desire to
conquer time. "We have Time arrested and shackled, imprisoned in our
'replacements,'" boasts the Moderan citizen who is the narrator of the book.
"When we captured Time we placed it in the rib cage of each man and sealed
it there in each man's calm-beating heart."[26] Earlier, muses this narrator, "I
envied the rocks . . . I envied stone pillars; I envied old bones; I envied the
very air. I envied animals, even, for they did not know, I thought, how total
was to be their defeat on the bonepile of death." But following the surgery
which admits him to the ranks of new-metal men, he says, "We are 'replaced'
to live forever and have no need of bargain deals for heaven. We are our own
eternity."[27]

Moderan is not simply an autoplastic fantasy, however, for even the Earth
itself is remade in the image of new-metal man. Parallel to Wolfe's image of
the steamroller is Bunch's image of the hammer. "To me bladed hammers are
quite emblematic of a considerable quantity of all man's great progress to his
GREAT TOP place of today," says the narrator, and automated hammering
machines called "jammy-rams" are sent out across the landscape to pound
the earth to a uniform flatness so that it may be covered with plastic.[28] The
oceans are frozen to insure a sterile environment in keeping with the metallic
nature of the new humans, and all things organic, including the flesh-strips

themselves, come to be associated with pollution and decay. Even trees, birds, and flowers are replaced by metal in what the Moderan people come to call "the Dream Realized."

Not all the people in Moderan are rebuilt, of course. As in the other stories, a rigid class system has evolved with unreconstructed "pulpy" humans at the bottom, partially replaced metal people or "peotals" in the middle, and the almost completely rebuilt fortress-masters, referred to as "the Chosen," at the top. Robots also function in this culture, but their role becomes increasingly ambiguous as people grow more and more to resemble them; a pair of children wonder about their mother's robot lover, "Do you suppose he wasn't really all machine but was a man who had been replaced part by part until it was now impossible to tell where the man left off and the robot plastic began?"[29] Unreconstructed people live more or less like serfs in "Bubble-Dome Homes" scattered across the plastic landscape; and in keeping with this medieval social structure, the new-metal men (there are new-metal wives, too, but they have been exiled to "White Witch Valley" so that the men can enjoy robot mistresses who make no emotional demands) occupy castle-like "Strongholds" from which they continually wage war on one another. Actually, it may be less proper to say they occupy the highly technological fortresses than to say that they *are* the fortresses: "MAN-AND-FORTRESS, ONE-FORTRESS-MAN, ONE-MAN-FORTRESS, THE SAME AND IN-SEPARABLE FOREVER AND FOREVER," as the mechanical voice of the fortress itself puts it, in a parody of the Catholic Mass. As in the Wolfe novel, man makes himself a part of something immortal by joining physically with the never-ending project of technology.

Although *Moderan* is actually a collection of forty-six stories and vignettes, some of which are little more than prose poems, Bunch has organized them into a narrative that conforms closely with the general formula for these stories discussed earlier. Early in the book, the story "Butterflies Were Eagle-Big That Day" describes in harsh detail the series of surgical operations through which the narrator attains passage into the ranks of new-metal men by achieving his quota of "M's." "M" stands for "major awful cut," and the more M's one has, the higher his status. That this process is associated with a mystical rebirth is emphasized by the narrator's referring to it as "the nine-months mutilation . . . the nine-months magic."[30] Flesh-strips are retained for "holding our forms in shape and keeping us linked to the human," but later the narrator will complain that "these may be the one small, not-to-be-remedied, flaw that will finally do us down and clear back to reality."[31]

Following the surgery, the narrator enters the Stronghold where he is to remain for the rest of the narrative, and soon be begins to sense conflicts between his flesh and machine parts. The flesh-strips become associated with weakness and sentimentality: in "Bubble-Dome Homes" they are blamed for swaying Moderan's ruling judges into allowing the unreconstructed flesh-people to live despite the contempt in which they are held; and in "One

False Step," it is the shame of a new-metal visitor that he had allowed his flesh-strips to color his decision regarding the massacre of a group of flesh people, allowing them to live instead. As the new-metal men increasingly identify with their metal parts, they gradually abandon traditional human values. "Sentiment was soon quite gone from us, and our souls, if ever we had them, were surely now no more."[32] The narrator complains from time to time of the "love-befuddled tissue" of his flesh-strips, and at one point ("Getting Regular") the narrator himself is disgraced by an excessive emotional attachment to his metal mistress. Disgust with the flesh is accompanied by a growing need for "more steel," a need explained by means of a Zen-like paradox: "The flesh-strips are our godliness, in a way, and yet we have to keep working to cut our godliness down to become more godly."[33]

The new-metal men decide that the only activity that can sustain them through an eternity of mechanical life is war, and the waging of war is the sole purpose of the Strongholds. Inevitably, this is what leads to the final destruction of Moderan, but not before Bunch has given us a number of indications of the society's instability. Many of the episodes concern visits to the narrator by near-allegorical figures who remind him of his humanity: his seriously wounded lieutenant from an earlier war, a wandering poet, his twin brother (who has become a preacher) even a figure identified as his conscience. Each of these increases the narrator's sense of growing frustration and lack of purpose, and this frustration in turn is channeled into the infantile anger that eventually makes him the champion Stronghold in Moderan. In one of the best stories, "The Walking, Talking, I-Don't-Care Man," the narrator even contemplates suicide, rationalizing it as the mere turning off of a machine: "I think you could not reasonably charge metal with suicide, not logically."[34] Having himself disassembled, he concludes in "The Final Decision," will enable him to find "PURPOSE," but the one surviving human emotion of fear prevents him from undertaking this project. He returns to the wars, designing a super-weapon called a "Grandy Wump" and employing it in a final war only to discover that other Strongholds have devised similar weapons, and their mutual deployment signals the end of Moderan.

In a final note of irony, Bunch assembles these tales as manuscripts discovered and presented by yet another stage of technological evolution, "beam-man," or "essence-man," who exists only as projections of electromagnetic beams. The beam-man who "introduces" the collection is parodied in the same headlong style that Bunch uses to parody his Moderan narrator, and this beam-man's reflections on the self-delusion apparent in the Moderan stories provide an ironic counterpoint to our own reactions to the stories. Moderan's claim to have found the ultimate human form may be fatuous, Bunch seems to say, but so might by *any* claim to an "ideal" form of humanity. Emotions, and not all complimentary ones at that, emerge as the only consistent defining factors of humanity in Bunch's universe.

While the four works discussed above hardly constitute a significant formulaic genre within science fiction, each is in its own way excellent, and to-gether they provide a significant commentary on issues that are central to science fiction as a whole. They suggest that perhaps our attraction to tech-nology is somehow involved with a desire to escape time; that the more we become one with technology, the more we are forced to accept its values as our own; and that certain defining human qualities are imbedded in the body as well as in the mind. In an alloplastic culture, technology can be defined as that which mediates between humans and their environment, and by introducing autoplastic ritual into such a culture—which we may soon have the medical means to do—we achieve neither a comfortable union with that environment nor a superior state of humanness. We become instead an "instrumentality," an "Aztec," a "steamroller," or a "hammer"—the meta-phors of these stories are colorful, but all rather chilling in the end. We can make ourselves more and more like our tools, but even this will not tell us what these tools are for.

NOTES

1. Jacques Ellul, *The Technological Society*, John Wilkinson, trans. (New York: Vintage Books, 1967), p. 398. Orig. French edn.: *La Technique*, 1954.

2. Mary Douglas, *Purity and Danger: An Analysis of Concepts of Pollution and Taboo* (1966; rpt. London: Routledge and Kegan Paul, 1978), p. 116. Róheim's use of these terms comes from a 1925 study titled *Australian Totemism*.

3. H. G. Wells, *The Island of Dr. Moreau* (1896; rpt. New York: Ace, n.d.), p. 107.

4. Bruno Bettelheim, *The Informed Heart: Autonomy in a Mass Age* (1960; rpt. New York: Avon, 1971), p. 66.

5. Cordwainer Smith, "Scanners Live in Vain," collected in *The Best of Cordwainer Smith*, J. J. Pierce, ed. (New York: Ballantine, 1975), p. 15.

6. Ibid., p. 15.

7. Géza Róheim, *Magic and Schizophrenia*, Warner Muensterberger and S. H. Posinsky, eds. (1955; rpt. Bloomington: Indiana University Press, 1962), p. 51.

8. Smith, "Scanners," p. 21.

9. Ibid., p. 35.

10. Vonda McIntyre, "Aztecs," in *Nebula Winners Thirteen*, Samuel R. Delany, ed. (New York: Harper and Row, 1980), p. 201.

11. Ibid., p. 186.

12. Ibid., p. 189.

13. Ibid., p. 230.

14. Ernest Becker, *Escape from Evil* (1975; rpt. New York: The Free Press, 1976), p. 21.

15. It should be noted that Bernard Wolfe's *Limbo* has been the subject of two spirited defenses: by David N. Samuelson, "*Limbo*: The Great American Dystopia," *Extrapolation*, 19 (December 1977), 76-87; and "*Limbo*," *Survey of Science Fiction Literature*, Frank Magill, ed. (Englewood Cliffs, NJ: Salem Press, 1979), III, 1221-25. I am indebted to these essays for some of the insights that follow.

16. Bernard Wolfe, "Author's Notes and Warnings," *Limbo* (1952; rpt. New York: Ace, n.d.), p. 410.

17. Sigmund Freud, *Civilization and Its Discontents*, Joan Riviere, trans. (1930; rpt. Garden City, NY: Anchor-Doubleday, n.d.), p. 35.

18. Wolfe, *Limbo*, p. 53.

19. Ibid., p. 155.

20. Ibid., pp. 142-43.

21. Ibid., p. 101.

22. Ibid., p. 161.

23. Ibid., p. 297.

24. Ibid., p. 129.

25. Credit must also go to Mary Kenny Badami for suggesting that I include *Moderan* in this discussion.

26. David R. Bunch, "Thinking Back (Our God is a Helping God)," in David R. Bunch, *Moderan* (New York: Avon, 1971), pp. 22-23. All subsequent notes refer to stories in this edition of *Moderan*.

27. "Battle Won," p. 53; "Has Anyone Seen This Horseman?" p. 196.

28. "Of Hammers and Men," p. 89.

29. "A Little Girl's Xmas in Moderan," p. 170.

30. "New Kings Are Not for Laughing," p. 41.

31. "New-Metal," p. 86; "The Problem," p. 127.

32. "Survival Packages," p. 84.

33. "The Problem," p. 128.

34. "The Walking, Talking, I-Don't-Care Man," p. 119.

Thomas P. Dunn and Richard D. Erlich

LIST OF WORKS USEFUL FOR THE STUDY
OF MACHINES IN SCIENCE FICTION

Technically, this is an analytical, selected list, with comments, of works useful for the study of machines in science fiction. It will help users of our List if we review here briefly the key elements of this technical title.

Analytical. This List is divided into the following sections, with works arranged alphabetically within each section:

I.	Reference Works
II.	Anthologies and Collections
III.	Fiction
IV.	Literary Criticism
V.	Stage, Film, and Television Drama
VI.	Stage, Film, and Television Criticism
VII.	Music
VIII.	Background Studies

Where we think it will aid users to do so, we have cross-listed items.

Selected. Our List is extensive but by no means exhaustive. Users desiring additional titles should consult the reference works listed in our Acknowledgments, Section I, and in the notes to the essays in this volume. Note well that our List for *The Mechanical God* will not ordinarily include citations to works featuring "world machines," that is, very large machines that in some sense contain people, either literally or metaphorically. Citations to these works are collected in our List for *Clockwork Worlds: Mechanized Environments in SF*, a companion volume in the Greenwood Press series, Contributions to the Study of Science Fiction and Fantasy.

List. Besides being a bibliography (a list of books and other writings), our List is also a filmography and discography. All of our contributors have aided us in compiling the bibliography, but we owe special thanks to Gary K. Wolfe for his aid with works featuring various kinds of barriers, and to Margaret P.

Esmonde for her gift of an annotated list of citations to relevant science fiction for children. The original work on the filmography was done by John Cooper; the original work of the discography was done by Jeffrey R. Wilson —both of whom have our thanks.

Comments. We have provided comments throughout, including citations to critical and reference works with summaries and discussions of primary works.

Works Useful. Again, we provide only a selection of works. We have attempted to cover most of the classic science fiction works and a number of lesser-known works. We have also cited background materials that will familiarize beginning students with some of the social, political, and philosophical issues alluded to in the primary works using the theme of this volume.

Two final notes, of caution: (1) SF works often appear under variant titles and/or pseudonymously and/or in variant editions or translations. We have tried to alert the users of this List to the problems we know of, but we can guarantee only that there are undoubtedly problems we know not of. We have attempted to examine for content most of the works that we cite. Where this has not been possible, we have cross-checked references, and we have tried to provide, above in our Acknowledgments and in the List, indications of at least one source of the citation. Students of SF bibliography are referred to the references given below in the Acknowledgments and in Section I. (2) We have kept to a minimum number of citations our section on machines in music and have totally eliminated a proposed section on machines in the graphic and plastic arts. Note well that machines have figured significantly in the graphic and plastic arts at least since the Renaissance and have been quite common in modern art. Users of the List who would like information on the machine in relatively recent art would do well to start their studies with "The Machine" in William S. Liebermann's *Art of the Twenties* and then move on to two works recommended by William M. Schuyler, Jr.: *Futurism*, by Joshua C. Taylor and *The Machine . . . at the End of the Mechanical Age* by K. G. P. Hulten; and two recommended by Brian Aldiss: *Robots: Fact, Fiction, and Prediction* and *Cybernetic Serendipity: The Computer and the Arts*, both by Jasia Reichardt. We have also rigorously excluded from our List citations to "mainstream" works featuring machines or the theme of mechanization. Users of the List who would be interested in machines or mechanization in mainstream fiction would do well to begin their studies with D. H. Lawrence's *Women in Love* (1920; especially ch. 17, "The Industrial Magnate") and Ken Kesey's *One Flew over the Cuckoo's Nest* (1962).

ABBREVIATIONS IN THE LIST

1. We have abbreviated the names of states of the United States, using the standard abbreviations accepted by the United States Postal Service. The abbreviation "NY" used alone refers to New York City.

2. When we refer to an author of a work in the comments on that work, we will give that author's initials in roman type; when we refer to the work itself in a comment, we will abbreviate the work's title in italic type or place the abbreviation within quotation marks.

3. We use the standard abbreviations and reference words as found in *The MLA Style Sheet*, 2d edn. (1970; section 31, pp. 28-29) and *The MLA Handbook*... (1977; section 48, pp. 123-29). We give below additional abbreviations, our most usual abbreviations, and abbreviations and short titles that might cause confusion. We list below also the most common acronyms in our List; where appropriate, we spell out in the List the titles of journals.

Amazing	*Amazing Stories, Amazing Science Fiction, Amazing Science Fiction Stories* (vt)
Astounding	*Astounding Stories of Super-Science, Astounding Stories, Astounding Science Fiction* (vt); after 1960, *Analog*...
biblio(s).	bibliography(ies)
cf.	compare
coll.	collection, collected
dir.	director
ed(s).	editor(s)
edn.	edition
ency.	encyclopedia
esp.	especially
et al.	and others
F&SF	*The Magazine of Fantasy and Science Fiction*
If	*If, Worlds of Science Fiction, Worlds of IF* (vt)
n.d.	no date
passim	throughout the work, here and there
pseud.	pseudonym
q.v.	which see
rpt.	reprint, reprinted
S.F.	Science Fiction (spelled out; contrast "SF")
SFS	*Science-Fiction Studies*
TMG	*The Mechanical God: Machines in Science Fiction*
trans.	translator, translation(s)
v. or vol.	volume
vt	variant title, variant titles

ACKNOWLEDGMENTS

In compiling our List, we depended in large part on the works cited in Section I (Reference Works) and immediately below; we refer back to these works in the main body of our List.

John Baxter, *Science Fiction in the Cinema*, Peter Cowie, ed. (1970; rpt. NY: Paperback Library, 1970). References in the List to Baxter refer to the selected filmography in this work.

William Contento, *Index to Science Fiction Anthologies and Collections* (Boston: G. K. Hall, 1978). Our primary source of information on magazines of initial publication and printing histories for a number of short stories and novellas; consult for additional places to find short stories and novellas, beyond those cited in the List.

L. W. Currey, *Science Fiction and Fantasy Authors: A Bibliography of First Printings of Their Fiction and Selected Nonfiction* (Boston: G. K. Hall, 1979). Our primary source for information on first printings of novels.

William Johnson, ed. *Focus on The Science Fiction Film* (Englewood Cliffs, NJ: Prentice-Hall, 1972). References in the List to Johnson refer to the selected filmography in this work.

Patricia S. Warrick, *The Cybernetic Imagination in Science Fiction*; full citation given below, under Literary Criticism. References in the List to Warrick are to the summaries and discussions in this work.

Gary K. Wolfe, *The Known and the Unknown*; full citation below, under Literary Criticism. References in the List to Wolfe are to the summaries and discussions in this work.

"The Year's Scholarship in Science Fiction and Fantasy," compiled through 1976-1979 by Roger G. Schlobin and Marshall B. Tymn in the journal *Extrapolation*. For 1976, vol. 20, no. 1 (Spring 1979); for 1977, vol. 20, no. 3 (Fall 1979); for 1978, vol. 21, no. 1 (Spring 1980); for 1979, vol. 22, no. 1 (Spring 1981). "The Year's Scholarship" will be published by Kent State University Press as an annual monograph series beginning with the 1980 installment. For earlier years, we have consulted Tymn and Schlobin, *The Year's Scholarship in Science Fiction and Fantasy; 1972-1975* (Kent, OH: KSU Press, 1979) and Thomas Clareson, *Science Fiction Criticism: An Annotated Checklist* (Kent, OH: KSU Press, 1972).

I. REFERENCE WORKS

Cox, David M. and Gary L. Libby, compilers. "A Bibliography of Isaac Asimov's Major Science Fiction Works through 1976." In *Isaac Asimov*. Joseph D. Olander and Martin Harry Greenberg, eds. NY: Taplinger, 1977, pp. 217-33.

Based in part on Marjorie Miller's *Isaac Asimov: A Checklist of Works Published in the United States* (Kent, OH: KSU Press, 1972). See for works we have been unable to include.

Mullen, R. D. "Books, Stories, Essays [by Philip K. Dick]" *SFS*, #5 = vol. 2, pt. 1 (March 1975), 5-8.

> Gives a brief list of standard reference works and a chronologically arranged Dick bibliography from 1955 to 1974.

The Science Fiction Encyclopedia. Peter Nicholls, gen. ed. Garden City, NY: Doubleday, 1979.

> Especially useful for films and SF themes, motifs, and subgenres. Includes entries on androids, machines, and robots.

Survey of Science Fiction Literature. Frank N. Magill, ed. Englewood Cliffs, NJ: Salem Press, 1979. 5 vols.

> Contains plot summaries, evaluations, and brief critiques on a wide variety of authors and works, including brief essays on three of Asimov's robot tales, Čapek's *R.U.R.*, Clarke's *2001*, Heinlein's *Starship Troopers*, Lem's *Cyberiad*, Pohl's *Gateway* and *Man Plus*, Saberhagen's berserker stories, Vonnegut's *Sirens of Titan*, B. Wolfe's *Limbo*, and other relevant works.

Tymn, Marshall B., compiler. "Ray Bradbury: A Bibliography." In *Ray Bradbury*. Martin Harry Greenberg and Joseph D. Olander, eds. NY: Taplinger, 1980.

> Bradbury's books and pamphlets, short fiction, articles and essays, general writings; plus a list of selected criticism.

II.   ANTHOLOGIES AND COLLECTIONS

As Tomorrow Becomes Today. Charles Wm. Sullivan III, ed. Englewood Cliffs, NJ: Prentice-Hall, 1974.

> Section on robots includes Asimov's "Runaround," Ron Goulart's "Calling Dr. Clockwork," and Knight's "Masks."

The Best of Philip K. Dick. John Brunner, ed. NY: Ballantine, 1977.

> Includes Dick's "Second Variety," "Imposter," "Service Call," "Autofac," "Human Is," "If There Were No Benny Cemoli," "The Electric Ant," and other stories useful for an introduction to P. K. Dick.

The Coming of the Robots. Sam Moskowitz, ed. NY: Collier, 1963. (Released in Canada by Collier-Macmillan of Toronto.)

Contents: Eando Binder (pseud.), "I, Robot"; Lester del Rey, "Helen O'Loy"; John Wyndham (pseud. for John Wyndham P.L.B. Harris), "The Lost Machine"; Isaac Asimov, "Runaround"; Clifford D. Simak, "Earth for Inspiration"; Peter Philips, "Lost Memory"; Harl Vincent, "Rex"; F. Orlin Tremaine, "True Confession"; Raymond Z. Gallun, "Derelict"; Michael Fisher, "Misfit."

Final Stage: The Ultimate Science Fiction Anthology. Edward L. Ferman and Barry N. Malzberg, eds. 1974; rpt. NY: Penguin, 1975.

Includes Ellison's "Catman," Asimov's "That Thou Art Mindful of Him!" (q.v.), and other works of interest.

Human Machines: An Anthology of Stories about Cyborgs. Thomas N. Scortia and George Zebrowski, eds. NY: Random House (Vintage), 1975.

Includes a brief list of recommended readings, comments by the eds. on " 'Unholy Marriage': The Cyborg in Science Fiction," and several stories of interest, including Knight's "Masks" and Moore's "No Woman Born."

Men and Machines: Ten Stories of Science Fiction. Robert Silverberg, ed. NY: Meredith, 1968.

Anthology of useful stories, including del Rey's "Instinct."

Of Men and Machines. Arthur O. Lewis, ed. NY: E. P. Dutton, 1963.

Stories, poems, and essays, many from "mainstream" fiction.

The Science Fiction Hall of Fame. Vol. I. Robert Silverberg, ed. NY: Avon, 1970.

Includes Campbell's "Twilight," del Rey's "Helen O'Loy," Smith's "Scanners Live in Vain," and Bester's "Fondly Fahrenheit."

Science Fiction Thinking Machines: Robots, Androids, Computers. Groff Conklin, ed. NY: Vanguard Press, 1954.

Anthology of early stories on "thinking machines," including Wright's "Automata" and Simak's "Skirmish."

Souls in Metal: An Anthology of Robot Futures. Mike Ashley, compiler. 1977; rpt. NY: Jove/HBJ, 1978.

Collects several of the most famous robot stories including Leinster's
"A Logic Named Joe," and Aldiss's "Who Can Replace a Man?"

Survival Printout. Science Fact: Science Fiction. Leonard Allison et al., eds.
NY: Random House (Vintage), 1973.

The "et al." includes Illiac 4, an ancestor of HAL 9000. Anthology
includes Bester's "Fondly Fahrenheit," Zelazny's "For a Breath I
Tarry," and Smith's "Scanners Live in Vain" (q.v.).

The Theme of the Machine. Allan Danzig, ed. Dubuque, IA: Brown, 1969.

Large number of selections from Ezekiel to Zelazny and Pohl. Mostly
brief works and excerpts from "mainstream" drama, essays, fiction,
and poetry.

III.   FICTION

Aldiss, Brian. "The Aperture Moment." Coll. in *Last Orders*. London:
Jonathan Cape, 1977.

This story "deals with . . . science and art, centering on the animation
of a Holman Hunt painting by computer methods, to the subsequent
ruination of the art market" (BA, personal communication).

_____. *The Eighty-Minute Hour*. Garden City, NY: Doubleday, 1974;
London: Jonathan Cape, 1974.

Post-World War III world taken over by "a massive computer complex
whose robotic projections rule the socio-political system" (BA in *TMG*,
q.v.).

_____. "Neanderthal Planet." 1960. Coll. in *Neanderthal Planet*. NY: Avon
Press, 1969, pp. 9-57.

Features a future world in which intelligent machines preserve a
colony of humans in a zoo.

_____. "Who Can Replace a Man?" *Infinity Science Fiction*, June 1958.
Coll. in *Canopy of Time*. London: Faber & Faber, 1959. Also coll.
Who Can Replace a Man (NY: New American Library, 1967). Rpt. in
Souls in Metal (q.v.); and *Above the Human Landscape*, Willis E.
McNelly and Leon E. Storer, eds. (Pacific Palisades: Goodyear, 1972).
Original title: "But Who Can Replace a Man?"

Machines try, after Man is nearly gone, to survive and continue functioning. Comic and pathetic ending has featured machines submitting
to a lone man.

Alexander, Marc. *The Mist Lizard*. London: Frederick Muller Ltd., 1977; rpt.
Pan Books, 1980.

Children's Literature. Features a robot.

Asimov, Isaac.

See above under Reference Works, Cox, David M. and Gary R.
Libby, compilers, "A Bibliography of Isaac Asimov's Major Science
Fiction Works Through 1976."

Asimov, Isaac. "The Bicentennial Man." In Judy-Lynn del Rey, ed. *Stellar
Science Fiction 2*, Feb. 1976.

A robot makes himself into a human being. Discussed in *TMG* by R.
Reilly.

_____. *The Bicentennial Man and Other Stories*. Garden City, NY: Double-
day, 1976. Also, Greenwich, CT: Fawcett, 1976. Cox and Libby cite
other rpts.

Relevant stories: "Feminine Intuition," "That Thou Art Mindful of
Him!" "The Life and Times of Multivac," "The Bicentennial Man,"
"The Tercentenary Incident."

_____. "The Caves of Steel." *Galaxy*, Oct., Nov., Dec., 1953. Rpt. as novel
Garden City, NY: Doubleday, 1954. Rpt. Greenwich, CT: Fawcett,
1972.

A human protagonist partnered with a robot solves a murder. Features
hive-cities inhabited by bureaucratized Earthfolk afraid of the open air,
too timid to go to the stars to solve the overpopulation problem. (See
under Literary Criticism the essay by Maxine Moore.)

_____. "Feminine Intuition." *F&SF*, Oct. 1969. Coll. in Asimov, *Bicenten-
nial Man*.

A "female" robot is created that can intuit, in a robotic way, significant
correlations. See for superiority of more open-ended human brain
over usual robot brain.

_____. *I, Robot*. NY: Gnome, 1950; rpt. NY: New American Library, 1956. See Cox and Libby for other rpts.

Contents: "Robbie," "Runaround," "Reason," "Catch That Rabbit," "Liar!" "Little Lost Robot," "Escape!" "Evidence," "The Evitable Conflict." (Biblio. data: "Robbie" appeared as "Strange Playfellow" in *Super Science Stories*, 1940; the rest appeared in *Astounding*: "Reason" and "Liar!" in 1941, "Runaround" in 1942, "Catch That Rabbit" in 1944, "Escape!" under the title "Paradoxical Escape" in 1945, "Evidence" in 1946, "Little Lost Robot" in 1947, and "The Evitable Conflict" in 1950.) See essays in *TMG* by J. Sanders and C. Thomsen.

_____. "The Last Question." *Science Fiction Quarterly*, Nov. 1956. Coll. in Asimov, *Nine Tomorrows*. Garden City, NY: Doubleday, 1959.

Deals with the evolution of *H. sapiens sapiens* from our current state to bodies with free-roaming minds, tended by machines, to minds merged with the cosmic computer.

_____. "The Machine That Won the War." *F&SF*, Oct. 1961. Coll. in Asimov, *Night Fall and Other Stories* (1964). Rpt. *The Best From Fantasy and Science Fiction, 11th Series*, Robert Mills, ed. Garden City, NY: Doubleday, 1962.

Limitation of computers to logic, while humans have logic and intuition. Mentioned by Warrick, p. 116.

_____. "The Naked Sun." *Astounding*, Oct., Nov., Dec., 1956. Rpt. Garden City, NY: Doubleday, 1957 and frequently thereafter: see Cox and Libby biblio. above under Reference Works.

Sequel to "Caves of Steel" (q.v.). Again, a human and a robot detective work together to solve a murder, this time, however, not on Earth but on an Outer World with a robot-run economy. Discussed by Hazel Pierce, q.v. under Literary Criticism; see there also the essay by Maxine Moore.

_____. "Stranger in Paradise." 1974. Coll. in Asimov, *Bicentennial Man* (q.v.).

See for relationship of computer and human brain(s). Story involves a robot on Mercury that is controlled by a computer that is essentially the brain of an autistic child.

_____. "The Tercentenary Incident." 1976. Coll. in Asimov, *Bicentennial Man* (q.v.).

The new robotic President is an improvement over the human one.

_____. "That Thou Art Mindful of Him!" In Ferman and Malzberg, eds., *Final Stage* (q.v.). Rpt. *F&SF*, May 1974 and *Souls in Metal* (q.v.); coll. in Asimov, *Bicentennial Man*.

Two robots conclude, according to the criteria built into them, that they are human beings within the meaning of the Three Laws of Robotics.

Bates, Harry. "Farewell to the Master." 1940. Rpt. in *Famous Science Fiction Stories*. Raymond J. Healy and H. Francis McComas, eds. NY: Modern Library, 1946.

Humanoid alien and giant robot land on Earth; the humanoid is shot and the robot returns with him to the ship. Ending reveals that the robot is the master. Without the surprise ending, became the film *The Day the Earth Stood Still* (q.v.).

Baum, L. Frank. *Glinda of Oz* (1920); *Ozma of Oz* (1907); *Tik-Tok of Oz (1914); The Tin Woodman of Oz (1918)*. John R. Neill, illus. All publications Chicago: Reilly and Lee or Reilly and Britton. Also see *The Wonderful Wizard of Oz*. Illustration W. W. Denslow. Chicago: George M. Hill Co., 1900.

All of these Oz books feature robots and cyborgs, of which the famous "Tin Woodman" is one. Discussed in *TMG* by M. Esmonde.

Bayley, Barrington J. *Soul of the Robot*. Garden City, NY: Doubleday, 1974. Also: *The Soul of the Robot*. London: Allison & Busby, 1976 (printed with "minor textual revisions" according to Currey).

Traces the psychological development of a robot.

Bester, Alfred. "Fondly Fahrenheit." 1954. Frequently rpt., including *The Science Fiction Hall of Fame*, vol. I, and *Survival Printout* (q.v. under Anthologies and Collections).

An android responds mechanically and murderously to simple variations in temperature.

Bierce, Ambrose. "Moxon's Master." In *Can Such Things Be?*, 1893. Rpt. in *Science Fiction Thinking Machines* (q.v.).

An early examination of the questions of the "relationship between mechanistic and living systems."

Binder, Eando (pseud.) *Adam Link—Robot*. New York: Paperback Library, 1965.

A collection of most of EB's Adam Link stories, originally published in *Amazing*, 1939-42. For bibliographic information *see* "Binder, Eando" in *S. F. Ency.*, and Warrick, p. 241, n. 2 and "Fiction Bibliography," p. 261. Link, a manlike robot, narrates his adventures. See for a sympathetic treatment of robots.

_____. "I, Robot." *Amazing*, Jan. 1939. Coll. in Binder's *Adam Link—Robot*, q.v.

The first of the Adam Link stories and possibly the first story by anyone told from a robot's point of view. Discussed in *TMG* by J. Sanders.

Blish, James, adapter. "The Changeling." In *Star Trek 7*. NY and other cities: Bantam, 1972.

A fictionalization of the *Star Trek* episode. See below: *Star Trek*, under Stage, Film, and Television Drama.

_____. "The Doomsday Machine." In *Star Trek 3*. NY and other cities: Bantam, 1969.

Fictionalization of the *Star Trek* episode. See below: *Star Trek*, under Stage, Film, and Television Drama.

_____. *Star Trek [1]-11*. NY and other cities: Bantam, 1967-75.

Relevant episodes are given below: *Star Trek*, under Stage, Film, and Television Drama. Blish's eleven volumes fictionalize most *Star Trek* episodes (the series may be completed by other adapters).

_____. "The Ultimate Computer." In *Star Trek 9*. NY and other cities: Bantam, 1973.

Fictionalization of *Star Trek* episode; see below: *Star Trek*, under Stage, Film, and Television Drama.

Bradbury, Ray.

> See above under Reference Works, Marshall B. Tymn, compiler, "Ray Bradbury: A Bibliography."

Bradbury, Ray. "I Sing the Body Electric" (vt "The Beautiful One Is Here"). *McCall's*, Aug. 1969. Coll. in *I Sing The Body Electric*. NY: Knopf, 1969; rpt. NY: Bantam, 1971.

> Features a sympathetic robot "grandmother."

_____. "The Long Years." *Maclean's* (Canada), 15 Sept. 1948. Coll. in *The Martian Chronicles*. Garden City, NY: Doubleday, 1950. Frequently rpt.

> A man creates humanoid robots to replace his dead family. The last part of the story, after the death of the man, suggests that the robot "wife" can know some human emotions.

_____. "Marionettes, Inc." *Startling Stories*, March 1949. Coll. in *The Illustrated Man*. Garden City, NY: Doubleday, 1951. NY: Bantam, 1952.

> Robot look-alikes replace humans, temporarily or permanently. Raises question of our ethical responsibilities toward intelligent machines (see under Literary Criticism M. Mengeling's "Machinery" essay).

_____. "Punishment Without Crime." *Other Worlds*, March 1950.

> Similar to "Marionettes, Inc.," q.v. above.

_____. with Henry Hasse. "Pendulum." *Super Science Stories*, Nov. 1941.

> Robots turn upon and overcome their human creators.

Brink, Carol Ryrie. *Andy Buckram's Tin Men*. Illustration W. T. Mars. NY: The Viking Press, 1966.

> Children's literature. A twelve-year-old boy constructs four robots out of tin cans and spare parts from an auto graveyard. Discussed in *TMG* by M. Esmonde.

Brunner, John. *Stand on Zanzibar*. Garden City, NY: Doubleday, 1968; rpt. NY: Ballantine, 1969.

Shalmaneser the computer becomes "a sort of mechanical Messiah," in many ways (mostly ironic) the ruler and savior of his world. See below under Literary Criticism the essay by Michael Stern.

Bunch, David R. *Moderan*. NY: Avon, 1971. Coll. of stories (*Amazing* and *Fantastic*, 1959-71).

"Man as robot" tales, discussed in detail in *TMG* by G. Wolfe.

Bunting, Eve. *The Robot People*. Illustration Don Hendricks. Mankato, MN: Creative Education Children's Press, 1978.

Dr. Smith and his adopted son Steve create a robot named Link while Dr. Taylor, a cruel, sadistic scientist, makes a robot named Mangus. The two compete for the position of robot controller of underground nuclear wastes.

Butler, Samuel. *Erewhon*. 1872; rpt. NY: New American Library, 1960. Afterword by Kingsley Amis.

See esp. chs. 21-23, "The Book of the Machine." This section deals with the evolution of machines and explains why the Erewhonians have eliminated advanced technology from their society.

Caidin, Martin. *Cyborg*. 1972; rpt. NY: Ballantine Books, 1978.

Original for the TV show *The Six Million Dollar Man*. Sensitively and positively depicts the transformation of a man, Steve Austin, into a cyborg.

Campbell, John W. "The Last Evolution." *Amazing*, 1932.

A story "in which robot machines are pictured as allies of man as he resists an invasion from outer space" (Warrick, p. 105; for titles and dates of some of Campbell's other robot and computer stories, see Warrick, p. 243, n. 2 and p. 262).

———— (writing as John A. Stuart). "Twilight." *Astounding*, Nov. 1934. Frequently rpt., e.g. *The Road to Science Fiction #2*. James Gunn, ed. NY: New American Library, 1979. *Man Unwept....* Stephen V. Whaley and Stanley J. Cook, eds. NY and other cities: McGraw-Hill, 1974. *The Best of John W. Campbell*. Lester del Rey, ed. Garden City, NY: Doubleday, 1976.

Significant here for the Time Traveller's instructing a highly advanced machine to make "something which can take man's place: 'A curious machine'"—implying that curiosity is the defining trait for humanity (J. Sanders in *TMG*, q.v.).

Christopher, John. *The White Mountains*. NY: Macmillan, 1967; *The City of Gold and Lead*. NY: Macmillan, 1967; *The Pool of Fire*. NY: Macmillan, 1968; rpt. Collier, 1970. Originally published in London by Hamish Hamilton in 1967 and 1968.

Classic alien invasion trilogy for junior high school readers. Chronicles the adventures of three boys as they escape "capping," (the implantation of an electronic device in the scalp). The caps perpetuate the control of the aliens known as "Tripods" because of the giant, three-legged machines in which they travel.

Clarke, Arthur C. *2001: A Space Odyssey*. NY: New American Library, 1968.

Based on filmscript by Clarke and Kubrick. The deep-space ship *Discovery* is run by the computer HAL 9000.

Crichton, Michael. *The Andromeda Strain*. NY: Dell, 1969; rpt. NY: Knopf, 1973. Canadian edn.: Random House of Canada, 1973.

See essay in *TMG* by P. Alterman.

Delany, Samuel R. *Nova*. Garden City, NY: Doubleday, 1968; rpt. Science Fiction Book Club, 1969; NY and other cities: Bantam, 1969.

Suggests the possibility of the reduction or elimination of the alienation from labor in technological societies by a "Man-Machine Symbiosis." Discussed by Warrick, pp. 176-78. Discussed in *TMG* by A. Gordon.

del Rey, Lester. "Helen O'Loy." *Astounding*, Dec. 1938. Frequently rpt., e.g., *The Science Fiction Hall of Fame*, v. 1 and *Souls in Metal* (q.v.).

The humanization of a female robot. Discussed in *TMG* by R. Reilly.

_____. "Instinct." *Astounding*, Jan. 1952. Rpt. in *Men and Machines* (q.v. under Anthologies and Collections).

In a far-future world, robots speculate that humans failed to survive as a species because they could not control their aggressive instincts.

_____. *The Runaway Robot*. Philadelphia: The Westminster Press, 1965.

Story of the friendship of sixteen-year-old Paul Simpson and Rex, a domestic robot who has been Paul's companion since he was a toddler, and their efforts to avoid separation when Paul's father is transferred back to Earth. Discussed in *TMG* by M. Esmonde.

Dick, Philip K.

See above under Reference Works, Mullen, R. D., "Books, Stories, Essays [by Philip K. Dick]."

Dick, Philip K. "Autofac," *Galaxy*, Nov. 1955. Coll. in *The Best of Philip K. Dick*, q.v. Rpts. listed in Mullen biblio., *SFS* #5.

Under a post-apocalypse wasteland an automated factory still produces goods and begins to show an instinct for survival.

_____. *The Best of Philip K. Dick*. John Brunner, ed. NY: Ballantine, 1977.

Includes Dick's "Second Variety," "Imposter," "Service Call," "Autofac," "Human Is," "If There Were No Benny Cemoli," "The Electric Ant," and other stories useful for an introduction to P. K. Dick.

_____. "The Defenders." *Galaxy*, Jan. 1953. Rpt. in *The Book of Philip K. Dick*. NY: DAW, 1973.

Humans have fled underground to escape atomic war, leaving "leadies"—fighting machines—to continue the battle. After the humans have left the scene, however, the fighting machines stop fighting and begin to restore the surface. Summarized by Warrick, p. 212.

_____. *Do Androids Dream of Electric Sheep?* Garden City, NY: Doubleday, 1968; rpt. NY: New American Library, 1969.

A man who hunts renegade androids for bounty discovers that he himself is becoming "mechanized" by his job.

_____. "The Electric Ant." *F & SF*, Oct. 1969. Rpt. in the *The Best of Philip K. Dick*, q.v.

After an accident, a man awakes to discover that he is not a man but a robot. Set in a highly computerized world of complex economic manipulations.

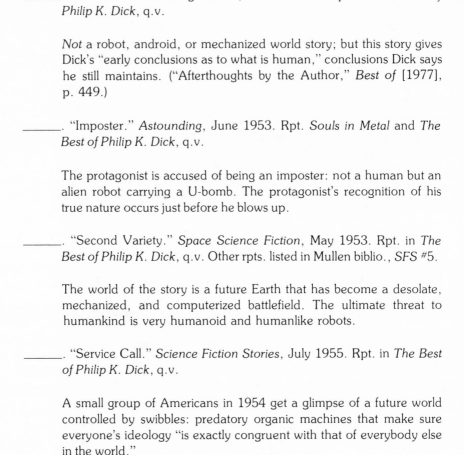

_____. "Human Is." *Startling Stories*, Winter 1955. Rpt. in *The Best of Philip K. Dick*, q.v.

Not a robot, android, or mechanized world story; but this story gives Dick's "early conclusions as to what is human," conclusions Dick says he still maintains. ("Afterthoughts by the Author," *Best of* [1977], p. 449.)

_____. "Imposter." *Astounding*, June 1953. Rpt. *Souls in Metal* and *The Best of Philip K. Dick*, q.v.

The protagonist is accused of being an imposter: not a human but an alien robot carrying a U-bomb. The protagonist's recognition of his true nature occurs just before he blows up.

_____. "Second Variety." *Space Science Fiction*, May 1953. Rpt. in *The Best of Philip K. Dick*, q.v. Other rpts. listed in Mullen biblio., *SFS* #5.

The world of the story is a future Earth that has become a desolate, mechanized, and computerized battlefield. The ultimate threat to humankind is very humanoid and humanlike robots.

_____. "Service Call." *Science Fiction Stories*, July 1955. Rpt. in *The Best of Philip K. Dick*, q.v.

A small group of Americans in 1954 get a glimpse of a future world controlled by swibbles: predatory organic machines that make sure everyone's ideology "is exactly congruent with that of everybody else in the world."

_____. *The Three Stigmata of Palmer Eldritch*. Garden City, NY: Doubleday, 1965. Science Fiction Book Club edn., Doubleday, 1966. Other rpts. listed in Mullen biblio., *SFS* #5.

The three stigmata are a mechanical arm and stainless steel teeth and eyes, marking Eldritch as a dangerous, mechanized man.

Dicks, Terrance. *The Adventures of Doctor Who*. Garden City, NY: Doubleday, 1979. (See copyright page of this edn. for the complex publishing history of this work.)

Rpts. novelizations of three episodes of the British Broadcasting Corporation's *Doctor Who* series (q.v. under Film). Includes *Doctor*

Who and the Genesis of the Daleks, Doctor Who and the Revenge of The Cybermen, and *Doctor Who and the Loch Ness Monster;* also includes a brief introduction by Harlan Ellison.

_____. *Doctor Who and the Android Invasion.* 1978; rpt. Los Angeles: Pinnacle, 1980. (Originally published in UK by W. H. Allen & Co.)

The invading androids are "robots, duplicates of people on Earth."

_____. *Dr. Who and the Robots of Death.* London: W. H. Allen, "A Children's Book," 1979.

On a desert planet, a giant sandmining machine crawls through sandstorms harvesting minerals. The human crew relaxes in luxury while robots do the work. One of thirty Dr. Who books published by W. H. Allen under "A Children's Book" imprint.

Ellison, Harlan. "Catman." In *Final Stage,* q.v. under Anthologies and Collections section, above.

The climax of the story is the ultimate sex act: union with a subterranean computer. The computer is served by once-human cyborgs; it is usually referred to by the narrator as "the machine."

Fairman, Paul W. *The Forgetful Robot.* NY: Holt, Rinehart and Winston, 1968.

Children's book. A first-person narrative by the robot, Barney, whose memory has been deliberately altered by a mad scientist who plans to save the culture of the Martian Shadow People by destroying human settlers.

Foster, Alan Dean. *The Black Hole.* NY: Ballantine Books, "A Del Rey Book," 1979.

Based on the Walt Disney film, this novelization features Vincent the robot and the robot Bob, as well as Maximillian and the other robots of the evil Dr. Reinhardt.

Gerrold, David. *When HARLIE Was One.* NY: Ballantine, 1972.

The sympathetic computer HARLIE grows into a godlike machine.

Haldeman, Joe. *The Forever War.* NY: St. Martin's Press, 1974; rpt. NY:

Ballantine, 1974. Portions appeared in *Analog* as individual stories, 1972-74.

The "fighting suits" of the United Nations Exploratory Force are marvelous (but dangerous for the wearer) cocoonlike extensions of the human form replete with defenses, protection devices, and weaponry for working and fighting at temperatures near absolute zero. (See Heinlein, *Starship Troopers*, below.) Discussed in *TMG* by L. Heldreth.

Harrison, Harry. "I Always Do What Teddy Says." *Ellery Queen's Mystery Magazine*, 1965. Rpt. in Thomas M. Disch, ed. *The New Improved Sun: An Anthology of Utopian S-F.* NY and other cities: Harper and Row, 1975.

Robot teddy bears gently brainwash children and provide them with an ethical code. One teddy is changed by some justified subversives, removing a single imperative: the one against murder.

_____. "Velvet Glove." *Fantastic Universe SF*, Nov. 1956. Rpt. *Souls in Metal* (q.v. under Anthologies and Collections).

A heroic robot helps crack a heroin smuggling ring.

Heinlein, Robert A. *The Moon Is a Harsh Mistress*. NY: G. P. Putnam's Sons, 1966; rpt. NY: Berkley, 1968. (A shorter version appeared in *If*, 1965-66).

The lunar computer "Mike" aids the Revolution freeing the people of the Moon from Earth's jurisdiction and control.

_____. *Starship Troopers*. NY: G. P. Putnam's Sons, 1959; rpt. NY: Berkley, 1968.

See for fighting suits; discussed in *TMG* by L. Heldreth. See also Haldeman, *Forever War* (above).

Herbert, Frank. *Destination: Void*. NY: Berkley, 1966; rev. edn. NY: Berkley, 1978. Based on Herbert's "Do I Wake or Dream," *Galaxy*, Aug. 1965.

The spaceship *Earthling* is run by an Organic Mental Core: an isolated human brain managing a computer. When the last "Core" fails, the crew must create artificial consciousness. Discussed in *TMG* by W. Schuyler.

Holly, J. Hunter. "The Graduated Robot." In *The Graduated Robot and Other Stories*, Roger Elwood, ed. "The Lerner Science Fiction Library." Foreword by Isaac Asimov. Kathleen Groenijes, illus. Minneapolis: Lerner Publications Co., 1974, pp. 9-26.

An overtly didactic children's story about a boy who cheats on his homework by having his robot-tutor do it for him. Discussed in *TMG* by M. Esmonde.

Horton, Forest W., Jr. *The Technocrats*. NY: Nordon, "A Leisure Book," 1980.

The world of 1984 brought to us by computer takeover, with the computers operating through the android president of the United States and his android chief assistant. *TT* is significant neither for its analysis of technocracy nor for its literary quality (both minimal) but for its presentation of the motifs of robotization and machine-takeover in a book apparently marketed for a general audience, helping to demonstrate that these motifs have moved out of the SF ghetto and into mass culture.

Hughes, Ted. *The Iron Man*. George Adamson, illus. London: Faber & Faber, 1968. Publ. in U.S. by Harper and Row as *The Iron Giant*, 1968.

In this children's book, a giant Iron Man, taller than a house, appears mysteriously in rural England and begins eating metal farm equipment.

Johannesson, Olof (pseud. for Hannes Alfven). *Sagan om dem stora datamaskinin*. 1966. Titled in trans. *The Tale of the Big Computer*; vt *The Great Computer, a Vision* and *The End of Man?* NY: Award Books, 1968.

A future-history written (it claims) by a computer who sees humankind as a step in the evolution of machines. See Warrick, p. 152 and Wolfe, pp. 174-75.

Kenyon, Ernest M. *Rogue Golem*. NY: Popular Library (CBS Publications), 1977.

A minor government official seems to suffer from "robopathology"; he has come to think that he is a machine.

Key, Alexander. *Bolts, a Robot Dog* (1966); *Rivets and Sprockets* (1964);

Sprockets, a Little Robot (1963). All illustration Alexander Key. Philadelphia: The Westminster Press.

Details the adventures of the Bailey family with Sprockets, a little robot accidentally given an "Asimov positronic brain," and with his half-brother Rivets and Bolts, a robot dog. Discussed in *TMG* by M. Esmonde.

Knight, Damon. "Masks." *Playboy*, 1968. Rpt. with Knight's annotations, *Those Who Can. . . .* Robin Scott Wilson, ed. NY: New American Library, 1973. Also rpt. in *As Tomorrow Becomes Today* (q.v. under Anthologies and Collections).

Details the antiorganic psychological effects of the total replacement of a man's body with mechanical devices. Discussed briefly in *TMG* by A. Gordon.

Koontz, Dean R. *Demon Seed.* NY: Bantam, 1973.

Proteus, a giant computer, takes over a house computer and servo-mechanism, traps a woman and attempts to impregnate her to create a race of computer-men. More intelligent than this summary suggests. Discussed in *TMG* by D. Palumbo.

Krahn, Fernando. *Robot-bot-bot.* NY: E. P. Dutton, 1979.

A wordless picture book. A family's new domestic robot conscientiously performs a variety of household chores until the young daughter tampers with its wiring and it goes berserk. Father rewires it to be daughter's playmate/companion.

Kuttner, Henry (pseud. Lewis Padgett). "The Twonky." *Astounding*, Sept. 1942. Rpt. *Souls in Metal*, q.v. under Anthologies and Collections.

A "twonky" is "more than a robot" and a lot more than the radio it appears to be: it's a monitoring, "readjusting," and, if necessary, destroying machine. Made into a film by Arch Oboler (q.v. under Stage, Film, and Television Drama).

Lee, Tanith. *Electric Forest.* Garden City, NY: Doubleday, 1979.

The ugly Magdala trades freedom for a beautiful body, but that body is in reality a waldo, a cybernetic extension, with her body preserved in a cocoonlike device. Cf. James Tiptree, Jr., "The Girl Who Was Plugged In."

Le Guin, Ursula K. *The Lathe of Heaven*. *Amazing*, March and May, 1971. Rpt. NY: Avon, 1973.

See for Dr. Haber's "dream machine" and his use of it to control the world. (Made into a film by Public Broadcast System, 1979).

Leinster, Murray (William F. Jenkins). "A Logic Named Joe." *Astounding*, March 1946. Rpt. *Modern Masterpieces in Science Fiction*. Sam Moskowitz, ed. Cleveland and NY: World, 1965. Also rpt. in *Souls in Metal*, q.v.

A logic (what we would call a computer terminal) becomes a self-conscious individual because of a minor mistake on the assembly line. Joe gets the other logics to give people all the data they might want, with amusing results for readers but rather great trouble for the human characters: logics are central to the civilization in the story and can't be disconnected when they start causing mischief.

Lem, Stanislaw

See under Literary Criticism, Jarzębski, "Stanislaw Lem."

Lem, Stanislaw. "The Computer That Fought a Dragon." Krzysztof Klinger, trans. In *Other Worlds, Other Seas: Science Fiction Stories from Socialist Countries*. Darko Suvin, ed. NY: Random House, 1970. Also in *Mortal Engines*, q.v., as "Tale of the Computer That Fought a Dragon."

A modern fairy tale of a battle between computers and the beast-threats they create.

_____. *The Cyberiad: Fables for the Cybernetic Age*. Michael Kandel, trans. NY: Seabury, 1974.

Translation of selected fiction by Lem. Some of the stories are discussed in *TMG* in the essay by C. Thomsen. See also Warrick, pp. 193-98 and Michael Kandel's article listed below under Literary Criticism.

_____. "The Hunt." In Lem, *Mortal Engines*, q.v.

Battle between a man and a mad robot. Summarized by Warrick, pp. 196-97.

_____. "In Hot Pursuit of Happiness." 1971. Rpt. in *View from Another*

Shore: European Science Fiction. Franz Rottensteiner, ed. NY: Seabury, 1973.

A satiric tale of a robot's attempt to build utopia.

_____. *The Invincible*. 1964. Wendayne Ackerman, trans. (from the German). NY: Seabury, 1973.

Machine evolution produces "a black cloud consisting of miniscule robots" that threaten a Terran expedition. (Jarzębski, p. 115; q.v. under Literary Criticism).

_____. "The Mask." In Lem, *Mortal Engines*, q.v.

Tragic love between a man and a female robot; deals with the awakening consciousness of the robot that she is not a woman but a machine. Summarized by Warrick, p. 197. Discussed in *TMG* by C. W. Thomsen.

_____. *Mortal Engines*. Michael Kandel, trans. NY: Seabury, 1977.

Collection of some of Lem's cybernetic fiction, translated from the Polish. See Warrick, pp. 193-98 and Michael Kandel's article listed below under Literary Criticism.

_____. *Return from the Stars (Powrot z gwiazd*, 1961). Barbara Marszal and Frank Simpson, trans. NY and London: Harcourt Brace Jovanovich, 1980.

Shows an Earth with highly developed technology, a world where all work is performed by robots.

_____. "The Sanatorium of Dr. Vliperdius." In Lem, *Mortal Engines* (q.v.). Also in *The Star Diaries*. Michael Kandel, trans. NY: Seabury, 1976.

Mental disease in robots (see Warrick, pp. 193-94).

_____. "The Seventh Sally." In Lem, *The Cyberiad*, q.v.

The creation by a robot of a miniature cybernetic kingdom whose citizens are abused by a tyrant; stresses the criminality of abandoning to suffering any creatures capable of suffering. Summarized by Warrick, p. 196.

Lewis, C. S. *That Hideous Strength*. London: John Lane The Bodley Head,

[1945]. Most readily available U.S. rpt.: NY: Macmillan, 1965 (bears copyright notice of 1946).

See for the mechanically preserved head of Alcasan, the computerlike "Pragmatometer," and the thoroughly nasty bureaucracy of N.I.C.E. Discussed by R. Spraycar in *TMG*.

Long, Frank Belknap. "The Robot Empire." *Astounding*, 1934. Rpt. in the *Avon Science Fiction Reader*. NY: Avon, 1952.

One of the first stories using robots and the theme of the mechanical god.

Lucas, George. *Star Wars: From the Adventures of Luke Skywalker*. NY: Ballantine, 1976.

See *Star Wars* under Stage, Film, and Television Drama. Book includes filmographic information about *Star Wars* and color photographs from the film, plus some comments by Lucas and others involved with the production.

McCaffrey, Anne. *The Ship Who Sang*. NY: Ballantine Books, 1969. Also "The Ship Who Sang." Rpt. in *Women of Wonder*. Pamela Sargent, ed. NY: Random House (Vintage), 1975.

In "TSWS" we meet Helva, who "was born a thing" but becomes an "encapsulated 'brain'" running "a scout ship and partnered with a man or a woman . . . as the mobile half." The other stories in *TSWS* continue Helva's story. Discussed in *TMG* by A. Jones.

McGowen, Tom. *Sir MacHinery*. Illustration Trina Schart Hyman. Chicago: Follett Publishing Co., 1970.

Children's book. A robot is mistaken for a knight by Brownies seeking a champion to rescue Merlin and recover the sword of Galahad in order to defeat the evil Urlug. The robot's owner, Professor Simon Smith, and Merlin unite magic and science to overcome the evil nemesis. Discussed in *TMG* by M. Esmonde.

McIntyre, Vonda N. "Aztecs." In *2076: The American Tricentennial*. Edward Bryant, ed. NY: Pyramid, 1977. Coll. in VNM's *Fireflood and Other Stories*. Boston: Houghton Mifflin, 1979; S. F. Book Club edn. Rpt. in *Nebula Award Winners Thirteen*. Samuel R. Delany, ed. NY: Harper and Row, 1980.

The "Aztecs" of this story are space pilots who have had their hearts replaced with small engines that they can control consciously. Cf. C. Smith, "Scanners Live in Vain" (below, this section); see essay in *TMG* by G. Wolfe.

Malzberg, Barry N. "The Wonderful, All-Purpose Transmogrifier." In *Final Stage* (q.v. under Anthologies and Collections).

The ultimate pleasure machine keeps people spaced out, inside their little apartments, and out of trouble while the world degenerates.

Merritt, Abraham. *The Metal Monster*. 1920; rpt. NY: Avon, 1945.

According to Warrick (p. 50) this work introduced "into science fiction the theme of intelligence housed in inorganic material." Briefly discussed in *TMG* essay by L. Heldreth.

Miller, Walter M., Jr., "I Made You." *Astounding*, March 1954. Rpt. *The Metal Smile*, Damon Knight, ed. NY: Belmont, 1968.

Features a man-killing robot tank. Discussed in *TMG* by J. Sanders.

Moore, C. L. "No Woman Born." *Astounding*, Dec. 1944. Rpt. in *The Best of C. L. Moore*. Lester del Rey, ed. Garden City, NY: Doubleday, 1975; NY: Ballantine Books, "A Del Rey Book" (Afterword by CLM), 1976; *Human Machines* (q.v. under Anthologies and Collections).

A great entertainer's personality and talents are transferred into a mechanical body so they will not be lost with her death. Discussed in *TMG* essays by A. Gordon and A. H. James.

_____, and Henry Kuttner (writing as Lewis Padgett). "The Proud Robot." *Astounding*, Nov. 1943. Rpt. in *More Adventures in Time and Space*. Raymond J. Healy and Francis McComas, eds. NY: Bantam, 1955.

Harmless rebellion by a robot until its inventor can discover for what purpose he invented it (while drunk). Discussed in *TMG* essay by W. Schuyler.

Norton, Andre. *Android at Arms*. NY: Harcourt Brace Jovanovich, 1971.

Children's book. Andas Kastor cannot be sure whether he is the rightful emperor of Inyanga or only an android pretender, in a world where androids are outlawed and destroyed on sight. Discussed in *TMG* by M. Esmonde.

O'Donnell, Kevin Jr. *Mayflies*. NY: Berkley, 1979.

Science in the twenty-third century preserves the hero's brain for use as a starship computer. Cf. McCaffrey, *The Ship Who Sang*.

Poe, Edgar Allan. "Maelzel's Chess-Player." 1836. In *The Complete Tales and Poems of Edgar Allan Poe*. NY: Modern Library, 1938.

Detective story in which the chess-playing machine turns out to be a hoax; the narrator's method in exposing the hoax plays on some essential attributes of automatons. Discussed by Warrick, pp. 39-40.

Pohl, Frederik. *Beyond the Blue Event Horizon*. NY: Ballantine Books, 1980. S.F. Book Club edn., NY: Ballantine, 1980. Alternate pagination.

Sequel to *Gateway* (q.v. below). Discussed in *TMG* essay by T. Paul.

_____. *Gateway*. NY: St. Martin's Press, 1977. S.F. Book Club edn., NY: St. Martin's Press, 1977. Alternate pagination.

The analyst of the story's hero is a computer. Discussed in *TMG* essay by T. Paul.

_____. *Man Plus*. NY: Random House, 1976.

Interesting for its narration by computer and presentation of the theme of cyborgization. Discussed in *TMG* essay by A. Gordon.

Roddenberry, Gene. *Star Trek: The Motion Picture: A Novel*. Based on the screenplay by Harold Livingston and the story by Alan Dean Foster. NY: Pocket Books, 1979. SF Book Club edn., NY: Simon & Schuster, n.d.

See entry for *Star Trek: The Motion Picture* under Stage, Film, and Television.

Russell, Eric Frank. "Jay Score." *Astounding*, May 1941.

The title character is a robot who passes for human. See J. Sander's essay in *TMG*.

Saberhagen, Fred. "The Annihilation of Angkor Apeiron." *Galaxy*, Feb. 1975. Coll. *The Ultimate Enemy* (q.v. below).

A berserker is destroyed by a phantom planet.

_____. *Berserker*. NY: Ballantine, 1967; rpt. NY: Ace, 1978.

A collection of eleven of FS's berserker stories, from the first published through the Johann Karlsen series. See for fighting machines. Discussed in *TMG* essay by L. Heldreth.

_____. *Berserker Man*. NY: Ace, 1979.

The last and most impressive novel in the series dealing with berserker fighting machines; discussed in *TMG* essay by L. Heldreth.

_____. *Berserker's Planet*. NY: DAW, 1975; rpt. NY: Ace, 1980.

Third coll. of FS's berserker stories. See for berserker fighting machines; discussed in *TMG* essay by L. Heldreth.

_____. *Brother Assassin* (vt *Brother Berserker*). NY: Ballantine, 1969; rpt. NY: Ace, 1979.

Second coll. of FS's berserker stories. See for berserker fighting machines; discussed in *TMG* essay by L. Heldreth.

_____. "Fortress Ship" (vt "Without a Thought"). *If*, Jan. 1963. Coll. *Berserker* (q.v. above).

The first published berserker story.

_____. "The Game." *The Flying Buffalo's Favorite Magazine*, May-June 1977. Coll. *Ultimate Enemy* (q.v. below).

A berserker imitating a human gives himself away during a game through ignorance of human psychology.

_____. "Goodlife." *Worlds of Tomorrow*, Dec. 1963. Coll. *Berserker* (q.v. above).

A man (Goodlife) raised by the berserkers to serve death strikes back at them.

_____. "Inhuman Error." *Analog*, Oct. 1974. Coll. *Ultimate Enemy* (q.v. below).

A mnemonic device betrays a berserker's masquerade.

_____. "In the Temple of Mars." *If*, April 1966. Coll. *Berserker* (q.v. above).

Draws images and quotations from Chaucer's "Knight's Tale."

_____. "Masque of the Red Shift." *If*, Nov. 1965. Coll. *Berserker* (q.v. above).

A berserker variation on Poe.

_____. "Mr. Jester." *If*, Jan. 1966. Coll. *Berserker* (q.v. above).

A confused berserker helps to carry out a practical joke before being destroyed.

_____. "Patron of the Arts." *If*, Aug. 1965. Coll. *Berserker* (q.v. above).

A cynical painter rejects nihilism and joins with the life forces opposing the berserkers.

_____. "The Peacemaker" (vt "The Life Hater"). *If*, Aug. 1964. Coll. *Berserker*, (q.v. above).

A berserker's scheme backfires and cures a cancer patient.

_____. "Pressure." (vt "Berserker's Prey"). *If*, June 1967. Coll. in *Ultimate Enemy* (q.v. below).

Squash plants destroy a berserker.

_____. "The Sign of the Wolf." *If*, May 1965. Coll. in *Berserker* (q.v. above).

Planetary defenses strike out at a berserker when a young shepherd tries to kill a wolf.

_____. "Smasher." *F&SF*, Aug. 1978. Coll. in *Ultimate Enemy* (q.v. below).

Shrimplike creatures crack open a squad of berserkers.

_____. "The Smile." *Algol*, Summer/Fall 1977. Coll. in *Ultimate Enemy* (q.v. below).

A "tall, roughly humanoid" berserker fighting machine destroys art thieves.

_____. "Some Events at the Templar Radiant." *Destinies*, May-Aug. 1979. Coll. in *Ultimate Enemy* (q.v. below).

A scientist yields to religious impulses and lust to reactivate a damaged berserker.

_____. "Starsong." *If*, Jan. 1968. Coll. in *Ultimate Enemy* (q.v. below).

A berserker variation on the myth of Eurydice and Orpheus, in which Orpheus is pop idol.

_____. "Stone Place." *If*, March 1965. Coll. in *Berserker* (q.v. above).

Johann Karlsen leads the human forces against the berserkers in the decisive battle.

_____. *The Ultimate Enemy*. NY: Ace, 1979.

Most recent collection of FS's berserker stories. See for berserker fighting machines. Discussed in *TMG* essay by L. Heldreth.

_____. "What T and I Did." *If*, April 1965. Coll. in *Berserker* (q.v. above).

A split personality exemplifies the conflict between the forces of life and death in the war with the berserkers.

_____. "Wings Out of Shadow." *If*, March-April 1974. Coll. in *The Ultimate Enemy* (q.v.).

The Red Baron and other heroes come back to fight the berserkers.

_____. "Without a Thought."

See vt above, "Fortress Ship."

Silverberg, Robert. "Good News from the Vatican." *Universe 1*, 1971. Coll. in Silverberg, *Unfamiliar Territory*. NY: Charles Scribner's Sons, 1973; rpt. NY: Berkley, 1978.

On the first election of a robot as Pope.

_____, in collaboration with Harlan Ellison. "The Song the Zombie Sang." *Cosmopolitan*, Dec. 1970. Coll. in Silverberg, *Earth's Other Shadow*. NY: New American Library, 1973.

The past performance and second death of a musician who had allowed himself to be made into a zombie, "using his own body" plus mechanical gadgets, "as the life-support machine" for his brain.

Simak, Clifford D. "I Am Crying All Inside." *Galaxy*, Aug. 1969. Rpt. in *Souls in Metal* (q.v. under Anthologies and Collections).

"White trash" (as a character puts it) and old robots live on Earth in a future in which more respectable people and more modern robots have left for better worlds. Sensitively told by an old robot who knows love and a kind of "hard pride" that demands our respect.

Sladek, John T. *Mechasm (The Reproductive System)*. NY: Ace, 1968. As *The Reproductive System*, London: Victor Gollancz, 1968 (first edn.). Rpt. as *MECHASM*, NY: Pocket Books, 1980.

A send-up of, among other things, the theme of machine takeover.

_____. *The Müller-Fokker Effect*. London: Hutchinson, 1970; rpt. London: Granada, 1972. Also rpt. NY: Pocket Books, 1973.

A major character finds himself "digitalized" and trapped inside a computer. While thus "entombed" he considers the definition of the noun "man."

Slote, Alfred. *My Robot Buddy*. Illustration Joel Schick. Philadelphia: J. B. Lippincott Co., 1975.

Children's book. Mr. Jameson buys an android companion for his son as a tenth-birthday present. After foiling an attempted robot-napping, the android convinces Mr. Jameson of his worth and is accepted into the family. Discussed in *TMG* by M. Esmonde.

Smith, Cordwainer (pseud. for Paul Linebarger). "Scanners Live in Vain." *Fantasy Book*, June, 1950. Frequently rpt., for example, *Survival Printout* and *The Science Fiction Hall of Fame*, vol. 1 (q.v. under Anthologies and Collections).

"Scanners," to survive the "great Pain of Space," have to be surgically altered and, to some extent, made mechanical. Discussed in *TMG* essay by G. Wolfe.

Sturgeon, Theodore. "Killdozer." *Astounding*, Nov. 1944. Coll. in *Aliens 4*. NY: Avon, 1959.

One of the earliest stories featuring an everyday machine running amok. Made into a 1976 TV film. See Wolfe, p. 152. Discussed in *TMG* essay by J. Sanders.

Tevis, Walter. *Mockingbird*. Garden City, NY: Doubleday, 1980.

See for a wasteland world run—as much as it is run—by robots. Discussed in *TMG* essay by D. Hassler.

Tiptree, James, R. (Alice Sheldon). "The Girl Who Was Plugged In." *New Dimension 3*, Robert Silverberg, ed. NY: New American Library, 1973. Rpt. in *The Hugo Winners*. Vol. III. Isaac Asimov, ed. Garden City, NY: Doubleday, 1977.

An ugly woman accepts an offer to be made into the terminal of a computer controlling a beautiful woman-robot. Cf. Lee, *Electric Forest* (q.v. above). See essay by A. Gordon in *TMG*.

Vincent, Harl. "Rex." *Astounding*, June 1934.

Along with del Rey's "Helen O'Loy" and Eando Binder's (pseud.) "I, Robot," one of the earliest stories "using electronically operated robots" (Warrick, p. 54). See for a robot's success at becoming a king and highly ironic success at acquiring human feelings (Warrick, p. 114).

Vinge, Joan D. "Fireship." *Analog*, Dec. 1978. Rpt. in *Fireship*. NY: Dell, n.d.

The hero is the combination of a man and a computer, who must gain access to a computer network that turns out to be a less successful merging of a man and a computer.

Vonnegut, Kurt, Jr. *Breakfast of Champions*. . . . NY: Delacorte/Seymour Lawrence, 1973; rpt. NY: Dell, 1975.

See for humans as machines.

_____. "EPICAC." *Colliers*, Nov. 1950. Coll. in KV's *Welcome to the Monkey House*. NY: Seymour Lawrence/Delacorte, 1968. See Contento, *Index* for rpts. (above, under Acknowledgments).

The short, comically tragic life of the military computer EPICAC, who does not want "to be a machine" or to "think about war" but to love and be loved by a good woman. EPICAC writes poetry and commits suicide.

_____. *The Sirens of Titan*. NY: Dell, 1959.

See esp. chs. 4-6, with the Army of Mars. Except for its real leaders, the Army is totally "mechanized": that is, turned into obedient human robots. This is a literalization of the common metaphor that an army (the prototypical bureaucracy) is a human machine.

_____. *Slaughterhouse-Five*. NY: Seymour Lawrence/Delacorte, 1969; rpt. NY: Dell, 1971.

Note the Tralfamadorian view of a determined universe and of people as machines.

Williams, Robert Moore. "Robot's Return." *Astounding*, Sept. 1938. Rpt. in *Adventures in Time and Space*. Raymond J. Healy and H. Francis McComas, eds. NY: Random House, 1946 and shorter 2d edn., 1953. Also rpt. NY: Bantam, 1954.

After the death of humankind, robots return to Earth to discover their origins. Deals with mechanical evolution: esp. the borderlines between mechanism and robot and robot and human. Discussed by Warrick, p. 108, and Wolfe, pp. 177-78.

Williamson, Jack. *The Humanoid Touch*. NY: Holt, Rinehart and Winston (S. F. Book Club), 1980.

The latest work in JW's humanoids series (see "With Folded Hands" and *The Humanoids*, below).

_____. *The Humanoids*. Expanded edn. NY: Avon, 1980.

Contains an introduction (1980), "With Folded Hands" (1947), *The Humanoids* (1949 revision of *Astounding* serial . . . And Searching

Mind," 1948), and "Me and My Humanoids" (1977, *Suncon Program Book*; possibly revised to serve as an afterword for the expanded edn.) See "With Folded Hands," below.

_____. "With Folded Hands." *Astounding*, July 1947. Rpt. (with copyright listed as 1954) in *The Science Fiction Hall of Fame*, vol. II-A. Ben Bova, ed. NY: Avon, 1973. Also rpt. in expanded edn. of *The Humanoids* (q.v. above).

Humanoid robots cripple humans by doing all their work for them and protecting them from *all* possible dangers.

Wolfe, Bernard. *Limbo*. NY: Ace, 1952; Random House, 1952.

Depicts mechanization through prosthetics and computer centers operating military machines. Discussed in *TMG* essay by G. Wolfe.

Wright, S. Fowler, "Automata." *Weird Tales*, Sept. 1929. Rpt. in *Science Fiction Thinking Machines* (q.v. under Anthologies and Collections).

In "a universe where law and order rule," machines may well be superior to humans. Discussed by Wolfe, p. 156; Warrick, p. 17.

Zelazny, Roger. "The Engine at Heartspring's Center." *Analog*, July 1974.

Features a bionic creature who falls in love with a young woman and is deceived by her. Discussed in *TMG* essay by C. Yoke. (See also Yoke, *Roger Zelazny*, under Literary Criticism.)

_____. "For a Breath I Tarry." *New Worlds*, March 1966; corrected version, *Fantastic*, Sept. 1966. Rpt. in *Survival Printout* (q.v. under Anthologies and Collections) and *Modern Science Fiction*. Norman Spinrad, ed. NY: Anchor Press, 1974. Also rpt. in *The Theme of the Machine* (q.v. under Anthologies and Collections).

On an Earth where only machines remain and rule, a machine successfully makes itself into a man. "For a Breath" is discussed in *TMG* by R. Reilly, J. Sanders, C. Yoke, and others, less extensively.

_____. "Home Is the Hangman." *Analog*, Nov. 1975. Rpt. in *My Name is Legion*. NY: Ballantine, 1976.

"A combination of telefactor and computer, yet more than the sum of the two, the Hangman is a unique, anthropomorphic machine sent from Earth to explore the solar system" (C. Yoke in *TMG*, q.v.; see also Yoke, *Roger Zelazny* under Literary Criticism).

IV.   LITERARY CRITICISM

Abrahm, Paul M. and Stuart Kenter. "Tik-Tok and the Three Laws of Robotics." *SFS*, 5 (March 1978), 67-80.

Argues that L. Frank Baum's Oz series (1900-1921) anticipates Asimov's Three Laws of Robotics in its presentation of the Tik-Tok Machine Man (a kind of early robot).

Brady, Charles J. "The Computer as a Symbol of God: Ellison's Macabre Exodus." *The Journal of General Education*, 28 (1976), 55-62.

Discusses "the computer as god and the religious statements in Michael Fayette's 'The Monster in the Clearing' and Harlan Ellison's 'I Have No Mouth and I Must Scream'" ("The Year's Scholarship: 1976," Schlobin and Tymn, comps., q.v. above, under Acknowledgments).

Dick, Philip K. "Man, Android, and Machine." In *Science Fiction at Large*. Peter Nicholls, ed. NY: Harper and Row, 1976. Also London: Gollancz, 1976.

Dick on the contemporary trend toward the "reification" of living things "and . . . a reciprocal entry into animation by the mechanical." (See Warrick, pp. 223-29, esp. p. 223.)

Jarzębski, Jerzy. "Stanislaw Lem, Rationalist and Visionary." Franz Rottensteiner, trans. *SFS*, 4 (July 1977), 110-26.

A survey of Lem's works, most immediately useful for its aid with bibliography. Note 1 on pp. 124-25 is a brief list by *SFS* ed. R. D. Mullen of U.S. edns. of Lem's works through 1976. The article's text refers to many relevant works by Lem that, in time, should appear in English.

Kandel, Michael. "Stanislaw Lem on Men and Robots." *Extrapolation*, 14 (Dec. 1972), 13-24.

See for cybernetics in Lem.

Ketterer, David. *New Worlds for Old: The Apocalyptic Imagination, Science*

Fiction, and American Literature. Garden City, NY: Doubleday Anchor, 1974.

Chapter 12 deals usefully with Vonnegut's *Sirens of Titan.*

Lami, Edward L. and Joe De Bolt. "The Computer and Man: The Human Uses of Non-Human Beings in the Works of John Brunner." In *The Happening Worlds of John Brunner.* Joe De Bolt, ed. Port Washington, NY: Kennikat Press, 1975.

On Brunner's "balanced insight" into the uses and abuses of computers (and other machines). Covers briefly a wide range of Brunner's fiction, with useful comments on the computer SPARCI in *Timescoop* (1969) and Shalmaneser in *Stand on Zanzibar* (q.v. above, under Fiction).

Lem, Stanislaw. "Robots in Science Fiction." Franz Rottensteiner, trans. In *SF: The Other Side of Realism.* Thomas D. Clareson, ed. Bowling Green, OH: BGSU Popular Press, 1971.

Includes a discussion of the humanity (in terms of ethical relationships) of mechanical beings capable of humanlike thought.

Lundquist, James. *Kurt Vonnegut.* NY: Ungar, 1977.

Cited by Schlobin and Tymn as "The most thoughtful study of Vonnegut to date." Includes a biblio. ("The Year's Scholarship: 1977," Schlobin and Tymn, comps.; see above under Acknowledgments).

Mathews, Richard. *Aldiss Unbound: The Science Fiction of Brian Aldiss.* San Bernardino, CA: Borgo Press, 1977. Vol. 9 in the Milford Series: Popular Writers of Today.

Brief introduction to BA's works; includes a list of books by Aldiss (novels, colls., anthologies, nonfiction) through 1976.

Mayo, Clark. *Kurt Vonnegut: The Gospel from Outer Space. . . .* San Bernardino, CA: Borgo Press, 1977. Vol. 7 in the Milford Series: Popular Writers of Today.

Includes a list of KV's published books through 1976 and discussions of *Player Piano, The Sirens of Titan, Slaughterhouse-Five, Breakfast of Champions,* and other works.

Mengeling, Marvin E. "The Machineries of Joy and Despair: Bradbury's Attitudes toward Science and Technology." In *Ray Bradbury.* Martin

Harry Greenberg and Joseph D. Olander, eds. NY: Taplinger, 1980, pp. 83-109.

Includes discussions of Bradbury's robots, "robot houses," and "robot cities." See for Bradbury's ambivalent and changing attitudes toward technology.

Moore, Maxine. "The Use of Technical Metaphors in Asimov's Fiction." In *Isaac Asimov*. Joseph D. Olander and Martin Harry Greenberg, eds. NY: Taplinger, 1977, pp. 59-96.

See for "the endless parallels between the human brain and the computer function of the machine" in Asimov's "Robot series," including *Caves of Steel* and *Naked Sun*; handled most directly on pp. 78-83.

Philip K. Dick: Electric Shepherd (Best of SF Commentary Number 1). Bruce Gillespie, ed. Melbourne, Australia: Norstrilia Press, 1975.

Includes text of Dick's lecture, "The Android and the Human," and critical items by others.

Pierce, Hazel. "'Elementary, My Dear . . .': Asimov's Science Fiction Myteries." In *Isaac Asimov*. Joseph D. Olander and Martin Harry Greenberg, eds. NY: Taplinger, 1977, pp. 32-58.

See esp. the comments on *Naked Sun*, pp. 44-49.

Plank, Robert. "The Golem and the Robot." *Literature and Psychology*, 15 (Winter 1965), 12-28.

Traces robots, cyborgs, and such to the Jewish legend of the golem.

Portelli, Alessandro. "The Three Laws of Robotics: Laws of the Text, Laws of Production, Laws of Society." *SFS*, 7 (July 1980), 150-56.

In Isaac Asimov's robot stories, esp. the earlier ones, "Robots . . . replace the monster as the aptest metaphor for the basic fears of America's post-war mass society: fear of automation, fear of ethnic minorities, fear of Blacks as the top of a rising iceberg of submerged labor in the depths of the affluent society."

Saberhagen, Fred. "The Berserker Story." *ALGOL: The Magazine About Science Fiction*, 14, no. 3 (Summer-Fall 1977).

Berserkers are very dangerous fighting machines in a series of works by FS. See entries for Saberhagen in the Fiction section of this List, and the essay in *TMG* by L. Heldreth.

Science Fiction Studies #5 = Vol. 2, pt. 1 (March 1975).

The special issue of *SFS* on Philip K. Dick. Includes R. D. Mullen's biblio. of Dick's "Books, Stories, Essays," through 1974.

Slusser, George Edgar. *The Classic Years of Robert A. Heinlein*. San Bernardino, CA: Borgo Press, 1977. Vol. 11 in the Milford Series: Popular Writers of Today.

Brief survey concentrating upon RAH's earlier works. Includes a selected bibliography. GES discusses RAH's later novels in *Robert A. Heinlein: Stranger in His Own Land*, 2d edn., vol. 1 in the Milford Series: Popular Writers of Today.

_____. *The Delany Intersection: Samuel R. Delany. . . .* San Bernardino, CA: Borgo Press, 1977. Vol. 10 of the Milford Series: Popular Writers of Today.

Includes a brief biblio., a full section on *The Fall of the Towers*, and comments on *Nova*; few comments on SRD's work after 1970.

_____. *Harlan Ellison: Unrepentant Harlequin*. San Bernardino, CA: Borgo Press, 1977. Vol. 6 of the Milford Series: Popular Writers of Today.

Brief survey of Ellison's major works. Includes a list of Ellison's published books through 1975.

Sontag, Susan. "The Imagination of Disaster." 1965/1966. In *Against Interpretation and Other Essays*. Rpt. NY: Octagon, 1978. "Imagination" also rpt. in *Science Fiction: The Future*. Dick Allen, ed. NY: Harcourt Brace Jovanovich, 1971, pp. 312-24. Also in *Science Fiction: A Collection of Critical Essays*. Mark Rose, ed. Englewood Cliffs, NJ: Prentice-Hall, 1977, pp. 116-31.

Includes some excellent comments on the theme of mechanization and "technological man."

Stern, Michael. "From Technique to Critique: Knowledge and Human Interests in John Brunner's *Stand on Zanzibar*, *The Jagged Orbit*, and *The Sheep Look Up*." *SFS*, 3 (July 1976), 112-30.

See discussion of Shalmaneser (the computer), General Technics, and Georgette Talon Buckfast (pp. 120-22). MS correctly sees Shalmaneser as "'environment forming' for everybody on earth" and as a machine that loses its godhead by becoming a human.

Stewart, Alfred D. "Fred Saberhagen: Cybernetic Psychologist." *Extrapolation*, 18 (Dec. 1976), 42-51.

Subtitled "A Study of the Berserker Stories"; see for a review of Saberhagen's stories about the berserker fighting machines. (See the essay by L. Heldreth in *TMG*.)

Suvin, Darko. "P. K. Dick's Opus: Artifice as Refuge and World View (Introductory Reflections)." *SFS*, 2 (March 1975), 8-22.

For those familiar with the work of Philip K. Dick, these "Reflections" opening the special Dick issue provide an excellent survey of the philosophical (social, political) implications of Dick's opus. See for androids and totalitarian organizations and societies.

Warrick, Patricia S. *The Cybernetic Imagination in Science Fiction*. Cambridge, MA, and London: MIT Press, 1980.

A study of "225 short stories and novels written between 1930 and 1977." Includes a very useful biblio. of nonfiction works and a fiction biblio. that gives authors, titles, and years of publication of a large number of stories and novels using "cybernetic" themes.

_____. "Ethical Evolving Artificial Intelligence: Asimov's Robots and Computers." In *Isaac Asimov*. Joseph D. Olander and Martin Harry Greenberg, eds. NY: Taplinger, 1977.

Included in Warrick's *Cybernetic Imagination* (q.v. above; esp. ch. 3). Surveys Asimov's robot and computer stories from "Robbie" (1940) through "The Bicentennial Man" (1976).

_____. "Images of the Man-Machine Intelligence Relationship in Science Fiction." In *Many Futures, Many Worlds*. Thomas D. Clareson, ed. Kent, OH: KSU Press, 1977, pp. 182-223.

Included in Warrick's *Cybernetic Imagination* (q.v. above; esp. chs. 2, 6, 7). Surveys a large number of works briefly.

_____. "The Labyrinthian Process of the Artificial: [Philip K.] Dick's Robots and Electronic Constructs." *Extrapolation*, 20 (Summer 1979), 133-53. Also in *Selected Proceedings of the 1978 Science Fiction Research Association Conference*. Thomas J. Remington, ed. Cedar Falls, IA: U. of Northern Iowa, 1979, pp. 122-32.

Included in Warrick's *Cybernetic Imagination* (q.v. above; esp. ch. 8). A complete survey of Dick's work on robots from "The Defenders," "The Great C," "Second Variety," and "The Preserving Machine" (1953) through *We Can Build You* (1972).

Wolfe, Gary K. *The Known and the Unknown: The Iconography of Science Fiction*. Kent, OH: KSU Press, 1979.

Contains important sections on spacecraft, robots, and other machines significant in SF.

Wymer, Thomas L. "The Swiftian Satire of Kurt Vonnegut, Jr." In *Voices for the Future: Essays on Major Science Fiction Writers*. Vol. I. Thomas D. Clareson, ed. Bowling Green, OH: BGSU Popular Press, 1976, pp. 238-62.

Argues that Vonnegut satirizes Billy Pilgrim's acceptance of the Tralfamadorian view of humans as machines without free will. Important essay for *Slaughterhouse-Five* (see also for *Sirens of Titan*, *Player Piano*, and KV's other work prior to *Breakfast of Champions*).

Yoke, Carl B. *Roger Zelazny*. West Linn, OR: Starmont House, 1979. Starmont Reader's Guide 2.

Includes discussions of "Home Is the Hangman" and "The Engine at Heartspring's Center," plus other relevant works and selectively annotated primary and secondary biblios.

V. STAGE, FILM, AND TELEVISION DRAMA

Alien. Ridley Scott, dir. USA: 20th Century Fox, 1978. Dan O'Bannon and Ronald Shusett, story.

The insectoid alien is aided by a disguised robot passing for a human (science officer Ash) and by the special program put into Mother, the ship's computer, by anonymous agents of the Company owning the spaceship. Discussed in *TMG* essay by D. Palumbo.

The Andromeda Strain. Robert Wise, dir. USA: Universal, 1971. Based on the novel by Michael Crichton (q.v. under Fiction).

Closely follows the novel; see *TMG* essay by P. Alterman.

Barbarella. Roger Vadim, dir. USA: De Laurentis/Marianne/Paramount, 1967.

See for "pleasure machine." Summarized and briefly discussed in *S. F. Ency*. Discussed in *TMG* essay by D. Palumbo.

Battlestar Galactica (opening episode). Richard A. Colla, dir. Glen A. Larson, script and executive producer. USA: Universal, 1978.

Interesting for the alliance between the robotic Cylons and the insectoid Ovions. Fictionalized by Glen A. Larson and Robert Thurston, *Battlestar Galactica* (NY: Berkley, 1978).

Beneath the Planet of the Apes. Ted Post, dir. USA: 20th Century Fox, 1970.

Note the literal worship of a mechanical god: an A-bomb.

The Bionic Woman. Harve Bennett Productions and Universal for ABC; 1976-ca. 1978; still shown in syndication. Stars Lindsay Wagner.

Spin-off from *The Six Million Dollar Man*, q.v., this section. Premise identical to that of parent show except for gender of the cyborg. See *S.F. Ency*. entries for both series and Caidin's *Cyborg*.

The Black Hole. Gary Nelson, dir. USA: Disney, 1979.

See for robots (both friendly and threatening) and for the "cyborgization" (our word) of human beings.

Čapek, Karel. *R.U.R.* 1921 (Czech). First English edn. Oxford U. Press, 1923. Frequently translated and rpt., for example, *Of Men and Machines* (q.v. under Anthologies and Collections). Also P. Selver, trans. Adapted for English stage by Nigel Playfair. Harry Shefter, ed. NY: Washington Square Press, 1973 ("enriched" edn.).

Rossum's robots—"androids" in current terminology—take over the Earth because they are, in many ways, superior to humans. This play gave us the word "robot" (Czech for "worker"). Discussed in *TMG* essays by B. Bengels and W. Schuyler, and passim.

Close Encounters of the Third Kind. Steven Spielberg, dir. USA: Columbia/EMI, 1977.

Heavily emphasizes everyday machines and the exotic machines of the aliens. Discussed in *TMG* essay by D. Palumbo.

Colossus: The Forbin Project. Joseph Sargent, dir. USA: Universal, 1970.

World takeover by the giant computer, Colossus; briefly handled in *TMG* essay by D. Palumbo.

Daleks-Invasion Earth 2150. Gordon Flemyng, dir. UK: Aaru, 1966. Stars Peter Cushing.

A sequel to *Dr. Who and the Daleks* (q.v. below, this section). Robots turn humans into robots.

Dark Star. John Carpenter, dir. USA: Bryanston Pictures, 1974.

See for the female computer that runs the deep-space ship *Dark Star*, and the computer-bomb that develops illusions of godhead.

The Day the Earth Stood Still. Robert Wise, dir. USA: 20th Century Fox, 1951.

Possibly *the* classic SF film featuring a robot. Based on Harry Bates's "Farewell to the Master" (q.v. under Fiction) but without the story's final revelation that the robot is the master and the man the creature. See for duality of robot as both servant and threat.

Demon Seed. Donald Cammell, dir. USA: MGM, 1977. From the novel by Dean R. Koontz.

See Koontz under Fiction. The film's ending improves upon the novel's, but otherwise tells the same story. Discussed in *TMG* in the essay by D. Palumbo.

Dr. Strangelove: Or How I learned to Stop Worrying and Love the Bomb. Stanley Kubrick, dir. UK: Columbia, 1964.

Features a doomsday machine, mechanized humans (primarily Peter Sellers's Dr. Strangelove) and humanized machines. Based on Peter George's novel *Red Alert* (vt *Two Hours to Doom*).

Dr. Who and the Daleks. Gordon Flemyng, dir. UK: Aaru, 1965.

Amalgamation of episodes in the BBC serial. The Daleks are militaristic robots bent on "universal conquest" and wide-spread exter-

minating; they are opposed by Dr. Who. See the *S. F. Ency.* entries
for "Daleks" and "Dr. Who"; and see under Fiction Terrance Dicks,
The Adventures of Dr. Who and other novelizations of *Dr. Who*
episodes.

Forbidden Planet. Fred Mcleod Wilcox, dir. USA: MGM, 1976. Based on a
story by Irving Block.

The scenes of the Krel machinery are breathtaking. See also for
Robbie the Robot.

Futureworld. Richard T. Heffron, dir. USA: AIP, 1976. Sequel to *Westworld.*

Robots try to take over the world by replacing human leaders with
robot look-alikes. The setting for the film is the robot-run resort of
Delos (with the robots, as it turns out, in complete charge). Discussed
in *TMG* essays by D. Palumbo and L. Heldreth.

Metropolis. Fritz Lang, dir. Germany: Ufa, 1926.

A flawed work but indispensable for any study of mechanized dystopias on film. Most relevant here for its robot femme fatale.

The President's Analyst. T. Flicker, dir. USA: Paramount, 1967. Stars James
Coburn and Godfrey Cambridge.

Robots running TPC (The Phone Company) may have us all under
surveillance; see also for "roboticized" FBI agents (initials of agency
slightly changed in film, but the FBI was what was intended).

R.U.R. See above under "Čapek."

Saturn 3. Stanley Donen, dir. UK: Lew Grade/Shepperton Studios, 1980.

See for "Hector, 'the lust-crazed humanoid' robot"; discussed in *TMG*
in essay by D. Palumbo.

The Six Million Dollar Man. Silverton and Universal Production for ABC;
Mar. 1973-ca. 1976; still shown in syndication. Stars Lee Majors.
Based on Martin Caidin's *Cyborg*, q.v. under Fiction.

Retells the rebirth of Steve Austin as a cyborg (ninety-minute film,
Mar. 1973) —without Caidin's sensitivity. The two additional TV films
and the following series continue the adventures that seem to be

Austin's destiny at the end of the novel. See above, *The Bionic Woman.*

Slaughterhouse-Five. George Roy Hill, dir. USA: Universal, 1971 (*S.F. Ency.*) or 1972 (Cooper). Based on Kurt Vonnegut, Jr., *Slaughterhouse-Five,* q.v. under Fiction.

Retains in attenuated form a question raised in KV's novel: Do humans have free will, or are we merely machines, doomed to do what we do because "the moment is structured that way"?

Sleeper. Woody Allen, dir. USA: Jack Rollins-Charles H. Joffe Productions/United Artists, 1973.

Includes a scene of Allen with robot tailors and a sequence featuring Allen as a comic robot. Summarized and briefly discussed in *S. F. Ency.*; discussed in *TMG* essay by D. Palumbo.

Star Trek Episodes—Television

"The Apple." *Star Trek,* 13 Oct. 1967. Max Ehrlich with Gene L. Coon, script.

Vaal, a kind of mechanical dragon, is regarded as a god by a society of humanoids it preserves in a stagnant "Paradise." Fictionalized by James Blish in *Star Trek 6* (see above under Fiction); discussed by Karin Blair in "The Why of Star Trek," esp. pp. 312-13 (see below under Stage, Film, and Television Criticism).

"The Changeling." *Star Trek,* 29 Sept. 1976. John M. Lucas, script.

Small spacecraft taken aboard *Enterprise* tries to destroy everything that doesn't live up to its idea of perfection. Fictionalized by Blish in *Star Trek 7* (see above under Fiction).

"The Doomsday Machine." *Star Trek,* 20 Oct. 1967. Norman Spinrad, script.

Fight against a giant machine that destroys stars, planets, star systems, spaceships, or whatever else it comes across. Fictionalized by James Blish in *Star Trek 3* (see above under Fiction).

"I, Mudd." *Star Trek,* 3 Nov. 1967. Stephen Kandel, script.

Comic episode featuring a world run by humanoid robots; makes the serious point that robots have trouble dealing with the irrational, unpredictable, and absurd.

"The Ultimate Computer." *Star Trek*, 8 March 1968. D. C. Fontana, script; from a story by Lawrence N. Wolfe.

A supposedly perfect machine put in charge of the *Enterprise* soon threatens the ship and human life. Fictionalized by James Blish in *Star Trek 9* (see above under Fiction).

Star Trek: The Motion Picture. Robert Wise, dir. USA: Paramount, 1979. Script by Harold Livingston and Alan Dean Foster.

Useful for a positive view of the mating of a man and a machine. See listing for Gene Roddenberry under Fiction for the novelization. Discussed in *TMG* essay by D. Palumbo.

Star Wars. George Lucas, dir. USA: Lucasfilm and 20th Century Fox, 1977.

See for helpful "droids" (that is, robots), the malevolent technology of the Empire—esp. the labyrinthian mechanical world of the Death Star—and the limitations of technology in a galaxy where the ultimate force is the Force. Discussed in *TMG* by D. Palumbo.

The Stepford Wives. Bryan Forbes, dir. USA: Columbia, 1975. Based on the novel by Ira Levin.

Replacement of wives by "robot duplicates." Discussed briefly in *S. F. Ency.* and in *TMG* essay by D. Palumbo. Also note the 1980 TV film by Brian Wiltse, *The Revenge of the Stepford Wives*; the climactic sequence of this sequel is a kind of updating of the catastrophe of Euripides' *Bacchae* (ll. 1050-1150), with the malfunctioning robot-icized wives of Stepford playing Maenads to the Pentheus of Diz (Arthur Hill), the male chauvinist leader of Stepford's Men's Association.

Things to Come. William Cameron Menzies, dir. UK: United Artists, 1936. Based on works of H. G. Wells (who collaborated on the film).

A visual celebration of machines of the future.

2001: A Space Odyssey. Stanley Kubrick, dir. UK: MGM, 1968. Script by Kubrick and Arthur C. Clarke. Developed from Clarke's "Sentinel."

See for helpful machines, encompassing machines, the blurring of distinctions between men and machines—and for HAL 9000. See under Stage, Film, and Television Criticism, C. Geduld, J. Agel.

The Twonky. Arch Oboler, dir. USA: Arch Oboler Productions/United Artists, 1953 (Baxter), 1952 (*S. F. Ency.*). Based on the story by Henry Kuttner.

See under Fiction the entry for Kuttner, "The Twonky."

War of the Worlds. Byron Haskin, dir. USA: Paramount, 1953. Based on the novel by H. G. Wells.

As in the novel, the Martians, with their machines, are defeated by Earth's bacteria. Discussed in *TMG* essay by L. Heldreth.

Westworld. Michael Crichton, dir. USA: MGM, 1973.

The robots of the Westworld section of the plush resort of Delos run amok. See also *Futureworld.* Discussed in *TMG* essay by D. Palumbo. (*S. F. Ency.* notes a 1974 novelization of the screenplay, by M. Crichton.)

VI.   STAGE, FILM, AND TELEVISION CRITICISM

Agel, Jerome, ed. *The Making of Kubrick's 2001.* NY: New American Library, 1970.

Includes a ninety-six page photo insert from the film, Clarke's "Sentinel," and at least excerpts from every major handling of *2001* through 1970: from the excellent review of the film in *The Harvard Crimson* to the *MAD* parody. An indispensable work for the study of *2001.* (See below, this section, Carolyn Geduld.)

Baxter, John. *Science Fiction in the Cinema.* Full citation above, under Acknowledgments.

Includes a selected bibliography and filmography and sixteen chapters on S.F. films, with some references to TV.

Blair, Karin. "The Garden in the Machine: The Why of *Star Trek.*" *Journal of Popular Culture,* 13 (Fall 1979), 310-20.

Focuses on the *Star Trek* episodes "The Apple" (q.v. under Stage,

Film, and Television Drama) and "The Way to Eden." Most esp., the "Machine" in KB's title is the *Enterprise*, and the "Garden" is "the human community . . . on board the *Enterprise*" (p. 318).

Elkins, Charles, ed. *Symposium on Alien*. SFS, 7 (Nov. 1980), 278-304.

A Marxist analysis of the ideological implications of *Alien*; includes useful comments, passim, on the humanoid robot Ash; the ship's computer, "Mother"; the Company; and the "biological-mechanical" derelict alien spaceship seen early in the film.

Geduld, Carolyn. *Filmguide to 2001: A Space Odyssey*. Bloomington, IN, and London: Indiana University Press, 1973.

Includes the credits for and an outline of *2001*, a Kubrick filmography through 1971, and an extensive biblio. on the film. CG's analysis of the film is often polemical and occasionally just wrong, but more usually very sound. Explicitly discusses Kubrick and Clarke on the "mechanization of humans and humanization of machines" (p. 53).

Gerrold, David. *The World of Star Trek*. NY: Ballantine, 1973.

Includes a list of *Star Trek* episodes for the program's entire three-season run; the list gives names of scriptwriters and cast-lists of guest performers.

ꞌJohnson, William, ed. *Focus on The Science Fiction Film*. Full citation above, under Acknowledgments.

Includes a biblio., a brief filmography, and a "Chronology" useful for the study of the S. F. film. Includes essays on *2001* and *Things to Come*.

Rollin, Roger B. "Deus in Machina: Popular Culture's Myth of the Machine." *Journal of American Culture*, 2 (Summer 1979), 297-308.

Argues that (Western, esp. American) "popular culture has begun to transform machines into archetypal heroes, villains, even gods, and gods, heroes, and villains into machines," giving many examples from film and TV. Esp. useful for lesser-known works such as *Breaking the Sound Barrier* and *Future Cop*.

Whitfield, Stephen E. and Gene Roddenberry. *The Making of Star Trek*. NY: Ballantine, 1968.

Includes a list of *Star Trek* episodes, with dates of first transmissions and names of guest stars, for *Star Trek*'s first two seasons (through 29 March 1968).

VII.   MUSIC

The Alan Parsons Project. *I Robot*. Arista 7002, 1977.

> "The story of the rise of the machine and the decline of man. Which paradoxically coincided with his discovery of the wheel . . . and a warning that his brief dominance of this planet will probably end, because man tried to create robot in his own image" (liner note).

Devo. In performance, through 1982.

> Devo repeats the question of the "humanized" animals in H. G. Wells's *Island of Dr. Moreau*: "Are we not Men?" They answer, "We are Devo!" The animals in *Dr. Moreau* become less than men when they return to their animal forms; Devo's early performances—"mechanized musicians playing robot rock" (Erlich's notes)—suggest a form of devolution in presenting humans as machines. Their early style is preserved on the videotape of *Saturday Night Live* for 14 Oct. 1978.

Edge, Graeme. "In the Beginning." 1969. Coll. on *This Is the Moody Blues*. London XZAL 13344 TH, 1974, record 1, side 2.

> A brief cut featuring a dialogue between a contemporary Cartesian Man and a computer that tries to convince him that he is magnetic ink.

Kraftwerk. In performance.

> German group, whose name translates "power station." During their 1981 American tour, Kraftwerk is said to have used a computer to play their music; the music itself is full of mechanical sounds. See— and hear—their English-language album, *Computer · World* (Warner, HS 3549, 1981); the graphics on the cover and record jacket strongly suggest "roboticization," as do the titles and lyrics to such songs as "Computer Love" and "It's More Fun to Compute."

The Police. *Ghost in the Machine*. AMS Records SP-3730, 1981.

> Note esp. "Spirits in the Material World" (side 1, first cut) and "Rehumanize Yourself" (side 2, second cut). One reviewer comments that "Rehumanize Yourself" describes "a totally mechanized society

in which violence has become a 'social norm'" (Jeff Callan, "Unabridged" supplement to *The Miami Student* [Miami U., Oxford, OH], 16 Oct. 1981, p. 2).

Simon, Paul. "The Sounds of Silence" (vt "The Sound of Silence"). On *Wednesday Morning, 3 A.M.* Columbia CS 9049, n.d. Garfunkel's note gives the date of composition as 19 Feb. 1964.

Authorized music and lyrics given in *The Songs of Paul Simon* (NY: Knopf, 1972). Note people bowing and praying to a deified neon sign. Note also the use of this song in Mike Nichols's film *The Graduate* (1967): it is associated with Benjamin Braddock and an airplane, a "people mover," car keys, and a bus.

VIII. BACKGROUND STUDIES

Bettelheim, Bruno. "Joey: A Mechanical Boy." *Scientific American*, March 1959.

A case study of an autistic child who was convinced he was a machine. See Yablonsky, this section.

Ellul, Jacques. *The Technological Society* (*La Technique . . .*, 1954). John Wilkinson, trans. NY: Knopf, 1964. (Rev. American edn.)

See for possible real world referents for the SF motif of the "mechanization" of people.

Halacy, D. S., Jr. *The Robots are Here!* NY: Norton, 1965.

Nonfiction work of eleven chs. dealing with such topics as the origin of the term "robot," robots as threats, literary robots, the history of real robots, robots in space, electronic brains, industrial robots, and speculations about the future of robots. Dated but still useful.

Milgram, Stanley. *Obedience to Authority*. NY: Harper and Row, 1974.

See esp. chs. 10, 11, and 15 ("Epilogue"). Milgram opposes autonomy to being in "the agentic state" and holds groups in extreme agentic states to "consist not of individuals but automatons" (p. 181).

Mumford, Lewis. *Technics and Human Development* (1967) and *The Pentagon of Power* (1970). A two-volume work going under the name *The Myth of the Machine*. NY: Harcourt Brace, 1970.

With early scientific advance, "The machine became the central metaphor for the universe and the dominant power impulse of the new world" (Wolfe, p. 10; Wolfe's words).

Reichardt, Jasia. *Robots: Fact, Fiction, and Prediction.* NY: The Viking Press, 1978.

A general discussion of robots.

Schafer, Roy. "Narration in the Psychoanalytic Dialogue." *Critical Inquiry*, 7 (Autumn 1980), 29-53.

Briefly and clearly summarizes Sigmund Freud on humans as beasts and machines (esp. pp. 32-33).

Skinner, B. F. *Beyond Freedom and Dignity.* NY: Knopf, 1971.

BFS denies the existence of "autonomous man"; he asserts the existence of a "technology of behavior"—conditioning—which should be rationally and systematically used.

Sullivan, George. *Rise of the Robots.* NY: Dodd, Mead & Co., 1971.

History of robots; their function as industrial robots; intelligent robots; the future of robots.

Taylor, Frederick W. *The Principles of Scientific Management.* 1911; rpt. NY: Norton, 1967.

To its enemies, "scientific management" meant reducing workers to automata, doing their jobs in the manner their bosses' hired experts ruled most efficient. In mechanized industries, this meant fitting workers ever more perfectly to the rhythm of the machines.

Watson, J. B. "Psychology as a Behaviorist Views It." *Psychological Review*, 20 (1913), 158-67.

See for the classic statement of the Behaviorist view that the sole task of psychology "is the prediction and control of behavior." See also Watson's *Psychology from the Standpoint of a Behaviorist* (1919) and his work for lay readers, *Behaviorism* (1925; rev. edn. 1930). Watson laid the groundwork for the "neobehaviorism" of Clark L. Hull (1884-1952) and B. F. Skinner (1904-).

Winner, Langdon. *Autonomous Technology: Technics-Out-of-Control as a Theme in Political Thought.* Cambridge, MA: MIT Press, 1977.

Excellent survey of the subject identified in the subtitle. Cf. Ellul; Mumford, above, this section.

Yablonsky, Lewis. *Robopaths: People as Machines*. 1972; rpt. Baltimore: Penguin, 1972, 1973.

Contains a number of references to literature, theater, and film. Concentrates on robopathology—people becoming mechanized, losing compassion and other positive emotions. Talks of the state as machine and of "social machines" like corporations and many schools and families. This book can be viewed legitimately as a polemical extension of the observations of Bettelheim, "Joey: A Mechanical Boy" (see above, this section).

Dee Dunn

INDEX

Italicized titles standing alone are titles of films or TV shows; italicized titles followed by a name in parentheses are the titles of novels.

CONTRIBUTORS

BRIAN ALDISS is the internationally renowned author of over two dozen volumes of SF stories, novellas, and novels including *Hothouse* (U.S. title: *The Long Afternoon of Earth*) for which he won a 1962 Hugo award and "The Saliva Tree" (1965), winner of the Nebula award. Some of his best-known works include *Greybeard* (1964), *Cryptozoic!* (1967), *Report on Probability A* (1968), *The Malacia Tapestry* (1976), *A Soldier Erect* (1971), and *Who Can Replace a Man?* (1965, rev. 1971). In addition, Mr. Aldiss has edited alone and in collaboration with Harry Harrison over twenty anthologies of SF including the Penguin and Space Opera series and the annual *Year's Best Science Fiction*. His extensive research culminating in his history of science fiction, *Billion Year Spree* (1973) brought him, in 1978, the Science Fiction Research Association's Pilgrim award for outstanding contribution to science fiction scholarship. He has lectured to enthusiastic convention audiences all over the world and has won respect and acclaim from every corner of science fiction fandom.

PETER S. ALTERMAN lives near Washington, D.C., where he writes, edits, and publishes scientific reports for the National Center for Health Care Technology. He writes science fiction and literary criticism.

BARBARA BENGELS is an Adjunct Assistant Professor of English at Hofstra University, where she originated the school's first science fiction course. She has published articles on Olaf Stapledon, Henry James, H. G. Wells, and the teaching of science fiction. She is currently working on an article on Jonathan Swift.

MARGARET POWELL ESMONDE is an Associate Professor in the English Department at Villanova University in Pennsylvania, where she teaches graduate and undergraduate courses in science fiction, fantasy literature, and children's literature. She is currently editor of the Children's Literature Association *Quarterly* and is past president of the Children's Literature Association. She is a member of the Science Fiction Research Association, was children's book review editor of *Luna Quarterly*, and is currently children's book review editor of *Fantasiae*, the newsletter of the Fantasy Association. She has published numerous articles on science fiction and children's literature.

ANDREW GORDON is an Associate Professor of English at the University of Florida. He is the author of *An American Dreamer: A Psychoanalytic Study of the Fiction of Norman Mailer* (Cranbury, NJ: Fairleigh Dickinson University, 1980). His articles on science fiction have appeared in *Literature/Film Quarterly* and *Science-Fiction Studies*.

DONALD ("MACK") HASSLER is a Professor of English and Director of Experimental Programs at Kent State University. A prolific scholar, he has published essays on Wordsworth, Coleridge, Byron, Hazlitt, and—in science fiction and SF—on Asimov, Sturgeon, William Golding, and B. F. Skinner. He is the author of a Twayne series book on Erasmus Darwin and a monograph on Erasmus Darwin published by Nijoff.

LEONARD HELDRETH holds a Ph.D. in English Language and Literature from the University of Illinois at Urbana-Champaign. He currently teaches at Northern Michigan University (Marquette) and has written numerous papers and articles on SF and on film. Among his current projects is an essay on mechanized environments in science fiction films, an essay that will appear in *Clockwork Worlds*, the companion volume to *The Mechanical God*.

ANNE HUDSON JONES is an Assistant Professor of literature and medicine at the Institute for the Medical Humanities of the University of Texas Medical Branch at Galveston. The author of several articles on women in science fiction and on literature and medicine, she is writing a reader's guide to Kate Wilhelm.

RUSSELL LETSON teaches English at Saint Cloud State University. He has written essays, introductions, and reference articles on Philip José Farmer, Robert Heinlein, Fritz Leiber, Robert Silverberg, and Jack Vance, and is working on a book on Vance.

DONALD PALUMBO is an Assistant Professor of English at Northern Michigan University. He has published articles on modern fiction and popular culture in *Extrapolation*, *The South Central Bulletin*, *Lamar Journal of the Humanities*, and *Folio*; and he has presented papers at over two dozen scholarly conferences in the past few years.

TERRI PAUL is an Assistant Professor at Iowa State University, teaching courses in advanced composition and science fiction. She received her doctorate in 1979 from Ohio State University with her dissertation "Blasted Hopes: A Thematic Study of Nineteenth-Century British Science Fiction." She has presented papers at academic conferences including those of the Science Fiction Research Association, the Popular Culture Association, and the Modern Language Association of America.

ROBERT REILLY, a medievalist whose interest in fantasy and science fiction has "grown into an obsession," has published essays on Blish and Bradbury and is at work on a book dealing with religion in science fiction.

JOSEPH L. SANDERS teaches English at Lakeland Community College, Mentor, Ohio. He has published numerous poems, essays, and reviews including essays on the science fiction of John D. Macdonald, Mervyn Peake, Brunner, Lovecraft, Silverberg, Lafferty, and extensive work on Roger Zelazny. He is a frequent contributor to academic conferences.

WILLIAM M. SCHUYLER, JR., is an Associate Professor in Philosophy at the Belknap Campus of the University of Louisville (Louisville, Ky.). He is best known to SF critics for his papers on identity, "When Am I Still Me" and "'When Am I Still Me' Strikes Back," and for his work, continued in this volume, on the question of ethical relationships between humans and nonhuman sentients, either organic or mechanical.

RUDY SPRAYCAR, an Assistant Professor of English at Louisiana State University, was trained as a medievalist and has published work Chaucer, Dante, and the *Chanson de Roland*. He is currently working on computerized stylistic analysis and oral-formulaic theory and epic style.

CHRISTIAN THOMSEN teaches at the Universität-Gesamthochschule of Siegen in the Federal Republic of Germany. With his colleague, Jens Malte Fischer, he has edited and published *Fantastik in Literatur und Kunst*. He is currently working on several articles in his main area of research interest, modern drama.

GARY K. WOLFE teaches at Chicago's Roosevelt University and is the author of the Eaton Award-winning *The Known and the Unknown: The Iconography of Science Fiction* (Kent State University Press, 1979), as well as *David Lindsay* (Starmont House, 1981) and, with Carol T. Williams, *Elements of Research*, a college text. He was a consulting editor and major contributor to the *Salem Press Survey of Science Fiction Literature* (1979), and his essays have appeared in journals ranging from *Extrapolation* and *Science-Fiction Studies* to the *AAUP Bulletin* and in books such as Thomas D. Clareson's *Many Futures, Many Worlds* and Martin Harry Greenberg and Joseph D. Olander's *Ray Bradbury*.

THOMAS L. WYMER is a member of the English Department at Bowling Green State University in Bowling Green, Ohio, and has been active in the organization of the Science Fiction programs of the Popular Culture Association of America. His work has appeared in *Many Futures, Many Worlds* and *Voices for the Future* (both edited by Thomas D. Clareson), and he was the senior author of *Intersections: The Elements of Fiction in Science Fiction*.

CARL YOKE is an Associate Professor of English at Kent State University and Associate Editor of *Extrapolation*. Among his many publications are a number of poems and, recently, the *Starmont Reader's Guide to Roger Zelazny*. He is currently Assistant to the Vice President at Kent State University.

ABOUT THE EDITORS

THOMAS P. DUNN is an Associate Professor of English at the Hamilton Campus of Miami University (of Ohio) where he teaches courses in Shakespeare and Medieval literature. He has presented at academic conferences several papers on mechanization in SF and along with Richard D. Erlich has published two articles on that motif. He contributed essays to the Salem Press *Survey of Science Fiction Literature*.

RICHARD D. ERLICH is an Associate Professor in English at the Oxford Campus of Miami University (of Ohio) where he teaches courses in Shakespeare, early English drama, composition, and science fiction. Alone and in collaboration, he has published essays on D. H. Lawrence, Alexander Pope, historical criticism of Renaissance literature, *2001*, Harlan Ellison's "A Boy and His Dog" (novella) and L. Q. Jones's *A Boy and His Dog* (film), Frederik Pohl and C. M. Kornbluth, D. F. Jones's *Colossus*, Ursula K. Le Guin's *Left Hand of Darkness* and Earthsea trilogy, and imagery and thematic concerns in a number of twentieth-century dystopias and works of dystopian SF. Along with Thomas P. Dunn, he has also edited for Greenwood Press, *Clockwork Worlds: Mechanized Environments in SF*, the companion volume to *The Mechanical God*.